Amos H. Hawley, Ph.D., University of Michigan, is
Kenan Professor of Sociology at the University of North
Carolina. He formerly taught at the University of Michigan
and the University of the Philippines. He is President of
the Population Association of America, and was Editor of
the American Sociological Association's series on issues and
trends in sociology. Dr. Hawley is the author of *Human
Ecology*, also published by The Ronald Press Company.

URBAN SOCIETY

AN ECOLOGICAL APPROACH

AMOS H. HAWLEY

UNIVERSITY OF NORTH CAROLINA

THE RONALD PRESS COMPANY · NEW YORK

Library of Congress Catalog Card Number: 79–155207
PRINTED IN THE UNITED STATES OF AMERICA

to Gretchen

Preface

This textbook presents in systematic form the concepts, theories, and research findings on urban phenomena. In so doing it explores the interrelations among the many kinds of urban knowledge, organizes them in an intelligible unity, and reveals the relevance of this synthesis for an understanding of society as a whole.

Organizing the material on urbanization calls for a guiding principle or an hypothesis, which can illuminate existing data and reveal their meaning. The position taken in this volume is that the form and content of man's collective life is a function of the efficiency of his means of transportation and communication. The tendency—noticeable in every historic society—for an urban organization to arise and flourish has been decisively influenced by man's progress in overcoming the frictions of space. Thus, far from being a static thing, urban organization is a process, a development, a transformation of an entire society.

Urbanization is the term used to describe that process. In fact, as a concept urbanization tends to become identified with a general theory of societal change and growth. At this time it would be presumptuous to present a mature theory of that nature, but I have indicated in this book what the outline of such a theory might be.

As with most efforts of this kind, the present volume has had assistance from a number of sources. I am especially indebted to the Carolina Population Center for providing me with unmolested writing time over three consecutive summers. Many of the tabulations in Chapters VII and VIII were made possible by the Social Science Research Council, under the program of its former Committee on Population Census Monographs. My good friends Everett Wilson and Basil Zimmer were kind enough to read and comment on parts or all of the manuscript. Helpful though they were, they should not be held culpable for any faults in the finished product. And last but not least I wish to thank the many cohorts of students who so patiently steered my thoughts into the patterns reported in the chapters that follow.

Amos H. Hawley

Chapel Hill, North Carolina
September, 1971

Contents

URBAN SOCIETY

AN ECOLOGICAL APPROACH

1

Introduction

The turmoil of the sixties brought our cities into the foreground of national attention in unprecedented fashion. What had been largely taken for granted suddenly demanded explanation. Legislators, government officials, community leaders, journalists, and laymen generally began pressing for answers to questions about the nature and causes of urban problems and about the future of cities. Whether the accumulated knowledge is sufficient for the solutions attempted and planned remains to be seen. In the meantime, it is imperative that we put the knowledge we do possess into as orderly a form as possible.

One of the lessons to be learned from a study of cities is that the novelty in the situation does not lie in the existence of a serious problem. The unusual feature is rather the extent of consternation about it. The problem itself is an old one—but in a new and more dramatic guise. In the Western world, the city has been almost continually in crisis for the past 150 years or more. The recurring crises are symptomatic of the profound revolution in man's way of living that has been in the making for a number of centuries and that is now at work in the non-Western areas of the world. In the nature of things, cities stand at the vortices of the currents and crosscurrents of broad-scale change that alter and reconstitute societies. It is to be expected, therefore, that the intermittent eruptions incidental to the uneven course of change should exert their most violent effects at these centers.

The impossibility of divorcing the city from the societal context in which it is embedded has an important bearing on the study of urbanization. The city represents a cross-section—kaleidoscopic, to be sure—of the whole of life. Hence it lends itself to as many interpretations as there

3

are predilections among its observers. Each of those might, in its way, be correct, though it is doubtful that all could be equally useful. In any case, if only because one cannot ride off in all directions at once, it is necessary that we adopt a single point of view and cast our analysis in its terms. In no other way can we hope to bring order into so complicated a set of circumstances and events. That is the purpose of the present chapter. But, in the interest of clarification, let us first examine some commonplace concepts.

THE CITY

Because of the close association between the words *city* and *civilization* it seems to follow that every culture described as a civilization must encompass at least one nodal point, or city. Indeed, cities or things that have looked like cities from a distance have existed throughout the settled life of man. That all such places are of the same order and are uniformly distinguishable from the not-city is open to question. Nevertheless, they have been so treated. Dismayed by the confusion that has prevailed, Edward Gibbon long ago remarked that, ". . . from the vanity of nations and the poverty of language, the vague appellation of city has been indifferently bestowed on Rome and upon Laurentium." [1] What, then, are the salient and distinctive features of the city? Among the numerous characteristics that have been stressed by different students, several have been mentioned often enough to merit special consideration.

To many the city is first and foremost a physical thing, a compact cluster of relatively permanent buildings. Archeologists are apt to convey such a notion, in part because of the paucity of other information at their disposal. [2] More than that, however, the accumulation of capital and the mastery of skills represented in the structures of a permanent settlement, especially one that has endured the ravages of time, stand in sharp contrast to man's modest achievements during his primordial existence. Lewis Mumford feels that there are certain essential physical elements, all of which had come into being by 2500 B.C. These include "the walled enclosure, the street, the house-block, the market, the temple precinct with its inner courts, the administrative precinct, the workshop precinct . . ." [3] All of that, as Mumford fully recognized, constitutes merely

[1] *The Decline and Fall of the Roman Empire* (New York: Modern Library), Vol. I, p. 43.

[2] Cf. Heinrich Schliemann, *Ilios: The City and Country of the Trojans* (New York: Harper and Sons, 1881) and Basil Davidson, *The Lost Cities of Africa* (Boston: Little, Brown and Co., 1959).

[3] *The City in History* (New York: Harcourt, Brace, Jovanovich, Inc., 1961), p. 90. According to Gustave Glotz, the acropolis and the agora—the fortification and the meeting place—are the essential elements of the city (*Ancient Greece at Work*, trans. by M. R. Dobie [New York: W. W. Norton Co., Inc., 1967], p. 12).

a shell, the kernel of which is the collective life of a group of inhabitants; yet without other evidence, it is not apparent what that collective life was like. The settlement might simply have been a fortification in which a powerful family and its retainers found protection from the peasant population on which it preyed. Or it might have been a military depot and refuge for disabled veterans; Alexander left some sixty such settlements strewn along his line of march across southwestern Asia. Clearly, the existence of a physical structure is no more than a first clue, though often a very suggestive one, that a city was actually present.

Population concentration, more often than physical structure, has been taken to mark the presence of a city. A city is assumed to exist wherever there is a relatively large, densely settled population. "A city," declared Botero late in the sixteenth century, "is said to be an assembly of people . . . And the greatness of a city is said to be, not the largeness of the site nor the circuit of the walls, but the multitude and number of inhabitants and their power." [4] The official censuses of many nations, including that of the United States, define a city as an aggregate that exceeds a certain size, though the minimum chosen for the purpose varies from as few as 150 persons to 20,000 or more, as is shown in Table 1. Such a definition, asserts one author, is "logically and etymologically unassailable." [5] Population size, however, as with physical structure, is at best a rough index, useful only as a first approximation. It can be quite misleading. A large aggregation might be simply that and nothing more. The presumption that great size indicates a way of life was accepted by W. F. Willcox, who defined a city as a place where population density is so great that agriculture is impossible, i.e., 1,000 or more per square mile.[6] Yet densities of that magnitude occur in a number of settlements of agriculturalists on the alluvial plains of Asiatic rivers. On the other hand, many places of both the past and the present that have been regarded as cities include some agriculturalists among their residents and some agricultural lands within their boundaries. Some cities of India have a sixth or more of their populations engaged in agriculture.[7] In Japan a number of cities in the middle range of size, from 100,000 to 500,000 population, have over half their lands devoted to farm uses. Peasant towns of Sicily, sometimes with as many as 30,000 inhabitants, are occupied almost entirely by agricultural day laborers. Obviously, population size alone is not a sufficient criterion.

[4] Giovanni Botero, *The Reason of State and the Greatness of Cities*. Trans. by P. J. and D. P. Waley and Robert Peterson (New Haven: Yale University Press, 1956), p. 227.

[5] Hope Tisdale, "The Process of Urbanization," *Social Forces*, 20 (1942): 311.

[6] "A Redefinition of City," in E. W. Burgess (ed.), *The Urban Community* (Chicago: University of Chicago Press, 1925), pp. 115–21.

[7] Roy Turner (ed.), *India's Urban Future* (Berkeley: University of California Press, 1962), pp. 68–69.

A third mark of the city—political autonomy—derives from ancient and venerable origins. When Theseus established Athens by uniting the twelve tribes of Attica, he formed a municipal government or city of which the tribesmen composed the electorate.[8] The territory embraced in their constituency was much wider and more thinly settled than we normally expect to find when the term "city" is used: It was actually a rural commune. While self-rule in settled aggregates had appeared before the founding of Hellenic civilization—in the Assyrian Empire, for example—the Greeks provided the philosophic rationale to a concept that has become a heritage of Western thought. Strictly speaking, the "city" is a local congregation of people who possess the right of self-government. It is a place occupied by "citizens." This feature appears frequently among the definitions listed in Table 1.

If, however, one were to attempt to determine merely by looking at settled places those that were cities in the sense just described, he would be as often wrong as right. During the early Middle Ages the walled town was usually a proprietorship held by a feudal lord. The populace had no voice in its government; they were inhabitants, not citizens. Later, the medieval town gained municipal status, only to lose it again with the rise of the national state. In the Western world municipal autonomy reappeared only in the third quarter of the nineteenth century. In most of the non-Western world today, what are called cities are actually administrative adjuncts of central governments, possessing few, if any, discretionary powers of their own. Even where municipal autonomy is prevalent, as in the United States, there are notable exceptions. Washington, D.C., is not a city in that sense. On the other hand, municipal powers are often granted to rural townships which in no other particular resemble cities.

But, while places that appear to be cities on other grounds lack self-rule, they are seldom without a set of administrative agencies through which day-to-day needs are served. The necessity for that usually impresses itself upon central governments for reasons of efficiency. The problems of densely settled places are unlike those either of open country or the nation as a whole. Furthermore, the problems have an urgency about them that demands immediate attention. Consequently a city is normally established in law or in governmental practice as a corporate entity of some kind with a set of administrative mechanisms and clearly defined jurisdictional limits.

A locality regarded as a city is often further characterized as an "urban" place. The meaning of the word "urban" is perhaps somewhat more

[8] Fustel de Coulanges, *The Ancient City: A Study of Religion, Laws and Institutions of Ancient Greece and Rome* (Garden City, N.Y.: Doubleday and Co., 1956), pp. 130–31.

Table 1. Urban Definitions Employed in Official Statistics
(Selected Countries, Latest Years Reported)

Country	Year	Urban Definition
Algeria	1966	Fifty-five of the most important communes having local self-government
Australia	1966	Population clusters of 1,000 or more with a minimum density of 500 per square mile
Austria	1965	Communes of more than 5,000 inhabitants
Brazil	1967	Urban and suburban zones of administrative centers of districts
Bulgaria	1968	Towns legally established as urban
Canada	1966	Cities, towns, villages of 1,000 or more population, whether incorporated or unincorporated
Chile	1969	Population centers which have definite urban characteristics contributed by urban and municipal services
Colombia	1964	Population living in nuclei of 1,500 or more people
Cuba	1966	Places of 2,000 or more inhabitants
Denmark	1964	Agglomerations 200 or more inhabitants
England and Wales	1968	Places classified as urban for local government purposes
France	1968	Communes with agglomerations of 2,000 or more inhabitants living in contiguous houses
Greece	1966	Municipalities with population agglomerations of 10,000 or more.
India	1961	Incorporated towns and all places having 5,000 or more inhabitants
Indonesia	1962	Municipalities, regency capitals, and other places with urban characteristics
Iraq	1965	The area within the boundaries of Municipal Councils
Japan	1965	Urban municipalities usually having 30,000 or more inhabitants
Malaysia	1968	An area with a population of 10,000 or more
Netherlands	1968	Municipalities with populations of 2,000 or more
Norway	1968	Town municipalities
Peru	1969	Capitals of districts and population centers with urban characteristics
Sweden	1965	Built-up areas with at least 200 inhabitants
Tunisia	1966	Population living in communes
U.S.S.R.	1969	City and urban type localities officially designated as such by the constituent Republics
United States	1970	Centers with populations of 2,500 or more
Venezuela	1967	Cities, towns, and 183 other localities with urban socio-economic characteristics

SOURCE: United Nations, *Demographic Yearbook,* 1968, pp. 317–322, and 1969, pp. 144–150.

vague than is that of "city," although it seems at the outset to have been clear and specific. According to Fustel de Coulanges:

Civitas and *Urbs,* either of which we translate by the word city, were not synonymous words among the ancients. *Civitas* was the religious and political association of families and tribes; *Urbs* was the place of assembly, the dwelling place, and, above all, the sanctuary of the association.[9]

But *urbs* has since been transformed into the adjective "urban" with which to denote some one or combination of properties of life in thickly settled places. There is some reason to believe that the transition appeared first as the word "urbane," meaning possessed of the manner, the refinement, or the sophistication of the city or town dweller. However that may be, "urban" came into general use as a characterization of the city during the seventeenth century and afterward. Thus the meanings of "city" and "urban" have been reversed. The former now applies to a certain kind of place and the latter refers to a quality of life that is typically found in such a place.

What is the quality of life described as urban and how does the town dweller acquire it? The answer lies in the position of the town as a center upon which are focussed the interests and the activities of a more or less widely scattered population. The center may be the seat of ecclesiastical and political institutions which extend their services over the surrounding countryside. Of greater importance in centering the attentions of outlying residents upon a town is its possession of a market and of a specialized class of traders. Some scholars have taken the latter to be the cardinal identifying features of a city. Gras would withhold the term "city" from any place that lacked those elements.[10] Max Weber also insisted that the market was essential to a city.[11] Henri Pirenne,[12] Gordon Childe,[13] and others have argued in a similar vein. The intervention of the trader between the producer and the consumer, which both Childe and Pirenne consider essential, raises the market to a level of development above the occasional fair. Where that occurs specialists of various kinds gather to serve not just the needs of the intramural population but all who are drawn to the market. In other words, a permanent market usually is found in company with administrative, religious, communication, and other services, some of which are necessary counterparts of commerce

[9] *Ibid.,* pp. 134.

[10] N. S. B. Gras, *An Introduction to Economic History* (New York: Harper and Row, 1922), p. 91.

[11] *The City,* trans. Don Martindale and Gertrud Neuwirth (New York: The Free Press, 1958), pp. 65–68.

[12] *Economic and Social History of Medieval Europe* (New York: Harcourt, Brace, Jovanovich, Inc., 1933), pp. 40–41.

[13] "The Urban Revolution," *Town Planning Review,* XXI (1950): 9–16.

and others of which simply find the place of congregation a convenient location in which to operate.

It is precisely this feature of a permanently settled place, i.e., of a town, that generates its urbane character. The flux of commerce brings together people from various cultures and backgrounds and requires that they learn to live and work together. They become detached from the parochialisms of locality and are led to dwell in a wider realm of experience. Moreover, out of necessity they become accustomed to pursue their needs and interests through relatively complex organizational arrangements in which indirectness of relationship and rationality of procedure are operating principles. These organizational arrangements are the basic ingredients of urban life; sophistication of outlook and of behavior are inescapable by-products of sustained participation in a market nexus.

THE URBAN CENTER

In the interest of brevity, let us now proceed to define *city* as a permanent, relatively densely settled and administratively defined unit of territory, the residents of which gain their living primarily by specializing in a variety of nonagricultural activities. Obviously, a unit of this kind cannot be self-sufficient; it is by definition interdependent with people living elsewhere who engage in different but complementary activities. This interdependence argues forcefully for a broadening of one's conception of the appropriate object of study to include the entire set of interrelationships by which a localized population carries on its daily life.

That is, what is denoted by "urban" is not confined to a densely settled place. It embraces the whole of an organization that is based upon a center of settlement. Both the scope and the complexity of such a system may vary between wide extremes. In some instances the organization appears to be contained mainly in the center with but feeble ramifications into the surrounding area. In others the network of interdependences reaches far afield and involves virtually all of the activities of a distributed population. Movement from the simple, highly localized unit to the complex and territorially extended system is a growth process. We shall use the term *urbanization* to refer to that process.

Accordingly, our attention in this volume will be addressed to the urban organization rather than to the city proper. An urban organization invariably has a city, or something closely resembling a city, at its core. But not all cities are the centers of urban organizations; some are simply appendages of other cities. For this reason the term "urban center" is preferable to "city" for most purposes. We shall adhere to that usage so far as is practicable. It will not always be convenient to do so, however. The term "city" is too firmly implanted in the language of official reports and of the literature generally to be uprooted at this late date. Nor does our preoccupation with urbanization exclude consideration of cities that are not urban centers. Their existence and function in an urban system need to be explained.

THE COMMUNITY

We have already anticipated the way in which this somewhat ambiguous term should be employed. Nevertheless, clarification may be served by further discussion.

Community ordinarily denotes a territorially localized population that carries on a collective life through a given set of institutions. There are, of course, other uses of the word.[14] For example, one often hears reference to "religious community," "professional community," or "international community." Each such use implies the existence of a population sharing a common characteristic. The commonality, however, need not be so specific. It may be a collection of diverse things, all of which are important to a group of people. So it is with the human community. The common interest concerns the system of interdependences together with the instrumentalities, including the territory occupied, that the system employs in its routine operation. Various forms of consensus pertaining to rules, procedures, and sanctions observed in the normal conduct of affairs are built into the system and constitute a further element in the commonality. The combination of interdependences, instrumentalities, territory, and norms defines a setting in which most specialized, common interests are developed and cultivated.

Structurally speaking, the community is a unit of local organization having a center and an outer zone, with the two connected by radial routes of travel. If the center posesses a market and various specialists whose activities serve the entire unit, it is at least an incipient urban center. Urbanness varies along two continua: it increases with the number and variety of linkages between central and scattered populations; and it increases as the amount of exchange with the external world grows in volume and diversity. From a functional standpoint the urban community is a mechanism for relating a local population to a larger universe of activity. On the one hand, through its organization it produces products, services, or information for export to other communities. On the other hand, its organization is adapted to receiving and distributing im-

[14] G. A. Hillery lists ninety-four definitions of "community" in his paper on "Definitions of Community: Areas of Agreement," *Rural Sociology*, XX (1955): 111–23.

ports, as well as locally produced goods and services, among its members. The two-way flows of interaction are decisive factors in determining the content of communal life.

As we shall see, the progress of urbanization renders the concept of community less and less useful. So long as the territorial scope of collective life is small in scale, the term has descriptive utility. Each local unit is more or less inclusive of the interests and activities of its members. But as the scale of organization increases the boundaries of locality become blurred and indistinct. Localities are merged and often absorbed in larger systems. If, in these circumstances, the term "community" continues to be used, it is with a large degree of arbitrariness. Of this there will be more to say in later chapters.

HUMAN ECOLOGY

The study of territorially based systems, of which the urban community is a prime example, is known as *human ecology*. More abstractly, this designation refers to a concern with the processes and the form of man's adjustment to environment.[15] The community is a generalized form of that adjustment. In the reasoning of human ecology, adjustment is accomplished, not by each individual's acting independently, but by means of a division of labor developed among a number of individuals. Adjustment is a collective achievement. The unit of observation, therefore, is a population; the adaptive organization, i.e., the division of labor with its various ramifications in social relationships, is the property of a population.

Environment, on the other hand, embraces all of the externalities that impinge on the life chances of a definable population. It includes not only the physical and biotic elements of an occupied area, but also the influences that emanate from other organized populations in the same and in other areas. In certain circumstances the latter acquires a more critical importance than the former.

The basic hypothesis of human ecology, then, is that, as a population develops an organization, it increases the chances of survival in its environment. The emphasis is upon organization. In its ecological applica-

[15] See Amos H. Hawley, *Human Ecology: A Theory of Community Structure* (New York: Ronald Press, 1950); Leo F. Schnore, "Social Morphology and Human Ecology," *American Journal of Sociology,* LXIII (1958): 620–29; O. D. Duncan and Leo F. Schnore, "Cultural, Behavioral and Ecological Perspectives in the Study of Social Organization," *American Journal of Sociology,* LXV (1959): 132–53; June Helm, "The Ecological Approach in Anthropology," *American Journal of Sociology,* LXVII (1962): 630–39; Julian Steward, "Cultural Ecology," *International Encyclopedia of the Social Sciences* (New York: Macmillan and The Free Press, 1968), vol. 4, pp. 328–36.

tion, organization is an inclusive concept. It refers to the entire system of interdependences among the members of a population which enables the latter to sustain itself as a unit. The parts of such a system—families, clubs, shops, industries, for example—cannot be self-sustaining; they can only survive in a network of supporting relationships. As easy as this is to say, it does not fully dispose of the question of how to define the boundaries of a system. The identification of the effective limits of organizational units is one of the persistent problems in human ecology. It is sufficient at the moment, however, to state that ecology is committed to dealing with the most inclusive unit manageable.

Thus the problems selected for study are of the order commonly characterized as macroscopic. This choice is in contrast to a microscopic type of problem, such as that concerned with a part of a system or, more particularly, an individual taken separately. There is no reason to infer *a priori* that either level of investigation is more or less preferable; the issue must be decided entirely on the basis of the problem at hand. But it is assumed that the variables applicable to an analysis of phenomena at one level have very little explanatory utility for phenomena that lie at the other level. Human ecology seeks its explanations among variables that are structural properties, demographic attributes, and features of environment, including interactions with other systems. The import of this theoretical position will become more understandable as one follows the exposition in succeeding chapters.

SPACE, TIME, AND ORGANIZATION

It should be apparent that the system of interdependences we have described as urban is a territorially based phenomenon. Indeed, that is its most obvious aspect. Spatial considerations in one respect or another will be, therefore, a continuing concern in this volume. For that reason it is desirable that we put the concept *space* in sociological perspective.

Man and his behavior are facts of nature. As such they share certain characteristics with other facts of nature. They occupy space, for example. Moreover, man relies on a great many things that are distributed over space: food, water, raw materials of all kinds. Were these necessities everywhere present in abundant supply, it is conceivable that the idea of space might never have occurred to man. They are not, of course, if for no other reason than that two or more finite things cannot exist in the same place at the same time. The very irregular distribution of the requisites for life is a fact that provokes in man's behavior a constant sensitivity to distances and locations.

Of more immediate importance is a second fact, namely, that space is an ever-present element in the fundamental interdependence among men.

There should be no need to document the inescapability of interdependence; it begins at biological conception and is omnipresent throughout life. That is why we describe man as a "social" animal. Stripped to its essential content, the word *social* means interdependence. It follows with simple logic that interdependence presupposes accessibility between the parties concerned. There can be no mutual support or exchanges unless individuals can come together with whatever frequency the business at hand may demand. Conversely, the distances that separate people affect the kinds of joint activities they can pursue. A family operates as a family only when its members are close together. When they are widely separated the family becomes something else, a kin group, a clan, or nothing at all. The universal tendency for human settlement to be nucleated, to live in clusters, which reaches its highest form in urban centers, maximizes interpersonal accessibility and therefore the opportunity for devising elaborate cooperative arrangements.

But space, as it is experienced in human collective life, is not a fixed quality. It is rather a function of the time consumed in movement. Man is a time-bound creature. He must eat and rest at regular intervals. These elementary requirements set limits on the time and energy available to him for other activities, including movement. Space may be thought of as a friction measurable by the time and the effort expended in getting from point to point. Where the friction is great the number of different things that can be done in the span of a day are few; conversely, the number and variety of activities can be increased as the friction is reduced.

Many of our notions of distance and space seem to have begun as measurements on a time dimension. In times past, long distances were calculated in number of days of travel: Herodotus described distances by the number of days required to move between points by "a man traveling light." The Roman *league* may have been the distance legionnaires could march in an hour's time. On the other hand, an acre originated as the area a man with an ox could plow in a single day. It is of interest to note that, despite revolutionary advances in overcoming distance, the 60-minute radius still defines the ambit of local life. Seldom has man been willing to devote more than an hour's time to trips that must be made every day. The distance that can be traveled in that interval has been extended from about 3 miles for the pedestrian to approximately 30 miles for the vehicular-borne rider. Beyond the 60-minute radius, interactions with a center are reduced to less than a daily periodicity. Through most of the nineteenth century and the early part of the twentieth, the team-haul distance—the distance a horse-drawn wagon could travel and return in the course of a single day, or about 12 to 15 miles—measured the scope of weekly trips to a center. More recent improvements in transportation, of course, have enormously extended the radius of occasional travel.

Moreover, efficiency in the overcoming of distance has been heightened by the development of means of sustaining indirect or mediated relationships.

The only means at man's disposal for pressing back the limits that time presents is through enlarging upon a division of labor with his fellows so that an increased number of activities can be carried on simultaneously. Such specialization produces a countereffect: the greater the number of complementary activities carried on by different people, the greater is the amount of time that must be devoted to exchanging and communicating. A characteristic solution to that problem has been a close concentration of the people engaged in high-frequency exchanges, forming villages, towns, or cities. As organization develops it becomes possible to economize further on time by delegating responsibility for movement to specialists: messengers, teamsters, dispatchers, and the like. The effect of organizational development in this respect rests in large part on the capability it affords for the acquisition and utilization of technological advances. Thus the man mounted on horseback can travel farther in an hour than can a pedestrian, but the maintenance and equipment of the horse imposes larger technical demands and consumes the time and effort of more people. The animal-drawn cart, though somewhat slower than the mounted rider, can carry much larger loads. Again, however, the cart presupposes skills in manufacturing and a knowledge of harnessing the animal that do not occur in very simply organized groups. Similarly, the four-wheeled wagon, the railway, the motor vehicle, and numerous other innovations that have contributed to the reduction of the friction of space have followed from the growth and elaboration of organized life.

For the time being, perhaps enough has been said to indicate that the meaning of space for man, the way in which it enters into his activity, grows out of his experience with time. As he has learned to economize on his use of time, he has been able to spread his activities over larger amounts of space. The conservation of time depends in turn on the extent to which man is able to elaborate his organization of complementing activities. Thus space, in a very large and important sense, is a derivative of organization. Urbanization is but one of the more conspicuous ways in which man has, through the development of organization, enlarged upon the territory from which he obtains the materials of daily life.

URBANIZATION AS A GROWTH PROCESS

In its most visible aspect urbanization is a process of increasing territorial scope of organization. The process is much more involved than that, of course. There are other factors that are also vital to a system; change must move concurrently in those respects as well. In short, growth in a phenomenon as complex as a community or a social system entails reciprocal effects among culture, population, territory, and organization. Unless change in one is accompanied by changes in the others, the results are not cumulative, that is, growth does not occur. Instead, the tendency to change is short-lived and the unit in question reverts to its original state.

The interrelations among the four factors or dimensions of a social system become apparent in analysis. Cultural accumulation, with which change begins, cannot proceed far without an increase in population. Additional people are needed to retain and to put to use a diversifying repertory of ways of acting. At the same time, more territory is required to supply the increased amounts of food needed to nourish an enlarging population and to provide the increasing variety of materials used in fabricating the multiplying items of material culture. Furthermore, the growing number, variety, and spread of activities presuppose an elaboration of organization to assure coherence among complementing parts. The more finely drawn the division of labor, the more imperative is the requirement for centralized mediating and coordinating institutions.

This paradigm outlines a rather generalized conception of an expansion process. At first glance urbanization might seem to be a special case of the general principle. Yet, although the process may be mounted on various scales, it seems that in all instances it unfolds from a center strategically situated with reference to access to its tributary area, on the one hand, and to external regions, on the other hand. The center is the locus of the organization that knits together dispersed activities and links them to what is being done in other places. Center and territory advance together, each supporting the other.[16]

It is not meant to imply that the growth of a territorial system follows a smooth or uninterrupted path. Historically, the process has ebbed and flowed. On some occasions it has subsided after a brief career. Elsewhere the process has advanced to a grand scale, only to end in dissolution. Invariably, however, expansion has sprung up in another quarter and has surged to still larger dimensions. The vagaries of the process are of interest. In the following chapters we shall explore how the process is initiated, the character of its movement, and how limits are imposed upon it.

Nor is expansion in any sense a simple matter. To speak of the growth of organization is to refer in a very cryptic way to a highly involuted sequence of events. Urbanization is a transformation of society the effects of which penetrate every sphere of personal and collective life. It affects the status of the individual and his opportunities for advancement, it alters

[16] See R. D. McKenzie, "Industrial Expansion and the Interrelations of Peoples," in E. B. Reuter (ed.), *Race and Culture Contacts* (New York: McGraw-Hill, 1934), pp. 19–33; Amos H. Hawley, *Human Ecology*, pp. 348–70; and Otis D. Duncan, "Social Organization and the Ecosystem," in R. E. L. Faris (ed.), *Handbook of Modern Sociology* (Chicago: Rand McNally, 1964), pp. 36–82.

the types of social units in which people group themselves, and it sorts people into new and shifting patterns of stratification. The distribution of power is altered, normal social processes are reconstituted, and the rules and norms by which behavior is guided are redesigned. Fundamental social changes of this order will be examined in later chapters as fully as the present state of knowledge permits.

A METHODOLOGICAL NOTE

The approach to the study of urbanization is both developmental and comparative. The intention here is to draw comparisons across the span of time as well as within historic periods. The process we identify as urbanization has a long history. In its beginnings it moved slowly and tentatively, gradually it gathered momentum, and since the turn of the nineteenth century the pace has accelerated rapidly. The urban center of gravity has shifted in the course of events from ancient Mesopotamia to the Mediterranean basin, then northward into Europe and, subsequently, to America and other areas over which European population has spread. Recently the long-quiescent areas of the world, the so-called developing nations, have entered into an era of extraordinary change in which urbanization is a conspicuous feature. Thus the process which at one time seemed to be peculiar to a particular cultural tradition has in the modern period taken hold of peoples of all places and cultures.

The persistence of urbanization, over many lapses and renewals, raises many questions on which an historical treatment can throw light, if not answer. Inasmuch as major social change carries forward elements from the past and mingles them with the new, a knowledge of an earlier period can contribute to an understanding of a later period. Therein lies the continuity that history represents. Historical inference, however, is a hazardous business, for often the parallels that impress turn out to be simply analogues. This risk must be accepted, for the excellent reason that we cannot take the historical process into a laboratory.

A more provocative issue concerns the repetitiousness of series of events in instances widely spaced in time and place. Does urbanization wherever and whenever it occurs reiterate a sequence of steps? If not, is it possible to determine which can be omitted and which cannot? And can one assess the consequences of skipping steps in a sequence? In short, is there a single process of urbanization, or are there several processes? These are questions that have long perplexed the student of change and continue to do so. At the very least, we will be able to sharpen these issues with references to specific empirical materials. But we can venture further than this to suggest that there are circumstances at work in the modern period to support a contention that there is an urbanization process of a sufficiently general character to be recognized in different kinds of societies. In any case, a comparative treatment will enable us to investigate that proposition.

There are other difficulties in addition to those that have been mentioned. Historical accounts were not compiled for the purposes of this volume. Hence desirable data are often inadequate or missing altogether. The situation is especially unsatisfactory for the ancient period, on which information exists largely as archaeological observations as of selected moments in time; there is little or no direct information on the process of change. Even so, these sources supply us with a large amount of descriptive data from which useful inferences can be drawn.

The later the period, the greater is the abundance of information about the dynamic factors involved in urbanization. As our inquiry takes us into the modern period, the need for reliance on history diminishes and disappears. Then the important question changes to what can be learned about the future from observations of contemporary trends.

SUPPLEMENTARY READINGS

GILMORE. HARLAN W. *Transportation and the Growth of Cities* (New York: The Free Press, 1953).

HAWLEY, AMOS H. (ed.). *R. D. McKenzie on Human Ecology* (Chicago: University of Chicago Press, 1969).

PARK, R. E. *Human Communities: The City and Human Ecology* (New York: The Free Press, 1952).

QUIGLEY, CARROLL. *The Evolution of Civilizations* (New York: Macmillan, 1961).

SCHNORE, LEO F. "Problems in the Quantitative Study of Urban History," in *The Study of Urban History,* ed. by H. J. Dyos (London: Edward Arnold, 1967).

2

Urban Organization
in the Ancient Period

THE BEGINNINGS OF SETTLED LIFE

Approximately 12,000 years ago a revolution was occurring in man's normal way of life, a revolution that appears to have been two or three thousand years in the making and even then was concentrated in only a few localities. Here and there in an elongated, semitropical zone reaching from central Asia through southwestern Asia and into northern Africa, men were becoming increasingly dependent on cereal foods. With the discovery of plant cultivation, formerly nomadic hunting and food-gathering bands drifted into permanent settlement in fertile river valleys. The permanence of settlement was secured by later developments in irrigation, in adapting the already domesticated animal to a plow, in metallurgy, in the use of the wheel in transportation, and in other innovations of the Late Neolithic.[1]

Permanence of settlement based on agriculture at once opened opportunities and imposed demands without parallel in man's experience. It presented an opportunity for unlimited cultural accumulation, for man was no longer limited to what he was able to carry about as he moved from place to place. Furthermore, the seasonality of agriculture freed him periodically for the cultivation of industrial skills and the extension

[1] See Robert J. Braidwood and Gordon R. Willey (eds.), *Course Toward Urban Life: Archaeological Considerations of Some Cultural Alternatives* (Chicago: Aldine Publishing Co., 1962).

of his knowledge. But the exploitation of that opportunity was made mandatory by the hazards of a sedentary life. Since he could no longer escape climatic and other environmental variations through moving his base of operations, man had to find ways of enlarging his mastery of environment. He had to accumulate tools and materials and to learn to store food surpluses to sustain him from one harvest to the next.

Thus, permanent settlement demands an increase in the variety of materials used in daily life. Its chances of flourishing are therefore enhanced where there is a diversity of environmental niches in close juxtaposition. Robert Adams describes several niches in the Mesopotamian alluvium. In addition to sections most suitable for wheat and barley cultivation, others were best adapted to garden and orchard crops and to cattle grazing, while the marshy lands supplied reeds for construction and fish as a food supplement.[2] Braidwood and Willey emphasize the importance of environmental differentiation for the emergence of permanent settlement in Mesoamerica.[3] It appears that specialization arises as an adjunct to a subsistence economy and from the efforts of a group to utilize its unique local resources.[4] Specialization is doubtless stimulated by the opportunity to exchange special products among mutually accessible groups, whether through a ceremonialized exchange of gifts or through direct barter. The complementation of one group's efforts by those of another raises the level of living of both to a higher degree of security. Having made this first step it then becomes possible, given appropriate conditions, for increased concentration on the production of particular items to call other specialists into being. These new phases might be concerned with mediating and administering the trade relationships, injecting new materials and products into the local exchange network, or providing services to workers engaged in crafts.

But the agriculturalist's immobility and his stores of wealth made him easy prey to marauding bands of nomads. For thousands of years settled areas were encircled by territories inhabited by these nomads, and a chronic state of warfare prevailed between the two.[5] It is probably that circumstance which gave rise to what later became towns. The recurring

[2] *The Evolution of Urban Society* (Chicago: Aldine Publishing Co., 1965), p. 48.
[3] *Op. cit.*, pp. 354–55.
[4] Alexander Lesser, "Social Fields and Evolution of Society," *Southwestern Journal of Anthropology*, XVII (1961): 40–48. Eric Lampard contends that "primordial urbanization most likely emerged in areas that contained diverse but closely juxtaposed sub-environments or cultures which, through social interaction, were symbiotically exploited." ("Historical Aspects of Urbanization," in P. M. Hauser and Leo F. Schnore [eds]., *The Study of Urbanization* [New York: John Wiley and Sons, 1965], p. 529.)
[5] Stuart Piggot, "The Role of the City in Ancient Civilization," in E. M. Fisher (ed.), *The Metropolis in Modern Life* (Garden City, N.Y.: Doubleday, 1955), pp. 5–17.

needs for defense led to the construction of fortified places in which settlers could gather in times of crisis and in which they could concentrate
and protect their stores of surpluses. Defensive requirements necessitated
a development of organization above what was required for day-to-day
production of sustenance. Thus a military establishment with centralized
powers of mobilization and command came into being. That defensive
organization, in turn, as it became permanent and professional, exacted
a cost paid in tithes or taxes levied on the peasants' product. It also encouraged specialization in weapon making, record keeping, administration, and other ancillary activities, all of which had to be supported from
the produce of the area. In time the military chieftain emerged as a
ruler with broad and often hereditary powers.[6] How that came about
initially is unknown, though the many instances in recorded history in
which a conqueror became a sovereign are probably illustrative of one
way in which the transition occurred. In any case, the appearance of a
ruling family and of a coterie of retainers superimposed upon a peasantry
marked the beginnings of a class structure based on functional differentiation.

Gordon Childe describes this protracted series of events, spread as it
was over several millennia, as "the urban revolution." It consisted in the
appearance in combination of ten entirely novel features:

1. Permanent settlement in dense aggregations.
2. Nonagriculturalists engaged in specialized functions.
3. Taxation and capital accumulation.
4. Monumental public buildings.
5. A ruling class.
6. The techniques of writing.
7. The acquisition of predictive sciences—arithmetic, geometry, and
   astronomy.
8. Artistic expression.
9. Trade.
10. The replacement of kinship by residence as the basis for member-
    ship in a community.[7]

How necessary each of the ten acquisitions was to the beginnings of
town life appears to be debatable. It has been observed, for example,
that writing failed to develop in prehistoric towns of Mesoamerica.[8] One

[6] This form of specialization appears to have occurred sometime prior to 3500 B.C.,
the approximate date of the oldest known archaeological remains of palaces and royal
tombs.

[7] "The Urban Revolution," *Town Planning Review*, XXI (1950): 4–17. In the
view of V. M. Masson the urban revolution was not so much a matter of the formation of large nucleated centers as of the emergence of professional specialization.
("The Urban Revolution in South Turkemia," *Antiquity*, XLII [1968]: 178–93).

[8] Eric Lampard, *op. cit.*

might question how fully residence has replaced kinship as a criterion
of membership in some of the cities of contemporary developing areas.
What should or should not be included in a list such as Childe's need not
detain us here. What is important is that an extraordinary transformation
in man's way of life did in fact occur.

Most of what can be said about the organization of collective life in
the early phases of permanent settlement is speculative, based on archaeological detective work (though recent and continuing advances are
building a firmer foundation for the speculations). It does appear, however, that many of the earliest townlike settlements might have been
military encampments. Quite possibly the ruler, with his administrative
bureaucracy and his military forces, had to move periodically from site
to site, not only to police and protect his domain, but also to supply his
establishment with food and provender since the level of productivity
and the transportation equipment were too primitive to permit a steady
flow of large quantities of materials to a single location. That incapacity
may be the reason why Egypt appears for several millennia to have been
a civilization without cities.[9] So it was, for example, with the Merovin-
gian and Carolingian kings in the early feudal period; instead of maintaining regular courts or capitals, they circulated over their territories
pausing long enough at fortified places to consume the stores accumulated
by their bailiffs.

THE PREHISTORIC TOWN

The earliest known towns of any consequence appeared in Mesopotamia, around 3500 B.C.[10] From there, town settlement seems to have
spread eastward into the Indus Valley and westward toward the Mediterranean Sea, perhaps following the diffusion of Late Neolithic technology.
To date, the largest of the Mesopotamian towns discovered has been Ur,
the home of Abraham, situated at the confluence of the Tigris and the Euphrates Rivers. But there were others, such as Lagash, Eridu, and Erech,
scattered along the upper reaches of the river valleys.

[9] John A. Wilson, "Egypt Through the New Kingdom: Civilization Without
Cities," in Carl H. Krailing and Robert M. C. Adams (eds.), City Invincible: A Sym-
posium on Cultural Development in the Ancient Near East (Chicago: The University
of Chicago Press, 1960), pp. 124–36.

[10] This point is controversial. Kathleen Kenyon believes that Jericho anticipated
Mesopotamian towns by some 1,500 years. ("Jericho and Its Setting in Near Eastern
History," Antiquity, XL [1956]: 184–97.) Robert Braidwood questions her evidence in "Jericho and Its Setting in Near Eastern History," Antiquity, XLI (1957),
73–81. See also Kathleen Kenyon, "Reply to Professor Braidwood," Antiquity, XLI
(1957), 82–84.

The excavated walls of Ur enclosed some 220 acres of land and are estimated to have sheltered 24,000 people.[11] Estimates of the populations of other Sumerian towns range from 2,000 to 20,000. (This point is discussed at length on pp. 33–35.) Although these were large populations for the period, they probably represented no more than 3 or 4 percent of all of the people within their respective localities. In general, agriculture as then practiced required the produce of forty to fifty workers for the support of one nonagriculturalist. The alluvial soils of the Euphrates River were unusually fertile, however, especially in the vicinity of Ur. The crops reaped were equal to eighty to one hundred times the amount of seed planted.[12] Still, the wealth represented in the construction of Ur suggests that it must have been built either on the strength of exorbitant taxation of the peasantry or on the spoils of war.

Physically, Ur was much like other Sumerian towns. The center was a citadel comprising the palace, a temple, monasteries and convents, and the granaries. The surrounding wall may have been as much for protection against the local people as against organized assaults from rival ruling groups, for there is reason to believe that Sumerian town dwellers were conquerors who had enslaved the indigenous residents. Hovering close outside the wall, enclosed in some cases by an outer wall, lived the craftsmen, the scribes, the domestic servants and other retainers of the ruling class. Within the outer wall there usually were gardens and pasture lands, for not infrequently a town had to withstand a siege; most cultivation, of course, occurred outside the walls. Streets were narrow and devious ways, marked out originally by animal movements, not unlike those of oasis towns in contemporary northern Africa. Congestion in the limited space forced houses to two and three stories, each built around an inner court with blank walls facing the street.[13] Evidently even within the town defensive precautions were necessary.

The marketplace was located not within the town proper, but outside it on the premises of the river harbor. It served mainly the purposes of intercity and interregional trade. The amount of intradistrict or local trade was negligible. Most residents of the town were landed proprietors who drew their material requirements from their farms or manors and who, therefore, had no reason to buy or sell among themselves. According to Oppenheim, in most of the Mesopotamian towns life was lived at a subsistence level. Real prosperity occurred only when a town was ruled by a victorious king who returned from forays rich with the spoils

[11] Gordon Childe, *What Happened in History* (New York: Penguin Books, 1946), p. 87. See also Leonard Woolley, *Ur of the Chaldees* (Hammondsworth: Penguin Books, 1952).

[12] Childe, *op. cit.*, p. 83.

[13] Wooley, *op. cit.*, pp. 126–27.

of war.[14] There was then a liberal distribution of wealth to art and architecture and to the cultivation of learning. But these periods of affluence were infrequent in the history of any one town.

Nevertheless, the leisure bought by the Mesopotamian townsman with the plunder of war enabled him to make remarkable cultural advances. Writing and record keeping, systems of numbers and time reckoning, mathematical and astronomical calculations, law and administrative procedures—these and many other elements of urban civilization made their first appearance in Mesopotamia. Among the advances were significant improvements in technology, especially in the domestication of plants. That these accomplishments were built from cultural borrowings is scarcely debatable. Trade in luxury goods was carried on with distant points over caravan routes and river courses; ideas and information invariably move with commodities. Warfare was also an agent in the diffusion of knowledge. How widely the cultural achievements were disseminated through the town populations is not apparent on the surface. Quite probably they belonged to the few rather than the many, though it is likely that as innovations were understood and their uses appreciated they became common property. Technological gains may have found their way into the universe of discourse long before the intellectual achievements were shared with the public.

The relationship of town to hinterland is a question on which archaeologists have little to say. Presumably the relationship was not carried beyond a rudimentary stage; that is at least suggested by the absence of a market for locally produced goods. Quite possibly the relationship involved merely an exchange of the outlander's labor on farms, irrigation systems, and construction for certain administrative services provided from the town. The ruler in the town, with the military and administrative apparatus at his command, was able to preserve peace and order over the lands under his jurisdiction, at any rate while his power was ascendant. He might also supervise the maintenance of irrigation works and the exercise of water rights. His gathering of surplus produce into public granaries created an emergency food reserve that could be redistributed as a dole in time of famine, if, that is, the elite had not by then consumed it all. The town was also a source of religious ministration, for government and religion were inextricably intertwined. It is not likely, however, that a relationship of the kind described could reach very far beyond the town precincts, probably not more than a few miles. Transportation and communication fell mainly upon the backs of men. The application of the wheeled vehicle, the war chariot, to cargo uses came late in the prehistoric period. Extensions of the narrow ambit of daily exchanges could occur

[14] A. Leo Oppenheim, *Ancient Mesopotamia: Portrait of A Dead Civilization* (Chicago: University of Chicago Press, 1964), p. 117.

only by diverting portions of the surplus produce to the feeding of larger numbers of porters and messengers.

For all of its limitations the order imposed by the town over the countryside roundabout undoubtedly established a measure of security and led, therefore, to a comparatively low death rate in the hinterland population. Where that occurred population increase would tend to crowd the land and to press hard against the productivity of the soil. Population was also swelled from time to time by expulsions of dissident elements, defeated factions, and delinquent debtors from the town, and more or less continuously by infiltrations from mountain and desert tribes.[15] The resulting stresses and political unrest were resolved often by colonization on reclaimed lands or in conquered territories. Not infrequently, however, instability infected the town and led to the overthrow of ruling families or so weakened the community that it fell prey to foreign invasion.

Some of the ancient towns occupied commanding locations, locations from which expansion was possible. Strategic locations were created by the intersections of actual or potential routes of travel, such as a crossing of overland routes or,[16] better still, a convergence of land and water routes. Sites of that kind had a twofold significance. The routes that fan out from such places [17] give the population so situated access to a wide variety of experiences and cultures. Consequently it is there that cumulative change tends to be most probable of occurrence and most rapid when it is begun. On the other hand, an intersection, particularly where different kinds of routes are represented, tends to interrupt flows of movement, as C. H. Cooley noted in his theory of transportation, causing population, wealth, and specialists to collect there.[18] Traders paused in the strategically located cities of ancient times not only to sell their wares but to be provisioned and rested for further travel. Their periodic appearances constituted a market for services to transients and encouraged local craftsmen to increase their production of high-value commodities that could be carried away as items of trade. Accumulations of capital from handicraft industry laid a basis for more ambitious undertakings. Usually, however, the transition of a settled place from a fortified rural center to an expanding town lagged until after colonization had planted the region with settlements.

15 *Ibid.*, pp. 82–83.

16 Long before it became the shrine of Islam, Mecca developed as a trade center by virtue of its location at the crossing of the principal east-west and north-south caravan routes. See Bernard Lewis, *The Arabs in History* (New York: Harper Torchbook, 1960), p. 34.

17 See Ernest Herzfeld, "The Highway System in the Near East from 2000 B.C. to 500 B.C.," in *Highways in Our National Life*, ed. by Jean Labatut and Wheaton J. Lane (Princeton: Princeton University Press, 1950), pp. 10–15.

18 "The Theory of Transportation," in *Sociological Theory and Social Research*, ed. by Robert C. Angell (New York: Holt, Rinehart and Winston, 1930), pp. 75 ff.

Miletus, on the coast of Asia Minor, is a case in point. Situated on an estuary of the Maeander River, it had access to the sea and to a rich agricultural country behind it. Eventually, after a number of failures, it managed to implant sixty or more colonies, mainly along the north shore of the Black Sea. With these Miletus developed a lucrative trade. Fleece and olives were brought into Miletus from surrounding districts to be processed and the products were sent out in exchange for grain. Many other items—locally made tools and luxury commodities obtained from remote sources—also entered into colonial trade. Numerous specialists appeared in Miletus—boatbuilders, metalworkers, shippers, middlemen, moneylenders, scribes. As the city grew it tightened its controls over its adjoining territories. But in time the estuary filled with silt and Miletus passed into decline.[19] Further south the Phoenician towns, Byblos, Tyre, and Sidon in particular, were engaged in similar expansive programs.[20] Subjected as they were to successive foreign dominations, they nevertheless managed to establish colonies as far west as Carthage and Sicily. As a trader and a pirate the Phoenician seaman had few peers in the Mediterranean.

The rise and fall of town-based territorial organization occurred repeatedly in the prehistoric period. In some places it was obliterated, as in the Indus Valley by as early as 1500 B.C.[21] Babylon overcame Ur and reigned as the metropolis of Mesopotamia for over one thousand years, before it was reduced to the status of a minor satrapy of Persia in the fifth century B.C.[22] In the meantime, towns had been spreading along the northern trade routes to the Caspian Sea and westward through Syria and the Levant to the eastern rim of the Mediterranean Sea. Most of these seem to have been military garrisons primarily, supported by tribute from the countryside and from the spoils of armed forays into adjoining districts. Predation was then a common business of town residents. Troy, for example, is believed to have lived from the tax imposed on the traffic portaging around the rapid currents of the Hellespont.[23] A few towns, such as Damascus and Jerusalem, became important trading and trans-

[19] T. R. Glover, *The Ancient World* (Hammondsworth: Penguin Books, 1944), pp. 59–60.

[20] Dimitri Barauki, *Phoenecia and the Phoenecians* (Beirut: Khayats, 1961).

[21] Two towns in the Indus Valley, Mohenjo-daro and Harappa, have been partially excavated. Both comprised three-quarters of a square mile of territory. Archaeological findings indicate a relatively high level of cultural development, but they are too incomplete as yet to tell us much about the character of urban life. (See Sir Mortimer Wheeler, *Civilizations of the Indus Valley and Beyond* [New York: McGraw-Hill, 1966].)

[22] A. T. Olmstead, *History of the Persian Empire* (Chicago: University of Chicago Press, 1948).

[23] Alfred Zimmern, *The Greek Commonwealth* (New York: Modern Library, 1931), p. 15.

shipment centers for luxury goods. Others, notably Susa and Persepolis, were founded as regional administrative centers of empire.

THE GREEK CITY

The Greek city is widely regarded as the most advanced expression of ancient urbanism. Its urban achievement has been overstated, however. For in the sixth century B.C. after a long period of development, it was little more than an agricultural village, according to Alfred Zimmern. It was inhabited mainly by cultivators of the soil who had, as the Greeks put it, "set up house together." [24] Its calendar, its drama and legends, and its round of activities, all reflected its close association with the land. The town had emerged as a fortress, an acropolis, where the countryfolk could shelter themselves from recurring invasions.[25] A space nearby, called the *agora*, served as a meeting place in periods of leisure. The agora was also used as a site for periodic markets. At best a very small fraction of its population could be supported in nonagricultural activity, perhaps not more than 2 or 3 percent. Greek soils were thin, rocky, and sparse. Resources of all kinds were meager. But Greece and the Mediterranean littoral constituted a compact yet greatly differentiated environment in which were fostered skills and products of many kinds and over which the Greeks could sow their colonies without serious difficulty. So they turned to trade and piracy as supplements to the grudging productivity of their lands. It was in this activity that the Athenians excelled.

In the fifth century Athens became the metropolis of Attica and of the entire peninsula. It was the center not only of a politically well-organized city-state but also of a far-flung trade network. The city bustled with increasing numbers of craftsmen, merchants, mariners, and emissaries and with numerous foreigners, some free and many enslaved. While most of the industry and business was conducted by domestic enterprises, the unattached worker, drawn largely from the ranks of vagabonds and exiles, appeared in growing numbers. So ramified became the structure of relationships and the transactions carried on that the old methods of payment in kind and exchange of a service for a service could no longer be tolerated. The introduction of coinage supplied the efficiency needed in the system. But in emancipating wealth from produce and in placing credit on a calculated basis, the use of money dissolved client relationships, divested the unfortunate of their lands, property, and often their freedom,

[24] *Op. cit.*, p. 77.
[25] André Bonnard, *Greek Civilization, from the Iliad to the Parthenon*, trans. by A. Lytton Sells (London: George Allen and Unwin, 1957), p. 22; and Carl Roebuck, *Ionian Trade and Colonization* (New York: Archaeological Institute of America, 1959), pp. 24–41.

and sharpened the differences between classes. Even so, there was justification for Pericles' claim that ". . . the magnitude of our city draws the
produce of the world into our harbor, so that to the Athenian the fruits of
other countries are as familiar a luxury as those of his own." [26] On the
other hand, his boast of Athens' hospitality to the trader and of its cosmopolitan character must have been intended as an invidious comparison
with neighboring city-states. Without those virtues Athens would not
have been more than an agricultural village.

One is tempted to conclude that the Athenians exhausted their aesthetic energies in the Parthenon and their political thoughts on abstractions, for the municipality was a mean affair.

The Athenians lived under the Acropolis, as many generations lived under
the spires of Oxford, in "squalid magnificence." So hard is it for the human
spirit to do two good things at once.

For, in spite of all of the talent at her disposal, asking for nothing better
than to do her bidding, her organization was more primitive than that of our
most backward country town. Water indeed she had, thanks to her tyrants:
although even that almost indispensable condition of Greek city life was not
extended to the Piraeus, which up to the time of the great plague relied wholly
upon cisterns. Her streets were narrow, crooked, dirty, unlighted, and ill-
paved. She had no sewers, or even cesspools, and over the whole department
of sanitation it is best to draw a veil. Most of the police were amateurs, and
the rest Scythian barbarians, the laughing-stock of freeborn citizens. Postmen
we do not expect, though the Persians, and later the Ptolomies, had a national
post. But it is a surprise, especially if we come fresh from the national systems
of education in Plato and Aristotle, to find that the Athens of Pericles paid no
attention whatever to her children . . . , and provided no national school-
masters except the citizens who drilled the recruits . . . Another surprise is
to learn that the city was too lazy to collect her own money. The imperial
treasury, where her ideals were vitally concerned, was carefully looked after in
every particular, and if the contributions were late there were officials to hasten
them in. But all the mere municipal moneys, the foreigners' poll-tax, the customs, the market dues, and all the various licenses, were simply farmed out to
"publicans," who made a profit on their contract.[27]

The disorder of the Athenian physical pattern must have been appreciated. When Hippodamus drew up the plan for Piraeus, Athens' port
city, he introduced the grid street pattern in which streets intersect at
right angles and at regular intervals. Apart from the appeal of its geometrical nicety, the grid pattern permits a maximum use of a limited
space. Whatever may have been the reason for Hippodamus' decision,
it did not extend to other aspects of the municipality. In congestion and
in its lack of public services Piraeus paralleled its parent city.

Athens' stature as a center of an urban community was no match for its
achievement as the hub of empire. Citizenship was restricted to members

[26] Thucydides, *The Peloponnesian War* (New York: Modern Library), p. 104.
[27] Alfred Zimmern, *op. cit.*, pp. 300–301.

of ancient phratries, exclusive of alien wives of members and of the children of such unions. The lack of citizenship imposed severe limits on one's participation in public life and his civil rights. While many of the city residents secured their sustenance directly from their landed estates, there were numerous market gardeners, weavers of coarse cloth, charcoal makers, and other producers who brought their products to Athens, hawking them in the streets and selling them from stalls in the agora. Exchanges were directly with consumers for the most part, though a growing number of retailers began to dominate the home trade, contrary to the practice in other Greek towns. Communications between center and hinterland were poor. Most of the roads were mere paths usable only for pack animals and porters. Athenian road commissioners and surveyors were appointed by lot and rarely, therefore, had any claim to competence. Most of the vehicular roads built under that arrangement ran to the ports, but a sacred way was extended to Delphi and another to Eleusis. These were seldom in good repair. Hence the costs of transporting heavy cargoes for distances of ten or twelve miles exceeded 40 percent of the value of the material.[28] The deplorable state of the roads is a commentary on the casual relations between center and hinterland. While the latter was a source of food for the former, Athens offered little in return. The relative absence of exchange relations with the hinterland may have been because most of Athens' substantial citizens owned rural estates from which they secured their livelihoods. The Greek city-state was a political unity to a much greater extent than it was an economic one.

Despite the growth of Athens and the increasing demands for manpower in its expanding economy, especially in its merchant marine, Attica was burdened with a chronic population problem. So was all of Greece. The rural sector yielded up surplus people in ever increasing numbers, barring the years of epidemics, for land scarcity closely limited the opportunities in agriculture. In the towns slaves and foreigners were cheaper than citizens, so there were few jobs for the displaced farmers. Colonization offered the only practicable alternative to civil strife or starvation. Between 479 and 431 B.C. some 10,000 families migrated to colonies.[29] That, of course, contributed to the growth of empire. But after the debacle of the Peloponnesian War and the loss of empire, Athenians (and other Greeks as well) had to resort to internal population controls. Infanticide was revived as a general practice.[30] In the fourth century B.C.,

[28] Gustave Glotz, *Ancient Greece at Work: An Economic History of Greece from the Homeric Period to the Roman Conquest* (New York: W. W. Norton & Co., 1967), pp. 291–93.

[29] William H. McNeill, *The Rise of the West: A History of the Human Community* (Chicago: University of Chicago Press, 1963), p. 257, fn. 5.

[30] A. H. M. Jones, "The Social Structure of Athens in the Fourth Century B.C.," *Economic History Review*, VIII (1955): 141–55.

colonization once more provided a means of escape for unlimited numbers of redundant people. Alexander was then overrunning the lands of south-west Asia and Egypt. While Greek youths filled his armies, settlers and their families followed in the wake of victory to settle the lands and occupy the new towns founded by the conqueror. Town-building surged eastward once more.

THE CITY IN THE ROMAN EMPIRE

With the rise of the Roman Empire, the city gained an unprecedented importance. The empire was an extraordinary administrative creation, and the city was the loom in which the strands of the system were woven together. No previous civilization was so thoroughly urbanized and no previous civilization developed so efficient an organization for exploiting the countryside in the interests of its urban centers. It was a civilization addressed to consumption. Nowhere was this more fully expressed than in the capital city itself.

Rome was a crowded place. The clutter visible in the remains of the Forum is unmistakable evidence of congestion. Almost one third of the space enclosed within the Aurelian Wall was devoted to streets, warehouses, the Palatine Hill, the Campus Martius, and other public uses.[31] For so many people to live in the space remaining required narrow streets and multistoried buildings. Of necessity, it was a city of pedestrians. The pedestrian made his way with difficulty through lanes and ways thronged with hucksters, business stalls that encroached upon the right-of-way, and householders on their daily trips to markets. If he had special business to attend to, he could find the potters clustered on Potter's Street or the brokers, drovers, glaziers, shoemakers, tailors, corn-dealers, and other specialists concentrated on streets named after their respective trades. The most diversified assortment of businesses could be found at the Forum, at least until business was driven back into the approaching streets by the construction in the Forum of temples, monuments, and government buildings. Only the bankers managed to maintain a commercial foothold in the Forum. Should the shopper be in search of finely wrought furniture, fair slaves, rare perfumes, and expensive ornamentations, he would head for the luxury market on the edge of the Campus Martius.[32]

Economic life was extensively subdivided. Although manufacturing was very small-scale and addressed almost entirely to goods for immediate consumption, a division of labor prevailed in each craft, sometimes within

[31] J. C. Russell, *Late Ancient and Medieval Population* (Philadelphia: American Philosophical Society, 1958), p. 65.

[32] Charles G. Herbermann, *Business Life in Ancient Rome* (New York: American Book Co., 1880), pp. 18–24, 43–49.

a shop, but usually by type of product. Among tailors, for example, some devoted themselves to shirtmaking, some to togas, some to women's gowns, and others to mending. So it was among shoemakers and even sculptors. Commerce was the dominating activity, however. It existed in myriad specialization and was supported by moneylenders, teamsters, warehousemen, bookkeepers, and others. Most of the artisans and businessmen were organized in guilds through which they sought to monopolize their trades and to serve as well their recreational interests.

Rome was an importer, not an exporter. The riches of the empire were drained into the city through military capture, state-controlled exploitations of farm lands, quarries, and mines, and the rapacious tax collections of publicans. The bulk of the enormous tribute extracted from its colonies was consumed in Rome. What found its way into the surrounding countryside flowed mainly to the villas and estates of the aristocracy. Since members of the Senate and others who aspired to high position were barred from direct engagement in trade, they acquired, if they did not already own, large landed properties in the vicinity of Rome and beyond. As a consequence most of the small farmers and free laborers had been displaced from the nearby hinterland, and the work was done by a slave labor force. The dispossessed drifted into the armies, into colonization, or into the laboring and indigent classes of the city. If there was an urban community reaching beyond the edges of the city—and information on these matters is woefully lacking—it seems to have comprised little more than the summer homes and estates of the upper class. The excellent roads that converged upon the city were not channels of reciprocity between city and country; they were essentially military thoroughfares. Rome was supplied mainly by sea and from the empire rather than from the hinterland.

But while the community of Rome was confined largely to its municipal boundaries, its empire exceeded anything previously known. Exploitations of its vast territories involved an enormous construction program. Roman administration brought into being hundreds of towns; it added to those established by the Greeks around the Mediterranean rim, planted more along interior waterways, and prompted the rise of others at frontier outposts. Many began as semipermanent military encampments. They were shaped in a standard pattern: rectangular enclosures with a gate in each side and a grid street arrangement within. As the encampment was converted into a permanent settlement, the location of the commandant's quarters at the center became the site of a forum. Markets, previously held outside the gates, moved into a ring and invaded the forum. In time a Colosseum and administrative buildings were added. Paris, Marseilles, Vienna, Cologne, Mainz, London, and innumerable lesser towns began with such a pattern. Administrators, merchants, dispossessed

Italian peasants, disabled veterans, and Romanized barbarians filled the growing towns and developed them into thriving centers.

"The Roman empire consisted," declared A. H. M. Jones, "with a few insignificant exceptions, of cities, that is, self-governing communities occupying a territory and almost always possessing an urban center. Geographically, the empire was a mosaic of city territories." [33] In the eastern empire there were 900 city territories; in the west, data for Gaul alone show the presence of 114. Most of these were based on small villages and towns, as in Africa, but not a few had centers of imposing size. The size and importance of a town depended primarily on the extent of administrative responsibility lodged there. Trier rose to importance when it became the seat of the praetorian prefecture of the Gauls. Owing to his residence, Trier acquired two arms factories, a woolen mill, and a mint. Later, when the prefecture moved to Arles, Trier declined. But in the majority of cases towns were small and their influences were confined to rather small territories.[34]

Roman administration had one serious flaw. It required that public officials, who were appointed for life, pay for municipal services and maintenance from their own pockets. As long as they could milk imperial revenues, the office was attractive. But when fiscal overseers were sent out to look after monies belonging to the state, administrative position lost its appeal. Many moved out of the provincial towns in the hope of losing eligibility for the position. Failing that, they passed the financial burden downward in more and more oppressive taxation. During the fourth century A.D., provincial towns began to decline as their upper classes, which included prospective appointees to public office, sought financial refuge in rural life.[35] Strenuous efforts were made to force their return to town residence to resume their responsibilities and to provide a livelihood for artisians and merchants. Some of the more burdensome obligations imposed upon the upper classes were relaxed. In the search for further municipal economies there appears to have been a decline of civic zeal. The maintenance of public buildings and streets was neglected. Walls were rebuilt when necessary on a more restricted circumference, indicating perhaps a loss of optimism for further town growth.

In the fifth century the decline and dissolution of the empire was becoming all too apparent. The extravagances of the imperial courts had

---

[33] *The Decline of the Ancient World* (New York: Holt, Rinehart, and Winston, 1966), p. 237.

[34] *Ibid.*, pp. 230–39.

[35] Collingwood attributes the decline of towns in Britain and in Gaul to the failure of the Romans in any way to improve the productivity of agriculture. Hence the towns sapped the wealth from rural areas and themselves eventually passed into poverty and decay. ("Town and Country in Roman Britain," *Antiquity*, III [1929]: 261.)

denuded the forests of Italy, wasted her agricultural lands, and impoverished the people. Population was depleted by losses from continuous wars, famines, and pestilence. Tuscany, Amelia, and neighboring districts were all but depopulated and the Po Valley was desolated. The always thin and overextended lines of communication within the empire could no longer withstand the mounting pressures from barbarian hordes. African grain-producing areas were lost to the Vandals. In Britain, Gaul, Iberia, and elsewhere, the countryside was overrun and despoiled; the imperial order was reduced to a shambles by repeated invasions. Urban life disappeared. The towns that were not obliterated reverted to agricultural villages.[36] The population of Europe, which had flourished under Roman administration, subsided to its primitive density once again.[37]

SIZES OF ANCIENT CITIES

The greatness of the past is easy to exaggerate. Actually the towns were comparatively small. Athens at its peak embraced but 612 acres of land, less than one square mile. In Rhodes there were 125 acres; in Antioch, 325 acres; Carthage, 721 acres; Damascus, 532 acres. Nineveh, Babylon, Byzantium, Alexandria, and Rome were the giants. But only the latter exceeded 5 square miles in scope. Population data are more elusive than acreage. Some reports seem credible. Memphis with 800 families and Egyptian Thebes with 2,400 are probably not inflated estimates. The figure of 50,000 population for Babylon may contain a substantial error. The 150,000 figure often cited for Athens in the fifth century B.C. is even more questionable; it must have pertained to the city-state as a whole rather than to the city alone.[38] Likewise, the 700,000 population estimated for Carthage, the 650,000 for Alexandria, and the 100,000 given for Antioch are most improbable. Such figures translate into densities of 100,000 or more people per square mile. Their wall-to-wall buildings, multistoried houses, and very narrow streets notwithstanding, it seems unlikely that so many people could be crowded together under the conditions prevailing. These are exceptional densities even for modern cities, despite their efficient transportation and superior public utilities. The principal limitation on size, however, lay in the availability of food supply. Not only did agriculture yield very small surpluses, transportation from producer to consumer was laborious and costly. The cart

[36] Gibbon, *Decline and Fall of the Roman Empire*, Vol. II (Modern Library, n.d.), pp. 150–51.

[37] See K. W. Taylor, "Some Aspects of Population History," *Canadian Journal of Economics and Political Science*, XVI (1950): 301–13.

[38] A. H. M. Jones estimated the total, including foreigners and slaves, at 124,000, basing his estimate on the consumption of grain. (*Op. cit.*, pp. 142–45.)

with solid wheels and an axle that turned with the wheels was a clumsy vehicle of small cargo capacity. Furthermore, without hard-surfaced roads, it was unusable in certain seasons of the year. At the time of Diocletian, in the third century A.D., a cartload of hay doubled its cost in 30 miles. Four-wheeled wagons were known as early as Ur, but they were so awkward that they were used mainly for ceremonial purposes, much like the ponderous temple wagons of modern India.[39] Water transportation was considerably cheaper than overland carriage. The Greek merchant vessel could carry as much as 7,000 bushels of grain at a speed of 65 or so nautical miles per day and at a cost that was no more than a tenth that of land transportation. This advantage was seldom realized, however. Losses at sea from storms and piracy raised shipping prices to all but unsupportable levels. The costs of imported foods were prohibitively high. Hence most maritime cities and towns lived on the produce of their territories and imported only in emergencies.[40]

Rome, of course, towered above all other ancient cities, by virtue of its imperial successes and its extraordinary administrative organization. The size to which it grew has been debated for years. Gibbon's method of estimate, based on counting houses and multiplying the number of houses by an average number of occupants per house, is an acceptable one. But he arrived at what seems an improbable figure: 1,200,000 people, or about 240,000 persons per square mile.[41] Apparently Gibbon used too large a number of residents per building and more people than lived in Rome proper. A more recent estimate, by Russell, places the maximum population of the city at 350,000.[42] Even that figure implies a density of 65,000 persons per square mile, a density of which Russell is dubious.

An estimating procedure might yield results, concerning city size, no less accurate than those from literary sources and quite a bit more instructive. High and low estimates of maximum sizes can be made on the strength of a few assumptions. The first assumption has to do with the amount of land needed to support each person. In a fairly recent study

[39] Wagons dropped out of use around the first century A.D., not to reappear for another 1,000 years. Still another 300 years were required to produce the pivoting axle and proper harness for the draught animal. Until then it was necessary to drag the front end of a wagon around a turn.

[40] A. H. M. Jones, *The Greek City from Alexander to Justinian* (Oxford: Clarendon Press, 1940), p. 261.

[41] Gibbon, *op. cit.*, Vol. II, p. 346. See also McNeill, *op. cit.*, pp. 359–60.

[42] Russell, *op. cit.*, p. 65.

According to R. G. Collingwood, the total population of the Roman Empire at the birth of Christ, that is, shortly prior to the date to which Russell's estimate pertains (*circa* A.D. 74), was 70 million. On that basis, the population of Rome constituted approximately five per cent of the Empire population. (*Op. cit.*, 261–71.) Earlier Julius Beloch had estimated the population of the Empire, in 14 A.D. to be 54 million people. ("Die Bevölkerung im Altertum," *Zeitschr. für Socialwiss.*, II [1899]: 505–14.)

the minimum size of a viable farm in Jordan was judged to be 30 acres of unirrigated land or 6 acres of irrigated land.[43] Soil fertility is better in other parts of the Near East, but perhaps Jordanian land productivity is more representative of what was realized in that part of the world some 2,500 to 3,500 years ago. In that event the support of each member of a 6-person household would require the produce of approximately 5 acres of unirrigated land, or of one acre of irrigated land. If it is further assumed that the maximum feasible distance over which food could be transported overland is 10 miles—about the greatest distance an animal-drawn cart could travel and return in a single day—a town located on a plain had access to about 300 square miles of producing territory, given the unlikely circumstance that all land within that radius was cultivable. Where a town was situated on a river serviceable as a transport route, the down-river distance over which food could be moved might be of the order of 50 miles. Then, in addition to the 300 square miles surrounding the town on the plain, there would be another 800 square miles formed by two 10-mile bands on either side of the river reaching 40 miles upstream from the town's 10-mile radial belt, making a total of 1,100 square miles of accessible producing land. One further assumption is needed; that is, that a town population engaged in nonagricultural pursuits cannot amount to more, in normal circumstances, than 10 percent of the total population of the area in which it is located. This is a rather generous allowance for the ancient period, as are, in fact, our other assumptions. The implications of this line of reasoning are shown in Table 2. In a land-locked area the largest town could accommodate as many as 3,800 people without irrigated cultivation and almost 9,000 if one third of the productive area were irrigated, though one might question where under the stated assumption the irrigation waters were to be obtained. Where a river bisects a plain the town center might vary from 12,000 to an upper limit of 32,800 people, depending on whether as much as one third of the land could be irrigated.

As previously suggested, these estimates err on the liberal side. Moreover, they are suggestive of average upper limits. Exceptions, of which Rome was the extreme instance, could and did occur. For the most part, however, it seems unlikely that towns occupied exclusively by nonagriculturalists could grow much above 33,000 people without either unusually rich producing areas under their domination or very oppressive taxation of their food producers. A wanton use of slaves could be a very effective substitute for the latter. It is also possible that exceptionally large pop-

[43] Charles Issawi and Carlos Dabezies, "Population Movements and Population Pressure in Jordan, Lebanon and Syria," *The Milbank Memorial Fund Quarterly*, XXIX (1951): 385–401.

**Table 2. Approximate High-Maximum and Low-Maximum Sizes
of Ancient Towns
(Given Assumptions of Location, Accessible Area, Soil
Productivity, and Proportion of Population in Town)**

Assumptions	For Intersection of Land Routes at Center of Plain	For Intersection of River and Land Routes at Center of Plain
Square miles of territory	300	1,100
Acres of territory	192,000	704,000
Population[a] of territory, if without irrigation	38,400	120,800
Size of town (without irrigation), if 10% of total population	3,840	12,080
Population[a] of territory, if 1/3 irrigated	89,600	328,800
Size of town (with irrigation), if 10% of total population	8,960	32,880

[a]Given an average household size of 6 persons.

ulations might occur as temporary deviations from a more modest average, as on the approach of hostile armies or on the eve of colonization.

Knowledge of other demographic features of town life is less abundant than is information on size. It is a fair surmise, however, judging from much more recent experience, that mortality in the ancient town was very high—probably of the order of 50 or more deaths per 1,000 people per year on the average. Life expectancy at birth must have been around 25 years.[44] Congested living, unrelieved by the most elementary knowledge of health and sanitation, could only produce high mortality rates. Epidemics were frequent and diet was generally inadequate. Hence maintenance of numbers, to say nothing of growth, had to rely on migration, whether through enslavement or through the movements of free men. The very widespread use of slaves suggests that rural sectors were not very dependable suppliers of population replacements for town losses.

SUMMARY

The earliest towns appear to have been aggregations of agriculturalists, mainly, who banded together for purposes of mutual aid, among which defense was not the least important. The physical and the social struc-

[44] Cf. Louis I. Dublin, Alfred J. Lotka, and Mortimer Spiegleman, *Length of Life: A Study of the Life Table* (New York: Ronald Press, 1949), p. 30.

ture of the town was elaborated wherever a governing elite managed to superimpose itself upon the agricultural subsistence economy. It was only then that full-time specialists began to appear as administrators, priests, recordkeepers, soldiers, and craftsmen. Although evidences of trade are found in the earliest-known settlements, the trader becomes more prominent where social differentiation and a luxury market have made their appearance. The clienteles of specialists and traders were almost exclusively townsmen and particularly those who comprised the elite: the ruling family or clique, rich landowners, military officers, and occasionally students. In other words, the nonagricultural residents of the towns made their livings not by providing services for the surrounding countryside, but by catering to the luxury demands of small fractions of the town populations. Wealth was drained out of the surrounding areas to support the towns and little or nothing was sent back in payment.[45] A few places achieved great importance as mercantile centers, notably Alexandria, Thessalonica, and Ephesus; even so, their relations with their hinterlands were tenuous. Thus early towns were urban centers in only the most incipient sense of the term. Later in the Hellenic and Roman civilizations the towns began to acquire more reciprocal relations with their tributary territories. But there, too, urban organization was rudimentary.

The limited capacity for urban development was traceable to two conditions. First, food production in the ancient period was not sufficient to support more than 4 or 5 percent of the population of an area in nonagricultural occupations, except in those localities where the soils were unusually fertile. Surpluses over and above the annual needs of the producing population accrued mainly by repression of its consuming habits through taxation or some other kind of assessment. Second, transportation was too slow and feeble to make possible a concentration of very large quantities of food at any particular point in space. It seems improbable that towns of much above 33,000 people could have arisen in ancient times; and then only at locations where navigable streams existed. The simple state of transportation also limited the facility of a central place in distributing services over surrounding lands. A radial distance of 3 miles may have measured the normal reach of a town's activities; 10 miles may have been near the maximum distance.

Expansion of the scope of influence of a center required the investment of increased amounts of subsistence goods in time and energy devoted to movement. The supply of subsistence materials available in the area about a town afforded a very small margin of excess that might be used in that way. But the produce of neighboring areas, if reduced to servi-

[45] A. H. M. Jones, *The Greek City from Alexander to Justinian,* p. 263.

tude by conquest, could sustain long lines of communication and light transportation. Characteristically, then, expansion reached far afield to establish rather unstable frontiers of exploitation long before there was an enlargement of a local system of community relations.[46] The latter, in fact, was delayed for many centuries.

On the surface the great cities of the ancient past seem to have been orthogenetic in character, in the sense used by Robert Redfield and Milton Singer.[47] That is, they were the expressions of the great traditions of culturally homogeneous peoples. And there, these cultural additions gleaned from frontier contacts and the movements of traders, armies, or pilgrims were transformed in terms of the respective cultural traditions, preserving in the midst of change a normative and theological continuity. If that were true, it was due no doubt to the slow pace at which cultural increments were accumulated. But that interpretation may also rest in some degree of the refractoriness of archaeological and legendary information. Continuities were frequently interrupted and the subjugation of cultural groups was a common occurrence. In some instances, the conqueror's culture tended to displace that of the vanquished people.

It is to be noted in conclusion that ancient towns have had many counterparts in more recent times. As late as the fifteenth century A.D. the towns of the Khmer kingdom (in modern Cambodia) were similar in many ways to those scattered across Asia Minor in the early years of Western history. They were cult centers in a theocratically ruled society, much like those of the Aztecs up to the time of the Spanish conquest. The towns in both of these recent instances served also as administrative centers of redistribution systems. The towns of western Africa, around A.D. 1000, were not unlike the mercantile centers of the Mediterranean basin of some twelve centuries earlier. Not only were the Hausa towns places of refuge for agriculturalists in periods of invasion, they were markets for local and interregional trade.[48] As empires rose and fell in the struggle for control of the gold trade, towns waxed and waned. Some achieved preeminence as centers of culture before subsiding once more to simple fortified aggregations of farmers.

SUPPLEMENTARY READINGS

BRIGGS, LAWRENCE P. "The Ancient Khmer Empire," *Transactions of the American Philosophical Society*, XLI (Philadelphia, 1951): 1–295.

[46] Ralph Turner, *The Great Cultural Traditions* (New York: McGraw-Hill, 1941), vol. II, pp. 1298 ff.

[47] "The Cultural Role of Cities," *Economic Development and Cultural Change*, III (1954): 53–73.

[48] Basil Davidson, *A History of West Africa to the Nineteenth Century* (Garden City, N.Y.: Doubleday, 1966), p. 88.

GLOTZ, GUSTAVE. *The Greek City and Its Institutions* (London: Routledge and Kegan Paul, 1950).

LOUIS, PAUL. *Ancient Rome at Work: An Economic History of Rome from the Origins to the Empire* (New York: A. A. Knopf, 1927).

WATERMAN, W. L. "On Inland Transportation and Communication in Antiquity," *Political Science Quarterly*, XLIII (1928): 364–387.

YEO, C. A. "Land and Sea Transportation in Imperial Italy," *Transactions of the American Philosophical Society*, LXXVII (1946): 221–244.

3

Urban Revival in the West

THE FEUDAL ORDER

Following the disintegration of the Roman Empire, after the fifth century, orientation of life in Europe came to a focus on the land. The loss of Mediterranean trade routes to Moslem expansion, the breakdown of administrative order within the continent, and the continuing invasions of rural folk from the east returned European society to an agrarian subsistence economy. There arose out of the turbulence of three hundred years or more a system of land tenure based on personal allegiances, supported with landed benefices. As these became hereditary, a rigid stratification of social life took form in which each stratum was bound to the land. At the top stood the family of a military overlord, whose lands were subdivided among warrior vassals who subdivided their allotments further among lesser warrior vassals. Finally at the bottom of the pyramid were the serfs, the beasts of burden of the military-agricultural system known as feudalism. In payment for the landed benefices each stratum was obligated to come to the support of the next higher stratum, particularly on occasions of military conflict.[1]

[1] An interesting technological explanation for the emergence of the feudal order traces it to the perfection of the stirrup. With that innovation, according to Lynn White, the heavily armored, mounted warrior became possible. Not only did the appearance of heavy cavalry revolutionize warfare, it called into being the feudal land tenure system. For the provision of the armor and weaponry and even the maintenance of the horse was so expensive that great wealth was required. In a moneyless society that meant large holdings of productive land. (*Medieval Technology and Social Change* [Oxford: Clarendon Press, 1962], pp. 1–38.)

Personal allegiances, however, seldom survive great distances for long periods of time.[2] Consequently Europe under feudalism was a patchwork of small domains, each jealously guarded from external intrusions and each ruled by the idiosyncracies of its suzerain. Over the whole lay the endorsement of the universal Church, a willing partner in the fashioning of a static system. Not infrequently churchmen and monastic orders vied with secular rulers as full participants in the existing order. Feudal society was intensely parochial and ultraconservative. In principle, every man had an assigned place and tradition was the arbiter of disputes. But that principle applied only within localities; among localities or domains relations were anarchic and predatory.

Perhaps there is no better illustration of the state of affairs in the early medieval period than the difficulties of travel. Journeys over the roads were hazardous in the extreme. No man of means dared venture abroad without a group of armed guards to protect him. The stranger was always in peril regardless of his rank. Moreover, "over a journey of a hundred miles, a travelling merchant might fall under a dozen different sovereignties, each with different rules, regulations, laws, weights, measures and money."[3] At every boundary there was a toll to be paid, and passage through a domain entailed the payment of various other kinds of fees. The organization of life seemed designed to preserve insularity and to encourage parochialism.

The settlement pattern comprised a multiplicity of small villages, around 100 to 200 people in each, among which were interspersed castles, monasteries, burgs, and ecclesiastical towns. Of these only the burgs and ecclesiastical towns bore any resemblance to an urban place. But burgs assumed many different forms as the Middle Ages wore on. In the early years, for example, the burg was mainly a fortified place where the produce of a lord's estate was collected and stored and where the lord stayed periodically to attend to the administrative needs of a particular district. A duke or a baron might own several estates, each with a burg and each under the immediate supervision of a castellan. The ecclesiastical town was usually a survival of a Roman town which, with the disappearance of Roman civil authority, had fallen to the administrative responsibility of a churchman. Not until late in the medieval period was that responsibility seriously contested, for towns were of such little consequence. By

---

[2] For this reason periodic attendances at the court of the king or overlord were usually demanded of his vassals. In the meantime the overlord with his retinue circulated over his territories, consuming the harvests of preceding seasons that had been stored in his granaries or imposing himself upon the hospitality of his vassals. The Japanese *shoguns* went further. They required that members of *daimyo* families remain in permanent residence in Edo as hostages to loyalty.

[3] Robert L. Heilbroner, *The Making of Economic Society* (Englewood Cliffs, N.J.: Prentice-Hall, 1962), p. 51.

then the town had become something akin to a proprietorship, as were the burgs from the beginnings.

The prevailing economy was subsistence agriculture. The townsman, no less than the agriculturalist, lived from the land. There was virtually no market for foodstuffs; those who were not producers lived in the households of producers. Food surpluses were rarely transported more than a few miles. Transportation had actually deteriorated following the fall of the Roman Empire. It was for that reason that a feudal lord found it necessary to circulate among his estates in order to avail himself of the produce from his lands; he stayed on with his retinue in each burg until the food accumulated there was consumed. More humble folk had no such opportunity. They had to live or die by what was produced in their localities. Die they often did, since famines were recurrent. Although famine was usually quite restricted in scope, there was no escaping it. Communications were poor and the movement of surpluses from adjacent areas was all but impossible.

Feudal lords lived from rents and dues collected in kind from their demesnes. Craftsmen and servitors as well as agricultural laborers were in bondage to the aristocracy.[4] There was little money in circulation, and little need for it. Still, a few itinerant traders braved the dangers of travel to carry silks, fine linens, dyes, perfumes, and other luxury goods, originating in the Near and Far East, to those who could afford to buy them. Their stopping points were the fairs held seasonally and annually outside the walls of the burgs or of the ecclesiastical towns.[5] Local people gathered on such occasions to barter their products and to enjoy the excitement of a holiday. In the fair the trader might expect to meet with customers for his rare goods, but he might also acquire handicraft products peculiar to a district to barter or sell in a neighboring district or at the next fair on his route. At the conclusion of a fair local life lapsed again into the simple routine of a self-sufficient existence.

So much for a highly simplified description of the context in which a number of broad-scale changes slowly accumulated their effects to produce a revival of urban life. The ferment at work in medieval Europe occupied some thousand years following the close of the fifth century A.D., though indications of the resurgence of city life began to be visible as early as the tenth century. Obviously we cannot here review all of the developments that occurred in that long span of time. Nor is it necessary for our purposes. Instead we shall deal only with certain trends that are especially pertinent to urban organization.

[4] Henri Pirenne, *Economic and Social History of Medieval Europe* (New York: Harcourt, Brace, Jovanovich, 1937), pp. 40–41.

[5] See J. M. Wallace-Hadrill, *The Barbarian West*, A.D. 400–1000 (New York: Harper Torchbook, 1952), pp. 80–81.

POPULATION GROWTH

Although the data are far from satisfactory, there is reason to believe that the numbers of people in Europe declined to a primitive level following the collapse of the Roman Empire,[6] and then, around the ninth century, began a slow but steady increase.[7] How this latter turn of events came about is a matter for speculation. No doubt the establishment of the feudal system stabilized the food supply and, for all of its harshness, provided a degree of protection to life that had not existed during the chaotic years preceding it. There is the further probability that the insularity of daily living shielded people from contagious diseases, which usually moved with the flows of traffic and trade. Furthermore, the relative absence of town life exposed a very few to the effect of unsanitary conditions engendered in congested living.

Fragmentary evidence from sources such as Charlemagne's Breviary, the English Domesday Book, and surviving records of poll taxes and house counts point to a continuous growth of population until the middle of the fourteenth century. The population of France, which had contracted to about 5 million in the tenth century, grew to approximately 20 million by 1340.[8] In England the number of people at the time of the Norman Conquest was around 1.8 million. Three hundred years later the number had increased to 2.7 million.[9] It is reasonable to assume that over the rest of western Europe similar growth trends were operating.

There were also indirect indications of growth. One of these consists in reports of increases in the numbers of the unattached or floating population, made up of runaway serfs, pilgrims, and dispossessed sons.[10] In a relatively static society a significant change in an element of that kind would certainly attract attention. There is a possibility, of course, that some part of the floating population were refugees from famine areas rather than increments in the population. Support for the growth inference comes from another and more persuasive line of indirect evidence.

[6] K. W. Taylor, "Some Aspects of Population History," *Canadian Journal of Economics and Political Science,* XVI (1951): 301–13. See also J. C. Russell, *op. cit.,* p. 36.

[7] K. F. Helleiner, "Population Movement and Agrarian Depression in the Later Middle Ages," *ibid.,* XV (1949): 371–72.

According to Russell the collapse of the Roman Empire might have been due to a visitation of the plague in 545, lasting intermittently for the next two centuries. Population was decreased by 40 to 50 percent, with the result that the sizes of armies could not be maintained at sufficient levels to carry out imperial policies. ("That Earlier Plague," *Demography,* 5 [1968], pp. 174–84.)

[8] K. W. Taylor, *op. cit.,* p. 302, and Abbott P. Usher, "The History of Population and Settlement in Eurasia," *Geographical Review,* XX (1930): 110–32.

[9] K. W. Taylor, *op. cit.*

[10] Pirenne, *op. cit.,* pp. 69–70.

That evidence is found in the spread of settlement over European lands. Until the eleventh century much of Europe was unoccupied; there were vacant lands in dense forests, mountain slopes, and low-lying river valleys. But in that century began a vigorous movement of land reclamation and internal colonization which gathered momentum in the century following. Leadership in the development fell mainly to monastic orders, notably the Cistercian and the Hospitallers. The latter order is reported to have cleared an area in one locality sufficient for the creation of forty villages within a 10-year period.[11] While less aggressive in promoting reclamation and settlement, feudal lords nevertheless welcomed and encouraged the clearing of their forests and the drainage of their swamps by eager settlers drawn from the footloose population. An indication of the receptive attitude toward the colonizers lies in the fact that they were allowed to retain their freeman status and were lightly burdened wih feudal dues.[12] The bringing of waste lands into use added greatly to the agricultural resources of Europe.

The presence of dispossessed sons in the floating population mentioned above deserves special attention. Under the practice of primogeniture, common among landed families of Europe, second sons and those of higher birth order were thrust out of the parental household upon death of the father and succession of the eldest son as head of the family. The cadets, as the younger offspring were called, had no recourse; they were forced to live by their wits in a social situation that offered few legitimate opportunities. They became beggars, brigands, mercenary soldiers, and traders. In time these persons, especially those who became traders, would prove to be the instruments of drastic changes in European society. A practice by which was preserved the equilibrium in a principal institution of the feudal system, the seignorial family, turned out to be the means of destroying the system.[13]

TECHNOLOGICAL CHANGE

The development and settlement of idle lands could hardly have advanced far without the occurrence of a number of technological innovations. Foremost among these was the adoption of the moldboard plow in the ninth and tenth centuries. Until then it was impossible to turn the heavy soils of northern Europe. The delay in the use of the moldboard plow, which had been known in Roman times, was due to a lack of ap-

[11] John H. Mundy and Peter Reisenberg, *The Medieval Town* (New York: Van Nostrand, 1958), pp. 28–29.

[12] Pirenne, *op. cit.*, pp. 60–70.

[13] J. J. Habakkuk, "Inheritance Rules and Economic Change," *The Journal of Economic History*, XV (1955): 1–13; and Pirenne, *op. cit.*, pp. 69–70.

propriate organization among peasants. For the plow required not one but four to eight oxen to draw it. Since few peasants owned so many, they had to devise an arrangement for pooling their capital resources. Furthermore, the old square-shaped field, based on the necessity of cross-plowing with the lighter tool then in general use, was unsuitable to the heavier plow. With the latter a single plowing was sufficient, though space was required in which to turn the plow. Consequently, a redistribution of land was essential so that fields could be plowed in long strips. The strips could then be assigned in rotation among the several owners of plow and oxen. The pooling of both equipment and land eliminated individuality of decision as to time and sequence of farm operation and led to the establishment of village councils to decide questions of land use and management.[14]

Closely associated with the adaptations attendant upon use of the mold-board plow was the substitution of three-field rotation for the two-field system of land use. The economies gained from that alteration were very substantial. In the first place, only one third instead of one half of the land needs to lie fallow in each season, resulting in an immediate increase in productivity of 16 percent with each planting. But since it permitted three plantings a year rather than two, the total effect was to double productivity. Furthermore, the three-field system raised the efficiency of agriculture by spreading work more evenly over the year; and the crop diversification it permitted added further stability to the food supply. Of particular importance in the latter connection was the possibility of using the spring planting for the production of animal food crops, particularly oats as food for horses. It was at this juncture, according to Lynn White, that the horse came into general use for the first time.[15]

The development of a supply of grain food coincided closely with three almost simultaneous inventions that greatly improved the load capacity of the horse: the horsecollar, the tandem harness, and the horseshoe.[16] With these, though roads remained impassable during wet seasons, the cost of overland transportation in dry seasons declined to a third of what it had been. Thus towns could obtain their food supplies and maintain rela-

[14] Lynn White, op. cit., pp. 43–44, and Charles Singer (ed.), A History of Technology (Oxford: Clarendon Press, 1954), Vol. II, pp. 86–93. William McNeill contends that the opportunity for this reorganization of agriculture arose in the havoc caused by Viking and Magyar raids. (The Rise of The West, p. 452.)

[15] Op. cit., p. 72. According to F. W. Maitland, the presence of three fields did not necessarily mean that two were planted each year. In eleventh century England two were left fallow as often as planted. A full transition to the three-field system was a protracted process of accommodation. (Domesday Book and Beyond: Three Essays in the Early History of England. [1897] [London: Fontana Library, 1969], pp. 425–26.)

[16] Lynn White, "Technology and Invention in the Middle Ages," Speculum, XV (1940): 141–56.

tions of other kinds over much larger territories than had formerly been possible. There also appears to have been, in central Europe at least, a regrouping of rural population in much larger villages.[17] In general, however, roads remained undependable for anything heavier than a light cart. The increased use of the horse appeared primarily in the multiplication of pack trains; bulk cargoes as well as high-value goods were moved in that manner. Networks of crude roadways linking towns to supply areas were developed and extended, though their maintenance was indifferently attended to. Hence the principal avenues of local transport were the inland waterways. River ports were established complete with quays, derricks, and storage sheds. Still, the multiplicity of tolls, on river as well as on overland traffic, tended to neutralize the benefits of technological gains in transportation.[18]

Thus technical improvements, especially in agriculture,[19] and population increase complemented one another in an interactive relationship. Population growth led to a clearing and settling of lands and thereby allowed a wider scope for the application of technical advances. The latter steadily augmented the food supply for the support of a larger population. But it appears that increase in agricultural productivity moved faster than population growth; it yielded a growing surplus for an enlarging proportion of non-agriculturalists. Many and perhaps most of the rising number of non-agriculturalists found employment in rural industries. It is known that a fine woolen cloth was being produced in considerable quantity in Flanders by the eleventh century, Burgundy was producing choice wines for export, shallow tin, lead, and copper mines were being worked over many parts of Europe, and in numerous districts local handicrafts were being cultivated beyond local requirements. The process of interstimulation that underlies these early industrial stirrings is cloaked in obscurity. There is little doubt, however, that technical advances involved more than the invention and improvement of tools; they also included new forms of organization without which in many cases the tools could not have been used. It is entirely likely that the medieval period was most prolific on the score of organizational innovation.

[17] Lynn White, *Medieval Technology and Social Change,* p. 67.
[18] As late as the end of the fifteenth century there were sixty-four tolls on the Rhine, thirty-five on the Elbe, and seventy-seven on the Danube where it passed through Austria. (Henri Pirenne, *op. cit.,* p. 87.)
[19] Many other technical gains occurred in the Middle Ages. The Germans contributed the wearing of trousers and furs, an easily heated compact house, feltmaking, skis, the use of soap for cleaning, butter as a replacement for olive oil, the making of barrels and tubs and the cultivation of rye, oats, and hops. Of signal importance was the invention of the crank, combining rotary and reciprocal motions, and its application to grinding, milling, and other kinds of machine operations. (See Lynn White, "Technology and Invention in the Middle Ages," pp. 141–56.)

THE REVIVAL OF TRADE

The trader was probably never entirely absent from the European scene during the darkest part of the medieval age. Wherever there are commodities to exchange and willing customers, the trader seems to appear. Certainly in the eighth century itinerant traders were wandering over the continent, visiting the fairs and the castles of nobility, catering mainly to the whims of the wealthy. The numbers of wandering merchants seem to have grown with the increase of population, the improvement of the food supply, and the development of rural handicrafts. As the supporting base for trade was enlarged more and more of the unattached population were diverted—from brigandage, mercenary soldiery, and other hazardous pursuits—to commercial opportunities. The relatively slow growth of trading activities was dramatically accelerated in the eleventh century.

The impetus to the rather sudden resurgence of trade came, paradoxically enough, from the religious Crusades. The Crusades drew off excess population from Europe and with it shattered the isolation of Europe from the Byzantine East. As the Crusaders assaulted the Moslem world, with the assistance and occasionally under the guidance of the Venetian merchants and shippers, they carried with them a demand for European goods for which they paid with exotic booty from pillaged towns. A flood of commerce across the eastern end of the Mediterranean was released, bringing into Europe not only increasing quantities of trade goods but also a supply of coinage in precious metals. Although Venetian shippers and merchants were the principal beneficiaries of the large-scale commercial relations with the East, many of the Crusaders shared in the spoils of war and thereby acquired capital for entrepreneurial ventures. They also brought back into feudal Europe a host of contrasting ideas about standards of consumption, the uses of money, techniques of doing things, and the propriety of alternative ways of life.

Feudal Europe was ill-prepared for the revolutionary implications of the growth of commerce. It was receptive to the goods and the coins carried by the merchant, but not to his notions of freedom, his lack of commitment to the established order, and his rational approach to routines of life. The traders' sophistication and the literacy they later acquired, not to mention their wealth, were an affront to a people of limited experience and doctrinaire convictions. For this reason, and because, too, traders lived beyond the pale of traditional morality, they were fair game for anyone who could prey upon them. Out of a need for protection traders often banded together in their travels and frequently hired armed guards. One authority on the medieval period attributes the origin of merchant guilds to the spirit of fraternity that arose from a sharing of experiences during their hazardous journeys.[20]

We pointed out above the multiplicity of tolls and feudal dues that obstructed transportation. The trader was taxed repeatedly as he traveled from district to district and taxed again when he paused to sell his goods. He was allowed no shelter in most towns and on the high roads he was unprotected from robbery and extortion. If he married a wife from the servile class, she remained in bondage, as did the children from the union. The prevailing doctrine of the "just" or "fair" price, meaning variously an exchange without profit or a profit approved by a buyer, was endorsed by the Church and enforced whenever it was convenient to do so. There were no sympathetic courts to which the trader could appeal and no consistent body of law that defined the terms of justice. Nothing less than a bold and intelligent man could survive in so inhospitable an environment.

Despite these impediments, trade flourished. It did so, as we have said, on the strength of population increase and of the progressive affluence of the agricultural economy. Of great importance was the development of rural handicraft industries. From that activity the trader found a rich supplement to his luxury traffic. Thus commerce diversified as it grew in volume. It insinuated itself into more and more nooks and crannies of the agricultural society. These changes were especially prominent along the routes leading north from the Alps through the Rhône Valley into Flanders and on into Scandinavia.

THE GROWTH OF TOWNS

Town life lay dormant in western Europe until late in the tenth century, and until a much later date in central and eastern Europe.[21] Prior to the revival of commerce most of the towns, such as they were, had been held as proprietorships by members of the feudal nobility, both clerical and secular. They resembled nothing so much as enlarged households of landed aristocrats.[22] The static character of the feudal order held the towns as well as the countryside in its grip.

[20] Fritz Rörig, *The Medieval Town* (Berkeley: University of California Press, 1967), pp. 19–20.

[21] It is reported that Cambridge, England, added an average of but one house per year during the two centuries beginning in 1086. (George G. Coulton, *Medieval Panorama* [London: Meridian Books, 1955], p. 285.)

[22] Pirenne describes the composition of the ecclesiastical town as follows: "It was composed of the clerics of the cathedral church and of the other churches grouped nearby; of the monks of the monasteries which, especially after the ninth century, came to be established, sometimes in great numbers, in the see of the diocese; of the teachers and the students of the ecclesiastical schools; and finally, of servitors and

Yet it was often at towns, as noted, that the occasional fairs were convened. There also merchants frequently would rest after their long trips and would bide their time while waiting for the passing of inclement seasons. Gradually merchant settlements developed, usually outside the town gates, for seldom was the merchant invited to share the protection of the walls.[23] The *faubourg*, or suburb, as those settlements were called, later surrounded itself with walls attached to the walls of the town.[24] There was then usually enough business in a locality to keep merchants or their agents in continuous employment at a given site. Furthermore, by that time, i.e., the twelfth century, the merchant class had become literate and was therefore able to centralize the control of long-distance trade from fixed points of settlement.[25]

The town with its merchant settlement came to be appreciated as having economic value, mainly as an extra source of income for a feudal lord, often as his only source of money income. Members of that class began to take the merchant under his protection. The counts of Champagne, for example, established fairs at Troyes, Provins, and elsewhere in their territories. These were carefully regulated; and, to assure their success, merchants were protected on the roads and in their business dealings.[26] In the twelfth century and afterward town-building was vigorously pursued. Many towns appeared spontaneously, with the blessings of feudal lords, on recently reclaimed lands and at mineral sites; others were launched as frankly speculative ventures. In all, nearly one thousand towns were added to the settlement pattern of medieval Europe.[27] The success of a town as a commercial enterprise was measured not only by the presence of a colony of merchants, but also by the extent to which the merchants were able to organize rural industries and bring them into the

---

artisans, free or serf, who were indispensable to the needs of the religious group and to the daily existence of the clerical agglomeration." (*Medieval Cities*, p. 66.) Speaking of the burg, Pirenne says: "Its population comprised, aside from the knights and clerics who make up its essential part, only men employed in their service and whose number was certainly of little importance. It was a fortress population. It produced nothing of itself, lived by revenues from the surrounding country, and had no other economic role than that of a simple consumer." (*Medieval Cities*, p. 75.) (Reproduced with permission of Princeton University Press; copyright 1939.)

[23] There is an interesting parallel in this respect in the Japanese castle towns. See John W. Hall, "The Castle Town and Japan's Modern Urbanization," *The Far Eastern Quarterly*, XV (1955): 48–49.

[24] Successive additions of this kind gave to later medieval towns a cell-like aspect, with each cell occupied by a different class of specialists.

[25] Fritz Rörig, *op. cit.*, p. 43.

[26] Sidney Painter, *Medieval Society* (Ithaca: Cornell University Press, 1951), pp. 76–77. Much earlier, Charlemagne had issued protective edicts for all travelers, but enforcement was ineffectual.

[27] Robert L. Heilbroner, *op. cit.*, p. 48.

towns where they could be supervised. To populate the new towns with a sufficient labor supply, the custom developed of granting permanent sanctuary to anyone who remained in a town for a year and a day. "City air," it was said, "made men free."

Town success depended also upon location. Many of the points at which people had habitually congregated for local market days or to celebrate religious occasions, such as at monasteries and fortified burgs, failed to emerge as the sites of growing towns. Although some of those places contained great concentrations of wealth, their situations were often remote from the ordinary streams of movement. Unless a town site lay athwart avenues of travel, the town had little prospect of growth. Originally, favorable sites occurred principally at coastal locations. Later, with the development of overland routes and the assurance of protection to the traveler, locations appeared in the interior of Europe, especially whenever land routes intersected navigable streams. In general, town growth was a winnowing process in which places with superior access flourished whereas others with poorer location were either relegated to subordinate positions or disappeared entirely. The locations of the principal urban centers in Europe, in the thirteenth century, are shown in Fig. 1.

THE EMERGENCE OF MUNICIPAL INSTITUTIONS

The growth of towns as commercial centers within a fabric of seignorial rights, overlapping jurisdictions, and administrative procedures adapted to a stagnant agricultural economy provoked a continuing conflict between the old order and the requirements of the emergent middle class. The demands of the merchants were simple. As listed by Pirenne, they included, first, personal freedom to come and go, to live where one wished, and to have wife and children emancipated from bondage. Second, a special tribunal was sought which would eliminate the excessive claims of numerous jurisdictions and the irrelevant complexities of archaic laws.[28] The merchant wanted, third, a uniform and rational penal code to which he could appeal with some hope of justice. Finally, he wanted to be freed from the multiplicity of fees and tolls which impinged upon his every act.[29] In short, the merchant demanded a set of municipal institutions which amounted to local self-government under the control of the merchant class. Since effective central governments had not yet come into being, the contest for the attainment of these objectives was joined

[28] See Sidney Painter on the administration of justice in the medieval town (op. cit., p. 87).

[29] Medieval Cities, p. 170. See also W. Cunningham and Ellen McArthur, Outlines of English Industrial History (New York: Macmillan, 1908), pp. 50 ff.

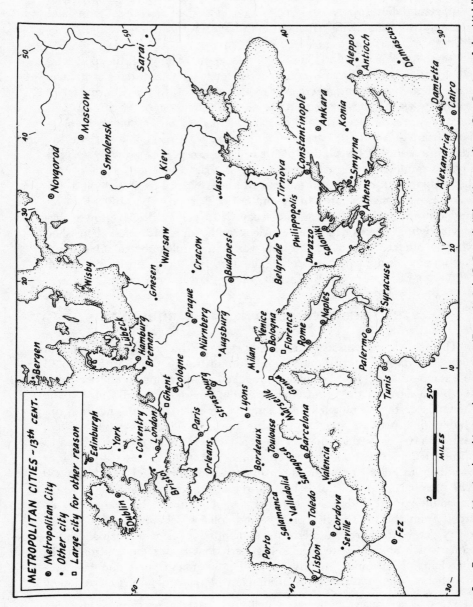

Fig. 1. European cities in the thirteenth century. (From Josiah C. Russel, "The Metropolitan City Region of the Middle Ages," *Journal of Regional Science*, II [1960]: 57. Reproduced with permission of the copyright holder and the author.)

locally in town after town.[30] The reform movement progressed through small concessions and violent clashes for a century or more. The landed aristocracy found itself poorly matched against the growing financial strength of the merchant group. In the Tuscan towns of Florence, Sienna, and Pisa the struggle was won early. There, after prolonged conflict, the bishops and feudal families were exiled to their rural estates and merchant-dominated communes were established.[31] As the movement spread across northern Europe the outcome was usually the same.[32] Municipal charters were wrested from feudal authorities, sometimes with the aid of a king who wished to embarrass and subjugate a recalcitrant aristocracy. Evidently feudal lords came to appreciate some advantages from town autonomy, for the charters extracted from them by the burghers were later used as models of charters voluntarily granted to *villes neuves* founded on reclaimed lands.[33]

The attainment of municipal autonomy, in Pirenne's view, marked the beginning of the city in the full sense of the word. A coherent civic order, in which impartial civil law could evolve, was established. It thus became possible to rationalize and standardize procedures and to extend them over the countryside so that the flows of communication and commerce would be relatively unimpeded by uncertainties and irregularities. It became possible, in other words, for the city to enter into a regularized partnership with its rural hinterland through an exchange of good and services. Out of necessity rather than altruism, the requirements of trade fostered and diffused a civility in human relations. If different groups of men are to constitute markets for the services of one another, they must be brought into a division of labor so that each has the wherewithal to purchase from the other. If functional interdependencies are to be relied upon, all parties must be treated as equals, at least before the law. Hence the city has usually been the enemy of serfdom and slavery. If the division of labor is to be raised to higher levels of productivity, opportunities for the cultivation of skills and for learning must be maximized. It is not surprising, therefore, that the humanist movement found its origins in the

[30] Gideon Sjoberg writes vaguely of the primacy of social power in the development of the city. He overlooks the fact, however, that the rise of the medieval European city entailed a transfer and reconstitution of power. See his *The Preindustrial City* (New York: The Free Press, 1960), pp. 85–86. See also Rörig, *op. cit.*, p. 56.

[31] In the tenth and eleventh centuries Florence was the scene of warring factions each with its fortified tower into which it retreated when bested in street fighting. (Ferdinand Schevill, *Medieval and Renaissance Florence* [New York: Harper Torchbook, 1963], vol. I, pp. 63–86.)

[32] In Germany variations in the process of town emancipation occurred in connection with whether the town developed on church, noble, or crown lands. But the end result, barring minor differences, was essentially the same in all instances. (J. W. Thompson, *Economic and Social History of Europe in the Later Middle Ages, 1300–1530* [New York: Appleton-Century-Crofts, 1931].)

[33] Pirenne, *Economic and Social History of Medieval Europe*, p. 70.

emergent city.[34] In short, the reforms obtained by the medieval merchant class harbored implications that reached far beyond anything intended. This is not to say that the respect of man for his fellow man and the decline of interpersonal violence were immediate outcomes of the rise of municipal institutions. On the contrary, the requisites for mutual dependence were often ignored or suppressed and only gradually did they penetrate men's consciousness. The process of learning how to live in an urban context has been a long and painful process. Nevertheless, the emergence of municipal institutions fulfilled one of the pre-conditions for a growth "take-off," to use Walt Rostow's term.[35] The universe in this instance, of course, was not a nation; it was a local territory accessible from a town site.

As cities achieved autonomy they began systematically to cultivate the local markets and rural industries within their reaches. Competition among Italian cities caused expansion to be an object of militant policy, pursued through armed conflict and culminating in the reduction of the loser to the status of a secondary center in the dominion of the victor. This was the fate of Pisa and Sienna as a result of their struggles with Florence. But just as often the objective was attained by virtue of the advantages of proximity, through the development of local road systems and the profferment of economic inducements. By one means or another each city came into possession of a *banlieue,* a belt of rural territory over which it presided as an urban center. In the thirteenth century the territory tributary to Metz included 168 villages; Rouen was the focus of activity for 35 villages; and the small city of Provins exerted influence over 8 villages.[36] In Germany the average town was the center of 30 to 40 villages,[37] but Lübeck claimed 240 villages in its dependent area. Russell's studies of city regions in the medieval period reveal some tendency toward a regular spacing of smaller places in the territories adjacent to larger ones.[38]

There was thus the beginning in the Middle Ages of what N. S. B. Gras, the economic historian, characterized as the "town economy." This referred to a unit of local organization, comprising the town as a nucleus and the surrounding lands to a distance of 10 to 20 miles, which with its

[34] Cf. Schevill, *op. cit.,* vol. II, pp. 317–18 and Rörig, *op. cit.,* p. 142.

[35] *The Stages of Economic Growth* (Cambridge: The University Press, 1963), pp. 36–58.

[36] Mundy and Reisenberg, *op. cit.,* p. 35.

[37] E. A. Gutkind, *Urban Development in Central Europe,* Vol. I. *International History of City Development* (New York: Free Press, 1964), p. 193.

[38] J. C. Russell, "The Metropolitan City Region of the Middle Ages," *Journal of Regional Science,* II (1960): 55–70. For example, in the vicinity of Leicestershire, in Domesday England, villages of 50 to 100 people were spaced about 1.8 miles apart; towns of 100 population were about 4.2 miles apart; and settlements of around 200 people were separated on the average by 8.8 miles (p. 62).

villages constituted the remaining component of the economic cell: "Town economy is an organization of producers and consumers who work out their dependence on one another and on the outside world through the agency of a town." [39] Many units of this kind became so ingrown, without any inducement such as walls or other physical barriers, that they became culturally homogeneous social units. The time consumed in walking to and from the town nucleus on market days and on other festive occasions left so little time for movement in other directions that the outer edges of the dependent area were effectively sealed off against competing influences.

The cleavage between city and country was not entirely bridged by the formation of a town economy. Although relations between the two were drawn much closer, the prevailing attitude in the city was often one favoring exploitation of the rural folk. The guilds engaged in monopolistic practices that were harsh and discriminatory in their effects on the peasantry. In many places industry in rural districts was banned and forced into the city. Peasants were often excluded from the city after nightfall unless under the patronage of a citizen. Wealthy landed families were sometimes accorded similar treatment. In northern cities they were banished from the walls. In the south, having once been exiled, landed families were later required to live in cities where their activities could be kept under surveillance. Urbanization of the countryside was launched in the medieval period but was left far from completion. In retrospect some justification for exploitative policies can be argued. Such an interlude seems to have been necessary for the accumulation of capital required for a later surge of development that could bring the agricultural population into a fuller partnership with the city. The Renaissance was doubtless financed, at least in part, through that means. Less conspicuous, however, was its ultimate contribution to industrialization.[40]

After the metamorphosis of towns into cities, medieval economy existed as a multiplicity of highly localized markets linked in networks of long-distance trading relationships. There was little in the way of organization unifying territories in the middle distances. Even long-distance trade remained hazardous, subject always to marauding princes, brigandage, and exorbitant taxes. England was first to acquire sufficient internal political order to permit a relatively free traffic among commercial centers. Even

[39] *An Introduction to Economic History* (London: Harper and Row, 1922), p. 109.
[40] See Miriam Beard, *The History of the Business Man* (New York: Macmillan, 1938), p. 160. This hypothesis has also been advanced by Robert L. Heilbroner, *The Great Ascent: The Struggle for Economic Development in Our Time* (New York: Harper Torchbooks, 1963), p. 79, and by Nathan Keyfitz, "Political-Economic Aspects of Urbanization in South and Southeast Asia" in *The Study of Urbanization*, ed. by P. M. Hauser and Leo F. Schnore (New York: John Wiley, 1967), pp. 265–310.

there very few places maintained commercial relations beyond their immediate market areas. Elsewhere, cities found it necessary to form leagues
for mutual protection. A dozen or more German and Baltic cities entered
into the powerful Hanseatic League in the thirteenth century. In the
following century there appeared the shorter-lived League of Swabian
Cities and the Rhenish League. But in that century political unification
began to develop on the continent, first in France after the termination of
the Hundred Years' War, then in the Netherlands and in Switzerland. In
northern Italy the eighty-odd city-states were gathered into ten larger
political units. The medieval city lost its autonomy with the emergence
of strong central governments.

SIZES OF CITIES

Judged by contemporary standards, the sizes attained by individual
cities were unimpressive. What would be regarded as a large village or
a modest-sized city today served in the medieval period as a major metropolis. One must bear in mind, of course, that agricultural practices
were still rather primitive, transportation was slow and costly, and industry had not advanced beyond a handicraft stage. Seen in that light, some
of the population figures presented in Table 3 are striking indeed. The
data shown in the table are of uneven quality; some figures are reasonably
dependable, others are rough approximations. Even so, they are the product of a laborious and painstaking effort at historical reconstruction.

The ranking of cities in order of size in Table 3 reveals something of
the historical sequence in which cities appeared and rose to ascendancy,
the variation in dates to which the figures pertain notwithstanding. As
noted in an earlier connection, city growth developed first in northern
Italy, then spread northward in western Europe and at much later dates
began to occur in central Europe. It should also be observed that most
of the dates follow the Black Death epidemic of 1349, which reaped a
holocaust in places of congested settlement. An enumeration in Florence
at the turn of the fourteenth century reported a population of 90,000,
almost twice the population shown in the table for 1381. The size of
Milan was reduced from 52,000, in 1300, to approximately 8,000, in 1482.
Thus many of the figures for dates after 1349 doubtless understate the
maximum sizes to which many cities had grown. On the other hand,
places not then deeply involved in the network of trade routes that had
been spreading over Europe were spared the ravages of the plague.

There remains some uncertainty about whether the population sizes
shown in Table 3 represent the numbers of inhabitants within city walls
or include also residents of outlying territory claimed by cities. Densities

Table 3. Estimated Populations and Areas of Selected Medieval Cities

City	Date	Population	Land Area (Acres)
Venice	1363	77,700	810
Paris	1192	59,200	945
Florence	1381	54,747	268
Milan	1300	52,000	415
Genoa	1500	37,788	732
Rome	1198	35,000	3,450
London	1377	34,971	720
Bologna	1371	32,000	507
Barcelona	1359	27,056	650
Naples	1278	22,000	300
Hamburg	1250	22,000	510
Brussels	1496	19,058	650
Sienna	1385	16,700	412
Antwerp	1437	13,760	880
Pisa	1228	13,000	285
Frankfort	1410	9,844	320
Liège	1470	8,000	200
Amsterdam	1470	7,476	195
Zurich	1357	7,399	175
Berlin	1450	6,000	218
Geneva	1404	4,204	75
Vienna	1391	3,836	90
Dresden	1396	3,745	140
Leipzig	1474	2,076	105

SOURCE: J. C. Russell, *Late Ancient and Medieval Population* (Philadelphia: The American Philosophical Society, 1958), pp. 60–62.

ranging up to and above 100,000 per square mile are questionable. A crowding of people that even approximated that figure could only have been achieved with an extremely intensive use of the land and at considerable cost for transportation. Rome stands out in the series as having an exceptionally low density. But Rome had been in decline for some centuries and had been devastated by the Normans in the eleventh century. It was enjoying some recovery as an administrative center for the Church during the twelfth century.

THE INTERNAL ORDER OF THE CITY

Since the beginnings of barbarian invasions of Europe the wall had been an indispensable element of town structure. The wall defined the living space available and supplied a rough outline of a physical pattern.

Within the wall of the old towns confusion appeared more commonly than order. Streets were narrow and winding and were densely lined with buildings that overhung and sometimes overarched the rights-of-way. Some of the newer towns, as on the eastern marches of Europe, had been planned and therefore possessed greater clarity of pattern. In general, however, the variation from place to place was so great that it would be misleading to suggest the existence of anything approaching a consistent physical pattern. Where there might have been one at an earlier time, growth and changing composition of the city obscured it.[41] Nevertheless, it is possible to identify a few common features.

At the outset two kinds of gathering places or nodal points were found in the town, one religious, the other political. The cathedral often stood opposite a main gate in the town wall, separated by a large open space or plaza. Its location spoke for the religious ministration of the town to the country. The plaza was the setting of religious festivals and other gala occasions. When commercial activities were allowed inside the gate, they congregated on and around the plaza. If a town were large enough, it might have two or three or more parishes, each with its church and smaller plaza. The political gathering point was marked by the palace of the reigning prince, a bishop of the church in some instances, a secular lord in others. There much of the population converged for employment and the hope of employment. Residences of other members of the elite were gathered close about the prince's palace.[42] While in general the streets were narrow, winding passageways suitable only for pedestrian and animal traffic, an avenue wide enough to accommodate wheeled vehicles led from the main gate to the political center.

As the merchant class rose to power the center of orientation in a city shifted in some instances to the *faubourg*. But there were cities in which the merchant class, at least its more successful members, left the outer settlement and preempted the residences of the older elite. Streets and districts came to be differentiated by trades and crafts, the members of each occupation tending to cluster their residences for mutual support and the promotion of common interests.[43] There was no separation of home

[41] For discussions of city patterns see Gutkind, *op. cit.*; R. E. Dickinson, "The Morphology of the Medieval German Town," *Geographical Review*, XXXV (1945); 74–97; and Cecil Stewart, *A Prospect for Cities: Studies Towards a History of Town Planning* (London: Longmans, Green and Co., 1952).

[42] According to Francis H. Parker, medieval London did not follow the pattern in which upper class houses were concentrated at the center. (*The Image of Opportunity and the Medieval Country Town*, unpublished doctoral dissertation, University of North Carolina, 1963.)

[43] Writing of Elizabethan London, M. St. Clare Byren says: "Printers were only just becoming associated with Fleet Street, which was still more famous for its taverns and its 'motions' or sideshows of all kinds. Paul's Churchyard was almost entirely appropriated by the booksellers, Bucklersbury by the grocers and apothecaries. East

from workplace; occupation was a family concern. Intramural transportation, moreover, was too inefficient to encourage daily commuting to and
from place of work, though most towns were so small that walking distances had no great influence on location. Whenever there were costs of
transportation to be borne, however, they were invariably imposed upon
the day laborers and the poor; the underprivileged were relegated to the
outer reaches of a town and sometimes beyond its walls. Any tendency
toward the development of an inclusive and symmetrical pattern in the
distribution of activities was offset by a compartmentalization of the enclosed space. Cell-like enclosures marked off by inner walls and accessible
to one another through gates that might be closed at night were commonplace. Thirteenth century Ratisbon (now Regensburg) comprised three
separate cells, one for royalty, a second for clergy, and a third for merchants. Elsewhere the subdivision was sometimes more elaborate.
Among the many compartments in Frankfurt were the Nuremburg Court,
the Compstella, the Braunfels, and numerous strongholds. From the beginning, it seems, town peace was always subject to interruption by violent clashes between contentious families and competing factions. Municipal institutions had not yet developed so far as to include an effective
police force. Only the foolhardy ventured into the streets after dark
without arms and company. Street lighting, fire protection, and other
municipal services were just as primitive as the policing service.

Surges of town growth exerted various effects on physical structures.
Growth was normally accommodated by adding cells to the cluster through
the incorporation of contiguous *faubourgs*. On occasion it became necessary to rebuild the main walls on a larger circumference. In that event
footings of the old walls were usable as rights-of-way for circular avenues.
But growth was seldom very great in amount. The limitations on town
size that had been in effect from ancient times remained in force through
most of the medieval era.

Congestion and the lack of sanitary facilities and knowledge made the
medieval city a malodorous place. Sewage was dumped into the streets
and the offal of slaughtered animals was allowed to rot where it was
dropped. Water purification was an unknown craft. Although street
paving was known from Roman times, its cost was high enough to dis-
courage a surfacing of thoroughfares. Consequently refuse accumulated
in heaps and puddles, serving as breeding grounds for vermin and as
food for rats. Occasional efforts to control waste disposal seem to have

---

Cheap was still famous for its cookshops, but the butchers were encroaching upon it
in addition to occupying most of the shops in St. Nicholas Shambles . . . Cook shops
shared Thames Street with the stock-fishmongers . . . Bread Street and Milk Street
indicated their inhabitants' callings by their names, as did Goldsmiths' Row . . ."
(*Elizabethan Life in Town and Country* [London: Methuen, 1957], p. 81.)

been undertaken largely for aesthetic reasons. Later, as civic interest developed, the guilds assumed responsibility for cleaning and maintaining their respective streets. Despite these efforts mortality remained high. There is no ground for believing that survival rates in the medieval city were significantly different from what they had been in ancient towns. The city continued to be a consumer of population; without migration the excess of deaths over births could soon reduce the medieval city to an uninhabited shell.

Just as there was no clear separation of residence from workplace, so there was no manifest demarcation between social and economic units. The family was the all-purpose unit, the cornerstone of society, as it had been from time immemorial. Whatever the interest or activity, the family was the vehicle for its pursuit in all reaches of society from the elite to the humblest class. Should the family be deficient in members for any enterprise, it recruited additional members through kinship equivalents such as adoption and the more tenuous apprenticeship. Marriage, a family-controlled arrangement, was used to link families in larger mutual-aid organizations, that is, to extend the kinship bond. But, under the secularizing influences of city life, families engaged in similar occupations combined without benefit of kinship surrogates to form voluntary associations known as *guilds*. The medieval guild was an adaptation of the corporation, borrowed from the monastic orders and the church fraternities to promote ritual celebrations, social services, and economic regulations of interest to its members. That form of organization spread from one handicraft industry to another, especially those whose products were consumed mainly in local markets. Out of the civic concern they engendered, the guilds became the chief regulatory agencies in the cities, even in the matter of approving and supervising candidacy for citizenship. As they grew stronger they established their sovereignty in communal governments. Eventually they fell under the control of their wealthier members. From that point on, monopolization and regulation of trade became their main functions. After the fourteenth century the guilds were increasingly subjected to central-government control and a consequent loss of influence.[44]

Not all of the working population was organized in guilds. In many cities the industrial entrepreneur had appeared, particularly in the manufacture of textiles—silks, woolens, and linens. He purchased quantities of raw materials from wholesale merchants and entered into mass production for foreign commerce. Hence, in Lucca, Florence, Ghent, Ypres, Brussels, Louvain, and other textile centers a class of wage-earners developed. Although "corporations" were formed within industrial segments

[44] Andrew Hacker (ed.), *The Corporation Take-Over* (Garden City, N.Y., Doubleday and Co., 1965), pp. 47–48.

of that group, they were unable to monopolize their occupations as were the guilds. Having few privileges and exposed as it was to the vicissitudes of markets and raw material supplies, this class of people constituted an urban proletariat. It was a source of unrest and turbulence and, in consequence, it was often the victim of violent repressive measures.[45]

Urban development in the West was arrested in the fourteenth century by the Black Death, which struck first in 1349, again in the 1360's, and intermittently for the next two hundred years or more. The growth of commerce and the circulation of people, both essential to urban development, opened the doors of Europe to the invasion and spread of the plague. Between one quarter and one third of the population of Europe succumbed to the disease in the fourteenth century alone. The numbers of people in cities, families, monasteries, and other institutions were so depleted that in a great many instances these social units could no longer operate as such. The havoc was aggravated by the flights of people from areas where the epidemic was in full course and by the bitter efforts on the part of people in other localities to turn aside the floods of refugees. Although a few districts were but lightly touched by the plague, its repercussions were generally felt. Trade was everywhere disrupted, organized life was imperiled, and the normal paths of cultural transmission were obstructed. Some elements of technology are known to have been lost temporarily, to be rediscovered only after the passage of several generations. The full consequences of the Black Death are impossible to measure. It has been estimated that at least a century was required for the replacement of population losses. Organizational and cultural restoration is more difficult to trace, for soon afterward Europe was visited by another broad-scale disturbance—an epidemic of warfare incidental to the political unification and expansion of national states.

SUMMARY

Medieval European cities arose in the uncongenial context of a feudal order. A revival of trade and an increasing productivity of agriculture created markets for goods and services and thereby raised the proportions of population that could depend on non-agricultural occupations. In the preceding chapter three requisites to town development were noted. Those were: (1) an agricultural surplus sufficient to support specialists in other occupations; (2) transportation adequate to the task of moving food and other bulky materials to concentration of population; and (3) a location of high accessibility which facilitates a convergence of traffic and communication on the town and permits an extension of influence

[45] Pirenne, *op. cit.*, pp. 185–88.

over a wide territory. The examination of European experience in the present chapter adds two more requisites for urban development to the list. One is the appearance of a class of venturesome individuals, i.e., entrepreneurs, who through their risk-taking and capital formation, stimulate industry, expand markets, and bring about the growth of an organization capable of integrating an enlarging economy. The second is a standardization of the terms of discourse—weights, measures, coinage, idiom, law, and the principles of justice, in order to enhance the efficiency of the circulation of goods, services, ideas, and information. The broader the area over which such standardization prevails, the greater are the possibilities of urban growth and development. Municipal institutions, as against feudal and ecclesiastical institutions, were essential to the realization of both of these requisites. In the absence of strong central governments, the merchant class sought to achieve a rational organization and a cultural generalization by its own powers. A necessary step under the existing circumstances was to replace the proprietorships under which feudal authorities held the towns with municipal communes adapted to the needs of commerce.

The importance attributed to trade in the rise of urbanism might seem to imply an assumption of economic determinism. On the contrary, however, trade is as much a social as it is an economic activity. In order for an exchange relationship to last beyond a chance encounter, some very fundamental understanding must be reached and some common procedures must be adopted by all parties. Communication is necessary; an appreciation of the culture of the one by the other is essential; mutual trust is imperative; and all participants must submit to a given set of rules. Trade creates numerous common denominators. Thus it is a source of civility among men and a great humanizing agent in their culture. Having acknowledged as much, it is still important to recognize that a city is basically an organization for the production and distribution of sustenance. Of course, sustenance is itself a many-faceted quality.

While the European city was developing a division of labor and an administrative organization befitting a center of a network of long-distance trading relationships, the Muslim city lay in comparative stability under the domination of foreign conquerors, the Mamluks.[46] The latter, content to live on their estates and to provide a minimum of services, divorced themselves almost entirely from urban affairs. The principal centers were subdivided into numerous quarters occupied in each instance by persons of similar kinship and village ties. In Damascus there were seventy such quarters, Aleppo included fifty or more, in Cairo there were thirty-seven; the lesser towns of Tripoli, Baalbek, and Namus had cor-

[46] Ira H. Lapidus, *Muslim Cities in the Later Middle Ages* (Cambridge: Harvard University Press, 1967), ch. II.

respondingly fewer. Trade and industry were harnessed to the needs and wants of the Mamluks and their appointed governors. Specialization was relatively undeveloped; nor was there a very clearly structured hierarchy in either the economy or the government. The *ulama,* or spiritual leaders, were also teachers, merchants, mediaries between the mass of the people and the overlords, and performers of numerous other professional roles. Their elite ranks were permeable from all sectors of the society, so loosely drawn were class lines. The towns owed their simple organization and their inertia to the Mamluk subjugation of the economy to their own consumer interests and to the concentration of power in the households of appointed officials. Town-hinterland relations were actually town-estate relations, for the Mamluks monopolized the cultivation and distribution of food supplies.

By contrast, a fairly close parallel to the town economy of the late twentieth century existed in China prior to the Communist revolution of the 1940's. A town served as the market, and social, religious, and political center for approximately eighteen evenly spaced villages. So fully did the affairs of the town and its service area engross the attention of the local people that the locality took on the aspect of a unique social and cultural universe. It acquired weights, measures, and a vernacular somewhat peculiar to itself; lineage systems were adapted to market area limits; marriage contracts were arranged exclusively within the area; and the temples likewise were supported solely by local residents.[47]

But there the parallel ends. The rural market center, around which life in its tributary area revolved, fell at the lowest echelon of a hierarchical system of centers through which a centralized administration exercised its controls. No such system had emerged in medieval Europe. The Chinese hierarchy, moreover, was an economic as well as a governmental one; actually the two institutional sectors were almost indistinguishable. Many forms of commerce were monopolized by the government and were used as sources of revenue.

SUPPLEMENTARY READINGS

ASHLEY, W. J. "The Beginnings of Town Life in the Middle Ages," *Quarterly Journal of Economics,* X (1896): 359–406.

BURKE, GERALD L. *The Making of Dutch Towns: A Study of Urban Development from the Tenth to the Seventeenth Centuries* (London: Cleaver-Hume Press, 1956).

GREENE, ALICE. *Town Life in the Fifteenth Century* (New York: Macmillan, 1894).

[47] G. William Skinner, "Marketing and Social Structure in Rural China," Part I. *The Journal of Asian Studies,* XXIV (1964): 3–43.

LOPEZ, ROBERT S., and RAYMOND, IRVING W. *Medieval Trade in the Mediterranean World* (New York: W. W. Norton, 1963).

NICHOLAS, DAVID M. "Town and Countryside: Social and Economic Tensions in Fourteenth Century Flanders," *Comparative Studies in Society and History,* X (1967): 458–485.

THRUPP, SYLVIA L. *The Merchant Class of Medieval London* (Ann Arbor: University of Michigan Press, 1948).

4

The Beginnings of
Modern Urbanization

With the fifteenth century, the pace of change in the Western world quickened noticeably. Large-scale events were in the making over most of Europe. One has only to recall that the period was distinguished by struggles for political power and the almost incessant clashing of armies, by overseas discoveries and explorations, and by the cultural upheavals of humanism and the Reformation. The course of urban development is often obscured by the high drama of these extraordinary occurrences. That at their roots lay the modifications in men's outlook and way of life cultivated in cities seems beyond question. It is no less reasonable to assume that the major processes at work in society reinforced the growing influence of urban centers on the history of Western civilization. Of these connections, however, relatively little is known.[1] But a few relevant circumstances stand out clearly enough to supply at least an outline of urban development during the period.

THE CITY AND THE STATE

In the latter part of the fifteenth century population growth was resumed once more. Losses occasioned by the Black Death were being made up and numbers here and there were rising above pre-plague levels.

[1] For comment on the inadequate knowledge about this period see F. J. Fisher, "The Sixteenth and Seventeenth Centuries," *Economica*, n.s. XXIV (1957): 2–18, and Dorothy George, *England in Transition* (Hammondsworth: Penguin Books, 1931), p. 9.

Growth was made possible, not by improvements in agricultural tools, for none seems to have occurred, but by various crop substitutions. Wheat was taking the place of less nutritious grains and garden vegetables and fruits were entering into the normal diet. The use of clover and of root crops for animal food was spreading so that greater amounts of meat were made available for daily consumption. Intensive cultivation was highly developed in the Netherlands and neighboring areas were seeking to copy her methods. In general, agricultural advances appeared along the coastal zones and in the river valleys; inland territory was relatively unaffected by the dietary innovations.

Of great importance in connection with the food supply were improvements in transportation. Significant advances appeared in water carriage. Improvements in ship rigging which permitted the use of the tacking sail, in ship design leading to sturdier vessels with larger cargo capacities, and in navigation instruments, notably the compass and the astrolabe, greatly enhanced the reliability and the versatility of water transportation. They made possible, of course, explorations in distant waters, but they had important local effects as well. A much more extensive coastal and riverine trade in bulky food stuffs ensued. In consequence the threat of famine was substantially reduced in regions accessible to navigable waterways. Overland transportation remained in its primitive state. The principal exception to this was the four-wheeled wagon with a pivoting front axle which appeared in the fifteenth century.[2] Its use, however, was confined almost entirely to the few paved streets of cities.

While land transportation languished, communication was revolutionized by the invention of the printing press in the fifteenth century. Access to the printed word was for a long time thereafter limited to the literate few, churchmen and merchants for the most part. Nevertheless, the resulting circulation of documents conveying ideas and information, technical as well as classical, gave enormous impetus to the diffusion of culture. No less important were the increased possibilities for storing and retrieving an accumulation of culture.

On the industrial side, water and wind as sources of power had come into general use. Streams were harnessed to local industries and windmills dotted the landscapes. The main beneficiaries of technical change at the time were the metals industries, especially those devoted to the production of military armament. Foundries for the casting of guns and cannon and enterprises engaged in making powder and shot became important sources of employment for village and small-town workers. Meanwhile, in rural districts mines and quarries multiplied to meet the demands of the metals industries. These industries were organized in small do-

[2] T. K. Drury and Trevor I. Williams, *A Short History of Technology from the Earliest Times to A.D. 1900* (New York: Oxford University Press, 1961), p. 202.

mestic enterprises and employed ancient handicraft methods. A similar situation obtained in the textile industry. The weaving of cloth was geared to the luxury market and the product was distributed over long-distance trade routes. There were no civilian mass markets for either fabricated metals or for textiles.

The earlier growth of trading centers such as Lübeck, Cologne, Antwerp, Paris, Lyons, Bordeaux, Marseilles, and London had superimposed commercial dominions upon the feudal anarchy. These developments awakened aspirations for political unification of contiguous economic regions and for the extension of sovereign jurisdictions as far as communications would permit. As always, trade and politics tended to move hand in hand. The thriving cities played a crucial role in the rise of the national state. Seeking to cast off the last remains of feudal restraints, the city burghers allied themselves with nascent monarchies and liberally supported them with loans of money.[3] In return the burghers could look forward not only to interest payments on their loans but also to preferential treatment in enlarged territories over which uniform coinages, weights and measures, legal provisions, and other facilitations of commerce would obtain. Political unification of feudal demesnes, however, collided as often as not with conflicting dynastic claims and with the competing interests of cities. The immediate outcome was war, which became endemic over most of Europe.

The consequences of warfare for urban growth varied with the way in which it impinged on different districts. Walter Dorn suggests that the formation of large armies created the first mass markets for textiles, metal products, and services of many kinds and for agricultural products.[4] Accordingly industry, trade, and transportation flourished in and around cities of expanding states. But where military needs furnished the sole basis for growth the gains tended to be transitory. Thus Alais, in France, and Suhl, in Saxony, prospered as military supply centers for awhile and then receded, to be surpassed by more favorably situated centers such as Nuremberg, Nancy, and Toulouse.

In areas of active hostilities the effects of war were usually disastrous. Conflict in the Netherlands, in the sixteenth century, is reported to have driven industry and capital across the Channel to England and northward and southward along the coast.[5] Antwerp never regained its stature as a

[3] Robert L. Heilbroner, *The Making of Economic Society* (Englewood Cliffs, N.J.: Prentice-Hall, 1962), p. 51.

[4] Dorn also suggests that the disciplined organization necessary in an army developed a model that was copied by industrial and administrative establishments. (*Competition for Empire, 1740–1763* [New York: Harper Torchbook, 1965], pp. 14–16.)

[5] John U. Nef, *Western Civilization Since the Renaissance: Peace, War, Industry and the Arts* (New York: Harper Torchbook, 1963), p. 78.

trade and industrial center. The devastation wrought in central Europe by the Thirty Years' War, in the seventeenth century, was ruinous. Military mortality was a small part of the loss. Much more serious were the sacking of towns and cities, the spoliation of agricultural areas, the mass flights of people, and the breakdown of organized life. Augsburg and Marburg lost half their populations. Berlin and Munich declined by one quarter. Leipzig was bankrupt. Thousands of villages disappeared and extensive districts extending from Strasbourg far to the northwest were denuded of residents.[6] A few cities, however, such as Bremen, Dresden, and Hamburg, emerged from the war stronger than before. The recurrence of wars later in the century in France, Spain, Poland, and elsewhere spread similar, if less disastrous, effects. England alone was spared the disorder of the period.

To make matters worse, some of the most catastrophic crop failures of European history were experienced in the seventeenth century. From Spain to Sweden food supplies repeatedly fell to minimum levels.[7] Malnutrition and the crowding of refugees in towns and cities led to renewed outbreaks of the plague. It was in this period, too, that large-scale migrations began, to the Ukraine, to Prussia, and to a lesser extent to the Americas. In short, during the seventeenth century population was once again in decline over most of Europe. Where it was not in decline growth was nearly imperceptible.[8] Yet in some areas, primarily in western Europe, the demands for manpower exceeded the supplies. Recruitment efforts to secure settlers and laborers for towns and nations were commonplace, armies sought their mercenaries from neighboring countries rather than from their own, and beggars, indigents, and the wives of soldiers were forced into industrial employment.[9]

According to Walter C. Scoville, the flights of Flemish, Brabantine, and Zeeland refugees to England, at the beginning of the Hundred Years' War, revitalized a decaying textile industry in the receiving country. They pioneered in capitalistic production and supplied the skills and manpower for a great surge of economic growth two centuries later. Another influx in the sixteenth century, this time of Flemish, Walloon, and Dutch Protestants fleeing the Spanish Netherlands, stimulated the textile, glass, paper-making, metallurgical, and agricultural industries of England. ("Minority Migrations and the Diffusion of Technology," *Jour. Economic History*, XI [1951]: 351–53.)

[6] C. V. Wedgewood, *The Thirty Years' War* (Garden City, N.Y.: Doubleday and Co., 1961), pp. 492–94; and *The New Cambridge Modern History* (Cambridge: The University Press, 1961), Vol. V, pp. 20–21.

[7] *The New Cambridge Modern History* (Cambridge: The University Press, 1961), Vol. V, p. 21.

[8] Herbert Moller, *Population Movements in Modern European History* (New York: Macmillan, 1964), pp. 19–41.

[9] F. L. Nussbaum, *A History of the Economic Institutions of Modern Europe* (New York: F. S. Crofts, 1933), pp. 112 ff.

Mumford contends that after the sixteenth century the multiplication of towns on the European continent ceased.[10] If so, it might have been due partly to the preemption by then of available sites for town locations. But there are also indications that the populations of many centers subsided somewhat. Employment opportunities were increasing most rapidly in rural industries situated at resource locations and were attracting town workers as well as displaced agriculturalists.[11] Political changes appear to have exerted an even greater effect on town growth. The emergent state was superseding the sovereignty of the city and was effectively imposing its will on formerly independent localities.[12] The consequences were felt in two directions. On the one hand, national boundaries were drawn without respect for preexisting market territories. Urban domains that overlapped political frontiers were broken up and left to reshape themselves as time and circumstance permitted. Some were successful in doing so; but the many that were not shrank into inconsequential provincial towns. On the other hand, the rise of national states caused urban increase to gravitate to political capitals. The older mercantile centers languished for want of traffic and trade.

London, Paris, Warsaw, Moscow, Naples, Lisbon, Vienna, and Copenhagen had attained populations of 100,000 or more in mid-seventeenth century and at the close of the century London and Paris passed the half-million mark. Sizes of these magnitudes, far greater than anything reached in the Middle Ages, resulted in part from intensive centralization of government controls over city and country alike and in part from the garrisoning of huge military establishments close by the courts.[13] Elaborate administrative bureaucracies arose as sovereign policy was extended over a widening array of civil affairs. Mercantilist doctrine, under which the state sought to regulate economic growth and colonial trade, alone required an immense amount of administrative supervision. Political expansion had moved far ahead of the expansion of urban organization. But only the mercantile centers were embarrassed by the turn of events. The subordination of municipal affairs to central government control had

[10] *The Culture of Cities* (New York: Harcourt, Brace, Jovanovich, 1938), p. 81.

[11] Sir George Clark, *The Seventeenth Century* (London: Oxford University Press, 1947), pp. 75–78.

[12] Writing of Amsterdam in the seventeenth century, Violet Barboure declared that city's commercial reign to be the last in which a veritable empire of trade and finance could be held by a city in its own right unsustained by the power of a modern state. (*Capitalism in Amsterdam in the Seventeenth Century* [Baltimore: Johns Hopkins Press, 1950], p. 13.)

[13] For an interesting account of centralization in France and its effects on the towns see W. H. Lewis, *The Splendid Century: Life in the France of Louis XIV* (Garden City, N.Y.: Doubleday and Co., 1957), especially ch. 7.

no appreciable effect on the provincial towns. They continued as before in their small domains and their mutual isolation.

While, as Nef has observed, the development of urban life since the preceding centuries had elevated Western societies of the sixteenth century to a comparatively high level in the arts, in government, and in sophistication generally,[14] these gains appear not to have spread broadly over the lands. Nor does it seem that a hundred years later they had penetrated deeply into the texture of local life. Consider Wedgewood's account of the state of affairs in central Europe just prior to the Thirty Years' War.

The outlook even of the educated was harsh. Underneath a veneer of courtesy, manners were primitive; drunkenness and cruelty were common in all classes, judges were more often severe than just, civil authority more often brutal than effective, and charity came limping far behind the needs of the people. Discomfort was too natural to provoke comment; winter's cold and summer's heat found European man lamentably unprepared, his house too damp and draughty for the one, too airless for the other. Prince and beggar were alike inured to the stink of decaying offal in the streets, of foul drainage about the houses, to the sight of carrion birds picking over public refuse dumps or rotting bodies swinging on the gibbets. On the road from Dresden to Prague a traveller counted above seven score galloweses and wheels, where thieves were hanged, some fresh and some half rotten, and the carcases of murderers broken limb after limb on the wheels.[15]

Civil life was still raw and uncultivated. A long period of disorder would follow before central governments would effectively monopolize the instruments of violence and bring peace and order to, at least, their own territories.

THE TECHNICAL REVOLUTIONS

The scene of urban development in the West shifted in the eighteenth century to England. A number of circumstances converged at that time and place to foster relatively rapid and cumulative changes. The problems of sovereignty resolved, internal peace and order reigned to a much greater extent there than elsewhere. Its insular position shielded England from much, though not all, of the turmoil on the continent. By the same token, it was able to capture an increasing share of foreign trade while promoting colonial expansion without the distractions of boundary disputes. While England's sheltered location had certain advantages, her proximity to the continent had others. In particular, the country was exposed to flows of ideas and experiences carried by refugees and travelers.

[14] John U. Nef, *Cultural Foundations of Industrial Civilization* (New York: Harper Torchbook, 1960), p. 71.
[15] C. V. Wedgewood, *op. cit.*, p. 15.

Hence the receptivity of English people to innovation was heightened and the probability of invention was raised accordingly. Finally, the country was well endowed with resources, especially the kinds of resources that were appropriate to the development of its rural industries.

But at the beginning of the century the condition of territorial organization in England still possessed a medieval character. There was not a single town other than London that had connections with the entire country.[16] Internal commerce was carried on in the periodic fairs and by the itinerant merchant who transported his goods by pack train. Roads were primitive and unprotected from the harassments of highwaymen. On the other hand, transportation by water along the coastline and in the estuaries was easy. Hence it was in those regions that development first began.[17] Port cities such as Bristol, Chester, Liverpool, and London, the latter because it was an administrative center as well, flourished on the coastal and especially the colonial trade. The benefits of trade, however, were shared by a rather small part of the country. Most of the goods that entered English ports was bound for transshipment to European markets. The interior of the country seemed to lie in the grip of stagnation.

In actual fact the appearance was deceptive. For a long time numerous subtle changes had been occurring in many places and in various spheres of activity. By midcentury their effects had accumulated to produce the major forward surge known as the Industrial Revolution. This term is much too narrow to adequately describe the transformation that took place. There were revolutions in transportation, in agriculture, in commerce, and in the mode of collective life, as well as in the industrial arts. Changes in each of these respects were contingent on supporting changes in the others.

Despite the poor state of the roads internal trade was growing in the early years of the eighteenth century. So also was the administrative organization of the nation. These two forces, both demanding easy access to all parts of the country, combined to bring about legislation permitting the construction of toll roads. The twenty years following 1745 were a period of feverish toll-road building. In that short space of time internal transportation was radically altered. The costs of haulage were reduced to a half of what they had been and the volume of traffic on the highways was doubled.[18] Road improvements were initiated in the vicinities of urban centers; they were subsequently extended into hinterlands, in some places quickly, in others only after a considerable lapse of time.

---

[16] Paul Mantoux, *The Industrial Revolution in the Eighteenth Century*, trans. by Marjorie Vernon (New York: Harcourt, Brace, Jovanovich, 1927), pp. 111 ff.

[17] See Adam Smith, *The Wealth of Nations* (New York: Modern Library, 1937), pp. 18–19.

[18] Mantoux, *op. cit.*, pp. 117–19.

As traffic increased so did the market for food for horses, the principal motive power for overland transportation. While this phase of change was taking place an era of canal-building opened. The new waterways short-cut the previous circuitous routes between raw-material producing areas and urban centers. Old river ports declined and new centers arose as remote districts were brought into fairly close reach of one another. Urban influence was carried out along the roads and the canals, penetrating the isolation of inland localities and opening new vistas for enterprise.

At the same time a revolution in agriculture was gathering momentum. Just as England had been borrowing handicrafts from the continent over the past centuries, it also imported agricultural experiences and practices. Enlightened travelers observed European methods of land drainage, the cultivation of pasturage and fodder crops for animals, the uses of fertilizers, methods of seed selection, and techniques of animal breeding. Some of these, such as Jethro Tull and Viscount Townshend, published their notes in pamphlets which were widely circulated.[19] A few, notably Arthur Young, traveled over the countryside of England as apostles of agricultural improvement. Increases in productivity, in both food and industrial products,[20] coincided with the enlargement of markets for grains and fodder to feed draught animals, for fibers for the growing textile industry, and for food to nourish the swelling town populations. Large landholders saw opportunities for cash incomes from what were merely subsistence farms. The prospect of commercial farming on a large scale was clouded by the existing organization of agriculture.

Most of the agricultural land was held by freeholders or yeomen whose titles to the land had been established through many generations by use and wont rather than by formal deed. In many instances their claims involved payment of an annual fee in kind to a landlord whose title was even more ancient. Crop lands were worked in the open-field system. That is, strips were consolidated in larger fields and managed by a village council which determined what, when, and how to plant. Although this arrangement had at one time been a vast improvement over preceding practices, it proved to be a serious impediment to change in the eighteenth century. The individual farmer could not respond to innovations without the consent of the council, for to do so would be to trespass on the rights of others. Interspersed among the yeomen's holdings were "waste" or common lands, the property of landlords. The common lands were used collectively for the pasturage of animals and for gleaning firewood. This practice, too, was governed by ancient rights.

[19] *The New Cambridge Modern History*, vol. V, p. 24.
[20] In 1710 the average weight of oxen was 370 lbs., of calves 50 lbs., of sheep 38 lbs. By 1795 their weights had increased to 800, 150, and 80 lbs., respectively. (Mantoux, *op. cit.*, pp. 165–66.)

Drastic action was required to break up the archaic organization of agriculture. The impetus came in a renewal of the enclosure movement that had been initiated in the preceding century. The new Enclosure Acts dealt first with the waste lands. As those were enclosed and given over to commercial crops the yeoman lost an important supplement to his livelihood. Later the acts encroached upon the small farmer's croplands in what amounted to forced sales.[21] The progressive absorption of small plots into large farms dislodged rural population and drove it from the land. The actual departure of many was stayed by a substitution of cottage industry earnings for agricultural income and by wage employment in road-building and canal-digging. But increasing numbers of displaced farmers gathered in the villages and there sank into poverty.[22] The commercialization of agriculture thus prepared the way for a wholesale redistribution of population. In the meantime the social costs of the change were borne by the people least able to afford them.

Population is rarely, if ever, constant when major social changes are in process. So it was in the period under discussion. Shortly after the middle of the eighteenth century the death rate entered upon a long-term decline as a result almost exclusively of gains in the amount, quality, and accessibility of the food supply. (Medical knowledge was to remain in its medieval state for nearly a century more.[23]) The reduction of mortality while the birth rate remained high and occasionally increased led to a widening excess of births over deaths and increases in the rate of population growth. Numbers grew slowly between 1700 and 1750, from 5,135,000 to 6,040,100, but in the next fifty years they leaped to 9,187,000, an increase of 52 per cent.[24] This was the opening phase of what has since come to be known as the "demographic transition."

Events in the eighteenth century, then, created a disposable population from displacements from the land, on the one hand, and from absolute increases in numbers, on the other hand. How that affected the pervasive poverty, which Gregory King had reported from his analysis of hearth tax returns of late in the preceding century, is not clear. The growth of pop-

[21] The enclosure movement extended into the nineteenth century. By 1843 it is estimated that half the arable land of England had been enclosed. (Arnold Toynbee, *The Industrial Revolution* [Boston: The Beacon Press, 1956], p. 30.)

[22] Toynbee reports an estimate of 181,000 yeomen having disappeared in the eighteenth century. (*Op. cit.*, p. 32.)

[23] T. McKeown and R. G. Brown, "Medical Evidence Relating to English Population Change in the Eighteenth Century," *Population Studies*, IX (1955): 119–41. Similar evidence of the origins of population growth is found in Indonesia (see Clifford Geertz, *Agricultural Involution: The Process of Ecological Change in Indonesia* [Berkeley: University of California Press, 1963]), and in Ceylon, Mauritius, and British Guiana (see Harald Frederikson, "Determinants and Consequences of Mortality and Fertility Trends, *Public Health Reports*, LXXXI [1966]: 715–27).

[24] See Toynbee, *op. cit.*, pp. 7–8.

ulation suggests that the situation had been relieved, though that may
have been nothing more than a Malthusian response to improvements in
sustenance. Some of the surplus population was doubtless taken up by
the domestic industry, road- and canal-building, and other rural employments. There was also some movement to urban centers and increasingly
toward foreign destinations. Still, there was no evidence of absolute rural
population decline at any time during the century.[25] Instead, the rural
areas were crowded with unemployed and underemployed people, partly
because under the poor laws then in effect the recipient of relief was
bound to his locality of residence and partly because there were not sufficient urban opportunities for the absorption of the surplus population.
In the latter part of the century the volume of internal migration grew
larger despite the restraints that were present. People, young people especially, crowded the towns and cities in anticipation of a better livelihood. The center of population shifted toward the Midlands.

Changes in transportation, agriculture, and population coincided with
the breaking of a number of bottlenecks in the development of industry
beyond the handicraft stage. A series of inventions, occurring within a
brief space of time, suddenly increased the amount of yarn for the textile
industry, solved the flooding problem in mine shafts, improved the quality
of fuels for metallurgy, and supplied a new source of power for manufacturing processes. Innovations in credit and banking and in methods of
financing through joint-stock companies—the precursor of the modern corporation—were also being introduced and improved.[26] This outpouring
of inventions stemmed not from independent actions of individual men,
though they are usually associated with particular names such as Ark-
wright, Hargreaves, Watt, Darby, Boulton, and others. These were rather
persons of energy and imagination who happened to appear opportunely
at the points where numerous lines of diffusion converged.[27] And as inventions were adapted to one sphere of industrial activity after another,
individuals too numerous to mention, many of them anonymous, added
further modifications and improvements.

It is important to recognize the interweaving of influences that transformed England's economy. Agricultural improvements made possible
the support of an increasing number of persons engaged in non-agricultural pursuits. How that may have affected inventive activity is too obscure a matter to be easily explored. The growth of non-agricultural
activities in towns and cities stimulated further agricultural innovations

[25] John Saville, *Rural Depopulation in England and Wales, 1851–1951* (London:
Routledge and Kegan Paul, 1957), pp. 8–21.
[26] T. S. Ashton, *The Industrial Revolution, 1760–1830* (New York: Oxford University Press, 1964), pp. 40–41.
[27] *Ibid.*, pp. 12 and 62.

and an extension of production for markets. The latter led to increasing crop specialization in producing areas, especially in the immediate hinterlands of large centers. The interaction between cities and agricultural areas was facilitated by increases in the efficiency of transportation, through first the toll roads, then the canal system and later the construction of all-weather roads. People and ideas as well as goods circulated at accelerating rates. Within and between cities industrial developments played upon one another in a spiraling process of change.

Sometimes it was a simple case of imitation, as when the principle of attenuating material by passing it through rollers was transferred from the iron to the textile industry, or when Wilkinson's method of boring cannon was turned to the making of steam-engine cylinders. Sometimes an advance in one sphere was a condition of progress in another, as when the development of coke ovens made possible the extraction of tar. Often two or more industries went hand in hand, each contributing to the forward movement of the other. Without the discovery of smelting with coke, which made it possible to supply larger and more intricate castings, Newcomen would not have perfected his engine; and without Newcomen's engine Darby could hardly have obtained the blast that was required to produce iron on the scale required . . . The invasion by the founders of the territory of the forgemasters made these look to new ways of reducing the cost of wrought iron; the introduction of the flying shuttle made it imperative for the spinners to seek out better methods of producing yarn; and the later improvements in spinning and weaving brought a new urgency to the search for quicker methods of bleaching and finishing.[28]

Agriculture, transportation, and industry presupposed an accumulation of capital. Such surpluses were produced originally by commerce, particularly foreign commerce. The mere existence of capital was not enough, however; means had to be devised for assembling it around particular projects, for controlling risks, and for the management of credit. Thus institutions addressed to the management and distribution of funds made their appearance.

An invention of no small consequence was the factory organization of production. This originated in the textile industry primarily as a way of reducing the pilfering of materials by cottage industry workers, though also as a means of regularizing production. Technological advances, however, soon raised the costs of tools above the capital resources that individual families could command. Capital requirements mounted rapidly in the power-driven textile industry and no less rapidly in the iron industry. Despite the early demonstration of its feasibility, the spread of factory production within and beyond those industries was a slow process, lasting into the twentieth century.[29]

[28] *Ibid.,* pp. 62–63.
[29] For a discussion of the social implications of the factory, see Chapter 6.

INDUSTRIALIZATION AND CONCENTRATION

The growth of markets and the increase of production advanced in a reciprocal relationship. Contingent as it is on the scope of the market, the scale of industry depends also on the extent of specialization. Thus skills were joined to extract and process raw materials, to fabricate and finish parts of tools and products, to assemble parts in finished products, all of which required numerous ancillary services. A functional integration of specialties could be most effective when the distances separating them were short, especially where local transportation was slow and inefficient. Specifications must be communicated and innumerable adjustments must continuously be made in order to achieve a close complementation of operations. In a word, the multiplication and specialization of industries led inevitably to their concentration in space.[30] That began in a regrouping of rural industries in and about urban centers. It extended into the elaboration of industry as mechanical technology developed.

The application of steam power to production gave further impetus to the centripetal tendency. Steam cannot be transported very far; it cools quickly and its energy is easily dissipated. Steam must be used where it is produced. Furthermore, coal, the fuel for the production of steam power, is consumed in use. Yet its bulk is such that transportation costs are relatively high, both in respect to carriage and to terminal facilities. Those costs can be minimized either by locating production close to the mines or by a number of users clustering together to share the charges for terminal facilities. The latter is often advisable because various other materials that originate from widely spaced sources also enter into production. Concentration tends to be cumulative. The location of one or more industries at a transportation terminal attracts other industries. Some of those may perform repair and maintenance services for the initial industries, others may engage in prior or subsequent stages in the production process, still others may use by-product materials. The concentration of complementary industries results in what are called "external economies"; collectively the assembled industries reduce the total production costs of each enterprise.[31] The cumulative tendency was noticeable in Manchester at an early date:

In 1795 Dr. Aikin observed that six foundries in Manchester were occupied in casting wheels and pipes for steam engines and shafts and that tinplate

[30] See Eric Lampard, "The History of Cities in the Economically Advanced Areas," *Economic Development and Cultural Change*, III (1955): 113.
[31] For a simple, lucid account of the cumulative localization process see Wilbur R. Thompson, "Urban Growth and Development in a National System of Cities," in P. M. Hauser and L. F. Schnore, *op. cit.*, pp. 431–90.

workers, braziers, and harness makers were engaged in making parts for spinning frames. From about 1817 a steady stream of engineers came to Manchester, and of them Richard Roberts, James Nasmyth, William Fairbairn, Joseph Whitworth and T. C. Herries founded machine-making factories whose output supplied the materials for the spread of the new industrial techniques through the north of England. The trades which could be utilized by the factories themselves were most susceptible to the influence of the cotton manufacture, and from the service of the industry and its population Manchester developed important railway, brewing, chemical, building, coal, and wholesale businesses.[32]

Industrial concentration had a like effect on population. As long as movement to and from work and for other daily purposes was accomplished primarily by walking, increases in the sizes of work units and in the sizes of the clusters in which they congregated resulted in dense concentrations of population. A multiplier effect operated in settlement concentration as well as in industrial concentration. People need services, especially when they no longer have space for garden plots and time for home industries. Retailers of consumer goods, repair services, innkeepers, entertainers, professional practitioners, and others add their number to the industrial population. By improving the amenities of a place the development of a service complement exerts a further attraction on industry and thus leads to another round of concentration effects. Presumably the process ends when the costs of internal communication approach equality with the advantages derived from concentration at a particular place.

The rate of city growth, then, increased sharply with the mechanization of industry. Not all towns participated in the growth, however. Those that were inappropriately located for industrial purposes subsided into villages or barely held their own. Among the towns that were favorably situated growth was uneven. "The iron towns grew more slowly than the cotton, and faster than the wool towns." [33] Among the great provincial towns at the beginning of the eighteenth century Bristol and Norwich were the largest, with approximately 28,000 population in each. York and Exeter came third and fourth, each with 10,000 inhabitants. Worcester, Nottingham, Leeds, and Hull had attained sizes of 8,000 population. Of these eight only Bristol and Leeds grew rapidly, more than tripling their populations during the century. A few smaller places, notably Liverpool, Manchester, Birmingham, and Sheffield, starting with populations of 4,000 to 6,000, increased tenfold or more in the course of the century. London nearly doubled its size, reaching 900,000 inhabitants. New industrial towns had appeared as well, especially in the suburban zones around

[32] Leon S. Marshall, "The Emergence of the First Industrial City: Manchester, 1780–1850," in The Cultural Approach to History, ed. by Caroline Ware (New York: Columbia University Press, 1940), p. 142.

[33] Mantoux, op. cit., p. 370.

London, Manchester, and Birmingham. By the end of the eighteenth century 17 percent of the total population of England and Wales lived in places of 20,000 or more people.[34]

Perhaps never before in man's history had that proportion risen above 5 or 6 percent. Not in every case was city growth based on mechanical industry. Industrialization spread its effects. The remarkable growth of Liverpool, for example, rested on its role as a port and transshipment point; raw materials from the colonies entered there and manufactured products funneled through Liverpool to foreign markets. Industrialization should be regarded as a feature of a total economy rather than of particular locations within the economy.

It would be a mistake to imply that the effects of the technical revolutions were limited to England and Scotland. The Low Countries across the channel were not far behind Britain in an industrial revolution of their own. English investors and industrialists had been establishing factories at various points along the coast and in northern France in the late years of the eighteenth century. France, in fact, had entered that century with a more promising industrial economy than that possessed by England. Her industrialization was frustrated, however, by recurring wars.[35] Manpower was squandered, markets were lost, and capital was drained away to unproductive uses.

THE FOUNDING OF COLONIAL URBANISM

It was not an accident that the movement toward urbanization in England and later on the continent coincided with the enlargement of empire. The expansion of trade and the beginnings of mechanical industry encouraged Europeans to search farther afield for markets and for riches that would add to capital accumulations. Since late in the fifteenth century they had been establishing outposts along the transoceanic rim. These overseas settlements were of three different kinds: trading stations along the densely populated coasts of India and southern China; sugar and spice plantations manned by slave labor in the tropics; and farm-family colonies of permanent settlers in the temperate belts.[36] In one way or another all of these ventures resulted in an exportation of urbanism, though nothing could have been further from what was intended.

[34] A. F. Weber, *The Growth of Cities in the Nineteenth Century* (New York: Columbia University Press, 1899), p. 47.

[35] J. L. Hammond and Barbara Hammond, *The Rise of Modern Industry* (London: Methuen and Co., 1925), ch. 3.

[36] R. D. McKenzie, "Industrial Expansion and the Interrelations of Peoples," in *Race and Culture Contacts*, ed. by E. B. Reuter (New York: McGraw-Hill, 1934), p. 23.

Of the several types of settlement the farm-family colonies proved to be the most fertile ground for the subsequent cultivation of an urban-centered society.

That outcome lay in the remote future so far as Central and South America were concerned. Since the sixteenth century Spain and Portugal had been sowing colonies under crown auspices along the coasts, mainly for the purpose of provisioning ships with water, food, and marine stores and for the transshipment of precious metals. Policy changed in the seventeenth century when the town came to be regarded as an instrument for the promotion of agricultural settlement. Towns were planted, often with poor judgment, where resources were thought to be abundant. Settlers were sent out to occupy and develop the lands in the hinterlands of town sites. Most of the settlers had little or no interest in towns, for they were land-hungry people who had known only an agrarian way ot life. Hence the struggles of the towns for people was an issue that hung always in the balance.[37] Town prosperity was further handicapped by their failure to develop a commercial reciprocity. Each was under the direct administration of Seville or Lisbon in economic as well as in political affairs. The unilateral exercise of bureaucratic controls went so far as to specify the ground plan of each town. Interference and domination by the mother country effectively prevented the development of a colonial economy. Only a few centers grew to any size therefore; Santo Domingo, Lima, and Mexico City, for example, rose to prominence as regional administrative centers.

Settlements on the North American coast exhibited certain similarities to these in America south of the Rio Grande. Towns were planted in underdeveloped country in the hope that they would stimulate settlement and cultivation in the surrounding country. Likewise, they were instruments of mercantilist policy. That is, the new towns were regarded as means of channeling a unilateral trade with the home country. However, instead of being under the direct control of a central government, the towns were established by landed proprietors who sought to use them to develop the chartered lands and thus to enrich the owners. This feature introduced an important element of variability in administration and in freedom to respond to opportunity.

The proprietary origins of the colonial towns in North America launched most of them as closed corporations. They were laid out according to preconceived plans and were empowered with far-reaching controls over their residents. Controls extended from the determination

---

[37] Richard M. Morse, "Latin American Cities: Aspects of Function and Structure," *Comparative Studies in Society and History*, IV (1961–62): 222–32; and "Some Characteristics of Latin American Urban History," *American Historical Review*, LXVII (1962): 317–38.

of qualifications for residence to the supervision of religious observance and, on occasion, to the regulation of dress and habits of consumption.[38] But medieval restraints of that order could not survive long. They were inappropriate to pioneer conditions and even more so to the growth of trade. Paternalistic rules fell into abeyance as control over town affairs passed into the hand of citizens.[39]

Commerce developed on the basis of natural resources in maritime hinterlands—furs, fish, and timber for shipbuilding in the northern colonies, marine stores, tobacco, and grains in the southern and central colonies. Trade grew from the direct exchanges with England into a flourishing intercolonial commerce reaching into West Indies markets.[40] The thickening of settlement in the hinterlands increased the demand for manufactured goods. It was not long before home industries sprang up to supply some of that demand and to process raw materials prior to exportation. The towns grew on the strength of the expanding local economies. As they increased in size their organizations were elaborated. Institutions for servicing commerce—banks, insurance companies, brokerages—appeared. Shipping firms and drayage contractors multiplied. Municipal governments began to broaden their purviews beyond keeping the peace and fostering commerce. Collective life was further enriched with voluntary associations concerned with religious, cultural, and nostalgic interests.

By 1730 the population of Baltimore and Boston had each reached 13,000, and Philadelphia had 11,000 inhabitants. New York, which had stagnated under Dutch rule in the preceding century, had grown to 8,000 population. The flour-milling and ship-building center known as Newport had increased to 3,800 people. To the south, two centers, Norfolk and Charleston, prospering from the West Indies trades, had attained population of 6,000 and 3,500, respectively.[41] Traffic across the north Atlantic, however, was far more conducive to town growth than was coastal or island traffic. Before the century was out Boston, New York, Philadelphia, and Baltimore had established themselves as the major trade centers of the colonies. Far away New Orleans, an outpost of France, was thriving on the fur trade. Other French trading posts had been planted at wide intervals along the Mississippi River, but these were to remain as mere villages until after the turn of the century.

[38] Charles N. Glaab and A. Theodore Brown, *A History of Urban America* (New York: Macmillan, 1967), pp. 8 ff.

[39] Carl Bridenbaugh, *Cities in the Wilderness: The First Century of Urban Life in America, 1625–1742* (New York: Ronald Press, 1938), pp. 468–69. See also Sigmund Diamond, "From Organization to Society: Virginia in the Seventeenth Century," *American Journal of Sociology*, LXIII (1958): 457–75.

[40] For a description of colonial trade see *Historical Statistics of the Unted States: From Colonial Times to 1957* (Washington: U.S. Government Printing Office, 1960).

[41] Glaab and Brown, *op. cit.*, p. 9.

Impressive though the growth of colonial centers along the Atlantic coast may have been, they contained but a small part of the total population. Settlement was primarily rural, with the village as the principal focus of orientation. In 1800 not more than 4 percent of the United Sates population lived in places of 8,000 or more. Three quarters of that fraction were concentrated in the four major mercantile centers, each with 24,000 or more residents. There was nothing in these facts to lead one to expect that the United States was to become one of the world's most highly urbanized nations.

GROWTH OF CITIES IN THE NINETEENTH CENTURY

Urban population increase after 1800 assumed such massive proportions that the ensuing one hundred years may quite properly be called the century of city-building in the Western world. The explanation of that extraordinary development must be sought in the rapidly accumulating and diffusing effects of the technical revolutions launched in the preceding century. A consequence of immediate importance was an enormous growth of trade, especially of local trade. Reductions in the cost of food and of manufactured products caused large proportions of the populations to abandon home-produced goods for market commodities. People were turning unreservedly, in other words, toward an urban way of life.

The expansion of local markets was stimulated further by yet another series of improvements in transportation and communication, each more dramatic than the one preceding. Telford's and McAdams' experiments in road construction culminated in a vigorous program, in England and Scotland, of converting dirt roads to hard-surfaced highways usable in all seasons of the year. As miles were added to the all-weather road system the volume of traffic mounted rapidly. While road systems were being rebuilt, on the continent as well as in England, the steam-powered ship made its appearance. By the 1830's it was in general use in coastal and river trade. The first and most significant effect of the steam vessel was felt in the local service rather than in the more spectacular transoceanic service. In eliminating the uncertainties of wind and current, regular traffic schedules could be introduced on inland waterways as well as between coastal ports. Urban influences were able to penetrate continental interiors far more effectively than was formerly possible. But no innovation equaled the railway in the thoroughness with which it linked hinterlands to urban centers. Within less than two decades after its inception, in the 1820's, the railway had completely overhauled the pattern of territorial relationships. Overland distances that had been measured in days and weeks were abruptly reduced to journeys of a few hours. Rural self-sufficiency gave way to specialized production for urban markets, and urban products and services flowed out over surrounding districts. Territorial relationships were drawn still more close in the middle of the century with the invention of the telegraph. This first step in the separation of communication from transportation made possible a centralized administration of widely scattered field activities and a closer timing of buying and selling transactions. Although these improvements, the railway and telegraph in particular, at first knitted the activities scattered over areas with radii of seventy-five to one hundred miles into compact economic communities, their long-distance utility soon dissolved regional and provincial insularities and welded nations into coherent functional entities.

It was no accident that the practice of systematic census enumeration was inaugurated while urban expansion and national integration were taking giant strides forward.[42] The rationalization of administrative and social affairs that necessarily accompanies increases in the scale of organized life demands accurate, current information about population and related matters. Thus from around the opening of the nineteenth century our knowledge of population begins to be lifted from hearsay to fairly dependable fact.

Admittedly, population numbers are a crude indicator of the extent and nature of urbanization. They are, however, one of the few means available for the purpose. There is the further problem that the minimum size required for a place to be designated as urban is, as was noted in Chapter 1, an arbitrary matter. But, if we use a minimum size of 20,000 population, we escape some of the uncertainties inherent in unrefined figures. On that basis the population of Europe, in 1800, was not more than 5 percent urban. At that date there were no more than twenty-one cities of 100,000 population and over in England and on the continent.[43] Another eight cities of that size existed outside of Europe: Mexico City and Rio de Janeiro in Latin America, Constantinople and Cairo in the Middle East, and Calcutta, Bombay, Hyderabad, and Madras in India.[44] On the whole probably not more than 2½ percent of the population of the world lived in places of 20,000 or more people in 1800.

---

[42] Occasional counts, usually of selected parts of populations, had been frequent in the past. But the periodic count of an entire population is a modern development. It began in Sweden in 1747, then in the United States in 1790, England and Wales in 1801, Belgium in 1829, France in 1835, Spain in 1857, Portugal in 1864, Germany in 1871, and Russia in 1897. At the end of the century only Albania among European countries was without a regular census.

[43] A. F. Weber, op. cit., pp. 449–50.

[44] There may have been three or four others in east Asia, such as Edo (Tokyo), Peking, Nanking, and Canton. Whether these were cities in the same sense is open to question. Edo, for example, was more in the nature of a dense concentration of villages than it was an integrated city. About the others less is known.

Table 4 presents data for selected European countries on the proportions of their populations in places of 20,000 or more from 1800 to 1890. It will be seen that England and Wales began the century with approximately 17 percent of its population urban, according to that standard. Increases occurred in every succeeding decade; increase was rapid up to midcentury and much less so thereafter. The acceleration of growth between 1841 and 1851 coincided with the enlargement of the railway network and the concomitant prosperity of the steel industry. Growth was concentrated largely in the steel-producing and port cities.[45] In 1891 over half of the nation's population occupied cities of 20,000 or more inhabitants.

Table 4. Proportions of Total Populations in Cities of 20,000 or More Inhabitants (Selected Countries and Dates)[a]

Year[a]	England-Wales	Holland	Germany	Belgium	Italy	Austria	Hungary	Sweden	France
1800–01	16.9%	—	—	—	4.4%	3.6%	2.3%	3.0%	3.9%
1810–11	18.1	—	—	—	—	—	—	—	—
1820–21	20.8	—	—	1.3%	—	—	—	—	—
1830–31	25.0	20.1%	—	—	—	—	—	—	4.5
1840–41	28.9	—	—	—	—	4.2	—	—	—
1850–51	35.0	21.7	—	5.2	6.0	—	4.6	3.4	6.0
1860–61	38.2	—	—	—	—	—	—	—	—
1870–71	42.0	—	12.5%	—	—	—	—	—	6.7
1880–81	48.0	—	18.1	—	—	9.6	—	—	—
1890–91	53.6	31.3	21.9	13.2	13.3	12.0	11.2	10.8	9.1

[a]Dates are approximate.
SOURCE: A. F. Weber, *The Growth of Cities in the Nineteenth Century,* Columbia University Press, 1899, pp. 47–119.

Urbanization was slower on the European continent. In the northwest, however, there was a fairly early imitation of British technological and industrial experience. That was possible because of the presence of large numbers of skilled workmen and of entrepreneurs with organizing ability, of an abundance of natural resources, and of early beginnings of the iron and steel industries.[46] Elsewhere in Europe these favorable circumstances did not exist in the same combination.[47] Handicrafts that might have been converted to industrial skills had not developed in Russia, Spain, Portugal, and the Balkans. Resource deficiencies circumscribed the exploitation of long-standing industrial traditions in Italy. The effects of these uneven limitations can be seen in the data of Table 4.

[45] A. F. Weber, *op. cit.*, pp. 55–56.
[46] H. J. Habakkuk, "The Historical Experience on the Basic Conditions of Economic Progress," *International Social Science Bulletin,* VI (1954): 189–97.
[47] Alexander Gerschenkron, "City Economics—Then and Now," in *The Historian and the City,* ed. by Oscar Handlin and John Burchard (Cambridge: M.I.T. Press, 1966), p. 58.

Urban growth was slower in Holland and in Germany, as may be seen in Table 4, though it was still substantial. The German data begin with the unification of the state, in 1871. No other nation in Europe attained corresponding degrees of urbanization. In fact, no other country had as large a proportion of its population urban at the end of the nineteenth century as had England and Wales at the beginning. It appears that the forces making for urbanization moved southeastward across Europe during the century. That is, the farther removed is each country from England the later and perhaps the more difficult was its industrialization.

Averages, such as those shown in the table, are apt to be somewhat misleading. In France, for example, which as a whole had the least amount of urban development of any European country, there were large disparities. In the northwestern section, in the neighborhood of the Austrasian coal fields, industrialization and the growth of cities flourished, while in the rest of the country towns remained much as they had been in the preceding century.[48] On the other hand, in Austria and Hungary most of the urban population resided in the capital cities; the increases resulted from the growth of governmental bureaucracies rather than from economic changes.

In the new republic of the United States urbanization followed a different course, for there was no preestablished settlement from which to draw population. New towns led rather than followed the settlement of the country. At the conclusion of the Revolutionary War the westward movement of settlement began in earnest. Outposts had already been established at Detroit, Louisville, St. Louis, and New Orleans. With the accession of the Louisiana Territory, in 1803, these became rallying points for land-hungry settlers. New town sites soon appeared at Erie, Pittsburgh, Cincinnati, and elsewhere along the Ohio, Mississippi, and Missouri Rivers. In every instance the new towns served as points of departure from which settlement fanned out over surrounding lands. The opening of the Erie Canal in 1825 speeded the flow of settlers westward and, for the first time, permitted a return flow of raw materials to eastern centers. Lake ports at Rochester, Toledo, Chicago, and Milwaukee soon appeared; the little village of Cleveland blossomed into a substantial town, and the river ports at Pittsburgh, St. Louis, Cincinnati, and Louisville were within a decade rivaling New Orleans as entrepôt centers. In the meantime access to western raw materials changed the old mercantile centers of the east to manufacturing centers. Trans-Appalachian commerce received a further stimulus with the laying of rail lines across the mountains. Established centers were drawn into a network of intercity

[48] See Eric Lampard, *op. cit.*, pp. 113–15.

relationships by the rail lines and new centers developed at division points along the routes, at Canton, Columbus, Dayton, Indianapolis, Grand Rapids, Peoria, and elsewhere. Inland cities beyond the reach of navigable water became possible for the first time. According to H. J. Habakkuk, the economic historian, high internal transportation costs in America led to the establishment of a great many more manufacturing centers than was necessary in England.[49] Moreover, distances were great, and many market areas for manufactured goods were relatively isolated from one another.

By 1860 the principal outlines of the urban pattern east of the Mississippi had been completed. All but a few of the present centers of 100,000 or more population in that section of the country had been founded. After the Civil War cities sprang up west of the Mississippi in rapid sequence along the newly completed transcontinental railways. Within a scant twenty years, by 1880, the urban network of the nation was virtually completed. The landward drift of the population passed its peak in 1890. From that date to the present the prevailing trend in population redistribution has been cityward.

Urban growth in the United States during the years from 1790 to 1900 is described in Table 5. It will be noted that the trend of increase was uninterrupted during the eleven decades. Growth was most rapid in the last half of the nineteenth century, instead of in the first half as was the case in England and Wales and northern Europe. In the first half of the century the groundwork for the political and economic organization of the nation was laid down; in the second half that organization matured rapidly with cities as its nodal points.

Although cities had been multiplying at strategic sites across the country since early in the century, it was not until the last half of the century that the main thrust of urban growth occurred. Industrialization was well under way long before then, for the exigencies of settlement in an undeveloped country demanded a large degree of self-sufficiency. Local industry was encouraged, too, by the high costs of imported products. Mechanization in agriculture as well as in industry proceeded much more rapidly than it had in England. The difference was due partly to the absence of old institutional restraints in the new country and partly to a chronic labor shortage.[50] It was that shortage that was responsible for a rising tide of European immigrants continuing for over one hundred years. Since by 1880 most of the good lands were occupied, most of the migrants from that date on congregated in cities. They contributed to urban

[49] *American and British Technology in the Nineteenth Century: The Search for Labour-Saving Invention* (Cambridge: University Press, 1967), pp. 63–64.
[50] *Ibid.*, pp. 23, 50 ff.

Table 5. Number and Percentage of the Total Population in Urban Places (By Size of Place, U.S. 1790–1900)

Number of Places

Size of Place	1900	1890	1880	1870	1860	1850	1840	1830	1820	1810	1800	1790
All places	1,737	1,348	989	663	392	236	131	90	61	46	33	24
1,000,000 plus	3	3	1									
500,000–1,000,000	3	1	3	2	2	1						
250,000–500,000	9	7	4	5	1		1	1				
100,000–250,000	23	17	12	7	6	5	2		1			
50,000–100,000	40	30	15	11	7	4	2	3	2	2	1	2
25,000–50,000	82	66	42	27	19	16	7	3	2	2	2	3
10,000–25,000	280	230	146	116	58	36	25	16	8	7	3	7
5,000–10,000	465	340	249	186	136	85	48	33	22	17	15	12
2,500–5,000	832	654	467	309	163	89	46	34	26	18	12	

Percentage of Total Population

Size of Place	1900	1890	1880	1870	1860	1850	1840	1830	1820	1810	1800	1790
All places	39.7	35.1	29.2	25.7	19.8	15.3	10.8	8.8	7.2	7.3	6.1	5.1
1,000,000 plus	8.5	5.8	2.4									
500,000–1,000,000	2.2	1.3	3.8	4.2	4.4	2.2						
250,000–500,000	3.8	3.9	2.6	4.0	0.8		1.8	1.6				
100,000–250,000	4.3	4.4	3.6	4.0	3.2	2.8	1.2		1.3			
50,000–100,000	3.6	3.2	1.9	2.6	1.4	1.2	1.1	1.7	1.3	2.1	1.1	1.5
25,000–50,000	3.7	3.6	2.9	2.0	2.1	2.6	1.4	0.8	0.7	1.1	1.3	1.2
10,000–25,000	5.7	5.5	4.4	2.4	2.8	2.4	2.4	1.9	1.3	1.5	1.0	1.2
5,000–10,000	4.2	3.8	3.4	3.3	3.1	2.6	1.9	1.8	1.6	1.6	1.8	1.1
2,500–5,000	3.8	3.6	3.2	2.8	1.9	1.4	1.0	1.0	1.0	1.0	0.9	

SOURCE: U.S. Bureau of the Census, *Population Census*, Vol. I, pp. 14–15, 1960.

growth directly by adding their numbers to urban populations and indirectly by supplying a large volume of cheap labor to new, lightly capitalized industries.

SUMMARY

In the tumultuous period of European history lasting from the fifteenth to the close of the nineteenth century, two currents of change were of particular importance for the progress of urbanization. The first of these was the movement toward political unification and the rise of national states. Uneven though the consequences of that development were, the general effect was to arrest localized expansion tendencies and to cause a concentration of urban growth in the capitals of new or enlarged states. A functional integration of the politically consolidated territories followed much later and only as transportation improved and the necessary administrative institutions were created.

The next great set of forces to impinge upon the urban phenomenon comprised the technical revolutions. Dramatic improvements in transportation, on both water and land, so reduced distances that formerly isolated areas could enter into regular exchanges with one another. The universe of economic, political, and social discourse was correspondingly enlarged. A revolution in agriculture increased the capacities of food-producing areas to support larger proportions of non-agriculturalists while at the same time dislodging large numbers of subsistence farmers for distribution to other sectors of economies. A third and more spectacular revolution occurred in the industrial arts as steam-powered tools were perfected and applied to one manufacturing process after another. Just as important as the new tools was the new form of production organization known as the factory. Accompanying these revolutions was an extraordinary surge in the growth of population, due mainly to improvements in the food supply. Population growth provided an enlarging market for goods and services and an increasing supply of manpower with which to staff a ramifying division of labor.

Specifically, city growth resulted from the enlarging scope of markets and the advance of specialization. As the former increased the basis of support for specialized activities, the latter congregated closely in space in order to minimize the time and costs of communications. The interaction of size and specialization progresses cumulatively up to the point at which the costs of congestion become prohibitively high. Cities grew to unprecedented sizes, first in England, then on the continent and in North America.

SUPPLEMENTARY READINGS

BRIDENBAUGH, CARL. *Cities in Revolt: Urban Life in America, 1743–1776* (New York: A. A. Knopf, 1955).

BUER, MABEL C. *Health, Wealth and Population in the Early Days of the Industrial Revolution* (London: George Routledge, 1926).

HARTWELL, R. M. (ed.). *The Causes of the Industrial Revolution* (London: Methuen & Co., 1967).

KUBLER, GEORGE. "Mexican Urbanism in the Sixteenth Century," *Art Bulletin,* XXIV (1947): 160–171.

SMITH, R. C. "Colonial Towns of Spanish and Portuguese America," *Society of Architecture Historical Journal,* XIV (1955): 1–12.

5

The Urban Center in the Nineteenth Century

The nineteenth century has been aptly described as the great city-building period of Western history. The forces working to that end began earlier, of course, but they were gradually transformed as Western culture accumulated. It was during that period that the shape of the urban center was laid down and that the far-reaching import of urbanization came into full view. As a matter of fact, when one refers to the nineteenth century city he should have in mind a place located more in a technological than in a calendrical chronology. It was a period characterized by a reliance on steam power, in transportation as well as in production. In that respect the nineteenth century city was still very much in evidence as late as 1920 in the United States and much later in Europe. Many of the contemporary problems in cities are at least partly due to the persistence into the present century of patterns created in the preceding one.

The urban center that developed in this era is commonly characterized as the "industrial" city. While that designation is appropriate in a general way, its application often obscures the true state of affairs. Not all "industrial" cities were or are seats of industry. "Industrialism" here refers rather to a technological regime which has extended its sway over the entire range of human concerns. Among its distinctive features are the increasing scale and scope of organized activity, the absorption of large and widely distributed populations into a single market nexus, and the progressive accommodation of the forms of human behavior to the conditions generated in that nexus. Thus all of the centers that flourished under the new power-driven technology took on broadly similar features, whether they were devoted primarily to commerce, administration, or some other specialization. All became participants in an industrialized society and to that extent may be properly regarded as industrial cities.

The designation "industrial," as opposed to "pre-industrial," refers to a difference of degree rather than of kind.[1] Wherever there is trade there must be industry of some kind, for otherwise there would be nothing to trade. Nor has the rise in the volume of industry in the modern age dispensed with the trader. What happened in history is that, as manufacturing became more mechanized and required larger accumulations of capital, the scale, and with it the ramifications, of industrial activity increased. Commerce became an adjunct of industry instead of the reverse as it had been for hundreds of years past. Accordingly the power and prestige of the industrial entrepreneur surpassed those of the mercantile entrepreneur.

THE CELLULAR CITY

As it developed in the latter part of the eighteenth and throughout the nineteenth century the industrial city took form as a dense, compact settlement.[2] Industrialization, we noted earlier, exerted a pronounced concentrative effect, the more so as it fostered a progressive specialization. Of necessity specialists must congregate in order to facilitate the communications and exchanges upon which they subsist. The radial distance over which closely interrelated activities could spread was initially no different from what it had been since ancient times. Except for an increased traffic in wagons and drays for heavy loads, the city of this period was a pedestrian city; it was confined, therefore, to a radius of not more, and usually less, than three miles. The anomaly of a series of striking improvements in the efficiency and the reach of long-distance transportation while short-distance transportation remained dormant in a primitive condition lasted late into the nineteenth century.

The accumulation of growth was guided by the localization of employing institutions. Old towns and cities in areas of long-established settlement were too densely occupied to accommodate further increases. Hence new institutions with their labor forces and attendant populations had no alternative to locations at the edges of urban units. In the new towns,

---

[1] Leonard Reismann takes the opposite view, though mainly as an expedient way of limiting the range of material to be treated. (*The Urban Process: Cities in Industrial Societies* [New York: The Free Press, 1964], pp. 16–20.)

[2] In 1898, when Chicago contained 1,690,000 inhabitants, half lived within a radial distance of 3.2 miles from the city's center. (Paul F. Cressey, "Population Succession in Chicago: 1898–1930," *American Journal of Sociology*, XLIV [1938]: 59.)

whether in the English Midlands or in the United States, there were usually unoccupied interior spaces for the absorption of growth increments. But after the available space was occupied, growth was forced to the peripheries. The difference between old and new in this respect was a matter of when accretion at the periphery became the prevailing mode of urban growth. Parenthetically, we note that the continuation of growth at the edges of old European cities usually led to a destruction of the ancient walls and other fortifications which had been reduced to anachronisms by the consolidations of national states.

A difference did develop as between old and new centers in reference to their street patterns. In many of the old centers of Europe streets were meandering lanes that followed the contours of hills and narrow ways that strayed off in whimsical fashion. Irregularity was the rule. The new towns of North and South America were laid out in grid patterns of right-angled, intersecting streets.[3] Peripheral growth simply added extensions to the grids. Whether the recurrence of the grid pattern in many parts of the world over time was a result of cultural diffusion from the plan for Piraeus prepared by Hippodamus in the fifth century B.C., as Stanislawski claims,[4] is a moot point in view of its appearance in both the Inca and the Aztec towns. More pertinent is the fact that a rectangular pattern makes possible a most intensive occupance of land space while also simplifying the movement of wheeled vehicles. In both regular and irregular street patterns, however, houses were closely built on lots of twenty- to thirty-foot frontages. In the pedestrian city, space could not be squandered on yards and open spaces about each house.

Additions at the edge proceeded in a ragged fashion. In some instances, owing to the easy availability of land, industries located in open country at a short remove from the built-up areas of cities, forming suburban-like clusters. The intervening space was usually promptly filled with construction, however, erasing all outward appearances of separation. Asymmetrical growth was most in evidence on the peripheries of port cities. The great dependence on water transportation during the early phase of rapid increase caused industry, and commerce as well, to gravitate to water locations. In consequence, urban agglomerations were drawn out laterally along the rims of estuaries, river banks, or canal routes.

The solid mass of buildings laced with streets and byways conveyed a false impression of unity in the early nineteenth century city. Its oper-

[3] Two notable exceptions in North America were Washington, D.C., and Detroit, both planned and developed with radial street patterns.

[4] Dan Stanislawski, "The Origin and Spread of the Grid-Pattern Town," *Geographical Review*, XXXVI (1946): 105–20. Compare for example, J. M. Houston, "The Foundation of Colonial Towns in Hispanic America," in *Urbanization and Its Problems: Essays in Honour of E. W. Gilbert*, ed. by R. P. Beckinsale and J. M. Houston (Oxford: Blackwell, 1968), p. 372.

ating structure is more accurately described as cellular. In this respect an ancient city pattern was repeated, though without the clear demarcations afforded by interior walls. The long hours of work that prevailed and the difficulties of getting about on foot narrowly circumscribed the ambit of daily life for most people. There was, in fact, little separation of home from work place. Of these who did work outside their homes in New York, in 1899, the average commuting distance was about one quarter of a mile.[5] But it has been conservatively estimated that not more than 23 percent of the workers in New York, as late as 1840, were employed outside their homes.[6] Thus the urban agglomeration was a congeries of more or less self-contained districts or quarters, each with its own industries and shops and other institutions. Within each district there was no clear separation of rich and poor. Employer and employee, if they did not share a place of residence, lived side by side.[7] Residential seclusion from the clamor and turmoil of congested living was a luxury that could be afforded only by a very small minority.

The cellular aspect of the city points to another structural characteristic: the absence of any marked degree of centralization, such as a central business district toward which the interests and activities of the residents were oriented. The major economic activities were spread along the water's edge. Shops and services were sprinkled over the city, varying in number and type from district to district with differences in the wealth and other characteristics of their residents. Highly specialized services and luxury shops, however, were usually concentrated close by residential areas of the wealthy and on streets the names of which denoted the types of specialties represented. A major reference point might be found at a political capitol, a cathedral, or a ceremonial plaza, but such places were infrequently attended by most people. Each enclave had its own gathering place such as a produce market, a church, or a cafe.

The various districts were often further set apart by each having acquired a more or less distinctive provincial or ethnic coloration. For each tended to serve as the destination of a migration stream from a particular rural area or foreign source. Then, as throughout most of history, migra-

---

[5] Allan R. Pred, *The Spatial Dynamics of Urban-Industrial Growth: 1800–1914* (Cambridge: The M.I.T. Press, 1966), p. 209.

[6] *Ibid.*, pp. 209–10.

[7] Speaking of Boston in the middle of the nineteenth century, Sam Warner says: "Throughout the tiny metropolitan region of 1850, streets of the well-to-do lay hard by worker's barracks and tenements of the poor; many artisans kept shop and home in the same building or suite; and factories, wharves and offices were but a few blocks from middle class homes" (*Streetcar Suburbs: The Process of Growth in Boston, 1870–1900* [Cambridge: Harvard University Press, 1962], p. 19); see also Paul Chatelain, "*Quartiers historiques et centre ville: l'exemple du quartier du Marais,*" in *Urban Core and Inner City*. Proceedings of the International Study Week, Amsterdam, 11–17 September, 1966 (Leiden: E. J. Brill, 1967), pp. 340–55.

tion flowed mainly along the lines of communication between kinsmen and erstwhile village associates. Through that means districts were differentiated by peculiar habits of speech, food preferences, recreational practices, and other elements of traditional cultures. The turbulence of urban life soon smoothed out such differences among the native born. But a foreign enclave preserved its uniquenesses into the second and third generation.

CENTRALIZATION

The beginnings of change in the cellular pattern appeared in the second decade of the century. That came about as a result of rudimentary improvements in local transportation. The twelve-passenger, horse-drawn omnibus was introduced in Paris, in 1819, and was imitated in New York twelve years later. This adaptation of the overland stage to urban purposes was quickly superseded by the horse-drawn street railway in New York, 1832. Not until after 1850, however, was its spread rapid. Then in the 1850's the horse car was adopted in Brooklyn, Boston, Cambridge, and Philadelphia in rapid sequence. In the next decade the horse-drawn, street railway appeared in Salford and Liverpool, in England, and in Chicago, Cincinnati, and Baltimore. By 1890 in the United States 28,000 cars were operating over 6,600 miles of track.[8] As a result the radius of urban settlement was lengthened from two or two and a half miles to three and three and a half miles and then to over four miles. Settlement was drawn out along the tracks into what had been open country. At the same time, converging rail lines contributed to a reorganization of the urban pattern inaugurated by the steam railway.

The establishment of a steam railway terminal in the interior of the city, usually close by the piers and warehouses serving water carriers, set in motion a redistribution process that ultimately produced a well-defined centralization of activities. Public buildings, central offices, banks, services to business and industry, hotels, and retail and personal service establishments gathered about the terminal to take advantage of the quick communication with hinterlands and with other centers. A zone immediately surrounding the railway station became the nerve center of a broadening urban network. It became also the focal point in the internal affairs of the center, though centralization could not progress far as long as the horse-drawn car was the only supplement to walking.

The concentration of business activities in the central district dislodged the prior occupants. Competition for central locations among specialized businesses and those catering to mass consumer markets forced land val-

[8] *Encyclopaedia Britannica,* vol. 8 (1963), p. 221.

ues in the central district to prohibitively high levels for residential and other low-intensive uses.[9] From 1840 onward the populations of inner zones of New York, Philadelphia, Boston, London, Liverpool, Leeds, Birmingham, and many large centers of Europe declined more or less continuously,[10] though islands of high and mounting densities remained for some time in the interiors. The outward movement of residential areas carried with it, of course, the zones of high rates of population increase.

For some time, however, the central business district together with the pattern of axial routes connecting it to the outer portions of the city constituted but a thin overlay on the cellular pattern. Some tendency on the part of population to sort itself into somewhat homogeneous residential groupings had begun to be manifest. Still, the process could not proceed very far as long as intramural transportation facilities remained in a simple state. Change was most apparent in narrow belts paralleling the axial thoroughfares. In the interstitial sectors between radial routes there was no appreciable alteration of the self-contained neighborhood.

The spatial reorganization in the urban center was greatly accelerated by the appearance of the electrified street railway. After two or three decades of experimentation the electric-powered street car was demonstrated to be feasible in Richmond, Virginia, in 1887. During the next thirteen years fifty-one American cities acquired trolley systems. And, by 1895, there were 850 systems operating with 10,000 miles of track.[11]

With twice the speed and more than three times the passenger capacity of the horse-drawn car, the electric railway enormously facilitated movement and communication. As systems were developed and elaborated, the effective radius of daily commutation was extended to as much as twelve miles from central business districts. While the doubling and tripling of the radius of daily travel produced as much as a ninefold increase in the potential areal expansion of a city's space, the actual effect was considerably less than that. The street railway's influence on settlement was linear rather than circular. It pulled settlement outward in bands lying along the rights-of-way. Tracks followed the level ground, skirting hills where necessary or seeking the gentlest slopes where rising ground

[9] "While the land within the first mile of State and Madison (in Chicago) increased in value from $819,000 in 1842 to $50,750,000 in 1856, a gain over sixtyfold, the greatest rate of increase came in the belts from one to four miles from State and Madison.

"The railroads had opened up the possibilities of land from one to four miles from the downtown section, and this area was largely subdivided into lots in this period." (Homer Hoyt, *One Hundred Years of Land Values in Chicago* [Chicago: The University of Chicago Press, 1933], p. 70.)

[10] A. F. Weber, *op. cit.*, pp. 459 ff.; Asa Briggs, *Victorian Cities* (London: Odhams Books, Ltd., 1963), p. 26; and Michel van Hulten, "In Search of the Urban Core of Amsterdam," in *Urban Core and Inner City, op. cit.*, p. 183.

[11] Charles N. Glaab, *The American City: A Documentary History* (Homewood, Ill.: The Dorsey Press, 1963), p. 178.

could not be avoided. The adjustments to topography gave each center a distinctive contour. Later engineering developments enabled electric cars to surmount steep inclines, after which settlement filled in many interstitial sectors. Formerly peripheral industrial districts became surrounded and enclosed by the enlarging city. Suburban developments, moreover, pushed out into open country like so many beads added to a string.

The outward thrust of urban aggregation had its complement in an increased centripetal drift. Street railways were able to concentrate far more people at a given point in far less time than had ever been conceivable with simpler forms of intramural transportation. Hence the spatial separation of home and work was lengthened and made more general in the population. The widening difference between the daytime and the nighttime distributions of urban residents measured a further impetus to the concentration of specialized activities, notably in the central business district. Other functions as well as work were in process of separation from the household and the vicinage. The central business district loomed steadily larger as the principal reference point and locus of dominance in the urban center. But the efficiency of the street railway in transporting throngs of people to the core district could not have been realized to the extent that it was had not the passenger elevator come into use after 1857. Thereafter the core district expanded vertically as well as horizontally.

THE CENTRAL BUSINESS DISTRICT

The commanding position of the central business district in the urban center rested on its monopoly of communications with the outside world and on the convergence in its precincts of the intramural transportation lines. Its position was further enhanced by the development of the telephone, which followed soon after the electric street railway. The telephone further simplified the spatial separation of administration from production activities while sustaining much closer interrelations than afforded by the telegraph. Administrative offices were thus able to concentrate in close juxtaposition to the interregional communication agencies and to ancillary services of various kinds. The rate of exchanges and of the general tempo of activity were sharply increased. Communication, transportation hub, administration offices, banks and money markets, and their innumerable supporting service agencies formed the seat of dominance for the entire community and the region beyond. Virtually every activity was supplied, financed, supervised or coordinated with other activities through the institutions concentrated in the central district. This concentration of power derived in no small degree from the superior access afforded by a central location.

Within the business district, agencies and institutions arranged themselves to further capitalize on the advantages of proximity. Clusters of various kinds appeared. Inasmuch as like units have similar location requirements, they congregated in selected locations and around them gathered various complementary units. In that way relations of interdependence and competition were interwoven. By being close together, like units could mutually support commonly used specialized services. They were also able to concentrate the market for their goods and services and thereby enjoy a larger volume of business. On the other hand, proximity enabled complementary units to pursue their respective interests more efficiently. A financial district, for example, was readily distinguishable; there were grouped banks, stock exchanges, brokerage houses, legal firms, and professional advisors to financial transactions. Interspersed among such establishments were restaurants, tobacco shops, job printing shops, messenger services, and other aids to daily business. In another locality theaters were concentrated and not far away were costumers, poster printers, film distributors, bars, restaurants, and flower shops. Wholesalers' display rooms were clustered here and corporate administrative offices there. Similarly, retail establishments formed loose groupings by type. Shoe stores gravitated toward a selected block or two, women's specialty shops to another location, furniture stores to still another, and so on.[12]

Under the influence of the street railway the local transportation system began to detach itself from the extra-local system as represented in the combination of railway and water routes. The tendency was most noticeable in the largest centers. From the beginning the two systems were modeled on the same pattern; they followed the same radial routes and shared the same terminal point. But as population spread over a wider area the location of the central business district proved to be far too eccentric for maximum accessibility, especially in centers located on waterfronts. Hence the central business district tended to move toward the geometric center of population, though the distance of removal was never so great as to make access to the steam railway terminal difficult. The point of convergence of traction lines moved in turn with the business district.

The shifting geometric center of residential population was not the only factor that encouraged a relocation of central business districts. A related influence was the great traffic density that developed in the vicinity of the terminals of intramural and interregional transportation systems. Hundreds of thousands of commuters and shoppers, electric railway cars, freight wagons, carriages, and other vehicles converged daily upon the

---

[12] R. M. Haig, "Toward an Understanding of the Metropolis, II. The Assignment of Activities to Areas in Urban Regions," *Quarterly Journal of Economics*, XL, (1926): 418 ff.

central district, causing all but immovable snarls of traffic. In the 1890's and afterward traffic congestion in downtown areas was regarded as a major urban problem. It led to efforts to clear streets by the construction of subways and elevated lines. A temporary solution was found in a separation of industrial from central office and commercial traffic. Further urban growth, however, soon re-created traffic congestion at the new locations.

MULTI-NUCLEATION

The bringing to completion of street railway systems accentuated a growth pattern that had been manifested earlier. As Richard Hurd had noted: "A continual contest exists between axial growth, pushing out from the center along transportation lines, and central growth, constantly following and obliterating it, while new projections are being made farther out on the various axes." [13] As a result the urban center tended to acquire a rather clear star-shaped configuration. Central growth followed radial growth as circumferential or "cross-town" street railway lines, intersecting radial lines, were built. Until that occurred, much of the interstitial spaces could not be fully occupied. Travel time to a destination included the walking time to a car stop as well as the time spent aboard a car in transit.

The intersections of heavily trafficked rail lines constituted breaks of flows and transfer points. At such locations, in accordance with a familiar principle, secondary business centers developed. These appeared at widely spaced intervals some five to six miles distant from the central business district. A further element, then, in the physical pattern of the walking *cum* street railway city was the multi-nucleation of its commercial services. In fact, the nuclei were more numerous than has been suggested thus far. Lesser, or tertiary, business districts were distributed over the entire built-up area at intervals of approximately three miles, and interspersed among them were corner service centers comprising two or three stores each. The entire set of service centers and subcenters resembled a hierarchy in size distribution, in territorial spread, and in the variety of services offered. At the top was the central district, providing the maximum range of specialized as well as many standard services; the next echelon was formed by a small number of secondary centers offering fewer specialized services but a wide assortment of commonplace services; a third level was composed of many smaller subcenters dealing only in the most standardized goods; and finally there were a great many neighborhood outlets catering to the daily consumption needs of residents.

[13] *Principles of City Land Values* (New York: The Record and Guide, 1903), pp. 39 ff.

RESIDENTIAL PATTERN

In the redistributions set in motion by the street railway, various other selective tendencies came into view. New housing was built at the outer edge of the city largely because of the availability of unoccupied and relatively inexpensive land there. The new housing was occupied for the most part by members of younger generations who left parental homes to marry and begin new families. As a result of the aggregate effect of that selectivity, the average age of population declined in successive intervals from the central business district. The outward movement of residents also gave freer play to the inclination of people to sort themselves into homogeneous clusters. In this respect the selective agent was usually income, for income determined the quality of housing that could be occupied and, too, the ability to pay the time and costs of longer distances to work and to other regularly visited destinations. That there were also invidious status distinctions at work in the segregation process is scarcely to be doubted.

The centrifugal movement of residences was a response to a push as well as a pull. The latter was the attraction of newer, more spacious home sites.[14] But behind that lay the obsolescence of old residential properties and rising land values. Obsolescence and rising land values were dual effects of the same cause, namely, the actual or expected encroachment of incompatible but high-rent-yielding land uses pushing outward from an expanding business district. When evacuation of old residential areas proceeded in advance of the actual appropriation of the land by high-intensive uses, the spaces were often held in speculation pending further rises in land values. In that event old homes were converted to rooming houses or subdivided into tiny apartments. A lucrative market for small, inexpensive and often substandard housing to accommodate the poor and the mounting influx of newcomers to urban life flourished with city growth. Lightly constructed, multistoried tenements were also built in areas of obsolescence to profit from the great demand for cheap housing. Population densities rose steeply in such districts from 8,000 to 9,000 to upward of 50,000 people per square mile.

In the American experience, the newcomers who filled the tenements and made over residence quarters in large numbers appeared first as immigrants from abroad. They created ethnic colonies in the inner sections of cities where cheap housing was available.[15] There they reproduced their native institutions and sought to preserve the past while adapting

---

[14] This trend was observed in nineteenth century London and was documented by Charles Booth. See Harold W. Pfautz (ed.), *Charles Booth on the City: Physical Pattern and Social Structure* (Chicago: University of Chicago Press, 1967), pp. 94 ff.

[15] A similar tendency was observed in London. See Pfautz, *op. cit.*, pp. 92–94.

to the new culture. Usually, however, early arrivals blended into the American population with the passing of generations and new foreign groups replaced those that had preceded them. A typical sequence of occupance in an inner locality began with Germans, followed by Irish, who in turn were replaced by Polish or Italian, and they by yet another eastern European group.

Centrifugal movements of industries also began to occur in the latter part of the century.[16] Plants that had been surrounded by dense growth and were cramped for space found it possible to relocate at peripheral sites without loss of contact with their working forces. In some instances low-cost housing for industrial workers was constructed in the neighborhoods of relocated manufacturing plants. The outward drift of industry and of working population moved generally along steam railway lines and to points where rail sidings for industrial freight could be cheaply provided. Industrial deconcentration in a relative rather than an absolute sense was much more evident. That is, new industries or additional plants of old industries were built at the outer edges of industrial districts. Each increment of that kind acted as a magnet for a further clustering of workers' homes and of stores and services catering to workers' needs. Thus while the inner zones were given over to low-income workers and their families, other concentrations of manual worker residences were spotted along the radiating steam railway lines. The low-income worker had to minimize travel time and cost to and from work as well as to find cheap housing.

European cities were less susceptible to changing settlement patterns than were American cities. The scarcity of cheap land held the cities to shorter radii and to greater average densities. For that and other reasons —perhaps the real or imagined insecurity of other opportunities for investment—land and buildings were a patrimony and were infrequently put on the real estate market. Obsolescence was a much slower process. Furthermore, internal communications developed rather slowly. Hence, middle- and upper-income groups remained in residential quarters through two and three generations and the tendency toward a regrouping in relatively homogeneous income clusters, visible in American cities, was much less pronounced. The poor were crowded, as often as not, to the extremities of urban centers.

MUNICIPAL SERVICES

The growth of the city in the nineteenth century usually far outdistanced its acquisition of utilities and services required for health, safety,

[16] See A. F. Weber, *op. cit.*, pp. 200 ff.

and comfort in congested living. A time lag was unavoidable, for what was needed had, in fact, to be invented and improved through numerous trials and errors. An urban technology was in its infancy, though there had been occasional contributions from very early times. Street paving, for example, was a fairly well-developed art, and streets in the older sections of most European and English cities were surfaced. But where city growth had been very rapid that elemental requirement was often neglected. Minneapolis, in 1880, had no paving on any of its 200 miles of streets. A decade later Chicago had surfaced no more than a third of its 2,048 street miles.[17]

Water supply and sewage disposal presented more novel problems. Municipal water systems began to appear early in the century, but they supplied small sections of their respective cities with water of very doubtful quality.[18] A water purification plant was built on the Thames, in 1829. Nevertheless, a severe cholera epidemic in London, in 1854, was traced to contaminated water. Typhoid was not eliminated as a threat to health in American cities until early in the present century. Sewage carried in open ditches in many places flowed or seeped into backyard wells. Early underground sewage systems were designed to dump their effluent into rivers and harbors with consequences that were extremely offensive, if not damaging to health. A water-borne sewage system was introduced in Hamburg in 1874, but other cities were slow to copy the improvement.

Other services were just as slow to develop. Until late in the century street lighting was confined to business districts and principal thoroughfares. Police existed mainly as a nightwatch in most places until midcentury. London organized a modern police force in 1829, and other large cities followed suit in subsequent years. Fire protection was left in the hands of volunteer companies into the 1840's.

Delays in providing needed municipal services can be but partly charged to lack of tools and engineering experience. There were also administrative and financing techniques to be developed and perfected. An attack on this problem was begun in the 1830's in England with the creation of the Borough and Corporate Towns Commission for the purpose of establishing appropriate boundaries for municipal taxing purposes, specifically in order to provide urban services.[19] Until after 1870 American cities were without the autonomy and taxing powers required to undertake large capital outlays. They had to rely on private enterprise for most of the utilities they required. Even under the best of conditions,

---

[17] Charles N. Glaab, *op. cit.*, p. 178.

[18] Blake McKelvey, *The Urbanization of America, 1860–1915* (Brunswick, N.J.: Rutgers University Press, 1963), p. 13.

[19] F. W. Freeman, "Boroughs of England and Wales of the 1830's," in R. P. Beckensale and J. M. Houston, *op. cit.*, pp. 70–91.

however, growth was so rapid that many a municipality was unable to keep abreast of its needs.

THE PROCESS OF LOCAL EXPANSION

In general the process of local expansion under the centralizing influences of steam and electric railway systems was from the center outward. The workings of the process were conceptualized by E. W. Burgess in his well-known concentric zonal hypothesis.[20] According to this proposition, concentration at the point of convergence of local transportation lines develops a pressure which forces activities outward more or less symmetrically. Growth of the central business district pushes ahead of it a belt of obsolescence occupied by light industries, warehouses, and slums. This transition zone, in turn, encroaches upon a zone of low-income housing, causing the latter to shift outward and to invade a belt of middle-income residential properties. The latter, finally, spills over into suburban territory and presses against a zone of high-income housing. The occupants of each inner zone tend to succeed to the space occupied by those of the next outer zone. At any moment in time, therefore, the distribution of land uses exhibits a ring-like appearance.

The conception of change employed in Burgess' proposition is known by the term *succession*.[21] This concept (borrowed from applications in studies in plant ecology) holds that change proceeds in an alternating series of stages in which growth is followed by equilibrium and then by growth and equilibrium again. How the process works in the growth of the city is subject to two interpretations. The more familiar one visualizes the alternation of change and equilibrium as occurring in each of several relatively homogeneous land use zones. Each zone settles into a fixed pattern which is resistant to pressures of change for a time, but eventually it yields to an invasion of a new type of occupant. This suggests that change is a series of impulses spaced at brief intervals through time. That may have been partially true of the history of American cities. Ebbs and flows of business activity seem to have produced spurts of growth and capital investment which laid down zones of renewal comparable to the rings of a tree. A second interpretation of the succession idea is that it pertains, not to zones, sections, or other localized areas in the city, but to the system as a whole. In this view, an urban system, including its center, changes in response to recent technological inputs until an

[20] "The Growth of the City: An Introduction to a Research Project," *Proceedings of the American Sociological Society*, XVIII (1923): 85–89.

[21] R. D. McKenzie, "The Scope of Human Ecology," *American Journal of Sociology*, XXXI (1926): 141–54, and R. E. Park, "Succession, An Ecological Concept," *American Sociological Review*, I (1936): 171–79.

adjustment is accomplished. At that point it returns to equilibrium. Growth is still cyclical, but the cycles are spread over longer spans of time. The internal distribution pattern of interest is that associated with the final equilibrium stage rather than that at one or more points in time during the maturation process. And that pattern is expected to conform to a relatively smooth gradient from center to periphery in which intensity of use varies inversely with distance from the center. In either case, whether viewed in the small or the large, the Burgess conception of growth should be recognized as a special case of a more general theory of expansion.

The notion of growth entering a city or a community at its business center and being distributed outward from that point is consistent with a concept of dominance [22] touched upon in an earlier connection. At the center are located those communal units whose functions are responsible for mediating the relations of the community with the external world. They thus set the conditions under which all other units must function; and to that extent dominance, i.e., a disproportionate share of the power contained in a system, belongs to them. Implied here, so it would seem, is a monocentered urban core. But, as pointed out, the city is often multi-centered. That, however, need not be contrary to the assumption of a principal, if not a single, center of integration. The elements of growth may enter through the central district to be transmitted directly to the immediately adjacent area and indirectly to outlying sections of the city through secondary and tertiary business districts. From every nucleus and subordinate nucleus growth pushes out ringlike increments. Even in those instances in which growth appears to occur by accretion at the edges, the regulatory influences may be exercised from the center.

A second assumption of the Burgess hypothesis appears to be that expansion proceeds uniformly in all directions from a point of origin. On the contrary, however, the linear effects of transportation lines tended, at least in the transportation regime that characterized the late years of the nineteenth century and the early years of the twentieth century, to draw cities into star-shaped patterns. Still, if distances were measured in time and cost rather than in linear units the distortions caused by transportation routes are minimized.[23]

As a formulation of growth the Burgess hypothesis was on sounder ground than as a generalized description of the spatial pattern of the urban center, though it is in the latter respect that the hypothesis has been

[22] R. D. McKenzie, "The Concept of Dominance and World Organization," *American Journal of Sociology*, XXXIII (1927): 28–42; and R. E. Park, "Dominance," in *Human Communities* (New York: The Free Press, 1952), pp. 159–64.

[23] J. A. Quinn, "The Burgess Zonal Hypothesis and Its Critics," *American Sociological Review*, V (1940): 210–18; and Amos H. Hawley, *Human Ecology* (New York: Ronald Press, 1950), p. 260.

most generally accepted. Burgess himself was partly responsible for that. His notion of zones derived from his observation of gradients. That is, density of occupance, quality or age of housing, front footages devoted to commercial land use, and various social characteristics such as poverty, delinquency, and broken families were observed to occur in decreasing frequencies (increasing in the case of housing quality) with distance away from the business center.[24] But a smooth gradient does not suggest zones unless one arbitrarily marks off class intervals along the curve. The language Burgess employed to describe his zones implied internal homogeneity in each case. As we have seen, however, the distribution of land uses or occupants over the urban area was more mottled than circular. Burgess was not unaware of this; he used the term "natural area" to refer to the patches of segregated uses or occupants. Nevertheless, the idea of homogeneity gained currency. It also attracted numerous critics.

Maurice Davie attacked the overly simple idea of a symmetrical distribution of land uses in concentric rings on the basis of a detailed study of New Haven, Connecticut, and an examination of land use maps for twenty cities.[25] He pointed to considerable heterogeneity within zones and many irregularities of pattern. Exceptions were also noted in European cities. Paris, according to Caplow, has no clearly discernible business center.[26] He explains that fact by reference to legislation limiting the height of buildings, in effect since the fourteenth century, which has prevented a great concentration of specialized services in any one locality. In a study of Budapest the author reported that the residential quarter of the nobility, rather than a business district, was the reference point around which land uses were arranged.[27] Case study findings such as these are interesting, but they are not a sufficient basis for criticism of a general hypothesis. Still another criticism took the form of a "sector theory." That is, land uses of a given type accumulate in radial extensions, forming elongated sectors of homogeneous uses.[28] These and other criticisms were provoked by a too literal interpretation of the zonal hypothesis. Had the gradient concept been described in more general terms, in terms of intensity rather than type of land use, much of the objection might have been obviated.

Another line of criticism has been concerned with the causal factors

[24] E. W. Burgess, "The Determination of Gradients in the Growth of the City," *Publications of the American Sociological Society,* XXI (1927): 178–84.

[25] "The Pattern of Urban Growth," in *Studies in the Social Sciences,* ed. by G. P. Murdock (New Haven: Yale University Press, 1937), pp. 133–61.

[26] "Urban Structure in France," *American Sociological Review,* XVII (1952): 544–49.

[27] Erdman D. Beynon, "Budapest: An Ecological Study," *Geographic Review,* XXXIII (1943), 256–75.

[28] Homer Hoyt, *The Structure and Growth of Residential Neighborhoods in American Cities* (Washington, D.C.: U.S. Government Printing Office, 1939), pp. 17 ff.

operating in the development of land use patterns. Burgess and other ecologists have been accused of relying too much on impersonal forces, such as competition, in their explanations of location choices. So the counter-argument has been put forth that sentiment, symbolism, and other non-rational elements are often of decisive importance in the choice of specific locations.[29] But, if the ecologists erred in one direction, the opposing view erred in another direction; it is unlikely that any simple factor lies at the roots of a location decision. In fact, if it were possible to lay bare the motivational anatomy of competition, it probably would be found to include various mixes of rational and non-rational elements, assuming an observer could sort them into such categories. More to the point, however, an explanation of a collective phenomenon cast in motivational terms hardly seems appropriate. Purposiveness in the individual has no necessary relationship to outcome in the aggregate. The more important question is: Under what condition do patterns of any given kind appear?

A different approach to an analysis of land value and land use determination is put in institutional terms by William Form. He observed that there are four congeries of groups involved in land development policy: the real estate and building business; large industrial, business, and utility firms; individual home owners and other small-scale users of land; and zoning boards, planning commissions, school boards, and other agencies of local government.[30] The interactions among these sets of units, according to Form, are affected by the resources each can command, the manner in which the set normally functions, the kind of internal organization each possesses, the pressures to which each is exposed, and the image of the city held by each set of groups. Although Form has little to say about how to treat the interactive process, it is obvious that his proposal adds depth to a causal analysis of land use patterns. There is a further step needed in such a study, however. That concerns the determination of the degrees of freedom possessed by each set of groups from the exigencies of cost consideration, transportation availability, and other kinds of accessibility requirements. It would also be necessary to know what factors influence the amounts of possible variability.

The concentric pattern is, of course, a descriptive formulation, not an explanation. As such it constitutes a useful first approximation. Its principal feature is the gradient concept. The description in profile of the relation of spatially positioned characteristics with distance from a central

---

[29] Walter Firey, "Sentiment and Symbolism as Ecological Variables," *American Sociological Review*, X (1945): 140–48; and *Land Use in Central Boston* (Cambridge: Harvard University Press, 1947).

[30] "The Place of Social Structure in the Determination of Land Use: Some Implications for a Theory of Urban Ecology," *Social Forces*, XXXII (1954): 317–23.

point has value for comparative purposes. Its slope gives an indication of the efficiency of local transportation facilities: the more gradual the slope, the greater the speed of radial movement and the wider the spread of components of the urban center. Gradients plotted in successive intervals of time for a given place, therefore, may be used to indicate the amounts of change in transportation efficiency.

The criticisms of the concentric zonal pattern could have been much more constructive had they raised questions relative to the theoretical specifications for such a model. It would seem, for example, that such a pattern would most probably appear where a virtually complete and highly integrated system obtains. In that circumstance all units of the system—corporate offices, industrial plants, retail stores, churches, households—occupy specific functional positions. All units, moreover, are responsive to influences that play upon the system and to the mechanisms that transmit those influences through the system. There is the further implication that the location of each unit is adapted to the function performed, and that a modification of the one is followed quickly by an appropriate adjustment in the other. Clearly, the organizational structure that most nearly fits a concentric spatial configuration is a hierarchical one. The integrating units occupy the center and their influence on the costs of occupying other locations in the area diminishes with distance from the center.

A model which relates organization of a system to its spatial pattern becomes a tool in comparative analyses. Exceptions to the model manifestly fail to conform to the conditions specified in the theory. The greatest disparity between an actual case and the model might be expected to occur where the so-called city is merely an unintegrated agglomeration. Some of the ancient Asian "cities," Edo, for example, appear to have been little more than loose concentrations of village-like settlements. In many other contrary instances two or more systems are juxtaposed in a single locality and are arbitrarily treated as one. Illustrations are found where the representatives of imperial powers have attached themselves to old native settlements and have constructed Western-style adjuncts to the preexisting patterns. Again, continuous growth may keep a process of redistribution in operation to such an extent that symmetrical patterns can be no more than a tendency. So it has been with many cities of the Western world.

TYPES OF URBAN CENTERS

It should come as no surprise that there is considerable diversity among urban centers. They differ as a result of the historical circumstances that existed at the time of their founding and initial growth phases, as a consequence of their subsequent growth histories, because of the locations they occupy, in respect to the extent that centralized planning guided their development, as an outgrowth of the functions they perform, and because of various other contingencies. In Europe new growth gathered about medieval structural survivals, while in American urban centers sprang up *de novo*. Centralized planning was the exception in Europe and North America, but was the rule in Central and South America.[31] Variety is found within a cultural area or an economic territory as well as among universes of relative internal homogeneity. Case comparisons, i.e., involving places considered individually, can always be expected to reveal differences.

It is highly probable that many of the differences among urban places that might be listed are for most purposes inconsequential. Conceivably, therefore, the variety could be reduced to a few categories or types of places. A number of efforts to find a classificatory principle from which a typology could be derived have appeared in the literature.[32] Most of those have resorted to the variable of functional specialization or the lack of it. All but one, however, have failed to observe a rather elementary distinction, namely, the dual orientation of an urban center. On the one hand, each urban center together with the organization of which it is the nucleus is engaged in the specialized production of one or a few products that are exported to other urban areas and regions. The product may be a manufactured commodity, a processed raw material, or a service such as education, recreation, or administration; whatever the export may be, it is the source of income by which the urban area is maintained. On the other hand, every center is a mechanism for distributing goods and services to the local population. In this latter respect all cities are or tend to be very much alike, a similarity which is affected by differences in size and in proximity to other places, but by little else. Cities differ mainly in their export functions, for it is usually on the strength of their unique advantages that they hold a position in a system of cities. Hence it is only in respect to the export function that a functional typology would seem

[31] The Latin American town was laid out, by directive from the Crown, as a rectangular grid with a plaza at its center. The Church, the administrative offices, and the homes of the elite—who were required to build town houses—faced the plaza. The residences of professional workers, shopkeepers, craftsmen, and army officers formed a second zone around the plaza. On the outskirts lived the agricultural laborers, the domestic workers, and others at the bottom of the social-economic hierarchy. (See Morse, *op. cit.*)

[32] See Chancy D. Harris, "A Functional Classification of Cities in the United States," *Geographic Review*, XXXIII (1943): 86–99; Grace M. Kneedler, "Functional Types of Cities," *Public Management*, XXVII (1945): 197–203; Victor Jones, "Economic Classification of Cities and Metropolitan Areas," *The Municipal Yearbook*, 1953 (Chicago: National Municipal League, 1953), pp. 49–57; and Howard J. Nelson, "A Service Classification of American Cities," *Economic Geography*, XXXI (1955): 189–210.

to be discriminating. The one classification that recognized that fact classified all places of 10,000 or more population in the United States, of 1950, as specialized in one or more of the following: manufacturing, wholesale trade, retail trade, education, public administration, transportation, military, and entertainment and recreation.[33]

The problem with a typology is that it is usually useful for a very limited range of problems, seldom more than one or two. A different typology is necessary for each new type of problem. This necessity arises in considerable degree from a lack of consensus as to what characteristics are critically important. In the absence of any real prospects for an all-purpose taxonomy of cities, a rigorously prepared classification hardly seems worth the effort, at least not in the present state of knowledge. Duncan and Reiss were fully aware of these difficulties. Their typology was developed for the express purpose of examining the social and economic characteristics of places as reported in the United States Census. But neither their nor any other typology has cast any light on the physical or spatial structures of urban places.

THE URBAN REGION

Until a fairly late date, each urban center needed a surrounding belt of agricultural land from which most of its daily food requirements could be obtained. Within that zone, scarcely more than a team-haul distance in width, were located the most prosperous farms. Competition for proximity to the urban market drove land values up close by the center and allowed them to taper off with distance away.[34] Differential land values tended to allocate land uses in relation to their capabilities for yielding returns high enough to cover land and transport costs and still produce a profit. Accordingly, an intensity-of-use gradient coincided with a land-value gradient. A German economist, von Thunen, conceptualized the pattern that emerged in the tributary agricultural zone as comprising four concentric rings devoted to a land use of different intensity.[35] These, in order of distance from a center, of use intensity, and of per-acre value, are (1) garden crop lands, (2) grain-producing lands, (3) pasture lands, and (4) land from which forest products are obtained. Needless to say, the pattern described by von Thunen represents another case of the dis-

[33] Otis D. Duncan and Albert J. Reiss, Jr., *Social Characteristics of Urban and Rural Communities*, 1950 (New York: John Wiley and Sons, 1956), pp. 387 ff.

[34] In 1815, when Cincinnati had a population of 8,000, land adjoining the town and to a distance of three miles sold for $50 to $150 per acre, within three to twelve miles prices ranged between $10 and $30 per acre, and beyond twelve miles the value fell to $4 to $8 per acre. (Pred, *op. cit.*, p. 154.)

[35] "Der isolierte Staat," in *Beziehung auf Landwirtschaft und Nationalökonomie* (Hamburg and Rostock, 1863).

tribution tendency put forth by Burgess' formulation; it is more apposite when regarded as a pattern of change than as a static pattern.

Stability of pattern seldom lasted for long in the nineteenth century. The extending tentacles of railway systems soon brought to the fore the economies of the long haul. The zone of agricultural self-sufficiency in the urban region was at first broadened and later was eliminated. Improvements in railway service enabled distant producers to compete with neighboring farmers for local markets.[36] In the competition many of the latter were displaced and their lands dropped from agricultural use, though they might have suffered no decline in soil fertility. The railway brought about a regional specialization of agricultural production on a national scale. Barring the presence of some special production advantage which enabled local producers to compete in interregional markets, lands in the vicinities of cities were used only for high value and perishable products.

Changes in the belt of land surrounding the urban center were also working in other directions. Rural industries addressed to the farmer's needs lingered on until late in the century before they were supplanted by urban products. Speaking of the English countryside, an observer commented:

Whereas heretofore the villager (a provincial craftsman, say) had been grappling adventurously and as a colonist pioneer with the materials of his own neighborhood—the timber, the clay, the wool—other materials to supersede the old ones were now arriving from multitudinous wage-earners in touch with no neighborhood at all, but in the pay of capitalists . . . What we saw was some apparently trivial thing, such as the incoming of tin pails instead of wooden buckets . . . If an out-house was boarded up with planed deal match-boarding from Norway instead of with "feather-edged" boarding cut out locally by sawyers one knew, who was to imagine what an upheaval was implied in this sort of thing . . . ? Seen in detail the changes seemed so trumpery and, in most cases, such real improvements. That they were upsetting old forms of skill . . . occurred to nobody.[37]

Again the railway was instrumental in bringing about the quiet revolution in rural life.[38] As crafts died away and agricultural lands fell into disuse, sons and daughters drifted off to the cities. In many cases villages were so depopulated that their institutions could no longer be sustained.

[36] After the completion of the railroads in the 1840's the New England farmer, who had but a short time before acquired a home market for his product, encountered severe competition from western producers of wool, beef, pork, wheat, and hay. The loss of markets was followed soon by declining labor supply through the out-migration of youth and then by the abandonment of farms. (P. W. Bidwell, "The Agricultural Revolution in New England," *American Historical Review*, XXVI [1920–21]: 683–702.)

[37] George Sturt, *The Wheelright's Shop* (Cambridge: The University Press, 1923), pp. 17–19, 153–54.

[38] See also A. F. Weber, *op. cit.*, pp. 188 ff.

The remaining people moved to surviving villages or followed their progeny into the city.

Concomitant with the extension of an urban center's influence over a widening hinterland there was a realignment of settlement units in a territorial division of labor within the expanding domain. Cities, towns, and villages acquired more or less specialized roles in an emerging system. Some performed manufacturing functions geared to more elaborate processes administered in the central city. Many others served as collecting points for locally produced goods to be shipped to or through the center and as distributing points for goods and services issuing from the center. The interrelations between the center and outlying settlements, however, were confined mainly to economic exchanges. Each locality preserved its identity and maintained a complement of institutions serving the daily and weekly interests of the people in its neighborhood. The railway was unable to effect as thorough a social as it did an economic integration of an urban region.

Within nearer distances, ranging up to twenty miles, a much closer interdependence between urban center and outlying settlement was possible. Villages and towns lying along transportation routes were transposed to suburban status and here and there new suburbs arose. The suburb changed its character during the century, however. In the early years it generally was an industrial concentration, often as congested, begrimed, and odorous as were the working class districts of the parent city.[39] It offered no attraction as an alternative place of residence for urban population. But transportation improvements fostered a new connotation for the term "suburb." It came to mean a place of clean and healthful living. We have already seen how the street railway pushed out contiguous clusters of settlement at the city's growing edge. The steam railway spread suburbs farther afield and spaced them at wider intervals. The outward movement to the detached suburbs was actually a small, highly selective migration. Few people other than the well-to-do were able to move leisurely to and from work or could afford the daily commutation fares. In the interstices between radiating rail lines there was no improvement of accessibility. A town twelve to fifteen miles from an urban center, but served only by a wagon road, could be as much as a day's travel from the center.

SUMMARY

The impetus to city growth exerted by the new industrialization occurred in the framework of primitive means of local transportation. The

[39] Asa Briggs, *op. cit.*, p. 28.

early nineteenth century city was a pedestrian city. As it grew, therefore, it could not preserve an internal unity; instead it assumed the form of a congeries of cells much as had large agglomerations in ages past though without the interior walls of the earlier period. Centralization began in the second quarter of the century as the horse-drawn railway made its appearance. The heightened access to the interregional transportation node fixed by the steam railway terminal at the water's edge led to a concentration of business and other activities. A central business district emerged as the radius of intramural travel lengthened. Another—and this time a major—thrust toward the advance of centralization came with the advent of the electrified street railway. Its speed and load capacity enabled it to concentrate more people at a given place in less time than was possible before. It also permitted a wider spread of settlement. The city pattern was extensively reorganized under the influence of the street railway. One further innovation of great importance was the telephone, which appeared near the end of the century.

With the concentration of specialized activities the central business district loomed larger as the focal point in the urban center. As that occurred the district tended to move closer to the geometric center of population. The intramural transportation center tended to separate from the interregional transport node. Functional clusters formed within the central business district, giving rise to financial, theater, and various kinds of retailing quarters. An accumulation of great traffic densities in central business districts was one of several factors in the growth of outlying service nuclei, or secondary business districts. Other factors were the distances over which residences were scattered and the intersections of traffic flows at convergences of radial and lateral street railway lines. While specialized activities were in the process of realignment the residential population moved centrifugally, also sorting itself into relatively homogeneous clusters. Both tendencies grew from the increasing separation of home from work place made possible by transportation and communication advances. Centrifugal movements of industry also occurred resulting in scattered industrial districts. The development of municipal services followed the emergence of critical needs by almost a half century. A new technology had to be acquired for the purpose, involving not only tools and engineering skills but also administrative and financial techniques.

The process of local expansion is a special case of a more general process of cumulative change. As formulated by E. W. Burgess, growth enters at a center and presses outward, effecting a selective redistribution of land uses. The lower the capability for intensive occupance of space, the greater is the distance of removal from a center. Accordingly, the distribution of uses reveals a gradient of declining intensity of use with distance. In Burgess' thinking the gradient was more steplike than continuous, suggesting the existence at any one moment of relatively homogeneous zones concentric with one another. The Burgess hypothesis, which was treated more as a pattern than as a process, was extensively criticized on the basis of case study findings. But the criticisms proposed no theoretical alternatives. A consideration of the theoretical implications of such a model offers a useful tool for comparative study. Efforts to create a typology of cities have failed to yield a classification having general utility. Only one such effort has ventured into an examination of the characteristics correlated with the city types identified.

Under the influence of the steam railway each urban center tended to carve out an economic area, with a radius of upwards from seventy-five miles, over which it exercised dominance. Agricultural self-sufficiency within such areas gave way, as rail service improved, to regional specialization in agricultural production. At the same time rural crafts were displaced by urban industries. Cities, towns, and villages in the tributary area became appendaged in a territorial division of labor integrated and administered from the principal urban center. In the near distances, suburbanization of residences of upper-income groups began to appear along rail lines.

SUPPLEMENTARY READINGS

DUNCAN, OTIS D., and BEVERLY. "A Methodological Analysis of Segregation Indexes," *American Sociological Review*, XX (1955): 210–217.

GLAAB, CHARLES. *The American City: A Documentary History* (Homewood, Ill.: The Dorsey Press, 1963).

McKELVEY, BLAKE. *The City in American History* (London: Allen & Unwin, 1969).

RANNELLS, JOHN. *The Core of the City* (New York: Columbia University Press, 1955).

SAMUELSON, PAUL. "The Business Cycle and Urban Development," in *The Problems of Cities and Towns*. Report of the Conference on Urbanism. Ed. by Guy Greer (Cambridge: Harvard University, 1942).

TILBY, A. W. "A Century of Suburbanization," *Edinburgh Review*, CCXLV (1927): 92–107.

WILLIAMSON, JEFFREY A. "Ante-Bellum Urbanization in the American Northeast," *Journal of Economic History*, XXV (1965): 592–614.

6

The Urban Social System of the Nineteenth Century

The physical and spatial pattern of an urban center is, to use Mumford's term, a "container" for its social system. It is fair to assume that the former tends to be an overt expression of the latter, and would do so were it not for the uneven course of change. During the nineteenth century both facets of the urban center were changing by fits and starts. Dislocations were probably as common as congruences. In any case, an understanding of changes in the physical structure hangs upon a knowledge of the transformation occurring in the social system. An urban center is preeminently a social system, or, more properly said, the nucleus of a territorially extended system. Hence the objective in this chapter is to present an analysis of the system in process of development.

SOURCES AND COMPOSITION OF URBAN POPULATION

How the populations of countries changed during their periods of industrial transition is fairly well established by now. Studies in historical demography have been filling in the details of trends that until recently had to be extrapolated from incomplete enumerations. But, as is so often the case, although knowledge pertaining to a large area may be reasonably accurate, its quality becomes more uncertain in each smaller subdivision of the inclusive area. So it is with urban places and particularly in reference to the components of population growth in such places. Yet there is enough scattered evidence to indicate the nature of the salient features of urban population change.

Cities persisted in their old role as consumers of population into the nineteenth century. Death rates, that is, remained consistently higher than birth rates, though the descriptive data on this matter are less than satisfactory. The decline of mortality which began in northwestern Europe in the third quarter of the eighteenth century seems to have had less of an impact on urban than on rural populations. So far as cities were concerned, improvements in the food supply appear to have been offset by recurring epidemics of typhoid, typhus, and smallpox and by occupational hazards. In London records of burials and baptisms indicated that deaths exceeded births by three to two until 1790.[1] The difference narrowed somewhat in following decades but it did not disappear. Near the end of that century death rates were higher in urban than in rural areas in England, France, and the United States; in fact, the larger the city, the higher was the death rate.[2] (See Fig. 2.)

Beginning after mid-nineteenth century, the birth rate entered upon its historic decline in the Western world. A partial description of the trend is given in Table 6. As the decline progressed the excess of births

Table 6. Average Size of Completed Family of Women Born 1841–65 and Reported as Married in 1911, England and Wales

Period of Birth of Women	Average Number of Live Births	Reduction in Average Family Size
1841–45	5.71	—
1846–50	5.63	0.08
1851–55	5.40	0.23
1856–60	5.08	0.32
1861–65	4.66	0.42

SOURCE: Royal Commission on Population, *Report* (London: H.M. Stationery Office, 1949), p. 24.

over deaths was slowly reduced and the rate of population increase subsided. But again the incidence of fertility change was different as between rural and urban areas, though this time the major effect occurred

[1] Dorothy George, *London Life in the Eighteenth Century* (New York: Harper Torchbook, 1964), p. 25.
[2] A. F. Weber, *The Growth of Cities in the Nineteenth Century*, pp. 343–45.

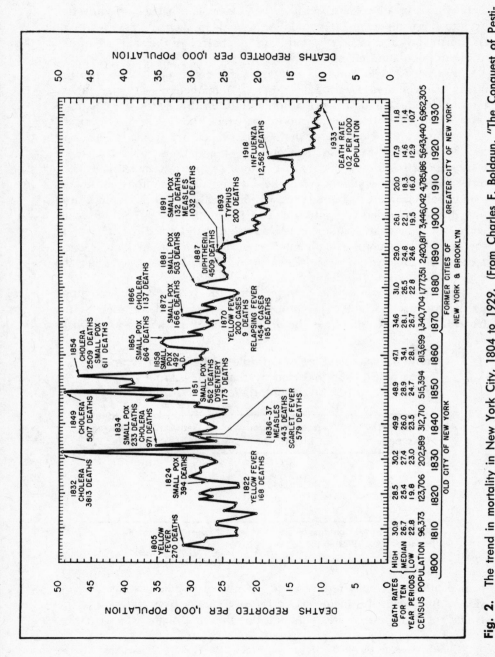

Fig. 2. The trend in mortality in New York City, 1804 to 1929. (From Charles F. Boldaun, "The Conquest of Pestilence," *Milbank Memorial Fund Quarterly,* XIII [1935]: 220. Reproduced with permission.)

in cities.[3] Urban birth rates declined through the remainder of that century and into the one following, whereas rural rates continued more or less unchanged. Hence the rural-urban birth rate difference widened progressively.[4] By 1920 an inverse relationship between the birth rate and size of city, as illustrated for the United States, in Table 7, was common in most Western countries.

Table 7. Children Aged 0–4, per 1,000 Women Aged 20–44 (By Size of Place and Nativity of Women, United States, 1920)

Size of Place	Native White Women	Foreign-Born Women
Total	538	779
100,000 and over	341	679
25,000–100,000	390	766
10,000– 25,000	434	861
2,500– 10,000	477	873
Rural area	720	998

SOURCE: Bernard Okun, *Trends in the Birth Rate in the United States Since 1870.* Johns Hopkins University Studies in Historical and Political Science, Series LXXVI, No. 1., 1958 (Baltimore), pp. 52–53.

Growth of urban population, therefore, was dependent almost entirely on net migration. In the early part of the period the failure of natural increase in cities could be charged to exorbitant death rates; in the latter part, after death rates had fallen, the deficiency was due to low and declining birth rates. Rural areas were the producers of population. The rising excesses of births over deaths supplied rapidly increasing numbers for resettlement in urban places and elsewhere. Surplus rural population was further inflated, and as was pointed out in Chapter 4, by displacements from agriculture consequent upon increases in sizes of farms and mechanization of agricultural operations.

The rural exodus resembled a refugee movement. It was far greater than cities could accommodate under the best of conditions of the time, for industrial economies were in their formative stages. Periodic depressions in business activity, moreover, contributed further to the numbers

[3] Two notable exceptions to this pattern of change appeared in France and Ireland. In France, following the introduction in the Napoleonic Code of the practice of equal inheritance of parental estates, birth rate decline began early in the century, in rural as well as in urban areas. In Ireland, after the famine of 1841, birth decline resulted from a steep rise in the age of marriage.

[4] A. J. Jaffe, "Urbanization and Fertility," *American Journal of Sociology,* XLVIII (1942): 48–60.

of unemployed and under-employed. A temporary solution was found in emigration to overseas destinations. Labor organizations and newly formed emigration societies subsidized migration of Englishmen to America.[5] On the American side business men and industrialists became increasingly active, especially after 1825, in soliciting skilled workers for their enterprises. The New England textile industry was built with English skilled workmen and managers, as was the mining industry in Pennsylvania and West Virginia and the iron industry in Pittsburgh.[6] At the same time the growing need for unskilled workers and for settlers in recently opened western territories created an insatiable demand for population. Labor recruiters, shipping firms, and hired agents of territories aspiring to statehood were aggressive stimulators of overseas migration. When English sources dried up these missionaries turned their attentions to the European continent. As they worked from the northwest toward the southeast they generated successive waves of migrants from different ethnic stocks. In the years between 1846 and 1920 almost 50 million Europeans moved abroad.[7] The important point here, however, is that the industrial transition in England and Europe was rendered much less painful than it might have been by the exportations of surplus rural populations abroad.

Gradually the multiplication of economic opportunities in English and, later, in continental urban centers was able to absorb local rural surpluses. The urbanward movement grew steadily in volume. In many places migrants outnumbered the locally born and in all growing centers they formed very substantial fractions of the respective populations. Net migration to Paris between 1851 and 1872 was 510,000, four times greater than the natural increase during those years.[8] In London, in 1881, the number of migrants was reported to be 1,164,071, in a population of 3,834,000.[9] A similar situation existed in most of the cities of Europe.[10] American cities had drawn heavily on the European flows. In 1870 the foreign-born population of San Francisco amounted to 47 percent of the total, to 41 percent in Chicago, 40 percent in New York, 32 percent in Boston, and 30 percent in St. Louis. At the end of the century one fourth of all urban population in the United States was foreign-born.

[5] Wilbur S. Shepperson, "Industrial Emigration in Early Victorian Britain," *Journal of Economic History*, XIII (1953): 181.

[6] Rowland T. Berthoff, *British Immigrants in Industrial Americas, 1790–1950* (Cambridge: Harvard University Press, 1953), chs. 3, 4, and 5.

[7] W. S. Woytinsky and E. S. Woytinsky, *World Population and Production: Trends and Outlook* (New York: Twentieth Century Fund, 1953), pp. 72 ff.

[8] D. H. Pinkney, "Migration to Paris During the Second Empire," *Journal of Modern History*, XXV (1953): 2.

[9] E. G. Ravenstein, "The Laws of Migration," Part II, *Journal of the Statistical Society*, XLVIII (1885): 187.

[10] *Ibid.*, LII (1889): 241–78.

Rural-urban migration within regions followed a general pattern, as Ravenstein was able to demonstrate.[11] It proceeded characteristically as a series of short-distance moves. Migrants to a given urban center originated primarily from the surrounding county or province. The places vacated by those persons were filled by migrants from areas further removed from the center, while persons from a third outer belt of territory replaced people who had moved a step inward. The number of migrants to a given center, therefore, diminished steeply with distance away from the destination. This pattern applies, of course, to unsolicited migration. It reflects the influence of distance on the spontaneous distribution of knowledge about a possible destination. Long-distance migration—overseas movements, for example—depends upon some form of migrant recruitment as a way of dissemination of information about destinations and how to get to them.

Rural displacement operated mainly on the young adults. The parent generation stayed on as agricultural workers or suffered the gradual attrition of handicraft industries. Their skills were not transferable to urban employments. The youth, however, not yet committed to traditional occupations, were available for relocation and adaptable to new techniques of work. Migration, whether over short or long distances, tends to be selective of young people. Thus in the populations of cities persons in ages ranging from 15 to 35 years became numerically preponderant, the more so where growth was rapid. Important consequences flow from this simple fact. Even though urban death rates were comparatively high and birth rates low, the age composition yielded an excess of births over deaths, albeit an excess which cannot be sustained without a continual replacement of the young through migration. It would seem also that the age composition of cities might have endowed them with an extraordinary vitality. Reasonable as that appears to be, it has not been possible to trace the dynamic propensities of urban centers specifically to the presence of large numbers of youth. Nor have studies of intelligence selectivity in rural-to-urban migration produced unequivocal findings.[12] The full significance of urban age composition has yet to be completely explored.

A second aspect of selectivity in migration pertained to sex. That differed with the length of the migratory journey. Females predominate in

[11] *Ibid.*, XLVIII (1885): 157–227.

Josiah C. Russell reports studies of migrations to medieval centers that followed the pattern described by Ravenstein ("The Metropolitan City Region of the Middle Ages," *Journal of Regional Science*, 2 [1960]: 67–68).

[12] Cf. Wilson Gee and Dewes Runk, "Qualitative Selection in Cityward Migration," *American Journal of Sociology*, XXXVII (1931): 254–65; Otto Kleinberg, *Race Differences* (New York: Harper and Row, 1935), pp. 176–96; A. H. Hobbs, *Differentials in Internal Migration* (Philadelphia: University of Pennsylvania Press, 1942); C. Arnold Anderson, James C. Brown and Mary Jean Bowman, "Intelligence and Occupational Mobility," *Journal of Political Economy*, LX (1952): 218–39.

short-distance migrations, males in long-distance moves. Since, in internal population redistributions short-distance moves were considerably more numerous than long-distance moves, city populations growing mainly from that source acquired disproportionate numbers of females. But cities that gained a substantial part of their increases from long-distance migration, such as did many American cities during the nineteenth century, had high proportions of males in their populations. In that respect they were not unlike frontier areas.

PROBLEMS OF TRANSITION

The transition from a village-agrarian to an urban-industrial regime has been a long-term process of almost continuous adjustment. Just as a precise date at which it began cannot be fixed, so there is no moment at which it can be said to have been completed. At no point was there a sharp break with the past, yet at nearly every point along the way there was novelty in unprecedented forms. Familiar institutions needed to be overhauled, and new institutions had to be created to accommodate the new forces at work. A full use of the technical culture that was being assembled in the nineteenth century could not be achieved until an appropriate organization was developed.

There was lacking, for example, a body of rules, orderly procedures, normative understandings, and means for the expression of civic concern which guide and facilitate the pursuit of the commonplace needs of urban residents. These elements of organization are not so much the underpinning of institutions as they are the stuff of which institutions are formed. It is not strange, therefore, that the latter were as undeveloped as the former. Hence the social costs incidental to rapid growth were high. Migrants from rural areas had no legitimate defenses against exploitation by landlords, employers, or others who might attempt to prey upon them. Welfare agencies that could provide a cushion against adversity lay far in the future. Some mutual aid could be expected from village associations that had been re-created in the city. But these traditional institutional groupings were scarcely adequate to the problems of the city. At an earlier time the guilds might have served the purpose; they, however, had outlived their usefulness. The one kind of institution that was present and influential was that which provided employment. Order diffused from the employing institution to the community. It prescribed most of the rules which regulated daily life, determined through its work schedule the rhythm of the diurnal round, and in its wage payments fixed the spending power on which other collective activities had to depend for their support.

The institutional inadequacies could be charged in considerable part to the absence of an effective local government. There was no conception of a responsible municipal authority. Local government was represented by an anachronistic medieval council. When its concern reached beyond the regulation of commerce, which was seldom, it was only to collect taxes for occasional street improvements, the support of an indifferent night watch, and a grudging contribution to the poor. In general, local needs were left to the discretion of national governments; legislative authority over localities was highly centralized. To move a central government on behalf of a locality required the intervention of industrialists or other influential individuals.

The reins of power had, in fact, shifted in a very large measure to the hands of the industrialists.

We will not stress the time-worn comparison between manufacturers and feudal lords, but they had this much in common, that certain localities, certain districts did belong to them. This was not only true of the factories which they ruled, but of the village or town into which they breathed life and prosperity, and of the county which came to depend on their industry; while the whole population more and more regarded them as its natural leaders. After the great landowners, to whom their titles gave an added ascendancy, the men who really counted were the spinners of Lancashire and Derbyshire, the ironmasters of Birmingham, of the Severn and of South Wales and the potters of Staffordshire. Whenever a question arose of carrying out some important scheme of public utility by which the whole district would benefit, they were the men with the greatest interest at stake, and ready to take the lead.[13]

When their interests were not at stake, however, they were as likely as not to ignore the needs of localities.[14] In the larger urban centers, or where large-scale industry had not been established, it was the merchant who ruled. Both manufacturers and merchants were slow to discover the connection between their prosperity and the welfare of the cities and towns in which their enterprises were located.

The lagging development of appropriate institutions had another part of its explanation in the naiveté of the newcomers to urban life. They had no knowledge of how to live in the new context, nor any of the civil discipline that would be required of them. There were many elementary things to be learned, such as that individual welfare depended on the welfare of an aggregate of anonymous persons, how to pursue personal ends through organizational means, and that it was necessary to be able to think in relatively general terms. These were not easy skills to acquire; to do so demanded the accumulated experiences of a generation or more. In the meantime, fresh influxes of unschooled arrivals from rural areas,

[13] Paul Mantoux, *The Industrial Revolution in the Eighteenth Century*, p. 404.
[14] See T. C. Parker and J. R. Harris, *A Merseyside Town in the Industrial Revolution: St. Helens, 1750–1900* (London: Frank Case & Co., 1959), pp. 181 ff.

technological shifts in industry and commerce, and cyclical swings in economic activity combined to postpone indefinitely the day of structural maturity.

THE RISE OF EXTRA-FAMILIAL UNITS

If one searches for a single organizing principle in the dynamics of urban development, he can do no better than settle upon the process of specialization. Specialization entails the breaking up of wholes, a refinement of parts, and their realignment in new combinations. Beginning as it does in the work sector of group life, the process spreads its effects into every distinguishable category and sphere of collective activity. And everywhere it generates similar consequences for the individual and for the social structure in which he pursues his daily affairs.

The extension of specialization, in the course of which traditional industries were subdivided and redistributed, proceeded first on a familial basis, much as it had in the past. Families concentrated more narrowly in various forms of retailing, tailoring, furniture-making, metallurgy, banking, personal services, and so on. Household enterprises proliferated and diversified as transportation improvements expanded the market, particularly the domestic market.

The growth of the market and technological change combined to increase the scale of production in a few industries beyond the capacities of the household enterprise. As we have noted before, the textile and the iron industries were the first to lend themselves to an extra-familial organization. The advent of the factory did not, however, bring a complete emancipation from early ways of doing things. Certain practices, developed in connection with the household unit of production, lingered on beyond the point of usefulness. The apprenticeship system, for example, persisted for twenty or thirty years despite the inconsistency of devoting some seven years to learning an unskilled task.[15] The deeply entrenched addiction to neoptistic customs took much longer to overcome. Nevertheless, a beginning had been made toward a reorganization of economic activity that would progressively remove that function from the household.

Although increases in the sizes of the social units in which men lived and worked became a prominent feature of urbanization under conditions of industrialization, the process moved much more slowly than is commonly thought. The invention of the factory was not followed by its immediate adaptation to all production processes. There were problems to

---

[15] See Ashton, op. cit., p. 77, and Neil Smelser, Social Change in the Industrial Revolution (Chicago: University of Chicago Press, 1959), pp. 104–5.

be resolved in the technical imperfections of power-driven equipment, in the procedures employed for mobilizing capital and limiting the liability of investors, in assembling suitable labor supplies, in developing management skills, and in transferring machine processes to successive handicraft industries. Even in the textile and iron industries the spread of the factory was gradual.

The first large textile establishment equipped with steam-driven machinery was opened in Manchester in 1806. There were fifteen of the same type in 1818. In 1823 there were probably 10,000 mechanical looms in the country. In 1850 the figure had risen to 50,000, although there still remained 250,000 hand looms in use in town and country. These were weaving cotton, a product for which mechanization was particularly suitable. Wool kept closer to tradition, and carpets were all woven by hand up to 1850. In 1830 the power-driven woolen loom was still an exception. The setting up of the mechanized silk industry apparently dates from the 1820's in Manchester, though it was not systematized until the end of the century.[16]

Elsewhere, exclusive of the iron industry, the typical production unit was a domestic enterprise in which a master craftsman worked with a journeyman or two and two or three apprentices. This was the state of affairs even where specialization was far advanced. Consider, for example, the small-arms industry of Birmingham in the 1860's:

Of the 5,800 people engaged in this manufacture within the borough's boundaries in 1861 the majority worked within a small district around St. Mary's Church. The reason for the high degree of localization is not difficult to discover. The manufacture of guns, as of jewelry, was carried on by a large number of workers who specialized in particular processes, and this method of organization involved the frequent transport of parts from one workshop to another.

The master gun-maker—the entrepreneur—seldom possessed a factory or workshop. Usually he owned merely a warehouse in the gun quarter, and his function was to acquire semi-finished parts and to give them out to specialized craftsmen, who undertook the assembly and finishing of the gun. He purchased materials from the barrel-makers, lock-makers, sight-stampers, trigger-makers, ramrod-forgers, gun furniture-makers, and, if he were engaged in the military branch, from bayonet-forgers. All of these were independent manufacturers executing the orders of several master gun-makers . . . Once the parts had been purchased from the "material makers," as they were called, the next task was to hand them over to a long succession of "setters-up," each of whom performed a specific operation . . . To name only a few, there were those who prepared the barrel for rifling and proof; the hardeners, polishers, borers and riflers, engravers, browners, and finally the lock-freers, who adjusted the working parts.[17]

[16] Charles Moraze, *The Triumph of the Middle Classes* (Cleveland: The World Publishing Co., 1967), p. 104.

[17] G. C. Allen, *The Industrial Development of Birmingham and the Black Country, 1860–1927* (London: Geo. Allen & Unwin, 1929), pp. 56–57, 116–17.

Industrialization began somewhat later in the United States, though once started.it progressed more rapidly than in England. Still, the average number of production workers per manufacturing establishment increased from eight, in 1849, to but twelve, in 1899. The average was depressed by the persistence of numerous handicraft enterprises. At the end of the century they comprised three fifths of all manufacturing establishments, but they accounted for only 11 percent of production workers in manufacturing. Factories, as distinct from handicraft shops, had at that time an average work force of twenty-one persons.[18]

Thus urban growth through most of the nineteenth century was built largely on the basis of a multitude of small enterprises.[19] They predominated in the food-processing, clothing, leather goods, furniture, and metal products industries. Factories of any kind employing as many as one hundred workers were rare until after 1850.[20] Nevertheless, an increasing number of workers were being drawn into units of relatively large and growing size. Of equal importance was the trend toward the reconstruction of industrial units as extra-familial organizations, an event which sometimes preceded and sometimes followed substantial increases in size of operations. The tendency, in other words, was for workers to pass to the dominion of organizations governed by impersonal and rationalized procedures.

The factory is a uniquely urban institution. Its deliberate specialization, its exclusive orientation to a market, its systematic application of rationalized processes, and its extra-familial basis of organization are alien to any other context. Profound changes in the structure of society followed upon the introduction of the factory. The success of the factory demonstrated a principle of organization that was copied widely in all reaches of society. Institutional specialization became so ubiquitous and so much taken for granted that it led to the unwarranted yet common assumption that individual behavior is compartmentalized in neat bins labeled economic, political, religious, social, and other. The disjunctiveness was an error in perception, a failure to see the whole because of a preoccupation with the parts.

REORGANIZATION OF THE FAMILY

The loss of its production function had profound consequences for the family. Deprived of the central concern which gave meaning and

---

[18] *Historical Statistics of the United States: Colonial Times to 1957*, p. 409.

[19] J. H. Clapham, *An Economic History of Modern Britain* (Cambridge: The University Press, 1932), vol. I, ch. 5, and M. H. Dobb, *Studies in the Development of Capitalism* (London: G. Routledge & Sons, 1946), pp. 263 ff.

[20] But from as early as 1839 the value added per worker in manufacturing had been increasing by 50 percent or more per decade. (See *Historical Statistics of the United States,* p. 139.)

order to its existence, the family underwent a radical change. No longer could each member, young and old alike, contribute to the prosperity of the household. One must gain a job in order to make a material contribution to the family, and jobs became steadily more selective of who held them. Thus external circumstances intruded to regulate the status pattern among family members. Similarly, kinship lost much of its meaning, for it ceased to provide a refuge from failure or an avenue to success as once it did. And, since the family and kin group were relieved of having to produce a labor force for domestic industry, the imperative was removed from child-bearing. Children were converted from a valuable resource to a charge against a wage or salary income. In time, therefore, the birth rate declined. Changes of these magnitudes, of course, occur not within but across generations. The household industry struggled on as a declining enterprise while the offspring drifted off to a new style of life.

Involvement in a monetary system advanced hand in hand with the participation of a growing proportion of the population in the market for consumers' goods and services. Reliance on money as a standard medium of exchange simplified and facilitated a progressive specialization of services of all kinds. Every such development tended to remove another function from the household. Food-processing, clothes-making, dwelling-construction, education of children, recreation, and numerous intimate services were absorbed by manufacturing establishments and service industries and were purveyed through retail outlets. In the process the household's activities were pared down to what might be called end functions, such as the final steps in the preparation of food, the repair and maintenance of clothing, the upkeep of residence quarters, and the like. The family was pushed along the path toward a specialization in consumption centered upon the one task in which it remained sovereign, the nurturing of children. Even in that its activities were tuned to, if not dominated by, an increasing number of institutionalized services.

The removal of functions from the household released repercussions in various directions. For one thing, it multiplied the number of destinations to be visited by household members, the number of trips to be made, and the amount of traffic on the streets. Again, in setting family members apart for short or long periods during the day it exposed them to a wide range of influences any one or more of which could have alienating effects. In short, while certain events were making it possible for the family to concentrate its energies on the nurturing and control of its members, other circumstances operated to weaken its ability to carry out those responsibilities.

These alterations of the position of the family in society brought with them significant internal changes. The wife of the family head, relieved on the one hand of the enervating burden of frequent reproduction and child care, and, on the other hand, of the drudgery of household industries, was able to turn to self-improvement and participation in activities outside the home. Her function in the household became more like that of the head, her husband, with the result that their statuses converged. The role of the children also changed. They ceased to be members of a household labor force, except in very minor respects, and their importance as sources of security for aging parents diminished as well. External interests and activities commanded increasing shares of their time. Parental influence over children weakened. Paradoxically, however, as parental influence declined, responsibility for the education and training of children was extended into progressively later ages. If nothing else, these shifts revealed the family to be a highly adaptable institution. No specialized institution could match its flexibility.

SPECIALIZATION AND STANDARDIZATION

Occupational and institutional specialization were mutually stimulating. Each further step in that direction inserted another link in a lengthening chain of dependences connecting the producer and the consumer, the originator and the ultimate user. Sequences of linkages among specialists, furthermore, became interwoven in a bewildering complexity of interdependences. The individual might know who supplied him his bread, but he had no knowledge of who built the baker's oven, who provided the credit or capital for the enterprise, who milled the grain, who cultivated the fields in which the grain was grown, or who transported the grain to the mill and from the mill to the baker. The intervention of intermediaries extended into the giving of charity, political participation, religious observance, and into a widening array of what had been personal concerns. It ceased to be imperative that the individual know all of the steps in the transfer of a service to him, to say nothing of who performed each step. It was necessary only that the flow of transactions be smooth and continuous. Yet the chances for disruptions and missed connections in so complex and delicately timed an apparatus were enormous. One kind of protection against the extreme vulnerability of such a system was the adherence of all participants to orderly procedures.

Specialization, then, gives rise to an elaborate set of rules and regulations. These comprise a major part of what was referred to earlier as the civil discipline that is mandatory in urban life. Rules within institutions differing with their respective functions, rules governing the relations between institutions, rules of the street—some formal, many informal—and rules regulating various responsibilities of individual to individual were multiplied and codified. Rules, of course, have to be administered and adjudicated. Hence new classes of specialists emerged to perform those functions, including police and local officials, managers and supervisors, and efficiency experts, dispatchers, and referees of many kinds.

Standardization is a necessary counterpart of specialization. Without that additional principle of order a complex structure of interdependences could not be reared. Close coordination of a multiplicity of different functions requires the utmost facility in communication and exchange. Common terms of discourse in language, coinage, and weights and measures, as remarked before, are essential. The requirement applies to much more than those obvious elements, however. What was needed was the development of a culture of standardization. Few things are more generative in that respect than is a monetary system. For it provides the means by which all wants, interests, and expectations are reduced to common, measured terms. The monetary system operates also as a powerful factor in fixing the rate and rhythm of organized activity. The amortization of capital outlays, the scheduling of interest payments, and the balancing of income with expenditures, all made visible and concrete in the pace of the machine, geared the activities of all participants to the calendar and the clock. Time units, therefore, were refined, made uniform, and introduced into every aspect of collective life, beginning with the family breakfast and ending in the determination of social policy.[21] Cost considerations dictate that the design of transportation equipment and other utilities be adapted to the average man. Interchangeability of parts, standard job descriptions and hence an interchangeability of workers, the adoption of a single organizing principle in the structures of groups and institutions, the specification of offenses and of the criteria of justice, these and other instrumentalities are both cause and effect of a pervading standardization which articulates the machinery of specialization.

CLASS AND SOCIAL MOBILITY

The massing of population in urban centers and the progressive subdivision of occupations and roles confused and blurred the distinctions by which men scaled and rated one another. In the rural society relationship to the land provided a simple and relatively immutable basis of classification with which most other invidious differences were rather closely correlated. But in the new social context there were no stable criteria on which a class system might be formed. Instead there were various criteria

---

[21] Standard time as we know it today had its inception at an international conference in 1875. In the same year a more subtle contribution to standardization was made when a department store in Paris introduced the single, take-it-or-leave-it, retail price in place of the old haggling and bargaining method of conducting exchanges.

with reference to which strata could be detected, such as occupation, lineage, rate of consumption, income or wealth, and social usefulness.[22] No necessary agreement existed among the strata observable in each of these attributes of individuals. Moreover. in the dynamics of urban development status criteria were constantly subject to modification and individuals were ever in the process of redistribution relative to the distinctions employed. The lines of classification were obscured further by the relative anonymity of life in the large aggregate. As a participant in the monetary nexus the individual could carry his prerogatives in his pocket in the form of cash money, and he was free to convert the latter to the former at will with no questions asked. Urbanization substituted for a class system a loose set of overlapping and fluid strata. At most it was an open system; movement among the strata was barred by no stigmata or predetermined limits of variability. There existed one glaring exception to this general state of affairs. That had to do with race or color distinctions. Because these markings did not disappear with movement into urban centers or with changes in occupation, income, or education, they could be and were used as criteria for discrimination. Within color categories, however, there were no sharply delineated class structures.

Yet, if the distinctions that set men apart in the urban context were less rigid and less visible than those experienced in peasant life, they could be none the less effective in the allocation of rewards and privileges. At the outset the industrial system contained no compensations for the insecurity of the wage job, no mechanisms for the sharing of risks other than a return to the farm household of one's rural kinsmen. Where the factory appeared, a broad gulf was opened between the machine-tender and the owner or manager of the establishment. The worker, as an interchangeable part in a machine process, could command few opportunities that would enable him to rise above his proletarian status. Until publicly supported education emerged, sometime after midcentury, there was no solid ladder by which the worker's children could climb to higher strata. On the other hand, in those industries in which handicraft skills persisted it was possible for the worker to set up business for himself, to amass wealth and, with the wealth, to avail himself and his family of educational and other cultural resources.[23] The invasion of those industries by mass production methods, however, steadily reduced the proportion of the population that enjoyed such opportunities. But no worker, whether laborer,

[22] Hans Speier, "Social Stratification in the Urban Community," *American Sociological Review*, I (1936): 193–202.

[23] Asa Briggs points to an interesting comparison between Manchester and Birmingham in the middle of the nineteenth century. Manchester developed as a factory center, Birmingham as a city of small enterprises. In the former there was little opportunity for vertical mobility; in the latter movement to higher levels of status was commonplace. (*Op. cit.*, pp. 188–9.)

shopkeeper, white-collar employee, or entrepreneur, was secure from the vicissitudes occasioned by large economic forces.

Upward mobility did occur, however, even from the ranks of workers whose skills had been absorbed by machines. It occurred not as often in the lives of the workers as in the accessions of their sons to the labor force. New industries drew their labor supplies from the young, who were not fixed in the habits of inappropriate occupational and industrial practices. Although the data in Table 8 pertain to a later period than the

Table 8. Percentage of U.S. Male Workers 45 Years of Age and Over in Selected Industries

Industry	1910	1930	Difference
Harness and saddle factories	38.1	68.9	30.8
Livery stables	29.2	52.6	23.4
Wagon and carriage factories	31.6	46.6	15.0
Piano and organ factories	21.9	45.6	23.5
Suit, coat, overall factories	21.0	42.4	21.4
Corset factories	18.4	33.5	15.1
Woolen and worsted mills	21.6	37.2	15.6
Brass mills	18.2	33.2	15.0
Blast furnaces and steel mills	16.0	26.6	10.6
Automobile factories	12.0	19.6	7.6
Electric machinery factories	12.3	18.8	6.5
Banking and brokerage houses	26.8	27.5	0.7
Public service	36.6	35.0	−1.6
Petroleum refineries	21.4	19.9	−1.5
Truck, transfer, and cab companies	22.1	19.8	−2.3

SOURCE: National Resources Committee, *The Problems of a Changing Population* (Washington, D.C., 1938), pp. 32–33.

one being discussed, they describe a mode of change that has been repeatedly experienced. Older workers stay on in old and declining industries, while the youth move into new and expanding industries. Economic growth and diversification fostered a capillarity in which those familiar with urban life ascended the occupational scale, their places at the bottom filled by newcomers to the system.

New opportunities increased exponentially. Every new addition to the industrial complex multiplied the number of interindustry mediating and technical services. And every further subdivision of an existing industry created a gap to be bridged by one or more specialists. Hence, the need for educational facilities to train specialists became more and more imperative. Entrepreneurs who sought better-trained workers and clerical and professional workers who wanted improved opportunities for their chlidren became aggressive advocates of public education. Commercial, civic, and scientific and technical associations operated as pressure groups on constituted authority. Their efforts brought success and in the years after 1870 public education spread rapidly from city to city, but at a much slower rate in the rural districts.

Industrial growth contributed in various ways to multiply the number and increase the proportion of higher status positions. We have already mentioned the increased requirement for technical services to industry. A further impetus came from the rationalization of processes and the growth of scale from which followed large growths of industrial administration. White-collar workers in industry multiplied steadily. At the same time advances in industrial productivity permitted a shortening of working hours, a reduction of the proportion of the population in the labor force, and a rapid expansion of the consumer sector of the urban economy. Establishments offering goods and services to individuals and households proliferated. Professional services multiplied, and local governments enlarged their ranges of functions in order to improve the amenities of life.

In other words, a reconstruction of the labor force occurred as a necessary feature of the industrialization process. That change has been described by John Hobson as "the normal law of the evolution of employment," [24] and by Colin Clark as the "morphology of economic growth." [25] Both refer to the historical tendency for the highest rates of increase in employment opportunities to occur first in primary industry (agriculture and mining), to then shift to secondary industry (manufacturing) after resources have been explored and developed, and finally to appear in tertiary industry (services in all forms) in the mature stage of economic development. Table 9 picks up this trend after midcentury in the United States. The constant decline in agriculture and related extractive industries is apparent. In the meantime, the proportion of the work force engaged in manufacturing and mechanical industries increased steadily though slowly. The tertiary or service industries, depending on how they are defined, already exceeded the secondary industries in 1870, and the margin of difference gradually widened in the following decades.

Increases in the relative numbers of professional, managerial, proprietary, and white-collar workers conferred a growing importance upon the sector of the population described, for want of a better term, as the middle class. What this term means in fact is that the statuses of the people concerned are neither devoid of opportunity for advancement nor endowed with unrestricted privilege. Between these extremes the range is wide and the category is amorphous. Intellectuals with and without wealth, capitalists and employers with and without advanced education, skilled and clerical workers with some savings, some education, or both,

[24] *The Evolution of Modern Capitalism* (London: Walter Scott Publishing Co., 1908, 1919), pp. 397–99.
[25] *The Conditions of Economic Progress* (London: Macmillan, 1940), pp. 337–73.

Table 9. Estimated Industrial Composition of the U.S. Working Force

Industry	1920	1910	1900	1890	1880	1870
Total	100.0%	100.0%	100.0%	100.0%	100.0%	100.0%
Agriculture, forestry, and fishing	27.6	31.6	38.2	43.4	50.0	53.5
Manufacturing, mechanical, and construction	30.3	28.5	24.8	23.7	22.1	20.5
Transportation, communication, and public utilities	7.3	7.1	6.7	6.0	4.8	4.2
Professional and related services	5.1	4.6	4.1	3.8	3.2	2.6
All other services and white-collar industries	27.0	25.6	23.8	21.3	18.4	17.8
Not classified	2.7	2.6	2.4	1.8	1.5	1.4

SOURCE: A. J. Jaffe and Charles D. Stewart, *Manpower Resources and Utilization* (New York: John Wiley & Sons, 1951), p. 192.

these and other combinations of statuses entered into the composition of the middle class. Heterogeneous as was this growing mass in the urban population, it became a powerful source of pressure for improved municipal services and publicly supported cultural opportunities. The extension of public education into the high school level, the founding of libraries, the inauguration of public welfare and health services, the provision of parks and playgrounds, and the insistence upon efficiency in municipal government were germinated as ideas and carried to fruition by the middle class.[26]

It is not unlikely that the rise of the middle class had a great deal to do with the reversal of the historic trend toward class inequality, which G. E. Lenski regards as one of the significant effects of industrialism.[27] The factors cited by Lenski as responsible for the reversal are interwoven as cause and effect with middle-class development. On the causal side are the specialization of function and of related technical knowledge together with the extraordinary increase in productivity. On the effect side are the spread of literacy and the equalization of opportunity that sometimes goes by the name of democratic ideology. To the latter should be added the promotion of many kinds of civil institutions to which reference was made in earlier paragraphs.

VOLUNTARY ASSOCIATIONS

Associations formed voluntarily about common interests have been a feature of urban life from a very early date. An exceptionally favorable

[26] Cf. Leonard Reissman, *The Urban Process: Cities in Industrial Societies* (New York: The Free Press, 1964), pp. 180–88.

[27] *Power and Privilege: A Theory of Social Stratification* (New York: McGraw-Hill, 1966), pp. 313–18, 398.

environment for the proliferation of such associations was present in the industrial city. Specialization multiplied the differentia among men far beyond what entered into the invidious comparisons on which social classes rested. Homogeneity among men is indefinitely subdivisible; it can be narrowed to the utterly inconsequential. Differences of experiences, of former associations, of avocational interests, of near and remote family connections, of hopes and fears appeared in limitless number. Each such difference where it was shared by three or more people could serve as the basis for formation of a voluntary association, and many were so used. Perhaps most common-interest groups were formed within class categories, but there were others that reached across class lines. The grouping about a common interest is an organizing principle with many applications.

A common genesis of voluntary associations is the occurrence of a threat brought against an interest or possession shared by a number of people. Those affected then pool their several strengths and resources to conserve their shared possession or to preserve the status quo. When the threat disappears, the association tends to languish and may eventually fall apart. But if the threat is chronic the association takes on properties of formal organization. The problems of maintaining communications among members and of administering group affairs give rise to a division of labor among officers and to a set of explicit rules and procedures. The threat may be as innocuous as the possible obscurity of persons distantly connected with an ancient event, such as represented in the Daughters of the American Revolution, or as critical as an impending loss of employment, one of many circumstances which brought labor unions into existence. Conflict has its organizational roots in the voluntary association. But the principle of organization is just as applicable to entertainment and avocation as it is to the opposing of change.

In early nineteenth century England clubs formed around the pub or the inn. Those occupied with serious pursuits sooner or later moved to other quarters as they assumed more formal structures and grew in membership. Burial associations, some of which later emerged as insurance firms, workers' unions, and emigrant aid societies, appeared in many cities. The more literate members of the populations formed associations devoted to philosophical interests, the promotion of statistics, social science concerns, the betterment of conditions of the working class, and the improvement of housing, sanitation and other civic matters. In cases where like associations had appeared in several cities, federation in national associations often followed.

In American cities the propensity for creating common interest association was, if anything, stronger than in England and on the continent. So thought Alexis de Tocqueville, at any rate. Americans were less hampered by tradition and less equipped with an institutional apparatus adapted to the needs of the new environment. No census was formally or informally undertaken of voluntary associations in urban places. But it is of interest to note that, before the century was past, local groups were entering into national federations. A partial description of the increasing scale of voluntary organization is presented in Table 10. The table shows only national associations that survived to the 1950's. Missing are numerous political clubs and parties that came and went and such influential bodies as the Ladies' Library Association, which promoted literacy and the public library, and the Wheelmen of America, an association of bicyclists which was instrumental in the good roads movement. The elevation of associations from local to regional and national scope undoubtedly followed improvements in transportation and communication and the progressive integration of American society.

THE URBAN SOCIAL SYSTEM

It is reasonable to expect that the urbanization process moved toward a systematic arrangement of the emerging institutions and organized groups. We have no clear conception, however, of what the system looked like. There is no theoretical consensus about the shape and content of a social system, urban or otherwise, and even less in the way of empirical description.[28] The most that can be accomplished under the circumstances, therefore, is to set forth certain speculations based on some very general ideas about social structure.

In the preceding chapter we observed that the conception of a social system implied in the concentric zonal pattern of land uses is that of a symmetrical hierarchy. In other words, the many units comprising the organization of an urban center are differentiated not by function alone but by the power inherent in the function and by the number of units representing each functional type. These differences are expressed in a set of layers that narrows from bottom to top. This notion may be used, as a point of departure at least, for present purposes. Several assumptions underlie the idea of hierarchy. The first is that there must be centralization of coordinating responsibility wherever a number of specialized units are engaged in a continuing cooperation. Second, the centralization of coordination usually falls to that unit whose function gives it the most direct and the most significant relationship to the external world. The unit that

[28] One interesting exception to the general neglect of the problem is presented by Roland L. Warren in *The Community in America* (Chicago: Rand McNally, 1963), ch. 9. But Warren's account is analytical rather than synthetic; it provides few clues concerning the shape of the inclusive pattern. Another exception is one put forward in Amos H. Hawley, *Human Ecology* (New York: Ronald Press, 1950), ch. 12. Some elements of that earlier formulation are repeated here.

Table 10. Date of Appearance of U.S. Nationally
(By Type of Association.

Date of Origin	All Associ- ations	Trade and Business	Labor	Agriculture	Educational and Cultural	Scientific and Technical	Gov't., Legal, and Public Affairs
1890–1899	331	64	21	20	19	20	13
1880–1889	217	43	19	22	10	19	8
1870–1879	119	13	6	15	7	9	6
1860–1869	52	7	4	6	3	2	–
1850–1859	36	3	2	3	1	2	1
1840–1849	33	1	1	2	2	2	–
1830–1839	12	1	–	–	–	1	–
1820–1829	13	1	–	–	1	–	1
1810–1819	66	–	–	–	1	–	–
1800–1809	1	–	–	–	–	–	–
Before 1800	14	2	–	2	–	–	–

SOURCE: *Encyclopedia of Associations.* Vol. I. *National Organizations*

mediates the relations between the external world and the internal system sets the conditions under which all other units must operate. Accordingly it exerts a disproportionate amount of influence in the system. Third, all other units are scaled and rated and arrayed relative to the coordinating unit in accordance with their degrees of removal from direct relations with the dominant unit. This is a conception of structure applicable alike to a group or to a cluster of groups. Presumably, in the urban social system individuals are the units within group structures, and groups are the units of the system structure.

The hierarchical model is altogether too simple, of course, to accurately represent the structure of an urban system. It differs from reality in several important respects. For one thing, it implies an equilibrium state in which closure is nearly complete. Nothing could be farther from the true situation. In the urban system disequilibrium is the normal condition. Moreover, contrary to the model, inputs from the outside are channeled not through a single unit but through numerous different units. In other words, the urban center is an open system and as such it is highly vulnerable to shifts and variations in the social environment. Since that is the case there is not a single inclusive hierarchy, but two, three, or more. Every unit that maintains a significant external relationship, i.e., that brings an appreciable amount of income, tends to have a number of units whose activities are contingent on its function. Each industrial establishment, for example, stands at the apex of a hierarchy involving wholesale, retail, and various service units. One of these subordinate separate hierarchies is represented in the municipal government, which through its many agencies supplies facilitating, policing, and certain maintenance services to the entire system. A peculiarity of the governmental hierarchy

**Organized Voluntary Associations
Colonial Times to 1899)**

Association							
Health and Medical	Social Welfare	Religious	Veteran and Patriotic	Fraternal and Ethnic	Hobby	Athletic and Sports	Other
18	6	25	22	54	9	10	30
13	9	24	3	30	6	4	7
7	13	7	1	19	–	5	11
3	1	3	2	12	–	–	9
5	–	5	1	3	1	–	9
4	1	4	2	5	–	1	8
–	–	4	–	1	–	–	4
1	1	3	1	–	–	–	4
–	–	1	1	3	–	–	–
–	–	–	–	1	–	–	–
–	–	2	2	5	–	–	1

of the United States (Detroit, Mich.: Gale Research Company, 1961).

is that its operations are confined to a clearly bounded jurisdiction. Other hierarchies are not so restricted; their key units operate in an unbounded territory of regional, national, or international scope. It is for that reason that the local governmental hierarchy is subordinate to the industrial-commercial hierarchy; it has little or no control over external circumstances.

The simple hierarchical model says further that interunit exchanges are direct trades of services or products for services or products. Accordingly, interactions or flows move up and down in the hierarchy and in no other way. That is true of primitive societies, of plantations, and of a few other small, rudimentary organizations. It cannot be true where there are two or more hierarchies as well as other units that do not fall neatly into a pyramidal structure. In the complex system goods and services move in one direction while a generalized medium of exchange, money, moves in an opposite direction. These counterflows move in cycles, a segment of each of which lies outside a given hierarchy. The several hierarchies are thus tied together through their sharing a given population of consumers or clients, by being dependent on a common set of services, i.e., for credit, transportation, protection, and by various lateral and diagonal linkages.

These limitations aside, the hierarchical model is a useful approximation of urban organization, if it is not taken too literally. In addition to the organizational form it suggests, it indicates where in a system to look for the seat of power and how the latter is distributed through the system. This calls to mind a complication of the structure which should not be overlooked. Whereas specialized institutional units are arrayed in vertical sequences to constitute the main scaffold of the hierarchy, there are also numerous coalescences among like units—occupations and individually held interests in some instances, institutional units in other instances—that lie horizontally in the structure. These are the voluntary associations mentioned earlier. They are among other things devices for mobilizing the powers of relatively weak units in order to at least match the power of stronger units. The important point of the moment, however, is that an urban system tends to be a complex network of relations among specialized institutions and voluntary associations and of federations of each.

It is complexity of this character that was being elaborated and ramified during the nineteenth century and subsequently. Advances in specialization, on the one hand, and increases in size, on the other hand, were almost continuously breaking up and recasting patterns of relationships so that the emergence of a coherent urban system was a tendency that was always imminent but never fully realized. At that time most of the flux occurred within urban centers. Since then other factors have gained sufficient importance to cause a broadening of the theater of urban system development. That is the subject of following chapters.

THE SOCIAL EFFECTS OF DENSITY

The development of organization made possible the support of great population densities in urban centers. At the end of the century average densities in the largest centers were reaching above 10,000 persons per square mile and in many centers there were districts where residential densities were as much as 100,000 per square mile. These very high ratios of people to space were found in areas occupied by poor people. But everybody contended with congestion in one way or another.

Observations such as these lead sooner or later to questions about the social significance of density. Some questions of that kind have rather obvious answers; others are much more difficult to deal with. It is obvious, for example, that the growth of density is productive of numerous economies, some tangible, some intangible. It reduces the costs of communication and thus facilitates the mutual complementation among persions with different capabilities. Specialization is possible only where a sufficient number of users of the given service or product are gathered together within reach of the specialist. Hence, other things being equal, the greater the density the greater the possible number of specialists that can be supported and the more complex may be the cooperative arrangements in which people may organize themselves. Another way of viewing the same set of facts is to recognize that opportunity may vary in a direct relationship with density. Differences of experiences, interests, and skills, i.e., individual differences, vary with population size; hence the larger the accessible population, the greater would be the chance of any one individual's gaining a new idea or a new point of view. Diversity also enhances the probability of success in new enterprises that might be launched.

The savings that can be realized with increases in density are encountered in many other respects, notably in the provision of utilities and public services of all kinds. The capital costs per foot for sanitary sewer and water mains, for electric power and telephone lines, for street surfacing and sidewalks, and for rubbish collection and delivery services can be reduced with increases in the concentration of users. Fire and police protection assessments per capital can also be less in denser aggregates. The relationships between unit costs and diversity are not as simple, however, as the preceding statements make them appear. Actual data often show that costs rise with density. Where that occurs it is often due to variations in the quality of service, a factor that is extremely difficult to standardize. More experienced or sophisticated populations may insist on higher levels of performance. Or higher quality of service may be advisable in greater densities to provide a larger margin of safety as protection against breakdowns. In any case, qualitative differences exist and enter into cost differences. On the other hand, cost comparisons fail to reveal tradeoffs that sometimes have to be made. That is, where densities are very high so much space has to be devoted to streets that other public amenities, such as space for parks, have to be neglected.[29]

The probability remains, however, that congestion generates costs apart from what might be attributed to qualitative improvements. At some point along a density continuum costs may exceed the benefits derived from proximity. Thickly crowded streets and overloaded telephone circuits cause delays and losses of time. High-intensity use may also raise repair and maintenance costs more than proportionally to the use value returned. There are other disutilities that are difficult to measure, such as offensive noise levels, polluted air, and other contaminations of the environment.

Much more difficult to establish, contrary to a widely held belief,[30] is the effect of density on health. The assumption that high morbidity and mortality rates can be traced directly to density in either housing or neighborhood flies in the face of contrary historical facts. Increases in longevity and declines in the incidence of tuberculosis occurred at the time urban densities were building to their highest levels. A careful review of the research literature on density and health led to the conclusion that crowding affects health indirectly through its influence on the social

[29] These and other costs of density are explored, albeit inconclusively, in Coleman Woodbury (ed.), *Urban Redevelopment: Problems and Practices* (Chicago: University Chicago Press, 1953), pp. 101–220.

[30] Allen M. Pond, "The Influence of Housing on Health," *Marriage and Family Living*, XIX (1957): 154–59.

environment in which physiological responses take place.[31] Stresses and strains arising in group situations may activate latent infections and thus raise morbidity frequencies. Or differences of background and experience may in competitive situations be associated with different disease rates. Other, less subtle correlates of density may be far more important than crowding, such as poverty, ignorance of sanitary practices, and improper dietary habits.

The causal connections between density and mental health are no less tenuous than are those concerning physiological health. To reason directly from animal studies, which show increasing frequencies of neuroses and antisocial behavior with increased crowding,[32] to hypotheses about human behavior is to make a long and questionable inferential leap. The conditions that bear upon individual behavior in the two kinds of populations are so different that comparability is negligible at best. How important privacy is to the human individual and how he responds to situations of prolonged and intense interaction depend on prior conditioning, the content of the existing situation, and on various other factors. An informal assignment of effects to causes, so common in much of the literature, is most unconvincing.[33] Much more carefully controlled research is needed before we can claim to possess any dependable knowledge about the effects of density on mental health.

In a very influential paper, Louis Wirth argued that the crowding in dense aggregations of heterogeneous individuals was responsible for a superficiality, anonymity, and transitoriness in social relationships.[34] Because of the social distances separating them, according to this line of reasoning, urban people are inclined to treat one another exclusively as means to ends and to resort to mutual exploitation whenever opportunity permits. Social anarchy reigns in the city. This characterization of urban life was an unfortunate distortion of the truth. It was true in the nineteenth century as it is now that an individual in a large urban center might encounter in the course of a day hundreds of other individuals, far too many for him to know or even to recognize. Under those conditions anonymity and impersonality in exchanges were the only assurances that an individual would reach a destination on time and get a day's work done. It was not true, however, that all of life was cast in that pattern. The opportunities for close association and intimate friendship were at

[31] John Cassell, "Health Consequences of Population Density and Crowding." Unpublished paper.

[32] See John B. Calhoun, "Population Density and Social Pathology," *The Scientific American*, CCVI (1962): 139–48.

[33] See James S. Plant, "Some Psychiatric Aspects of Crowded Living Conditions," *American Journal of Psychiatry*, IX (1930): 849–60.

[34] "Urbanism as a Way of Life," *The American Journal of Sociology*, XLIV (1938): 1–24.

least as numerous as they were in the rural village. In fact, the difference between rural village and urban vicinage was not great for most of the working class population; small incomes or language barriers isolated them from the larger community. Most of life was lived within a few blocks of residential places. An important difference did appear in the middle and upper classes. They lived farther from their work places and traveled more widely in the city. Hence they were not forced to accept the associates thrust upon them by proximity; they were free to exercise whatever selectivity appealed to them. For them the neighborhood was part of a much larger sphere of choice rather than an area of intense and exclusive association.

R. D. McKenzie's conclusions from an intensive study of neighborhoods in a medium-sized, midwestern city shortly after the close of the nineteenth century are enlightening.[35] He noted that neighborhood sentiment depended on a locality's having physical demarcations which set it apart from the larger community and having a relatively homogeneous and stable population. But such a sentiment could rarely be sustained over an area of more than two blocks. Despite the most favorable circumstances, however, general interest and participation in neighborhood affairs and projects require "the hard work of a few energetic promoters." Needless to say, it would be a mistake to conclude from these observations that the residents of the areas studied enjoyed no personal associations.

SOCIAL SIGNIFICANCE OF SIZE OF URBAN CENTER

Population density and population size have much in common. Where areas may be assumed to be constant, their only difference is that one is a relative and the other an absolute measure. Even where constant area does not obtain, density and size are fairly closely correlated. That is because most cities in the Western world developed under more or less comparable conditions. Much of what was said about the social implications of density therefore applies also to size. The larger the place, the greater is the amount of specialization that can be supported.[36] The number and variety of stores and shops, of commercial services, of religious denominations, and of leisure time and cultural opportunities of all kinds increase with size of place. Virtually every functional characteristic varies

[35] "The Neighborhood: A Study of Local Life in the City of Columbus, Ohio," *The American Journal of Sociology*, XXVII (1921): 145–68, 344–63, 486–509, 588–610, 780–99.

[36] For an early tabulation of characteristics of cities with population size see W. F. Ogburn, *Social Characteristics of Cities* (Chicago: The International City Managers' Association, 1937).

systematically with the number of people residing in urban centers. This variation does not imply that size of population is a cause of the properties associated with it. Rather is size a necessary condition; it is a factor in the absence of which certain other things cannot occur.

But there are a number of variables that are not size-linked. Most demographic characteristics, though they may show a correlation with size at one point in time, have no necessary dependence on size. They owe their correlation to adventitious processes which may or may not be repeated. The average number of years of school completed, for example, usually increases with size of place. The relationship is a result, however, of two historical trends: one, the relatively late development and spread of educational opportunities, which benefited the young primarily; and two, the urbanward redistribution of population which drew most heavily on young people. Thus educational differences were a result of age composition, not city size. Variations in the number of males per 100 females, sizes of households, proportions of population in the labor force, birth and death rates, and other demographic traits may be correlated with size, but they are actually transitory effects of the redistribution process.

Most of what is known about the significance of size of places has been learned from cross-sectional studies. Tabulations of characteristics by size of place for a given moment in time, such as that shown in Table 11,

Table 11. Percentage Distribution of Occupations
(By Size of City, Germany, 1882)

Size of City		Occupations					
	Total	Agriculture	Manufacturing, Mining	Trade, Commerce	Liberal Professions	Laborers	Other
All Germany	100	42	36	10	5	2	5
Cities 100,000+	100	1	47	27	11	5	9
20,000–100,000	100	3	53	20	11	4	9
5,000– 20,000	100	10	54	16	9	4	7
2,500– 5,000	100	26	49	12	5	3	5
Rural area	100	64	24	5	2	1	4

SOURCE: A. F. Weber, *The Growth of Cities in the Nineteenth Century*, Columbia University Press, 1899, p. 315.

are instructive and useful for many purposes. They are much less informative about the correlates of growth. Indeed, it is highly questionable that any inferences about the effects of subsequent changes can be drawn from such a tabulation. An observer in Germany, in 1882, might have reasoned that as small places grew to larger sizes their occupational distributions would change to conform to those of larger places of that date, if he could also assume that the historical conditions which prevailed during the growth of the large places would be repeated with little or no modification during the growth of small places. The assumption is too tenuous to be credible. A more satisfactory basis for knowledge about the significance of changing size lies in observations of the growth careers of successive cohorts of places. Here too, of course, an historical sampling issue is involved.

Although the empirical work falls short of what is needed, the theory is clear enough. According to a very general principle, growth requires changes in the relative sizes of the parts of the growing entity. For, as size or volume increases, destructive stresses develop at certain critical points in a structure. Compensatory changes must occur, if the structure is to survive.[37] Applied to an urban system this principle suggests that, with increases in population size, other things remaining constant, the costs of the communication needed to preserve the integrity of the whole increase more than proportionally. As costs of internal communication begin to exceed the advantages of size, one of two results becomes inescapable. Of these one is a return to scale; that is, the system resolves itself into smaller units within which the costs of maintaining integration are not excessive. This accounts for the cellular city pattern described in the preceding chapter. The alternative involves a change of form of the system permitting the attainment of higher levels of efficiency in administration and the communications among the parts. This does not happen automatically. It depends upon the acquisition of appropriate technical and organizational improvements that are most likely to occur in the centers having strategic locations at the intersections of transportation routes.

Elements that enter into a change of form by which an enlarged population is able to preserve if not to enhance its cohesiveness have been discussed in earlier parts of this chapter. They include increased specialization, a centralization and consolidation of administrative functions, and the improvement of transportation and communication technologies. The center of an urban system, more particularly the organization located at the center, grows increasingly important as the total system becomes larger.

The problems of maintaining an effective structure in the course of growth have suggested to some that there might be an optimum size of urban place. Optimum size refers to a population which yields the greatest possible benefit at minimum cost. Presumably, as size increases, the quality judged to be beneficial increases: at first more rapidly than population and then more and more slowly, tending toward a zero rate of increase. If diagrammed, the pattern of growth would resemble a flattened S-shaped curve. The optimum size would fall at the second point of flexion in the curve.

---

[37] For expositions of this principle in various analogous phenomena see Mason Haire (ed.), *Modern Organization Theory* (New York: John Wiley, 1965), ch. 10, and Kenneth Boulding, "Toward a General Theory of Growth," *Canadian Journal of Economics and Political Science*, XIX (1953): 326–40.

In this, as in other uses of the optimum concept, a number of critical assumptions are involved. One of these is that all other things are constant. The "other things" in this instance refers to the knowledge, skills, and tools possessed by the population. Unless it can be assumed that the cultural repertory is constant, there is nothing to bend the curve in the direction of a lessening rate of increase. The diminishing returns may be regarded as preliminary to a fragmentation of the system should growth continue. The constant-culture assumption may have been tenable for rather lengthy periods in earlier historical epochs, but it would be extremely difficult to defend its application to the nineteenth century. Second, optimum theory assumes that the beneficial quality, such as it may be, is a function of population numbers alone. The assumption is manifestly a vast oversimplification. Numbers are variously constituted with reference to age, sex, health, occupational skills, previous experience, and so on. They are also organized in different ways, productively or otherwise, efficiently or inefficiently. The effect of numbers can obviously vary over a wide range of possibilities, as wide as the spread of differences in these internal properties. To adopt either or both of these assumptions is to bring the issue close to the verge of circularity; it suggests that specialization causes specialization, organization causes organization. Finally, there is the question of which of the many qualities that might vary with size is the preferred or optimal one. This, of course, can be resolved arbitrarily for the purposes of analysis; for other purposes its resolution poses a far-from-simple problem of public policy.

Apart from the theoretical problems, there is as yet no empirical evidence to support an optimum urban concept. On the contrary, such data as are available indicate that the elaboration of organization is capable of varying continuously with population size.[38] The concept may still have meaning for individuals, however. Some people do not like large places; others object to small places. There are preferences: for locations by the sea, in the mountains, or elsewhere; for places with a cosmopolitan culture; for places that are growing rapidly; and for many other kinds of urban places. Each person may have his own optimum size of place, though he can be cruelly misled should he be guided by size alone.

INNOVATION

Although urban life bound the individual in a much more intricate and ramified network of dependences than he had ever before experienced, it also provided him with an unparalleled opportunity for expression. It emancipated the individual mind from the lethargy of tradition and the

[38] See O. D. Duncan, "Optimum Size of Cities," in *Cities and Society*, ed. by Paul K. Hatt and Albert J. Reiss, Jr. (New York: The Free Press, 1957), pp. 759–72.

censure of parochial ways. By being thrust into a company of strangers who were more concerned with what he could do than with what he was or had been, the person was stimulated to cultivate whatever resources he possessed. The impersonality and transiency of interrelationships had a positive as well as a negative influence. So it was also with the tendency toward the standardization of behavior. While that drift may be seen as a movement toward monotonous conformity, it had an opposite and perhaps more significant effect. Uniformity in the terms and conditions of discourse widens the universe of communication and thereby exposes the person to a great variety of experiences. The volume of information he can absorb and use is correspondingly enlarged. His intellectual mobility is enhanced, moreover, by his being relieved of the necessity of making innumerable small decisions to small ends. Standardization is a facilitating factor of inestimable importance; it is the cultural counterpart of a high rate of mobility.

The social circumstances underlying innovation were probably least favorable in the cellular city. Poor communications sealed off segments of the urban population in residential and employment enclaves.[39] Even there, however, specialization was in process, and specialization is the measure of one of the principal currents of innovation. Functional differentiation tends to dissolve communication barriers by bringing specialists into frequent interactions with one another. As that happened in the city of the early nineteenth century the frequency of interchanges increased more than proportionally.

The environment, of course, in this instance the urban context, sets the conditions and supplies the raw materials for interactions among individuals. The growing urban center gathered into itself the cultural achievements of its region and leavened the mass with foreign ideas and practices. Innovation in the arts, in intellectual perspectives, in political thought, and in the ordinary routines of living were virtually inescapable. If nothing else, the very dependent status of the urban center placed a premium upon industrial and commercial innovation in order to make secure an otherwise tenuous position. But, short of a vigorous exercise of repressive powers, change cannot be contained in any one category of activity; other spheres of interest are infected by the same ferment.[40]

[39] Industrial segregation may also have simplified labor opposition to technological change, as Sam Warner suggests was the case in early Philadelphia. ("Innovation and the Industrialization of Philadelphia, 1800–1850," in The Historian and the City, ed. by Oscar Handlin and John Burchard [Cambridge: M.I.T. Press, 1966], p. 68, fn. 7.)

[40] Repressive powers have often been applied, inadvertently or otherwise, to prevent change. Evidently Chinese cities in the eighteenth century were not centers of innovation, though they were market centers. The elaborate, rigid, and often corrupt bureaucracy milked the merchant of his capital and stifled initiative at its source. (See Rhoads Murphey, "The City as a Center of Change," Annals Assoc. Amer. Geographers, XLIV [1954]: 347–62.)

Despite the importance of the matter, there have been very few systematic studies of the influence of urban centers on innovation. From his study of Philadlphia in the first half of the nineteenth century, the historian Sam Warner concluded that large cities of northeastern United States were not "major invention environments." The innovative environment was the region rather than a particular type of locality: "Every town in the region had its tinkerers; talented inventors sprang up everywhere, both amateurs and professionals." [41] One would like to know more about the achievements of the small town inventors, where they found a sympathetic reception for their innovations, and how their numbers compared with those working in the nearby metropolis, before accepting Warner's conclusions.

A more adequate study dealt with the frequency of patents obtained on industrial inventions in 1860, 1880, and 1900 in the sixteen rapidly growing cities of the United States. Patent data, rough and partial as they are, indicated that the frequency of inventions exceeded the expected ratios to population by as much as three to one in New York, Chicago, Pittsburgh, and Cleveland, and by two to one in a number of other cities, including Philadelphia. The author of this study, Allan Pred, concluded that the suggestion that invention is a locational accident is without any foundation in fact. Further, the incidence of invention and innovation is "some function of both the size and the rate of growth of cities." [42] While the data in Table 12 pertain to a later period, they again show a relationship between invention frequency and size of place.

CITY AND COUNTRY

During the nineteenth century urban centers were spreading their tentacles of influence into their surrounding areas with increasing effect. Farm and village were brought into economic dependence on one or another urban center in a growing number of respects. Yet the dependence was limited to exchanges of goods. Distances were too great for a frequent dialogue between city and country on matters that were not of vital concern. In fact, urban life ended abruptly at a city's boundaries except in the narrow suburban bands drawn out along railway lines. The urban-rural difference widened over most of the century. Large cities came to resemble one another much more closely than they did their adjacent rural areas.[43]

In the urban center growth and change moved in a rapid and disorderly

[41] *Ibid.*, p. 64.

[42] *Op. cit.*, pp. 105–12.

[43] W. F. Ogburn, *Social Characteristics of Cities* (Chicago: International City Managers' Association, 1937), pp. 32–35.

Table 12. Index Numbers of Ratios of Patents to Population (By Size of Place, 1940)

Size of Place	Invention Index
All places	100
Metropolitan districts	
2,000,000 or more	130
1,000,000–2,000,000	110
250,000–1,000,000	101
50,000– 250,000	77
Non-metropolitan urban places	
25,000– 50,000	97
5,000– 25,000	69
2,500– 5,000	34

SOURCE: W. F. Ogburn and O. D. Duncan, "City Size as a Sociological Variable," in *Contributions to Urban Sociology,* eds. E. W. Burgess and Donald J. Bogue (Chicago: University of Chicago Press, 1964), p. 143.

fashion; old beliefs and practices were under almost continuous challenge as nothing seemed secure against the spirit of innovation. In the countryside, the much slower pace of change produced no sharp breaks with the past. The family farm and the family-operated enterprise in the village yielded slowly to the influences that seeped out of the cities. Population was too thinly scattered to permit any very great departures from simple collective activities. Thus the rural areas became identified with the traditional, the memorable, and the moral, and the city came to be regarded as the home of things quixotic, radical, and amoral.

It is not surprising, therefore, that the nineteenth century city invited a stream of criticisms from intellectuals of the period. Thomas Jefferson looked upon the city as antithetical to democracy, a view that must have been reinforced by his observations of the revolutionary mobs in Paris. His appreciation of technology, however, led him later in life to acknowledge the necessity of the city as a manufacturing center. Many who followed Jefferson were more harsh in their judgments. Emerson, Thoreau, Hawthorne, Melville, Henry Adams, and Henry James regarded the urban center as a violation of nature, a breeder of crime and disorder, and an affront to the dignity of man.[44] In some, notably Henry Adams and Henry James, the negative attitude rested on a cultural snobbishness;

[44] Morton and Lucian White, *The Intellectual Versus the City* (Cambridge: Harvard University Press 1962).

they objected to the city's attraction for the foreigner, for it threatened to dissipate the Puritan tradition. Superficially, all such criticisms and fears had a foundation in fact. The city of the time was unquestionably a confused, tumultuous, and disorderly place. But, as usual, romanticism is long in its view of the past and short-sighted as to the future. The critics were afraid of change and unable to perceive the creative forces at work. Whether or not the critics were the cause, they were certainly the heralds of an anti-urban attitude that has permeated political and social thought down to the present.

Nevertheless, the differences between urban and rural were steadily being reduced. In the preceding chapter we commented on the decline of rural industries as a consequence of factory-made products. Changes were also taking place in the ways in which those products reached the consumer. At first products were distributed to village stores by rail and were thence sold to consumers. In the latter half of the century a direct link between city merchant and rural consumer was created by a rapid spread of mail-order merchandising. The success of mail-order firms dissolved the monopoly of local markets that had been enjoyed by village merchants. That could not be complete, however, as long as postal service stopped with general delivery through village post offices. Merchants, who were often sources of credit, could exercise a surveillance over who was shopping where and take punitive steps when their interests were at stake. But this last control disappeared with the introduction of rural free delivery in the 1890's.[45] The new door-to-door mail service had far greater importance than its effect on retail practices. It linked farm and other households directly to cities and opened channels for an increasing variety of contacts. One of the important by-products was the stimulus it supplied to a road improvement movement in the rural areas surrounding cities.

SUMMARY

The events involved in the development of urban society are much too numerous and too interconnected to be fully treated in a space as short as this chapter. It has been possible to do little more than touch upon some of the main currents of change that entered into the elaboration of the social system. Instead of attempting a point-by-point condensation of what has been said, it might be more helpful to extract the general trends that are implicitly or explicitly represented in the discussion.

In order to accommodate an increasing number of people and to make

[45] Theodore K. Noss, *Resistances to Social Innovation as Found in Literature Regarding Innovations Which Have Proved Successful.* University of Chicago, doctoral dissertation, 1944.

use of the accumulation of culture, particularly the new mechanical technology, a reorganization of the units of society was necessary. This took the form of a substitution of an extra-familial for the familial unit. The extra-familial unit gave free play to the progress of specialization, to the application of complex tools to production processes, and to the adaptation of social processes to impersonal forces emanating from markets and other external sources. The substitution began in manufacturing industry and spread widely through society as specialization invaded one sphere of activity after another. As the family lost functions to extra-familial units it no longer had to produce and maintain a labor supply. Hence its size could be reduced and its birth rate allowed to decline. The status structure of the family was also set upon a path toward reconstitution.

In the transition to a different basis of organization several other important trends appeared. One was a progressive differentiation that spread beyond occupation into numerous characteristics of people. This produced a new stratification system and, in addition, a multiplication of like-interest or voluntary groups. Organization was thus elaborated along vertical and horizontal dimensions. The organization of the urban system assumed a multi-hierarchical form, depending on the number of units that occupied major roles as producers of income for the system. Lying across and woven through the several hierarchies and the units composing them appeared numerous like-interest groupings to constitute a horizontal layering of units. The system as thus constituted was an open system, exposed, that is, to inputs through numerous channels from the outside. The increasing specialization by which this complex system was created also involves a progressive standardization of culture, a tendency which becomes pervasive in many, if not all, sectors of society.

Increases in density produced numerous economies and also, after density exceeded a certain magnitude, mounting costs. No convincing balance sheet of economies and costs has been prepared. But with or without changes in density, growth of size raises communications costs involved in maintaining integration of the system. To prevent these from becoming prohibitively high, efficiencies must be introduced into the organzation of the system. These occur as further specialization, centralization of control, and improved mechanisms for administering communications. An important benefit associated with increasing size appears to be higher probabilities of innovation.

It is extremely improbable, if not impossible, that a transformation of the kind described in this chapter could have occurred without significant improvements in transportation facilities and the consequent enlargement of territory and of population accessible from a central point. Only thus could the scale of organized activity be enlarged and the capacity for employing and accumulating technical culture be increased.

SUPPLEMENTARY READINGS

ALEXANDERSSON, GUNNAR. *The Industrial Structure of American Cities: A Geographic Study of Urban Economy in the United States* (Lincoln: University of Nebraska Press, 1956).

JANOWITZ, MORRIS. *The Community Press in an Urban Setting* (New York: The Free Press, 1952).

LYND, ROBERT and HELEN M. *Middletown: A Study in Contemporary American Culture* (New York: Harcourt, Brace, Jovanovich, 1929).

SPENGLER, EDWIN H. *Land Values in New York in Relation to Transit Facilities* (New York: Columbia University Press, 1930).

THERSTORM, STEPHAN, and SENNETT, RICHARD (eds.). *Nineteenth Century Cities: Essays in the New Urban History* (New Haven: Yale University Press, 1969).

WILENSKY, HAROLD L., and LEBEAUX, CHARLES M. *Industrial Society and Social Welfare* (New York: Russell Sage Foundation, 1958).

7

The Rise of the Metropolitan Community

The nineteenth century was a period of regional and interregional expansion based on advances made in the efficiency of long-distance, bulk-haul transportation. The twentieth century was to be a period of local expansion in which dramatic improvements in short-distance transportation and communication would be the chief facilitating factors. Why the latter followed so long after the former may be explicable as an historical accident. Or it might be in the nature of technological progress that innovations appear first in large clumsy forms before they can be reduced to smaller, neater, and more efficient units. In any event, the process of local expansion has occupied all of the years of the present century thus far and is not yet concluded. It has involved a reconstitution of the old compact urban community on a new territorial basis and a different pattern of functional as well as spatial alignments. The change has been too sweeping and too costly to have occurred in a brief interval of time. Nor can it be described and analyzed in a few words. This chapter will be devoted to an examination of the major redistribution trends released in the expansion process. Following chapters will take up some of the organizational changes in greater detail.

THE REVOLUTION IN SHORT-DISTANCE TRANSPORTATION

In the late decades of the nineteenth century, a number of significant changes in the technology of transportation and communication began to appear. The telephone had been demonstrated to be practicable and the new companies were rapidly enlisting subscribers. Costs of transmitting electric power were being reduced to the point where it was becoming a feasible household utility. Intracity pipelines for water, sewage, and gas were being extended from the inner to all sections of urban centers. In the last decade of the century the motor vehicle made its appearance on city streets.

For some decades, reaching into the first quarter of the twentieth century, these improvements were restricted to the preexisting boundaries of cities. The restriction was due at first to the concentration in cities of people with sufficient means to afford the new luxuries. But as their costs were lowered so that they could be diffused more widely, their spread was then retarded by the lagging development of the necessary capital installations. This was especially true of automobile usage. As late as 1921 only some 13 percent of the roads outside of United States cities were hard-surfaced. Nevertheless, motor vehicles registered increased from 8,000, in 1900, to 10,500,000, in 1921, or from one per 10,000 of the population to one for every 10 persons. Country doctors, farmers weary of the long wagon trek to service centers, and mail carriers on the recently established rural free delivery mail routes were instrumental in spreading automobile usage over the countryside despite the deplorable state of the roads. These events coincided with a gathering centrifugal thrust from the interiors of urban centers. Residential settlement was spilling over municipal boundaries and flowing out along radial routes in increasing volume. Pressures at the center were produced by the growth of business and industry and the rising streams of rural to urban migration.

The superiority of the motor vehicle in short-distance transportation derived from its speed and flexibility in use and from its low cost per mile of travel. Previously the sixty-minute radius seldom exceeded six miles. In principle, that afforded the urban center a scope of 100 square miles, but in actuality very few were larger than twenty square miles. The motor vehicle extended the hour's travel distance to approximately twenty-five miles and opened a zone of accessibility amounting to some 2,000 square miles. Moreover, free of fixed routes and therefore of fixed schedules, the automobile and the truck could be moved in any direction and at any time, used for door-to-door pickups and deliveries, and employed in small lot or small passenger cargoes. This flexibility depended, of course, on a huge public investment in streets and roads.

Within relatively short distances, the motor truck proved incomparably cheaper than the railway. Costs for equipment and maintenance were much lower. Its independence of elaborate terminal facilities eliminated an expensive cost item. In the railway freight rate structure that item was prorated by trip length in such a way that the longer the trip, the lower was the ton-mile cost. Hence costs of motor truck haulage started low for the shortest distance and rose steeply and proportionately with distance, while railway costs started high for the shortest distance and increased less than proportionally with distance. Within a radius of 150 to 250 miles the motor truck had a clear competitive advantage; beyond that distance the railway was the superior competitor. The truck's advantage also extended to quicker loading and unloading, enabling it to offer speedier service. The differences in efficiency are shown in Table 13. Although the truck could make deliveries more quickly even beyond

Table 13. Elapsed Hours Within Specified Lengths of Haul of Shipments by Highway and Railway

Length of Haul	Highway	Railway
Under 50 miles	4	28
50 to 100 miles	9	33
100 to 200 miles	13	38
200 to 300 miles	18	45
300 to 500 miles	27	57
500 miles and over	51	85

SOURCE: National Resources Committee, *Technological Trends and National Policy* (Washington, D.C., 1937), p. 184.

250 miles, the advantage on that score was neutralized by comparatively high costs. Slower though it was in the long haul, the railway's operating costs enabled it to prevail, especially in the transportation of large bulk cargoes. The practical significance of these differences is that, whereas formerly distant merchants could compete effectively in local markets, after the advent of the motor truck local merchants had a distinct advantage in their local markets over their remote competitors.

Thus the large urban center carved out a tributary region over a radial distance of as much as 250 miles. Through its banking, marketing, transportation, and other services it became the administrative center for industry and commerce located within its enlarged domain. Relocations and other adjustments to the strategic position conferred upon the metropolis by the motor truck and the telephone led to specialization in localities and districts. The region became an economic unity "characterized by territorial differentiation and specialization of parts which are functionally integrated in a sensitive balance of space and of time relations." [1]

Local expansion created a new kind of urban center at the core of the enlarged and more highly integrated urban region. Instead of the dense, compact settlement unit laid down in the preceding century, there emerged a new, much more diffuse type of communal unit. Not only was the territorial scope of the sixty-minute radius increased to approximately twenty-five miles, the frequency and intensity of interactions within that expanded area were multiplied several-fold by the motor vehicle, the telephone, and other changes that facilitated communications. Some insight into the integrative effects of the new means of conducting interrelationships is provided in Table 14. It is to be noticed that the gradient falls away rather sharply beyond the twenty-five-mile margin.

Table 14. Subscriptions to Detroit Daily Newspapers and Toll Telephone Calls
(Per 100 Population, by Miles Distant from Detroit, 1931)

Miles from Detroit	Newspaper Subscriptions	Toll Telephone Calls
0 to 25	40.2	147.9
25 to 50	24.1	26.2
50 to 75	11.1	7.0
75 to 100	8.1	4.7

SOURCE: R. D. McKenzie, *The Metropolitan Community* (New York: McGraw-Hill Book Company, Copyright © 1933). Used with permission of McGraw-Hill Book Co.

Within the enlarged radius of daily communications, villages and open country settlements that had lived more or less aloof from the large center nearby were in a short space of time incorporated into an urban community. Their stores and services were thrown into a losing competition with those of the metropolis, their professional workers and specialists migrated to the hub of activity, and even their amusements were displaced by the greater attractions offered at the center. Commuting residents, recently moved from the central city, mingled increasingly in their local affairs. Village institutions were replaced by standardized services, distributed through chain outlets and branch offices, and supplied and administered from the metropolis.

[1] R. D. McKenzie, *The Metropolitan Community* (New York: McGraw-Hill, 1933), p. 81.

With the coming of the improved roads and the motor vehicle, Linden (Michigan) was brought within an hour's travel time of Flint . . . Farmers were no longer dependent on the produce marketing agencies in Linden. They could deliver farm products with their own vehicles to buyers in a much larger retail market than a village could offer. Linden declined as a farm trade center . . . Daily newspapers published in the larger city began to circulate in Linden. Retail merchants turned to Flint for their wholesale purchases. Even more important, Linden workers were absorbed into the Flint labor force. In 1900 employment in Flint on the part of Linden residents was impossible without a change of residence. But in 1930 twenty-nine workers, 14 per cent of the gainfully employed commuted daily to Flint by motor vehicle. That proportion had increased to 46 per cent by 1950.[2]

This vignette provides enough of a glimpse for the moment into a process repeated many times over in the immediate hinterlands of metropolitan cities. Some of the villages and small towns survived as residential settlements for the families of commuting workers, some acquired industry and grew rich on the suddenly augmented tax base, a few became the homes of medical or educational institutions, and others disappeared to be remembered only by lingering place names. Territorial differentiation followed in one form or another as the central city spread its influence over the expanded area. To view this phenomenon through the window of official statistics requires a digression here to consider the problem of definition.

THE PROBLEM OF DEFINITION

The concept of the metropolitan area lends itself to various definitions. As has been noted, it may apply to an enlarged area of local life, i.e., with a radius of twenty-five to thirty miles, or it may refer to a much broader area in which the scattered activities have come under the administrative supervision of a metropolis. The former is what is usually denoted when the term *metropolitan area* or *metropolitan community* is used; *metropolitan region* is ordinarily reserved for the latter.

In principle the metropolitan community, as well as the metropolitan region, is delineated by the frequency with which outlying residents and institutions transact their affairs in the metropolis, whether through direct visitation or through indirect means of communication. Such frequencies, we have seen, decline in gradient fashion with distance from the center. Thus figuratively speaking, one might rotate a gradient on its center and sweep out a zone in which the residents routinely engage in a given frequency of communication with the center. The zone of daily frequencies

[2] Amos H. Hawley and Basil G. Zimmer, "Resistances to Unification in a Metropolitan Community," in *Community Political Systems,* ed. by Morris Janowitz (New York: The Free Press, 1961), pp. 150–151.

comprises the metropolitan community; zones of lesser frequencies fall in the region. Theoretically sound as this mode of definition appears to be, it presents certain practical difficulties. To the observer, for example, the boundaries located in the manner described are ephemeral. They correspond to no political demarcation or, unless there happens to be a sea coast or mountain range nearby, to no physical impediments. A boundary is visible only through the application of rather refined means of observation. A functional boundary of that kind is also somewhat fluid; it shifts from time to time as the influence of a metropolis is extended or retracted.

For these reasons an operational definition of the metropolitan area is employed by the U.S. Bureau of the Census. This represents a compromise between the advisability of using territorial units for which official information is conventionally reported and the desirability of approximating the scope of territory functionally integrated with an urban center. Accordingly, in the United States the metropolitan area for which data are routinely tabulated and reported is a county having an urban center of 50,000 or more people and all contiguous counties that can be shown to have close functional relations with the county containing the urban center.[3] It should be added that this definition is but the most recent of a series of different ones used in preceding censuses. Revisions have been made partly in recognition of the changing organization of American society, but partly also in deference to political pressures exerted on the Bureau of the Census. The designation "metropolitan" confers prestige, or so it is believed.[4] Thus the number of areas, which stood at 212, in 1960, had become 228 by 1967 (Fig. 3). Because so much information is reported in metropolitan area units, there is no escaping use of the Bureau of the Census definition. The Bureau's frequent changes of definition, however, complicate any analysis of trends. A resolution of that difficulty requires that the decennial series be standardized on some one definition. Much of the following discussion of trends is based on an application of the Bureau's 1950 definition projected backward to 1900 and forward to 1960 and 1970.

This is an opportune point at which to mention another area concept introduced in the census of 1950 and carried forward in succeeding cen-

---

[3] In some instances two contiguous cities with a combined population of 50,000 or more within 20 miles of one another are recognized as a single central city. Criteria of functional integration among country units require of the adjacent counties at least 75 per cent of the labor force in non-agricultural employment and 15 per cent of the workers employed in the central city county, or that 25 per cent of those working in the adjacent county live in the central city county. (Bureau of the Budget, *Standard Metropolitan Statistical Areas* [Washington, D.C., 1961], pp. 3–5).

[4] See Henry L. Shryock, "The Natural History of Metropolitan Areas," *American Journal of Sociology*, LXIII (1957): 163–70.

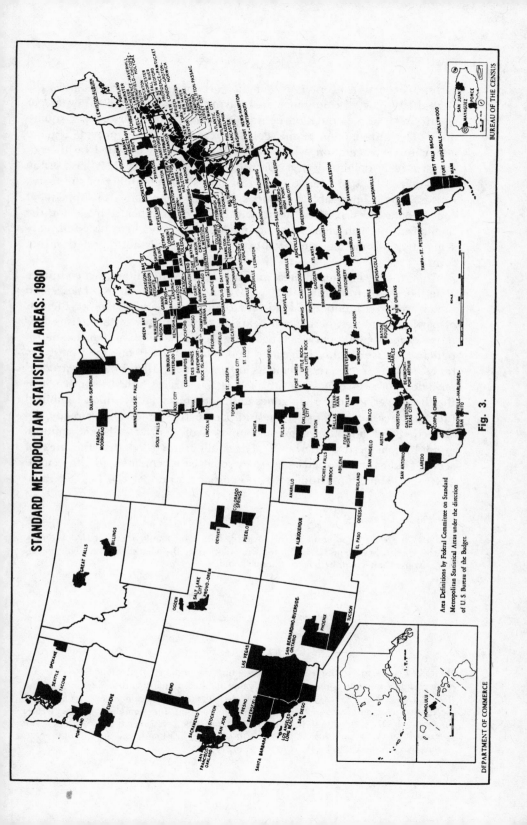

STANDARD METROPOLITAN STATISTICAL AREAS: 1960

Area Definitions by Federal Committee on Standard Metropolitan Statistical Areas under the direction of U.S. Bureau of the Budget.

Fig. 3.

BUREAU OF THE CENSUS

DEPARTMENT OF COMMERCE

suses. The new concept is called the "urbanized area." It includes the central city plus all contiguous area having approximately 500 houses per square mile, or a population density of around 2,000 persons per square mile. The introduction of this concept was intended to provide a more adequate representation of the built-up area than is afforded by the administratively delimited city. Useful as that innovation is, it has certain limitations. That is, defined in density terms, comparability in successive census years is impossible to achieve. It is also impossible to supplement census data for urbanized areas with data from other sources, for the boundaries of such areas have no official status anywhere else and, consequently, information generated by other agencies is not reported in that form.

Central city, urbanized area, and standard metropolitan area constitute a nested set of territorial units with concentric boundaries. These lend themselves to a number of kinds of urban investigation. One of these is of particular interest here, for it bears on the adequacy of the census definition of metropolitan area. Proceeding on the assumption that the metropolitan area is a highly integrated and relatively self-contained entity so far as its daily service requirements are concerned, Allan Feldt constructed an index [5] of self-sufficiency for each of ten service industries in each of the three overlapping urban zones and a summary index which combined the measures for each zone. In addition to the three zones already described, Feldt added two more composed of tiers of adjacent counties around each metropolitan area. His findings revealed that the area of service industry self-sufficiency is in some cases confined to the central city (e.g., Hamilton-Middletown, Kenosha, Lorrain-Elyria, Ogden, Pitts-

---

[5] This index is $I = \dfrac{e_i/p}{E_i/P}$, where e represents local employment in a given industry, p is the total population of the locality, E is total employment in that industry for the United States, and P is the total population of the United States. The ten indexes were then combined in a summary index:

$$S = 1{,}000 - \dfrac{\dfrac{\sum\limits^{10} w_i[100 - I_i]}{\sigma}}{\dfrac{10}{\dfrac{\sum w_i}{\sigma}}}$$

the only new term in which is w_i, representing the proportion of all local service industry employment in industry i. The value of the summary index S can vary from 0 to 1.0; the closer to 1.0, the greater is the degree of self-sufficiency. (*The Local Ecological Community: An Investigation of Relative Independence in an Urban Society.* Ph.D. Dissertation in Sociology, University of Michigan, 1962, and "The Metropolitan Area Concept: An Evaluation of the 1950 SMA's," *Jour. Amer. Stat. Assoc.,* XXL [1965]: 617–36).

field) and in others it reaches to the limits of the urbanized area (e.g., Altoona, Brockton, Detroit, Pittsburgh, Rockford). In these cases the Census Bureau's metropolitan area definition overstates the scope of local territorial unit. In many others (e.g., Akron, Buffalo, Canton, Chicago, Philadelphia), the metropolitan area definition is appropriate in that it embraces the area of self-sufficiency. For still other localities it is necessary to include the first ring of adjacent counties and in one or two cases the second ring of counties. These latter are described as "underbounded metropolitan areas."

METROPOLITAN POPULATION GROWTH

The separation of the discussions of population shifts and changes and of the relocations of functions in metropolitan areas is justifiable only on grounds of convenience. The interrelations between the one and the other are much too close to support a claim for independence. Movements of industry, commerce, and other activities are both cause and effect of population growth and distribution. Nevertheless, the demographic aspects of metropolitan development are sufficiently important to warrant an intensive consideration.

The population of the United States has been concentrating in what are currently designated as metropolitan areas since prior to 1900. Table 15, in which the trend from 1900 to 1970 is shown, casts some light on how the growth of metropolitan population has come about. It also obscures some important facts. The increase has occurred in two ways. One results from including in the figures the population of areas that have qualified as metropolitan in each successive census. Whereas at the beginning of the century there were but 61 qualifying areas, the number of areas rose to 84 in 1910, to 109 in 1920, to 189 in 1960, and finally to 202 in 1970.[6] The columns headed "Constant Criteria" show the redistribution of population as affected both by absolute changes in numbers of people and changing definition of territory. On this basis it may be noted that in 1900–10 metropolitan areas gained twice as many people as did nonmetropolitan territory, but in the last decade of the series, 1960–1970, the latter actually lost population. By the measure used, in the last decade shown all population growth in the nation, exclusive of Alaska and Hawaii, accrued to metropolitan areas.

The second means of growth, alluded to in the preceding paragraph, is an actual increase in the number of people within the area defined as

[6] Amos H. Hawley, Beverley Duncan and David Goldberg, "Some Observations of Changes in Metropolitan Population in the United States," *Demography*, I (1964): 149. All values referred to here and shown in Table 15 are based on the 1950 Bureau of the Census definition which has been applied to earlier and later years.

Table 15. Growth of Metropolitan and Nonmetropolitan Population

Decade	Conterminous United States, Total	Constant Criteria		Constant Area	
		Metropolitan	Nonmetropolitan	Metropolitan	Nonmetropolitan
Numerical Increase, in Millions					
1900–10	16.0	10.6	5.4	7.5	8.5
1910–20	13.7	11.5	2.2	8.5	5.2
1920–30	17.1	16.0	1.1	12.4	4.7
1930–40	8.9	5.9	3.0	5.0	3.9
1940–50	19.0	17.6	1.4	14.4	4.6
1950–60	27.8	27.5	.2	21.6	6.2
1960–70	22.8	18.7	4.1	17.9	4.7
Percentage of Increase					
1900–10	21	44	10	31	16
1910–20	15	33	4	25	9
1920–30	16	35	2	27	8
1930–40	7	10	5	8	6
1940–50	14	26	2	21	7
1950–60	18	32	0	25	10
1960–70	13	17	6	16	7
Percentage Distribution of Increase					
1900–10	100	66	34	47	53
1910–20	100	84	16	62	38
1920–30	100	94	6	72	28
1930–40	100	66	34	56	44
1940–50	100	92	8	76	24
1950–60	100	99	1	78	22
1960–70	100	82	18	78	22

SOURCE: Hawley, Duncan, and Goldberg, *op. cit.*, p. 149.

metropolitan as of the beginning of each decade. The trend computed in this way is shown in the columns headed "Constant Area," in Table 15. It may be seen that the amount of increase in metropolitan areas did not exceed that in nonmetropolitan areas until 1910–20; thereafter the rate of growth was more than twice as great in the former in all decades but one, the depression decade of 1930–40. In the last thirty years of the seven-decade period, metropolitan areas absorbed three quarters or more of all population increase in continental United States. The decline in the metropolitan growth rate in the 1960–1970 decade, assuming the 1970 preliminary figures are indicative, was due very likely to a further enlargement of the area over which metropolitan growth is spread. Such a trend has been gathering momentum since early in the century.[7]

It is important to recognize that the period of rapid metropolitan growth was also a period in which the full effects of farm mechanization were being manifested. Farm productivity had caught up with national population growth around the turn of the century and thereafter moved steadily ahead. Given the inelasticity of the market for agricultural products, there could be no other result than an increasing surplus population

[7] *Ibid.*, p. 154.

in rural areas. Fortunately, metropolitan areas were able to provide employment opportunities for most if not all of the rural surplus. Rural-to-urban migration became an increasingly prominent feature of population change. Some of the trends at work in that connection are shown in Table 16.

Table 16. Percentage of Change in Selected Components of U.S. Agriculture and of Population
(By Decades)

Decade	Value of Farm Machinery per Worker	Farm Productivity per Worker	Workers in Agriculture	Land in Farms	Population U.S. Total	Population Metropolitan
1890–00 ⎫	–	⎧14.1⎫	–	56.4	20.7	–
1900–10 ⎬	363.5	⎨ 2.3⎬	– 0.9⎰		21.0	31.3
1910–20 ⎭	–	0.3	–	14.0	14.9	24.6
1920–30	0.1	10.6	– 7.0	3.2	16.1	26.8
1930–40	42.6	27.6	–12.6	7.5	7.2	8.1
1940–50	198.4	34.5	– 9.6	9.2	14.5	21.2
1950–60	117.0	64.7	–28.9	1.3	18.4	25.2

SOURCE: Bureau of the Census, *Historical Statistics of the United States* (Washington, D.C.: Government Printing Office, 1960 and 1965).

Although metropolitan population growth has been spread over a progressively larger number of areas since 1900, the fact remains that most of the increase has accrued to a rather small number of areas. In the 1900–10 decade the New York area captured over a fourth of all metropolitan increase, while a half fell to five areas: New York, Chicago, Philadelphia, Pittsburgh, and Boston. In the next decade eight areas accounted for one half of all metropolitan population increase. The number of areas having that share of the total increase dropped to six in the 1920–30 decade, then increased to nine in the decade following. Thereafter the number of areas responsible for 50 percent of metropolitan increase expanded to thirteen and then to eighteen.

The uneven distribution of population growth is observable in another way. Fourteen areas, all but one of which were established before 1900, have constituted the nuclei of clusters of metropolitan areas.[8] That is, in 1960, each of the fourteen had three or more smaller areas located within 100 miles of its central city, including some seventy-five areas in all. Although, as Table 17 shows, the growth of the fourteen clusters lagged behind the growth of all metropolitan population after 1930, they have in every decade absorbed no less than three fifths of all metropolitan growth and they have contained 69 percent or more of the total metro-

[8] Boston, New York, Philadelphia, Baltimore, Washington, Cleveland, Detroit, Pittsburgh, Cincinnati, Chicago, Atlanta, San Francisco, Los Angeles, Dallas.

Table 17. Percentage of Increase, Percentage of All Metropolitan Increase,
and Percentage of All Metropolitan Population
(In Selected Clusters of Metropolitan Areas)

Decade	All Metropolitan Population	Washington–Boston[a]	Chicago–Buffalo[b]	Total for 14 Large Clusters
Percentage Increase				
1900–10	31	29	34	32
1910–20	25	18	37	26
1920–30	27	20	30	28
1930–40	8	6	4	7
1940–50	21	13	10	18
1950–60	25	16	20	24
1960–70	17	15	9	17
Percentage of All Metropolitan Increase				
1900–10	—	48	24	79
1910–20	—	36	35	80
1920–30	—	32	28	78
1930–40	—	30	12	64
1940–50	—	23	11	60
1950–60	—	22	17	66
1960–70	—	26	11	75
Percentage of All Metropolitan Population				
1900	—	52	22	78
1910	—	48	23	76
1920	—	43	25	75
1930	—	38	25	73
1940	—	39	24	72
1950	—	34	22	70
1960	—	30	20	69
1970	—	28	20	75

[a]Washington – Baltimore – New York – Philadelphia – Boston.
[b]Chicago – Detroit – Cleveland – Pittsburgh – Buffalo.
SOURCE: U.S. Bureau of the Census

politan population. On the other hand, it is apparent that their positions
of preeminence are gradually being undermined as metropolitan organization diffuses over the country. That is noticeable in the largest metropolitan agglomeration, which Jean Gottmann described as "Megalopolis" [9]
—the Washington–Baltimore–Philadelphia–New York–Boston complex,
and in the Chicago, Detroit, Cleveland, Pittsburgh, Buffalo complex.
Their shares of metropolitan growth have declined by almost half
since 1900–10. The proportion of the total metropolitan population
claimed by the northeastern "megalopolis" has shrunk from over 50 percent to less than 30 percent. The second great complex, stretching along
the Great Lakes from Buffalo to Chicago, has maintained greater stability,

[9] *Megalopolis: The Urbanized Northeastern Seaboard of the United States* (New
York: The Twentieth Century Fund, 1961).

though it, too, shows signs of yielding to the widening spread of metropolitan organization.

The slowing down of growth is limited to relatively few areas and those are among the oldest and largest metropolitan areas, situated for the most part in the northeastern part of the country. A small number, most of which were situated on the Pennsylvania coal fields, actually declined during each of the past two decades.

Size and age of area have also been associated with the way in which growth has occurred. The larger the area, the greater was the proportion of growth, in the 1960–70 decade, that was gained through net migration, as shown in Table 18. Similarly, the newer the area, by and large, the greater was the dependence on migration for growth. It is unlikely, however, that migration will contribute as much to metropolitan growth in the future as it has in the past. The rural sources of migrants are drying

Table 18. Percentage Distribution of Increase by Source of Increase and by Size and Age of Metropolitan Area, 1960–70

Size and Age of Metropolitan Area[a]	Total Change	Natural Increase	Net Migration
All areas	100.0	72.7	27.3
Before 1900	100.0	84.9	15.1
1900–1920	100.0	60.4	39.6
After 1920	100.0	45.9	54.1
1,000,000 and over	100.0	81.4	18.6
Before 1900	100.0	86.7	13.3
1900–1920	100.0	41.7	48.3
After 1920	–	–	–
500,000–1,000,000	100.0	59.8	40.2
Before 1900	100.0	74.9	25.1
1900–1920	100.0	66.9	33.1
After 1920	100.0	32.2	67.8
250,000–500,000	100.0	76.4	23.6
Before 1900	100.0	75.7	24.3
1900–1920	100.0	111.2	−11.2
After 1920	100.0	8.0	92.0
Under 250,000	100.0	44.3	45.7
Before 1900	100.0	180.6	−80.6
1900–1920	100.0	23.9	76.1
After 1920	100.0	62.8	37.2

[a]Date when central city first attained size of 50,000 population.
SOURCE: U.S. Bureau of the Census, *Census of Population,* 1970.

up in the United States. Migration is becoming increasingly a matter of inter-metropolitan movements. The general tendency in that respect doubtless will continue to be toward the southwestern part of the country.

When metropolitan areas are classified by their 1950–60 growth rates, it is possible to observe how population characteristics are altered by the circumstances that underlie demographic changes. Thus in the upper panel of Table 19 it may be noted that, where growth rates are low, pop-

Table 19. Percentage Distribution of Amounts of Population Change in 1950–60 (By Characteristics of Population, by Growth Rate of Metropolitan Area)

Population Characteristics	U.S. Total Population	Metropolitan, 1950—Per Cent Change							Non-metro-politan
		50 and Over	40–50	30–40	20–30	10–20	0–10	Less than 0	
Age of population (total)	100	100	100	100	100	100	100	–100	100
Under 18 yrs.	62	45	54	53	66	71	112	2	66
18–65 yrs.	23	46	36	40	21	10	–46	–129	10
65 yrs. and over	15	9	10	7	13	19	34	27	24
Nativity and color (total)	100	100	100	100	100	100	100	–100	100
Native white	110	82	64	81	80	64	57	24	120
Foreign white	–24	6	0	2	–2	12	35	–29	–24
Non-white	14	12	36	17	22	24	8	–94	6
Education[a] (total)	100	100	100	100	100	100	100	–100	100
Under 5 yrs.	–11	34	5	–1	–1	–6	–70	–149	–40
5–12 yrs.	69	29	65	58	54	23	83	67	97
13 yrs. and over	42	39	30	43	47	83	84	–18	43

[a]Population 25 years of age and over.
SOURCE: U.S. Bureau of the Census, *Census of Population,* 1960.

ulation increase is concentrated in the dependent classes, i.e., persons under 18 years of age and over 65 years of age. High-growth-rate areas tend to gain persons who are in the productive years of life. Again, the higher the growth rate, the larger is the proportion of the total increase that is composed of native white population. This tendency is offset to some extent by the seemingly erratic behavior of the non-white population. Non-whites, in the latest census decade shown, avoided both very slowly and very rapidly growing areas. Instead, they were attracted to areas with modest to high rates of increase. Foreign-born whites, of course, are a declining segment of the total population. It appears that the least educated have either followed high growth rates or high rates have occurred where the most poorly educated propagate rapidly. By contrast, the most highly educated have tended to congregate where growth rates are low.

Metropolitan growth trends have continued into 1970 with no interruption.[10] As settlement units they loom ever larger in the national pattern

[10] U.S. Bureau of the Census, *Trends in Social and Economic Conditions in Metropolitan Areas,* Current Population Reports, Special Studies, Series p-23, No. 27 (Washington, D.C., 1969), p. 2.

of population distribution. Their proportion of the total population has changed from one third, in 1900, to almost two thirds, in 1970. This shift represents the form taken in the twentieth century by the long-term urbanization process. When the term "urban" is now used to designate a type of place it should refer to a metropolitan community rather than to a city.

POPULATION REDISTRIBUTION WITHIN METROPOLITAN AREAS

Population growth is almost invariably accompanied by a redistribution of numbers. Opportunities for settlement at a given time are rarely the same as those that prevailed at an earlier time. The redistribution movement within metropolitan areas has been from the beginning a centrifugal drift. As noted earlier, urban population increase has usually collected at peripheries while inner sections have declined in numbers. What was true of centers is true also of enlarged units. Still, the centrifugal movement did not appear immediately. In the early years of metropolitan development between two thirds and three quarters of all metropolitan increase was absorbed by central cities. Central growth appeared to occur at the expense of outer areas, as the data in Table 20 indicate.

Table 20. Ratios of U.S. Population Increase in Concentric
Distance Zones Within Metropolitan Areas to
Population Increase in Central Cities

Decade	Metropolitan Total	0–10 Miles	10–20 Miles	20–30 Miles	30 Miles and Over
1900–10	0.973	0.933	0.849	0.825	0.969
1910–20	0.976	1.019	0.851	0.773	0.812
1920–30	1.029	1.262	0.994	1.021	0.948
1930–40	1.035	1.164	1.103	1.035	1.033
1940–50	1.063	1.283	1.111	0.932	1.100
1950–60	1.118	1.345	1.427	1.118	1.328

SOURCE: U.S. Bureau of the Census, *Census of Population,* 1600's through 1960.

Actual population losses were recorded in some outlying localities while others barely held their own with very modest growth rates.[11] As may be seen in Table 21, losses were general in localities with the poorest transportation to central cities, especially in the early decades. High growth rates favored places with rail and highway access, but in later decades rail access proved unnecessary for rapid growth.

[11] See also Amos H. Hawley, *The Changing Shape of Metropolitan America* (New York: The Free Press, 1956), p. 49.

Table 21. Percentage of Change of Population in a Sample of Outlying Localities in Metropolitan Areas (By Type of Transportation Access, Distance Zone, and Decade)

Transportation Access and Distance Zone	1940–50	1930–40	1920–30	1910–20	1900–10
Highway and railway					
5–10 miles	38	17	57	22	39
10–15	60	18	62	28	16
15–20	23	15	39	28	24
20–25	50	7	36	35	13
25–30	25	12	37	45	46
30–35	24	7	5	19	30
35 and over	45	6	13	14	7
Highway only					
5–10 miles	69	47	21	12	36
10–15	75	35	57	16	–5
15–20	68	27	53	12	10
20–25	70	19	15	28	15
25–30	22	4	–4	–3	–4
30–35	19	–1	4	4	0
35 and over	32	20	2	–6	6
Railway only					
5–10 miles	–	–	–	–	–
10–15	–	–	–	–	–
15–20	–	–	–	–	–
20–25	31	8	–5	–9	9
25–30	2	–8	3	8	–18
30–35	8	–4	–21	–8	6
35 and over	4	–9	–1	4	–9
Neither highway nor railway					
5–10 miles	–	–	–	–	–
10–15	27	15	–2	–11	5
15–20	20	9	30	–6	–1
20–25	14	12	–4	–4	–5
25–30	1	2	–5	–5	–7
30–35	11	10	13	6	0
35 and over	–3	5	–8	–10	–2

SOURCE: Amos H. Hawley, *The Changing Shape of Metropolitan America,* New York: Free Press, 1956, p. 111.

In general, the larger and the older the area, the earlier did growth in outlying areas begin to exceed that in central cities. High growth rates moved outward in a regular progression, like a ripple caused by a pebble dropped into a pool. Although the 0–10 mile belt around central cities has remained the zone of highest growth rate, growth rates in excess of those in central cities have spread over more distant zones since 1930. The pattern of dispersion of growth which appeared first in the largest metropolitan areas became common in all sizes of areas after 1920, though the outward movement proceeded at a much slower pace in the smaller areas.

Population deconcentration [12] in a relative sense—outlying areas growing more rapidly than central cities—became general, as suggested, after 1920. The trend is described in the top three lines of Table 22. In 1920–30 outlying zones increased at rates 50 percent higher than central city rates. During the next two decades the differential leaped to almost three to one. After 1950 outlying area growth rates averaged five or more times higher than central city rates.

The remaining lines of Table 22 describe the onset of deconcentration of metropolitan population in successive age cohorts of areas as defined by the dates at which central cities first attained sizes of 50,000 or more inhabitants. Central cities that reached minimum metropolitan size before 1870 were experiencing deconcentration as early as the first decade of the present century. The same trend appeared in areas "born" between 1880 and 1900 in the 1920–30 decade, and in still later decades for the more recently established areas. But those that attained metropolitan status after 1930 and 1960 were still in their concentration phases in the 1950–60 decade. After 1960 all classes of areas entered upon deconcentration trends. Note should be taken of absolute losses in the oldest central cities during the latest decade.[13]

The accelerating dispersal of urban population turned relative deconcentration to absolute deconcentration after 1950. Population densities increased in central cities of all age classes, but one, until 1950, as shown in Table 23. Thereafter the number of people per square mile declined. A fact to be underscored is that density reductions began in the newer metropolitan centers at much lower peak densities than those reached in older centers. Perhaps never again will urban centers have reason to attain great sizes and densities before deconcentration begins. Nor is there any reason to believe that the growth experience of the older metropolitan areas will be repeated by the newer ones.

Some of the inconsistencies that appear in a comparison of Tables 22 and 23 are explained by the data in Table 24. Differences in success with annexation account for the growth peculiarities.[14] The central cities of areas that were deconcentrating in the relative sense during 1950–60 were

[12] Deconcentration is used here in preference to decentralization. The dispersal of physical objects, such as people, residences, and other appurtenances, is not to be confused with the gathering into fewer institutions of the reins of administrative control over society. The two processes can and do occur simultaneously. Whatever the descriptive terms used, a clear distinction between them should be observed.

[13] Cf. Leo F. Schnore, "The Timing of Metropolitan Decentralization," *Journal American Institute of Planners*, XXV (1959): 200–206.

[14] Cf. Leo F. Schnore, *The Urban Scene* (New York: The Free Press, 1965), pp. 114–33.

Table 22. Percentage of Increase of Population in Metropolitan Areas (By Date of Inception of Metropolitan Area and by Type of Place [Constant Area])

Date of Metropolitan Area Inception and Type of Place Within Areas	1960–70	1950–60	1940–50	1930–40	1920–30	1910–20	1900–10
All areas							
Total	16.3	24.7	21.2	8.3	26.7	24.2	31.6
Central cities	4.8	7.0	12.9	5.3	22.6	25.6	41.9
Remainders of areas	29.1	48.3	34.4	13.3	34.8	21.5	30.7
1850 and before							
Total	13.1	15.3	12.6	5.8	21.8	17.2	29.0
Central cities	-2.1	-2.9	6.3	4.2	15.4	17.1	27.5
Remainders of areas	29.2	42.3	23.3	8.7	35.2	17.5	31.6
1860							
Total	15.6	22.8	24.2	7.4	28.1	24.8	28.9
Central cities	-5.5	-3.4	10.3	3.9	22.2	22.4	24.6
Remainders of areas	31.7	60.1	51.4	15.3	45.3	33.1	42.8
1870							
Total	8.7	19.4	16.2	5.3	31.2	37.6	37.0
Central cities	-9.5	-4.5	8.2	1.1	26.2	43.1	37.1
Remainders of areas	21 2	48.5	27.8	12.1	40.4	27.6	36.8
1880							
Total	13.5	23.2	16.8	3.7	22.4	24.0	27.6
Central cities	9.8	7.9	12.0	1.4	19.0	31.8	36.4
Remainders of areas	18.7	49.2	26.4	8.7	30.7	8.4	13.1
1890							
Total	22.7	32.7	28.1	15.5	41.0	28.0	34.8
Central cities	7.1	14.3	16.4	9.6	31.8	28.7	40.2
Remainders of areas	36.1	68.3	47.3	26.8	62.8	26.8	23.7
1900							
Total	15.7	19.8	21.3	5.5	15.8	23.9	42.1
Central cities	-1.7	13.0	19.1	2.4	14.8	29.2	60.9
Remainders of areas	29.6	27.2	23.8	9.1	16.9	17.6	24.8
1910							
Total	18.4	28.2	32.4	10.6	26.5	35.0	—
Central cities	16.6	25.7	28.0	7.8	36.6	45.4	—
Remainders of areas	20.8	31.8	39.3	15.0	12.6	23.4	—
1920							
Total	18.1	36.9	27.1	10.4	34.6	—	—
Central cities	13.2	29.7	14.3	10.2	39.6	—	—
Remainders of areas	22.9	44.6	45.8	10.7	27.3	—	—
1930							
Total	23.1	38.5	33.0	18.9	—	—	—
Central cities	21.4	-4.3	28.5	16.6	—	—	—
Remainders of areas	24.7	85.7	38.1	21.5	—	—	—
1940							
Total	23.6	52.3	51.0	—	—	—	—
Central cities	22.1	91.9	48.5	—	—	—	—
Remainders of areas	26.3	10.4	53.6	—	—	—	—
1950							
Total	22.8	26.1	—	—	—	—	—
Central cities	12.2	32.0	—	—	—	—	—
Remainders of areas	31.8	19.1	—	—	—	—	—
1960							
Total	33.9	—	—	—	—	—	—
Central cities	27.0	—	—	—	—	—	—
Remainders of areas	40.6	—	—	—	—	—	—

SOURCE: U.S. Bureau of the Census, *Censuses of Population.*

**Table 23. Population per Square Mile in Central Cities of Metropolitan Areas
(By Date at Which Central City Population Reached 50,000)**

Date Central City Population Reached 50,000	1960	1950	1940	1930	1920	1910
1850[a]	14,531	14,991	14,382	13,898	12,275	11,358
1860	13,252	14,264	13,338	13,093	11,538	9,545
1870	10,368	11,982	11,925	11,843	13,641	11,696
1880	5,357	7,206	7,077	7,096	7,058	5,448
1890	5,315	5,685	5,273	4,943	4,203	4,473
1900	4,472	5,372	4,806	4,650	4,147	3,336
1910	3,056	4,690	4,991	4,964	—[b]	—[b]
1920	3,688	4,711	4,559	4,582	—	—
1930	3,668	5,353	5,288	—[b]	—	—
1940	2,842	4,260	5,034	—	—	—
1950	3 408	3,449	—	—	—	—

[a]And prior to 1850.
[b]No area data available.
SOURCE: U.S. Bureau of the Census, *Census of Population*, 1910 through 1960.

**Table 24. Percentage of Change of Population in Metropolitan Areas
(By Type of Area and by Location of Change in Population,
1950–1960 and 1960–1970)**

Type of Metropolitan Area	Number of Areas	Increase, Total Metropolitan Area	Central City Increase			
			Total	Due to Annexation	In Central City Area of 1960	Area Annexed as Percentage of 1960 Area
All areas[a]						
1950–1960	162	25.2	9.0	8.1	0.9	45.3
1960–1970	189	16.3	5.0	4.1	0.9	27.5
Deconcentrating areas						
1950–1960	123	23.7	3.7	4.0	–0.3	25.8
1960–1970	148	16.1	2.5	2.2	–0.3	22.0
Concentrating areas						
1950–1960	39	39.2	54.7	43.4	11.3	136.7
1960–1970	41	18.5	22.6	16.4	6.2	72.2

All areas conform to 1950 definition of Standard Metropolitan Areas.
SOURCE: U.S. Bureau of the Census, *Census of Population*, 1950, 1960, 1970.

only moderately successful in adding to their incorporated territories—
the land they were able to annex in that decade added only 26 percent to
their 1950 area. In fact, nine tenths of the population increase that occurred in central cities of metropolitan areas existing in 1950 and before
was acquired through annexing occupied territory. Areas that were concentrating, relatively speaking, in the 1950–60 decade more than doubled
their incorporated space (150 percent) through enlarging their boundaries. Had they not done so, the new as well as the old areas would have
fallen into the deconcentrating category; four fifths to three quarters of
their population increase was acquired by means of annexation. Thus a
metropolitan area can be experiencing a relative concentration of its pop-

ulation while the density within its central city is declining.

It is possible to pursue an analysis of variations in deconcentration rates and patterns in considerable depth. Every significant characteristic of metropolitan areas will tend to show a deconcentration pattern more or less peculiar to itself. This is not the place to enter into an exhaustive analysis along these lines. One additional variable, however, is worth noting, that is, the type of specialization in the economic base. Specialization, for the purpose at hand, is measured in a sample of areas by the extent to which employment in each of eleven industrial categories exceeds the expected employment, i.e., the average for all metropolitan areas.[15] Any ratio which exceeds the expected ratio by an arbitrary 20 per cent or more is regarded as indicating specialization. By this means it is possible to identify metropolitan areas specialized exclusively in manufacturing,[16] in manufacturing, trade, and service combined,[17] in transportation and wholesailing,[18] and in service industries including one or more personal and business services, education, public administration, recreation, and trade.[19] Growth trends for each of these classes of areas are shown in Table 25.

Manufacturing areas have had a somewhat erratic growth history. They ended the seventy-year period with less than the average rate of increase. Although the first half of that period was marked by a pronounced centripetal drift of population, deconcentration began abruptly in 1930–40 and has progressed rapidly ever since. Areas with a more diversified economic base, those specialized in manufacturing, in trade, and in service, have had greater continuity of growth. They, too, have fallen behind the average growth rate of metropolitan areas. Deconcentration began earlier in areas of this class and has maintained a rapid pace through the last fifty years. Areas specialized in transportation and wholesaling industries have pursued a rising trend of increase until 1960, surpassing the average rate in each of the past three decades. Deconcentration started in the 1920–30 decade and, while the growth differential as between central cities and remainders of areas has been substantial, it has not been extreme. Central cities in these areas have preserved a vigor which contrasts sharply with central cities of the first two specialization classes. Metropolitan areas specialized in service industries other than

[15] This measure is a compound ratio of employment in a given industry in a metropolitan area divided by the population of the area over the total employment in that industry in all metropolitan areas divided by the total population of areas.

[16] Brockton, Pittsfield, Allentown, Worcester, Flint, Detroit, Gadsden, Wheeling.

[17] Baltimore, Beaumont, Cedar Rapids, Cincinnati, Jackson, Michigan, Lorain, Philadelphia, Syracuse, Toledo, Winston-Salem, Waterloo, Trenton, Scranton.

[18] Columbus, Ohio, Denver, Green Bay, Houston, Little Rock, Nashville, New Orleans, Roanoke, St. Joseph, Savannah, Wichita.

[19] Austin, Los Angeles, Macon, Mobile, Ogden, Sacramento, San Jose, Springfield, Ill., Tampa.

Table 25. Percentage of Increase of Population in Metropolitan Areas
by Type of Specialization
(By Type of Place and by Census Year [Constant Area])

Type of Specialization and Type of Place	1960–70	1950–60	1940–50	1930–40	1920–30	1910–20	1900–10
Manufacturing							
Total	19.9	20.4	19.3	6.5	41.1	47.0	33.8
Central cities	–4.8	–5.4	11.7	2.3	45.3	97.0	51.4
Remainders	39.8	48.5	29.1	12.5	34.6	19.1	–7.6
Manufacturing, trade, service							
Total	10.8	19.4	15.5	3.6	16.6	16.4	20.8
Central cities	–1.4	0.3	10.0	2.1	9.4	20.9	18.0
Remainders	22.0	48.3	25.2	6.3	33.6	6.9	26.9
Transportation, wholesale							
Total	23.3	37.5	32.9	15.5	32.4	21.9	19.1
Central cities	13.2	29.0	27.1	10.9	28.5	22.6	25.8
Remainders	46.2	68.8	53.3	35.4	54.0	17.1	–19.5
Service							
Total	27.5	58.0	50.0	24.1	102.6	68.2	196.0
Central cities	20.6	35.6	37.7	29.5	87.5	64.9	211.5
Remainders	33.2	82.1	65.9	17.6	123.9	73.6	172.7

SOURCE: U.S. Bureau of the Census, *Census of Population*, 1900 through 1970.

transportation and wholesaling have sustained exceptionally high growth rates before subsiding in 1960–70, though the rates have declined appreciably over the years since 1900. The trend toward deconcentration which began in 1910–20 was reversed momentarily in the 1930–40 decade and then resumed its course afterward.

The confinement of attention in the preceding pages to metropolitan growth in the United States is defensible mainly on grounds of the existence of more voluminous information over a longer span of time for that country than is available for any other.[20] There is the further fact that metropolitan expansion elsewhere in the world has been delayed by a slower adoption of the new forms of short-distance transportation and communication. Still, despite much lower frequencies of automobile ownership, rates of metropolitan deconcentration in Canada and the United Kingdom have been comparable to those in the United States.[21] On the European continent, changes in local transportation have been rapid since World War II. Effects on population growth and distribution of the same order as those in the United States are far advanced in the

[20] A delimitation of the metropolitan areas of the world, based exclusively on measures of population density, is presented in International Urban Research, *The World's Metropolitan Areas* (Berkeley: University of California Press, 1959).

[21] Yoshiko Kasahara, "A Profile of Canada's Metropolitan Centers, *Queen's Quarterly*, LXX (1963): 303–13, and Leo F. Schnore, "Metropolitan Development in the United Kingdom," *Economic Geography*, XXXVIII (1962): 215–33.

Copenhagen area and in the hinterlands of many other large centers of Western Europe.[22]

THE REDISTRIBUTION OF INDUSTRY

The long-term trend in the distribution of non-extractive industry displays both centripetal and centrifugal currents. There has been no interruption to the concentration in or about substantially sized cities. The movement had been selective, with the result that in many metropolitan areas complexes of closely interdependent firms have formed.[23] These sets of complementary industries have introduced an element of inertia into the distribution pattern. Nevertheless, a shift has occurred in the direction taken by the long-term drift of industry. Technological changes, such as the substitution of electric for steam power, and the development of lighter materials industries as represented in plastics and electronics, have favored inland metropolitan areas rather than the older areas situated at deep-water transportation locations.[24] Consequently, the industrial center of gravity in the United States has moved toward the southwest. The movement has proceeded mainly by new industries appearing in new locations rather than through interregional relocation of old industries.

Starting later but proceeding concurrently with the centripetal process has been a localized centrifugal redistribution of industry. As early as mid-nineteenth century, congestion in cities began to force industrial establishments toward urban peripheries. After 1899 industrial relocations were spilling over central city boundaries with increasing frequency and scattering to adjacent suburban sites.[25] This trend was slowed by economic depression and war-time materials shortages and then was accelerated rapidly after 1955. Wage jobs in manufacturing located in central cities declined from 63 percent of the metropolitan total, in 1940, to 51 percent in 1960.

The relocations of industry have not conformed to a uniform pattern in

[22] Aage Aegeson, "The Copenhagen District and Its Population," *Geografisk Tidsskrift*, LIX (1960): 210, and Robert E. Dickenson, *The City Region in Western Europe* (London: Routledge and Kegan Paul, 1967), ch. 6. See also Harold Lind, "Internal Migration in Britain," in *Migration*, ed. by J. A. Jackson (Cambridge: The University Press, 1969), pp. 74–98.

[23] Raymond Vernon, "Production and Distribution in the Large Metropolis," *Annals of Amer. Academy Political and Social Science*, CCCXIV (1957): 18.

[24] This corresponds to an expectation of Colin Clark ("The Distribution of Labour Between Industries and Between Locations," *Land Economics*, XXVI [1950]: 136–44), though for somewhat different reasons than those put forth by Clark.

[25] Daniel B. Creamer, *Is Industry Decentralizing?* (Philadelphia: University of Pennsylvania Press, 1935), pp. 10 ff. See also Evelyn M. Kitagawa and Donald J. Bogue, *Suburbanization of Manufacturing Activity Within Metropolitan Areas* (Chicago: University of Chicago Population Research and Training Center, 1955).

all size classes of metropolitan areas. As may be observed in Table 26, only in the largest size class is there evidence that wage jobs have tended to seek a distribution comparable to that of population. But that is more true of the long run than it is of the short run; between 1919 and 1939 the trend followed a contrary direction. In other size classes the two distributions—wage jobs and population—have become less congruent. In areas ranging from 250,000 to 1,000,000 population, wage jobs have gravitated to suburban cities of 10,000 or more population, while in the smallest size class wage jobs have been concentrating in central cities. Using establishments instead of jobs makes it apparent that in every size class the distribution of industry has been departing increasingly from that of population. It should be recognized that the measure used in Table 26, the

Table 26. Coefficients of Dissimilarity[a] for Wage Jobs and Establishments in Manufacturing Relative to Population Within Metropolitan Areas (By Size of Area)

Size of Area	Wage Jobs			Establishments		
	1958	1939	1919	1958	1939	1919
1,000,000 and over	9.3	17.3	14.1	15.7	19.4	8.9
500,000–1,000,000	13.0	6.8	8.3	15.6	12.0	12.6
250,000– 500,000	23.3	12.3	6.6	15.6	16.4	6.2
Under 250,000	23.6	24.2	19.0	12.6	15.4	11.6

[a]The coefficient of dissimilarity states half the sum of the percentage point difference between matched percentage distributions, i.e., for manufacturing wage jobs and for population, in which the class intervals are: central cities, other incorporated places of 10,000 or more population, and remainders of areas. It indicates the proportion of one of the two variables which would have to be redistributed to obtain a distribution identical to that of the second variable.

SOURCE: Computed from data in U.S. Bureau of the Census, Censuses of Population 1920, 1940, and 1960, and Censuses of Manufacturing, 1919, 1939, and 1958.

coefficient of dissimilarity, does not enable us to distinguish industrial movements from population movements; it merely describes the amount of difference at selected points in time.

Three factors have been instrumental in the deconcentration of industry in recent decades. These are the changes in space requirements of manufacturing, improvements in short-distance transportation and communication facilities, and in the spread of urban amenities, including street and utility networks, over outlying areas. The outward movement has attracted the large plants primarily, particularly those requiring specially designed buildings. A continuous, assembly-line mode of production is more satisfactory if laid on a single horizontal level. Hence the single-story building has replaced the multi-storied building. But the single-story building uses much more ground space and involves much greater cost for land. The assembling of land in sufficient quantity for a large sprawling building in a densely occupied area has proved to be too costly and time consuming to be worth the effort. Furthermore, space for parking workers' automobiles, in amounts rivaling that occupied by buildings, has become mandatory. These enlarged space requirements can be easily and rather inexpensively obtained in the suburban belt.

The more abundant and cheaper lands would not be accessible, of course, had there not been significant improvement in local transportation and communication facilities. With the motor vehicle in general use and an extensive network of paved road surfaces, a plant can draw its working force from a radius of twenty-five miles or more. Furthermore, the increased reliance on the motor truck for short-haul freight transfers has made a peripheral location far more convenient than a central location. In fact, the motor truck affords so close a timing of complementary industrial processes carried on in spatially separated plants that metropolitan streets and roads have become extensions of assembly lines. Inventory costs, created in the past by the necessity of stockpiling materials and parts, have been greatly reduced. The shrinkage of local distances, moreover, has permitted a spread over the metropolitan area of the external economies that were formerly available only in the close quarters of congested industrial districts.[26] The problem of maintaining access to the many services an industrial operation must have is simplified further by the telephone. Thus the administrative function may remain in a central location and in intimate contact with financial, legal, advertising, and numerous other services, while the space-using production function can occupy a low-cost location more easily accessible to suppliers and the labor force.

Of no small importance in the deconcentration of industry is the presence of urban services in outlying areas. Industrial establishments need water, sewer, police and fire protection, a road network, and other services supplied by government. These utilities, along with schools, churches, shopping centers, and recreational opportunities, are needed also by the labor force. For though the workers can be drawn from a wide area, there is apt to be a high worker turnover where work trips are over-long. Workers tend to shorten their daily journeys to work as much as is consistent with the needs and costs of family accommodations. Thus industrial plants cannot wander far beyond the growing edge of the expanding metropolitan organization. Until fairly recently necessary urban services and facilities were available only in the larger suburban municipalities.

[26] Edgar M. Hoover and Raymond Vernon, *Anatomy of A Metropolis* (Cambridge: Harvard University Press, 1959), pp. 49–53.

But in late years they have been much more widely provided in small towns as well as in unincorporated territory. There is still great unevenness in that regard as a result of differences in tax bases among local jurisdictions.

The outward movement of large space users leaves the interiors of central cities to small industrial establishments. Many of these are industries that do not require specialized buildings. Some are new enterprises struggling for survival on small amounts of capital. Some are old industries held at their locations by the distribution of a particular labor supply or by a dependence upon complementary industries. There is still an important place, especially in the very large central city, for the industry engaged in unstandardized processes subject to frequent product changes.[27] These are the kinds of industries that comprise the so-called external economies. They now serve a metropolitan area rather than just a highly localized market.

THE CONCENTRATION OF ADMINISTRATION

As mentioned previously, while producing activities were moving in one direction, administrative and related functions have moved in an opposite direction. In New York City, for example, manufacturing jobs declined by 42,000 between 1947 and 1955, but jobs in finance, insurance, and real estate, to say nothing of jobs in corporate offices, increased by 28,000.[28] A continuing trend toward the centralization of administrative control, incidental to an increasing scale of industrial organization, has also contributed to a large volume of space occupied by central office activity. Mechanization of clerical and other administrative tasks has increased the space required per office worker, thus adding further to the amount of central office space occupied.[29] As we shall see in a later connection, central office functions are not uniformly distributed among metropolitan centers; a few centers contain disproportionate amounts of that class of activity.

White-collar employment is a mixture of many varieties. Much of it is engaged in small-scale enterprises with many different location requirements. Much of it, too, is held in large central offices of industrial and commercial corporations. In any short interval of time there are movements and countermovements in the distribution of the administrative working force. An illustration is provided in Table 27, which shows those that occurred in a six-month period during 1968 in a sample of 145 metro-

[27] See Robert M. Lichtenberger, *One Tenth of A Nation* (Cambridge: Harvard University Press, 1960), pp. 39 ff.
[28] Raymond Vernon, *op. cit.*, p. 25.
[29] Hoover and Vernon, *op. cit.*, pp. 106–12.

Table 27. Square Feet of Office Space Placed on and
Removed from the Market
(1975 Buildings in 145 Cities, by Type of Change,
United States, May to October, 1968)

Type of Change	Placed on Market (−)	Removed from Market (+)	Net Change in Occupancy
(1) Business terminated or new business	281,833	821,349	539,516
(2) Moved to or from other cities	266,794	273,288	6,494
(3) Moved to or from outlying zone	371,171	186,432	−184,748
(4) Moved to other locations in same city	1,469,578	961,005	−508,573
(5) Change in space rented: no move	238,031	1,228,856	990,825
(6) Added to or subtracted from supply of available space	1,399,753	251,687	−1,148,066
(7) Total	4,027,160	3,722,608	−304,552

SOURCE: *Skyscraper Management*, 53 (November, 1968), p. 12.

politan central cities. The decline of about 8 percent in the total amount
of space occupied (row 7) was due largely to changes in the supply of
available space (row 6). In that time interval the supply was reduced;
in another interval it might be increased. Such changes are often due to
shifts in the location of the central business district, such as the uptown
movement that has occurred in Manhattan since 1950. Contractions and
expansions of space occupied are indicated in rows 4 and 5. Some of the
contractions may be associated with moves to outlying zones (row 3), as
where, for example, record storage is moved to cheaper quarters while
the administrative function remains in the central area. Still, the relatively small amount of outward relocation of office activity may be a har-
binger of more significant relocations. On the other hand, the large
increase in space occupied by new tenants (row 1) may reflect the centralization trend mentioned earlier.

THE REDISTRIBUTION OF RETAIL BUSINESS

Retail and service establishments have followed close on the heels of
the centrifugally moving population and industry. During the preeminence of mass transportation carriers in the intramural flows of urban
areas, the central business districts of central cities held undisputed ascendancy as shopping and service centers, especially for unstandardized

goods and specialized services. The motor vehicle and the telephone introduced radical changes into shopping habits. The multiplicity of demands on the consumer's travel and errand time has favored shopping locations where the quick stop and the fast start are possible. Hence the outlying and the suburban shopping centers, with their acreages of off-street parking space, have risen as serious competitors to the central business district and the old secondary business districts of the inner city. By the end of the 1930 decade outlying shopping areas were already rivaling the older retail centers in shopping goods sales and had moved ahead in sales of automobiles, furniture, and hardware.[30] In the last twenty years an estimated 2,500 shopping centers were constructed,[31] and the trend in that direction has not yet abated.

The effects of the dispersion of consumer services on the central business district are apparent in Table 28. There is no exception to the decline of the central district's position of importance, though it is still dominant in most metropolitan areas. Most of the declines shown in the table are absolute as well as relative. In a few instances, however, such as New York, San Francisco, Dayton, and Austin, the actual amounts of sales in the central business districts increased, while the percentage of the metropolitan areas sales was reduced. Whether these departures from the general tendency can be sustained is problematical. More than likely they cannot. The probability is that the position of the central district will continue to be eroded in the deconcentration process. Erosion is neither a simple nor a smooth process. It is an outcome of many interacting factors, some of which retard the movement, others of which accelerate it. Population growth rates, patterns of industrial relocation, changes in population composition, and other modifications in an area affect the position of the central business district.[32]

But if we consider the distribution of business activity in relation to the distribution of population, as was done with manufacturing industry (Table 26), it is found that the movements in one have almost kept pace with the movements of the other. Table 29 indicates that only in respect to retail establishments has a dissimilarity in the distributions widened appreciably. Thus it appears that population and merchandising and service industries move in fairly close association with one another. There is but a very small time lag involved in the mutual adjustment of their patterns of distribution.

[30] Walter Isard and Vincent Whitney, "Metropolitan Site Selection," *Social Forces,* XXVII (1949): 253–69.

[31] U.S. Department of Commerce, *Survey of Current Business* (January, 1961), p. 32.

[32] For an interesting analysis of some of these variables see John Caspari, "Metropolitan Retail Structure and Its Relation to Population," *Land Economics,* XLIII (1967): 212–18.

Table 28. Central Business District Retail Sales as Percentage of Metropolitan Retail Sales
(By Type of Goods, Selected Metropolitan Areas, 1948 to 1967)

Metropolitan Area	Convenience Goods					Shopping Goods				
	1967	1963	1958	1954	1948	1967	1963	1958	1954	1948
New York	1.0	10.9	11.5	12.1	NA	26.6	27.9	33.9	38.3	NA
Chicago	3.9	4.1	4.7	5.0	NA	15.9	18.9	23.3	28.2	NA
Los Angeles	1.4	1.6	2.2	2.8	NA	6.0	7.9	11.3	15.2	NA
Detroit	1.9	2.6	2.9	4.2	5.8	11.7	16.1	23.0	29.9	43.8
Philadelphia	4.8	5.5	6.0	6.6	9.0	19.1	25.5	34.6	40.3	50.6
Baltimore	3.2	3.3	4.6	6.3	NA	18.3	21.2	33.7	42.7	NA
Boston	4.0	5.2	5.4	6.2	NA	21.7	27.8	34.0	42.0	NA
Cleveland	4.2	4.7	6.0	6.8	9.4	21.3	28.1	41.1	50.3	61.2
Cincinnati	4.4	5.2	7.7	7.9	10.2	26.2	37.4	51.4	59.2	63.8
San Francisco	6.3	7.7	8.2	8.6	NA	20.0	24.1	28.9	31.4	NA
Milwaukee	3.3	3.6	3.7	4.5	NA	18.7	23.9	30.1	39.6	NA
Minneapolis	4.6	5.2	7.3	8.6	NA	20.6	29.8	40.1	47.0	NA
Dayton	3.8	4.6	6.5	9.6	NA	32.4	47.0	62.4	66.5	NA
Rochester	4.3	6.0	9.9	12.0	15.0	35.2	45.2	65.1	75.1	79.1
Kansas City	3.6	4.2	4.8	6.8	9.4	16.8	23.0	34.7	45.1	54.9
Atlanta	5.6	6.7	8.3	10.2	NA	26.1	37.5	56.8	59.7	NA
Birmingham	7.8	9.7	12.1	14.0	18.3	38.1	50.2	62.4	70.7	72.2
Seattle	4.5	5.5	7.6	10.3	NA	27.2	37.5	44.5	52.4	NA
Denver	4.3	5.4	8.0	10.2	NA	19.2	25.5	40.4	50.5	NA
Austin	6.3	8.0	12.1	15.1	26.1	28.0	36.8	73.9	76.9	88.1

NA means "not available."
SOURCE: 1958 Census of Business, *Central Business District Statistics,* Summary Report. BC 58-CBD 98 (Washington: U.S. Bureau Census, 1961), *Major Retail Centers:* Summary Report. BC 63-MRC-1 (Washington, 1965), and *Major Retail Centers in Standard Metropolitan Statistical Areas:* United States Summary. BC 67-MRC-1 (Washington, 1967).

The decline of the central business district as the preeminent shopping center does not mean, however, that its demise is at hand. On the contrary, we have seen that it has shown considerable vitality as a location for central office functions. There are some indications that it may grow even more important in that respect. In any case, so long as the central business district continues to be a major employment center it will also continue to be an important shopping center.

SUMMARY

In the metropolitan area, as in the urban center before it, expansion proceeds through two countervailing processes, the one centrifugal, the other centripetal. The centrifugal movement scatters people, residences, churches, schools, establishments retailing goods and services, and indus-

Table 29. Coefficients of Dissimilarity for Wage Jobs and
Establishments in Retail, Wholesale, and
Service Industries Relative to Population
(By Size of Metropolitan Area)

Type of Industry and Size of Area	Wage Jobs		Establishments	
	1958	1939	1958	1939
Retail				
1,000,000 and over	15.0	15.4	11.9	10.7
500,000–1,000,000	22.9	14.5	10.7	3.8
250,000– 500,000	24.6	22.4	14.8	5.3
Under 250,000	23.6	21.7	12.3	6.7
Wholesale				
1,000,000 and over	30.0	27.0	27.2	26.5
500,000–1,000,000	32.2	25.3	28.0	23.1
250,000– 500,000	24.8	27.0	26.5	25.3
Under 250,000	29.5	27.5	12.4	22.0
Service				
1,000,000 and over	26.1	23.5	15.1	18.2
500,000–1,000,000	25.1	21.6	13.7	10.5
250,000– 500,000	29.7	27.0	20.0	15.5
Under 250,000	26.5	25.2	14.8	15.4

SOURCE: U.S. Bureau of the Census, *Census of Business,* 1939 and 1959.

tries more and more widely over the area lying within a sixty-minute commuting radius of the central city core. Dispersion has led to a thickening of settlement, first in belts of land adjoining central cities and later in successively more distant rings of territory. The creeping spread of the urban component was regulated in the early stages by the rate at which local road systems were extended and elaborated. Whether there was any particular sequence in which residences, services, and industry followed the development of road systems is not known, though there was doubtless a cumulative interaction among the redistributions of these several classes of occupants.

The centripetal movement has concentrated administrative offices and institutions, the services that cater to administrative tasks, and the retailing of expensive and fashionable commodities in the central business district of the central city. This movement has been associated with a less conspicuous centralization of control over the metropolitan system. The spatial rearrangement is an external manifestation of a functional reorganization of an enlarging community. Centralization, however, no longer requires as dense a concentration of coordinating and administrative agencies as once it did. The entire pattern has become more open in the interiors of urban cores as well as the outlying sections. This is well illustrated by the spread of many kinds of professional services. These, too, have been in process of regrouping at locations easily accessible to motorized clienteles. Melvin Webber is unquestionably correct in his view that "the walking-precinct type of central business district, with its restricted radius, its compactness, and its fixed routed transit service, is not the only effective spatial pattern for face-to-face communication." [33] In a more diffuse settlement pattern, of which Los Angeles may be the prototype, vehicular movements consume no more time than walking in a congested place such as Manhattan. It is conceivable that the temporal pattern remains fairly constant while the spatial pattern changes.

Available data are not yet sufficient to permit one to follow the process of metropolitan reorganization in satisfactory detail. A cross-sectional study of forty-four metropolitan areas, as of 1960, provides some insight into how far the relocations have progressed. Using a method devised by O. D. Duncan and his associates,[34] Louis Loewenstein constructed indexes of concentration for eight types of land use relative to five concentric zones in the areas studied.[35] The values of the index range from −1.000 for full concentration in the outermost ring through zero for an even distribution over the five zones to +1.000 for complete concentration in the innermost ring. The resulting averages for the forty-four areas are as follows:

Manufacturing	.2800
Transportation	.3520
Professional service	.4064
Personal service	.4816
Finance, insurance, and real estate	.6896
Retail	.7344
Wholesale	.7276
Public administration	.8400

It is apparent that lands occupied by manufacturing, transportation facilities, and personal and professional services were, in the early 1960's, rather widely scattered over metropolitan areas. Still highly concentrated, on the other hand, were public administration, wholesale, retail, and finance, insurance, and real estate. The fact that all of the indexes indicate some tendency toward centrality should not escape notice.

It is clear that the deconcentration of urban functions has not yet

[33] "Order in Diversity: Community Without Propinquity," in *Cities and Space: The Future of Urban Land,* ed. by Lowdon Wingo, Jr. (Baltimore: Johns Hopkins Press, 1963), p. 45.

[34] P. M. Hauser, O. D. Duncan, and Beverley Davis Duncan, *Methods of Urban Analysis: A Summary Report* (San Antonio: Air Force Personnel and Training Research Center, 1956).

[35] "The Location of Urban Land Uses," *Land Economics,* XXXIX (1963): 407–20.

eliminated the gradient variation in land use intensity. At least one study has demonstrated that land values are still highest in the central business district and taper off as distance is increased.[36] While secondary districts in central and outlying areas have grown in their competitive power, the central district retains its position as a focus of orientation. The advantages of an early start and the existence of a street system designed to maximize its accessibility enable the central district to preserve its edge of superiority.

This is not to say, of course, that gradient aspects of land use have not changed in the process of metropolitan development. They doubtless have become flatter and more extensive, whether represented in land values, in density of land use, or in amounts of specific kinds of land use. The continuous improvement of transportation and communication have attenuated many of the advantages of proximity. How far that tendency may be carried in the future cannot be ascertained now. As the gradients have become flatter they have become smoother. The peaking at intervals where gradients pass through clusters of non-residential land uses is no longer as high as once it was.

SUPPLEMENTARY READINGS

BOGUE, DONALD J. *Metropolitan Growth and the Conversion of Land to Non-Agricultural Uses* (Oxford, Ohio: Scripps Foundation, 1956).

DICKENSON, ROBERT E. *City Region and Regionalism* (New York: Oxford University Press, 1947).

LAZERWITZ, BERNARD. "Metropolitan Community Residential Belts, 1950 and 1960," *American Sociological Review*, XXV (1960): 245–252.

LIND, HAROLD. "Internal Migration in Britain," in *Migration,* Sociological Studies 2. Ed. by J. A. Jackson (Cambridge: The University Press, 1969), pp. 74–98.

STACEY, MARGARET. *Tradition and Change: A Study of Banbury* (London: Oxford University Press, 1960).

THOMPSON, WILBUR R. *A Preface to Urban Economics* (Baltimore: Johns Hopkins Press, 1965).

[36] Warren R. Seyfried, "The Centrality of Urban Land Values," *Land Economics,* XXXIX (1963): 273–84.

8

The Changing Spatial
Orientation of
Metropolitan Residents

The distributions of population, industry, business, and other urban components described in the preceding chapter are the surface features of a fundamental reorganization at work in the expanding urban community. The greatly enlarged range of choice in location decisions afforded by the improved means of short-distance movement has implications for every kind of individual and collective activity. Many of these have already become evident in the emergence of new behavior patterns. Many others are still inchoate. The march of change, though all too rapid in some respects, is in others slowed and deflected by the persistence of anachronisms such, for example, as remnants of the compact city design laid down in the nineteenth century. Even without the presence of resistances and irregularities in change, reorganization would still be a continuous process as long as improvements in transportation and communication are added to existing technology. In this and the following chapter we shall explore the emerging metropolitan organization as fully as the present state of knowledge permits. Because of the magnitude of the changes involved, it will be advisable to divide the material between two chapters. The present chapter will deal mainly with changes in the spatial aspects of the enlarged community. The chapter following will be concerned with shifts of social structure.

POPULATION MOBILITY

It would seem that the great improvements in the facilities for movement might have reduced the need for mobility of modern populations over that of earlier ones. People are now able to remain at a given location and enjoy access to a wide assortment of jobs and opportunities. It is no exaggeration to say that the products and the knowledge of the world can be made available anywhere in a metropolitan area without the necessity for a residence change. In the light of this fact it is interesting to note that in recent years residence changes in the United States have involved an average of 10 percent of the population 5 years of age and over per year. At that rate the entire population could be completely redistributed in a ten-year period. But we have no comparative data that tell us whether such a rate is high or low.[1] The rate does give a somewhat inflated notion of the amount of movement. Persons 5 to 15 or 18 years of age, who comprise approximately one fifth of the total population, are not migrants in the same sense that older persons are; they merely accompany the movements of their parents. Were these eliminated from the data, a rather different result could be obtained.[2]

Data on the lifetime migration histories of the American population have recently become available. This information pertains to the population 18 years of age and over and describes the number of political units —cities or counties—in which individuals have lived for at least one year. They are shown in two ways in Table 30: by place of birth, and by place of present residence. Contrary to popular belief, the residents of large metropolitan centers have been less mobile than the residents of any other kind of place. Almost half (46 percent) of the persons born in central cities of 500,000 or more inhabitants were still living there in 1958 and had lived in no other place. The average number of places of residences of big-city people over the span of their lifetimes was less than two. In general, metropolitan people have not been much more migratory than nonmetropolitan people. The percentage distributions shown in Table 30 conceal many intergroup differences. The white population, for example, has been much more stable than the non-white, and old people have accumulated more places of former residence than have younger ones. In all such groups, of course, the most frequent residence changes occur

[1] Comparative data involving the United States, Canada, England and Wales, Scotland, and Japan, for the period around 1960, however, indicate that residence changes in the United States are 25 to 30 percent more frequent than in the other countries considered. (Larry H. Long, "On Measuring Geographic Mobility," *Journal of the American Statistical Association,* 68 (1970): 1195–1203.

[2] Attention should be called to the fact that in every United States census since 1850, 68 to 70 percent of the population is reported as living in the state of birth. (U.S. Bureau of the Census, *State of Birth.*)

Table 30. Percentage Distribution of Number of Places of Residence
of Population 18 Years of Age and Over
(By Place of Birth and Place of Residence, 1958)

Place of Birth	Number of Places of Residence							
	Total	1	2	2	4	5	6 or More	Median Number
Metropolitan								
500,000 and over	100	46	25	14	7	3	5	1.67
50,000–500,000	100	35	25	18	9	5	8	2.07
2,500– 50,000	100	28	29	20	11	5	8	2.29
Rural nonfarm	100	44	20	16	9	4	7	1.79
Rural farm	100	22	29	23	12	5	9	2.46
Nonmetropolitan								
2,500–50,000	100	21	28	21	12	6	12	2.56
Rural nonfarm	100	23	25	20	12	7	13	2.58
Rural farm	100	20	30	22	12	6	9	2.51
Place of Present Residence								
Metropolitan								
500,000 and over	100	38	37	14	6	2	3	1.82
50,000–500,000	100	25	32	18	10	6	9	2.28
2,500– 50,000	100	13	29	26	14	8	10	2.82
Rural nonfarm	100	18	28	23	13	7	11	2.64
Rural farm	100	35	24	21	11	4	5	2.14
Nonmetropolitan								
2,500–50,000	100	19	28	21	13	7	12	2.65
Rural nonfarm	100	23	24	20	13	7	13	2.61
Rural farm	100	44	19	18	8	4	7	1.83

SOURCE: U.S. Bureau of the Census, "Lifetime Migration Histories of the American People," *Current Population Reports: Technical Studies.* Series P-23, No. 25 (Washington, D.C., 1968), Tables 4 and 8.

within political units and are not, therefore, represented in the data of the table.

THE SIFTING AND SORTING OF POPULATION

As has been shown, the outlying or suburban zones of metropolitan areas have been growing much more rapidly than their central cities. In fact, a substantial part of suburban population growth has been supplied directly from central cities. Approximately two thirds of all present suburban residents formerly lived in central cities. In the 1955–60 residence changes reported by the U.S. Census of 1960, three residents of central cities moved to suburban locations for every one suburban resident who moved to a central city (Table 31). The net gains in the suburban zone resulting from population exchanges with central cities have been highest in the slowest-growing and oldest metropolitan areas. These are the same places for the most part; they also include in their number most of the

Table 31. Percentage Distribution of Residents in Sample of Metropolitan Areas Who Lived in Different Houses in 1960 and 1955 (By Growth Rate and Age of Area)

Type of Residence Change	Per Cent Population Change: 1950–60					
	All Areas	Over 40	30–39	20–29	10–19	Under 10
Total	100	100	100	100	100	100
Central cities to suburbs	11	10	10	14	12	8
Suburbs to central cities	4	5	4	4	3	4
Outside metro areas to suburbs	16	20	12	11	13	11
Outside metro areas to central cities	12	16	18	10	6	8
Within suburbs	25	23	16	25	30	31
Within central cities	32	26	39	36	36	38

Type of Residence Change	Date Central City Attained 50,000 Population					
	All Areas	1940 and After	1920–1940	1900–1920	1880–1900	Before 1880
Total	100	100	100	100	100	100
Central cities to suburbs	11	8	8	10	11	14
Suburbs to central cities	4	5	4	4	5	3
Outside metro areas to suburbs	16	15	27	9	17	11
Outside metro areas to central cities	12	17	21	20	13	6
Within suburbs	25	19	19	14	26	29
Within central cities	32	36	21	43	28	37

SOURCE: U.S. Bureau of the Census, *1960 Census of Population, Census Tracts.*

largest places. Metropolitan areas of these kinds are usually more fully developed in their suburban zones; that is, street networks, urban services, and governmental organization are more adequately prepared for the accommodation of urban populations.

To some extent the imbalance between centrifugal and centripetal streams is a function of the ways in which such areas grew in the past. Until recently both rural-to-urban and overseas migrants, who together supplied a very large proportion of urban growth, settled in central cities; and only much later, sometimes not until the second or third generation, did the migrant or his progeny move into the suburban zone. But with the decline of migration as the principal source of urban growth, internal migration has become increasingly a matter of inter-metropolitan movement. The present tendency is for rural-to-urban migrants to select central cities as destinations, while interurban migrants terminate their moves in suburban zones more frequently than not. A common migration pattern proceeds from nonmetropolitan localities to the central cities of small metropolitan areas and from the latter to the suburban zones of larger metropolitan areas. Table 31 indicates that, the more rapidly growing and the newer the area, the greater is the tendency for migrants from the outside to settle in central cities, while, conversely, migrants to areas that have been growing slowly and have been in existence for a relatively long time are more inclined to settle in suburban zones. In passing, the high frequencies of residence changes within central cities and within suburban areas should be noted; these moves comprise three fifths of all metropolitan moves. There is a milling process that gradually swirls population toward the outer boundaries.

Intra-metropolitan moves exhibit pronounced tendencies toward selectivity.[3] This is especially marked in the residence changes that occur between central cities and suburbs. In the suburbanward stream young families, comprising husband, wife, and school-age children, predominate. On the other hand, in the smaller streams that terminate in central cities the prevalent types of households include couples whose children have matured and have left the parental home, families broken by death and divorce, and single persons. These differences are reflected in the reasons given by persons who have made such moves. Over half of the reasons given for moving from central cities to suburbs have had to do with a quest for privacy, cleanliness, safety, and greater space in house and yard. For these amenities families are willing to sacrifice accessibility and to assume higher residence costs. Persons moving inward to central city destinations are in search of lower housing and utility costs and improved accessibility.[4]

The family life cycle pattern of residence changes points to a change in attitude toward the dwelling place on the part of a large and probably increasing proportion of the population. Whereas the place of residence was once looked upon as the family seat for two or more generations, the house has come to resemble a garment to be put on and off at each turning point in the family's life cycle.[5] The young couple usually starts married life in an apartment, moves to a small house as children begin to appear, shifts to a larger home in the suburbs as the family reaches its maximum size, and returns to small residential quarters, often in the cen-

---

[3] For an early discussion of this tendency see R. D. McKenzie, *The Metropolitan Community* (New York: McGraw-Hill, 1933), pp. 179 ff.

[4] Amos H. Hawley and Basil Zimmer, *The Metropolitan Community: Its People and Government* (Beverley Hills, Calif.: Sage Publications, 1970), pp. 31–33. There is no evidence to indicate that family-size differences as between central cities and suburbs are due to anything other than selectivity. When birth rate comparisons are standardized for age differences there are no significant fertility differences remaining. (*Ibid.*, p. 18.)

[5] Peter Rossi, *Why Families Move. A Study of the Social Psychology of Urban Residential Mobility* (New York: The Free Press, 1955), pp. 177 ff.

tral city, when the children leave to establish homes of their own. This pattern is a generalized one and, therefore, in need of certain qualifications. In small metropolitan areas, where the suburban zones are poorly supplied with urban services, there is no clear-cut evidence of selectivity. Again, the types of people attracted to large suburban municipalities of old metropolitan areas are indistinguishable from those moving to central cities.

Although a selection of household types has been a fairly consistent aspect of intra-metropolitan movement for several decades, there has been in recent years a noticeable shift occurring in the social-economic characteristics of households moving to suburban residences. Formerly, commuting time and costs and the individual outlays required for sewer, water, and other necessary services limited suburban residence to people in upper social-economic levels. Limitations of that kind have all but disappeared. The deconcentration of industry has scattered blue-collar as well as white-collar jobs widely over outlying territory. The proliferation of shopping centers has made commercial services accessible at many locations spotted over metropolitan areas. Similarly, the spread of schools and churches, the completion of street and public utility networks, the nearly universal use of the automobile, and the elimination of local telephone toll charges have removed most of the remaining barriers to suburban settlement by middle- and lower-middle income categories. Consequently, blue-collar workers and others in similar income ranges have been moving suburbanward in ever increasing numbers.[6] No longer is it correct to regard suburban residence as a prerogative of the affluent members of society or as a haven reserved for the aspiring "organization man."

Still, income selectivity on the part of suburban zones has not entirely disappeared. As a matter of fact, at all occupational levels suburbanward movement appears to skim the top off the income range. This is observable in Table 32, which reports results from the study of six metropolitan areas mentioned earlier. Quite possibly the differences shown here would be greater had they been adjusted for age composition differences. It would appear that there are still cost-of-living differences as between suburbs and central cities. These may be due to the higher costs of newer and more spacious residential properties and to the greater amount of transportation expense. In view of the comparative lack of rental housing in suburbs there is also a larger initial demand on wealth for down payments on homes. On the other hand, the centripetal movers tend to have

---

[6] Since 1966 the rate of change of blacks in suburbs has exceeded the rates for the white population, though the sample on which that observation is based is too small to be dependable. (U.S. Bureau of the Census, "Trends in Social and Economic Conditions in Metropolitan Areas," *Current Population Reports: Special Studies,* Series P-23, No. 27 [Washington, D.C., 1969], p. 3.)

Table 32. Median Annual Incomes of Household Heads
(By Size of Metropolitan Area, Occupation,
and Residential Experience)

Size of Area and Occupation of Household Head	Lived Only in Central City	Moved to Suburbs from Central City	Lived Only in Suburbs	Moved to Central City from Suburbs
Large areas: Milwaukee and Buffalo				
Professional, managerial, and official	$6,845	$5,940	$5,434	$6,799
Clerical and sales	4,409[a]	5,742	4,849	4,686
Craftsmen and foremen	4,930	5,653	5,917	5,390
Operatives and service	4,581	5,434	4,957	4,895
Laborers	3,781	5,607	6,257[a]	2,357
Medium-sized areas: Dayton, O. Rochester, N.Y.				
Professional, managerial, and official	$5,765	$7,391	$7,042	$6,311
Clerical and sales	5,044	5,133	5,499	4,740
Craftsmen and foremen	5,208	5,917	4,524	5,040
Operatives and service	4,475	4,813	4,740[a]	4,004
Laborers	3,679	3,982	4,036[a]	4,524
Small areas: Saginaw, Mich., and Rockford, Ill.				
Professional, managerial, and official	$6,283	$7,530	$6,040	$6,474
Clerical and sales	4,957	5,777	4,914	4,849
Craftsmen and foremen	5,031	5,151	5,499	5,694
Operatives and service	4,379	4,819	4,686	4,524
Laborers	3,440	4,524	4,524[a]	3,744

[a]N is 10 or fewer.

SOURCE: Amos H. Hawley and Basil Zimmer, *The Metropolitan Community: Its People and Government,* Beverly Hills, Calif.: Sage Publications, 1970, p. 44.

lower incomes than the non-movers. A comparable income selectivity is found within education classes. If such differentials were to persist, central cities would be left with increasing proportions of their populations in the lowest income classes.[7] The relative position of New York City in its metropolitan area with reference to per capita income, to cite one of the more fully documented cases, declined steadily from 1939 to 1956.[8] Urban renewal efforts and private developments are inducing a small number of well-to-do people to return to the central city. But there is not yet any indication of a trend of that kind sufficient to compensate for the losses to suburban areas, as some observers would like to believe.[9] What

[7] A similar finding emerged from a European study. See Sidney Goldstein, "Some Economic Consequences of Suburbanization in the Copenhagen Metropolitan Area," *American Journal of Sociology,* LXVIII (1963): 551–64.

[8] Rosalind Tough and Gordon D. MacDonald, "The New York Metropolitan Region: Social Forces and the Flight to Suburbia," *Land Economics,* XXXVIII (1961): 329.

[9] Editors of *Fortune, The Exploding Metropolis* (Garden City, N.Y.: Doubleday, 1957), pp. 10–11.

is true today, however, may not be true tomorow. There is no reason not to expect further changes in the pattern of income selectivity.

Various other kinds of selectivity have also operated in the centrifugal movement of population. Most important among these is education. Suburbanward migrants have completed one to two years more formal education on the average than have central city residents. When this loss is considered in conjunction with the departure of the more financially and occupationally successful citizens, it would seem that central city populations are suffering some impairment of their ability to deal with civic issues and problems. As we shall later see, however, the suburbs may not have benefited to the extent expected.

Some of the effects of selectivity on composition of residential population are shown in Table 33. The first two columns show rather clear

Table 33. Selected Characteristics of U.S. Population (By Size and Type of Place, 1960)

Size and Type of Place	Age Percentage Under 15	Age Percentage 65 and Over	Population per Household	Median Years of School	Population Labor Force Male	Population Labor Force Female
Urbanized areas						
3,000,000 or more						
Central cities	25.9	10.0	2.9	10.3	78.9	39.8
Other incorporated places	30.9	7.9	3.3	12.0	82.3	35.3
Urban fringes	30.5	6.1	3.6	12.0	81.8	31.0
1,000,000 to 3,000,000						
Central cities	27.3	10.2	2.9	10.4	78.0	41.2
Other incorporated places	31.7	7.8	3.3	12.1	81.5	34.6
Urban fringes	33.5	6.2	3.5	12.2	83.0	33.6
250,000 to 1,000,000						
Central cities	29.4	9.6	3.0	11.0	78.2	39.0
Other incorporated places	32.7	7.8	3.3	12.0	80.3	34.7
Urban fringes	35.1	5.8	3.5	12.1	82.5	33.6
Under 250,000						
Central cities	30.2	9.2	3.1	11.1	77.7	38.8
Other incorporated places	30.9	8.8	3.3	11.3	77.3	34.4
Urban fringes	34.5	6.0	3.5	11.5	81.0	34.4
Outside urbanized areas but in metropolitan areas						
25,000 or more	29.5	8.3	3.2	11.0	79.4	36.3
10,000 to 25,000	32.2	8.5	3.3	11.4	78.9	34.4
2,500 to 10,000	32.7	8.9	3.3	11.1	78.5	33.7
Rural nonfarm	34.3	6.9	3.6	10.6	77.4	29.6
Farm	32.1	10.0	3.6	9.2	79.7	29.6
Outside urbanized areas and outside metropolitan areas						
25,000 or more	30.2	7.7	3.1	—	76.8	38.3
10,000 to 25,000	30.2	10.0	3.1	—	75.3	37.2
2,500 to 10,000	34.3	6.9	3.1	—	74.7	35.6
Rural nonfarm	33.5	9.7	3.4	—	71.6	28.5
Farm	32.9	9.2	3.6	—	77.8	22.4

SOURCE: U.S. Bureau of the Census, *Seventeenth Census of the United States*, 1960.

age gradients in all sizes of urbanized areas; the proportion of people under 15 years of age rises from the central city through incorporated places and into urban fringes. The proportion 65 years and over follows an opposite slope. These patterns of age variation are repeated in the size classification of places outside of urbanized areas but within metropolitan areas. They are a function, of course, of the distribution of family types as noted earlier and as represented in the average sizes of household shown in the third column of the table. Young and growing families seek the more spacious residential areas. Again, educational achievement corresponds to the age pattern. So also does labor force participation. The opposing patterns for males and females reflect a combination of circumstances. The higher ages of males in the larger cities means more frequent instances of retirement and hence lower labor force rates. On the other hand, the higher participation rates for females in the larger places are due partly to a greater prevalence there of mature families which release women for employment outside the home, and partly to lower family incomes which women try to supplement.

The outward movement is also changing the political composition of suburban and central city electorates. As shown in Table 34, small gains

Table 34. Percentage Distribution of Political Party Affiliations of Household Heads (By Size of Metropolitan Area and Residential Experience)

Size of Area and Political Party Preference	Lived Only in Central City	Moved to Suburbs from Central City	Lived Only in Suburbs	Moved to Central City from Suburbs
Large areas: Milwaukee and Buffalo—				
Total	100	100	100	100
Republican	24	30	35	37
Democratic	41	38	35	36
Independent	24	26	21	24
Don't vote	4	—	3	1
No answer	7	6	6	2
Medium-sized areas: Dayton, O., and				
Rochester, N.Y.—Total	100	100	100	100
Republican	33	34	47	43
Democratic	40	35	23	25
Independent	21	24	22	26
Don't vote	3	3	4	2
No answer	3	3	4	4
Small areas: Saginaw, Mich. and				
Rockford, Ill.—Total	100	100	100	100
Republican	34	32	37	34
Democratic	38	35	30	41
Independent	18	23	19	18
Don't vote	4	2	6	4
No answer	6	8	8	3

in Democratic party strength and small losses in Republican party support occurred in the suburban areas in medium- and small-sized metropolitan areas. The shift in the outer zones of large areas was negligible, though there the central cities gained Republicans. These redistributions conform to a trend extending back to 1948 in the nation at large.[10] It is doubtless the residential movements of blue-collar workers that is carrying a two-party system to suburban areas.

DIFFERENTIATION OF RESIDENTIAL AREAS

The selectivity apparent in the movements to and from suburban areas is not a new phenomenon. It has been operating within the built-up areas of cities, since the inception of mechanized intramural transportation. Now the process operates over a wider area than was formerly possible, differentiating residential areas outside of as well as within central city boundaries. The greatly improved facility in movement and communication has speeded the process and carried it to greater extremes.

The parallel between inner-city zone and suburban zone extends further than is often thought to be the case. The homogeneity of the suburban zone, for example, has been erroneously inferred from the homogeneity within individual territorial units. In point of fact, however, the adoption of specialized roles by villages, towns, and rural districts situated close by large urban centers began early in the course of metropolitan development. The territorial reorganization of industry and business, as was described in the preceding chapter, has been a continuing trend down to the present. The recent changes in suburban selectivity impinge unevenly on outlying territory, contributing still further to the differentiation within that segment of the metropolitan area.

Heterogeneity exists in the distribution of suburban growth. The larger the place, the lower has been its growth rate.[11] Suburbs of 50,000 or more population, in fact, are very much like central cities in growth rates as well as in other demographic characteristics. A difference relative to central cities widens in each smaller size of place category. There are also differences of growth rates within suburban territory by distance from the central city. That has changed over time. The highest growth rates, once characteristic of the space within 5 miles of the central city, have moved outward and are now in the 15- to 20-mile zone.

Diversity among places in relation to distance from central cities has been shown to obtain in a number of population and residence character-

[10] Bernard Lazerwitz, "Suburban Voting Trends: 1948 to 1956," *Social Forces*, XXXIX (1960): 29–36.

[11] Amos H. Hawley, *The Changing Shape of Metropolitan America: Deconcentration since 1920* (New York: The Free Press, 1956), p. 25.

istics. In his study of eleven metropolitan areas, in 1950, Kish found a marked degree of differentiation among minor civil divisions close to central cities and a reduction in the extent of diversity as distance increased.[12] His observations pertained to the proportions of the male labor force in professional and in semiskilled occupations, the proportion of non-white households, dwellings in need of major repairs, average monthly rental value of dwelling units and proportions of voters who voted for Democratic candidates in the last previous election. Schnore, in his analysis of 1960 data, was able to distinguish between employing and residential suburbs and an intermediate class.[13] He noted that these three classes differed consistently in a large number of respects, such as ethnic composition, fertility rates, ratio of dependent to producing members of the population, socioeconomic status, and growth rates.

The pattern of differences among places might be expected to change over time, for metropolitan areas are still in process of accommodating their structures to the greatly enlarged scale of local distances. Yet there is persistence in the midst of change. Farley's study of the average levels of educational attainment of suburban residents revealed that the ranking of places on that measure was not appreciably different in 1960 from what it had been in 1920. Change in ranking was due mainly to growth of population; growth tended to accentuate the distinctiveness of individual places.[14] His finding is reminiscent of Homer Hoyt's "sector" theory of city growth. According to that argument, it will be recalled, areas of the city tend to retain their characteristic features even as they are extended radially in the course of growth.[15]

Continuity of distinguishing characteristics among localities, whether within the central city or beyond its boundaries, has its roots in a number of inertia factors. The housing supply, variously clustered as it is by age, type, and cost, sorts people into fairly lasting social-economic enclaves. Governmentally imposed zoning restrictions and subdivision development practices have helped to shape that distribution pattern. The presence of industry, having also been guided to its location in part at least by zoning regulations, stamps an additional characteristic upon its own and adjacent localities. Industry also affects the fiscal resources of places to an important degree. Suburban units having industrial establishments

[12] Leslie Kish, "Differentiation in Metropolitan Areas," *American Sociological Review*, XIX (1954): 388–98.

[13] Leo F. Schnore, *The Urban Scene* (New York: The Free Press, 1965), ch. 9. See also Marjorie C. Brazer, "Economic and Social Disparities Between Central Cities and Their Suburbs," *Land Economics*, XLIII (1967): 294–302, and R. D. McKenzie, *op. cit.*, p. 180.

[14] Reynolds Farley, "Suburban Persistence," *American Sociological Review*, XXIX (1964): 38–47.

[15] *The Structure and Growth of Residential Neighborhoods in American Cities*, pp. 17 ff.

within their jurisdictions have tax bases that are much richer than are places without industry. That, in turn, tends to influence locational decisions of various other institutions. In short, the accumulation of physical structure establishes the character of a locality for an indefinite period of time. The difference between inner city areas and suburbs in this respect is due largely to the timing and speed of change.

STRATIFICATION AND THE RESIDENTIAL PATTERN

The differentiation of residential areas is to a very large extent a spatial manifestation of social stratification. Social distances tend to be expressed in physical distances. Perhaps the most competent demonstration of this phenomenon is in a study executed by O. D. Duncan and Beverley Duncan.[16] While their study dealt only with a single place, Chicago, it has the virtue of pertaining to the entire metropolitan area as then defined. Using the simple measure for comparing two distributions described earlier,[17] with census tracts as the units of observation,[18] the results shown in Table 35 were obtained. It is evident in the first column that the occupational groups at the extremes of the scale were the most highly segregated, i.e., their distributions differed most radically from the distribution of all workers. Clerical workers, on the other hand, were the least segregated. The status of clerical workers was and is still ambiguous; they are somewhat better educated than craftsmen and foremen, but their earnings are lower. The remaining columns of the table describe how dissimilar were the distributions of each pair of occupations. Thus professional workers and managers, officials, and proprietors were residentially distributed in a fairly similar pattern. The separation of professional workers widened in comparison with each succeeding class of occupation and is shown to be greatest where laborers are concerned. This scale effect tends to appear as one goes down the occupation list, though it becomes somewhat blurred in the lowest categories. Again the status of clerical workers is seen to not be in accord with its white-collar character.

In a second study, conducted in the Wilmington, Delaware, metropoli-

---

[16] "Residential Distribution and Occupational Stratification," *American Journal of Sociology*, LX (1955): 493–503. See also Eugene S. Uyeki, "Residential Distribution and Stratification, 1950–1960," *American Journal of Sociology*, LXIX (1964): 491–98.

[17] Half the sum of the percentage point differences between two percentage distributions in both of which the classes are ordered by the same principle. The index of segregation compares each occupation against all other occupations taken together. The index of dissimilarity compares pairs of occupations.

[18] A census tract is a segment of urban space delimited for statistical purposes and comprising roughly 8,000 to 12,000 residents. The Chicago Metropolitan District contained 1,178 census tracts.

Table 35. Indexes of Segregation and of Dissimilarity Among Residential Distributions of Major Occupational Groups, Chicago Metropolitan Area

Major Occupation Group	Index of Segregation	Index of Dissimilarity							
		Professional, Technical Workers	Officials, Managers, Proprietors	Sales Workers	Clerical Workers	Craftsmen, Foremen	Operatives	Service Workers	Laborers
Professional, technical, and kindred workers	30	—	13	15	28	35	44	41	54
Managers, officials, and proprietors	22	—	—	13	28	33	41	40	52
Sales workers	29	—	—	—	27	35	42	38	54
Clerical and kindred workers	13	—	—	—	—	16	21	24	38
Craftsmen, foremen, and kindred workers	19	—	—	—	—	—	17	35	35
Operatives and kindred workers	22	—	—	—	—	—	—	26	25
Service workers	24	—	—	—	—	—	—	—	28
Laborers, except farm workers	.35	—	—	—	—	—	—	—	—

SOURCE: Adapted from O. D. Duncan and Beverley Duncan, *op. cit.* "Residential Distribution and Occupational Stratification," *American Journal of Sociology,* LX (1955); Tables 2 and 3.

tan areas, education appeared to be a more discriminating influence on the quality of housing occupied than was occupation.[19]   Once again the ambiguity of the clerical vis-à-vis the skilled worker or craftsman was evident. Taken together, these findings confirm further what is generally assumed to be the case: the criteria of status are not consonant with one another; and so long as they are not, the existence of social class is questionable.

Divergences among rank criteria, such as occupation, income, and education, are partly responsible for the less than complete homogeneity found in residential areas. Various other factors also contribute to a mixture of types. One of these is the symbiosis that exists among certain strata. Janitors, for example, occupy basement quarters in apartment houses inhabited by middle- and upper-income groups, and domestic servants live as close as possible to the residence of their employers.[20] The flow of change may be of even greater importance. Change occurs in the amenities of areas as a result of the encroachment of objectionable land uses or shifts in the accessibility of the locality to other parts of the urban system. But the turnover of residents is not instantaneous. The speed with which one population type succeeds another depends on many local circumstances; as long as there is some delay, heterogeneity will increase before there is an approach once again to relative homogeneity.

Change also occurs in the meaning of familiar rank criteria. As Kurt Mayer and others have shown, the ranges of differences in income and in education in the United States have narrowed significantly over the past few decades. Differences in behavior patterns which once were associated with rank position, as in habits of consumption and mortality and fertility rates, are disappearing.[21] Needless to say, should invidious rankings vanish, no residential clustering on such a basis could exist. But that eventuality lies far in the future. In the meantime new criteria for scaling social "worth" might be introduced.

Residential districts in growing urban areas are continuously exposed to change. In an earlier chapter it was pointed out that the growth of the central business district pushed a belt of obsolescent properties ahead of the advancing edge. The residential buildings adjacent to that belt lose their attractiveness for family life as nonresidential uses encroach upon their locale. In recent years the scope of residential obsolescence has

[19] Charley Tilly, "Occupational Rank and Grade of Residence in a Metropolis," *American Journal of Sociology*, LXVII (1961): 323–30.

[20] The manner of defining areas is responsible for some heterogeneity. Census tracts, which are extensively used for the purpose, are composed of square blocks in cities and in outlying areas of larger space bounded on four sides by roads. In each case opposite faces of such rectangles are often occupied by contrasting land uses.

[21] "Diminishing Class Differentials in the United States," *Kyklos: International Review for Socal Scence*, XII (1959): 605–28, and Christopher Jencks and David Riesman, "On Class in America," *The Public Interest* (Winter, 1968): 65–85.

widened well beyond the reach of central business district influence. It develops, too, from other points in an urban area such as industrial sites and the locations of secondary business districts.

The life cycle of residential districts has been described as a series of stages by Hoover and Vernon.[22] Stage one is characterized by new, single-family residences and a relatively low density of settlement. In stage two new construction in the district shifts to multiple-residence units, some of which replace original single-family units. Population increases and alters its composition toward an enlarging proportion of small families and childless couples. Downgrading of the district begins in stage three in which old housing, both single and multiple family units, is adapted to a greater density of occupance than was contemplated in the initial design. New construction has stopped; open land has long since been occupied and speculators are now biding their time for a rise in land values. It is usually in this stage that the district is taken over by an ethnic or minority group. It soon acquires the designation of a slum. At this point the properties sink steadily into disrepair, partly, as Jane Jacobs has pointed out, because credit agencies have been unwilling to lend money for their rehabilitation.[23] Stage four is marked, say Hoover and Vernon, by a thinning out of population due to the scattering of members of the younger generation and to demolitions of decrepit buildings. Finally the renewal stage, number five, is reached. In this stage the land passes to a new class of uses. That may be high-rise apartments or nonresidential uses, such as for stores and shops, office buildings, or parking lots.

There is no necessity that the life cycle of residential districts should have precisely five stages or any other number. Nor is there any definite duration of the stages. An area may remain at the threshold of stage four indefinitely, where, for example, an underprivileged group has nowhere else to go. Discrimination against blacks has preserved their segregation in districts of dilapidated and unsanitary housing. Similarly, there is nothing automatic in the progression to a renewal stage. Areas have remained in a state of blight in some cities for years. On the other hand, with external assistance, such as the federal government's urban renewal program, the transition of an area to another use can be effected in a short period of time.

TRAVEL PATTERNS

As population, industry, and commercial establishments have spread more widely over metropolitan areas, the flux of daily movement has be-

[22] *The Anatomy of a Metropolis,* pp. 192 ff.
[23] *The Life and Death of Great American Cities* (New York: Random House, 1961), pp. 294 ff.

come a much more prominent feature of urban life. It was remarked elsewhere that the separation of work from place of residence became steadily more prevalent during the nineteenth century. By the second decade of the present century the average distance from home to work place was 1.5 miles, if the finding from a Chicago study may be taken as representative.[24] Subsequently work-trip distance lengthened rapidly, and by 1960 such distances averaged 4.7 miles. Traffic origin and destination studies conducted in a number of urban areas during the 1950's measured the work trip in minutes rather than in miles. Distances varied from 15 to 30 minutes on the average, depending on the size of the territory encompassed by the boundaries of urban units. Since then, work-trip lengths have doubtless increased somewhat. For work places have continued to scatter over metropolitan areas, a great amount of expressway mileage has been constructed, and multiple-car ownership has become more common. The centrifugal movement of blue-collar residences, however, have tended to shorten work-trip distances for that element of the population.

The methods of getting to and from work in the United States, in 1960, are shown in Table 36. Almost two thirds of the workers rely on the pri-

**Table 36. Percentage Distribution of U.S. Labor Force
(By Method of Transportation to Work
and Place of Residence, 1960)**

Type of Place of Residence	Auto or Car Pool	Railroad and Subway	Bus or Street Car	Walk	Worked at Home	Not Reported	Total
Total	64	4	8	10	7	7	100
Urban	64	5	11	10	3	7	100
Urbanized area	62	7	13	8	3	7	100
Central cities	55	9	17	9	3	7	100
Urban fringe	74	3	8	7	3	5	100
Other Urban	71	0	2	16	4	7	100
10,000 and over	71	0	3	15	4	7	100
2,500–10,000	72	0	1	17	3	7	100
Rural	63	0	1	10	19	7	100
Nonfarm	72	0	1	11	8	8	100
Farm	37	0	1	6	51	5	100

SOURCE: U.S. Bureau of the Census, 1960, *Census of Population.*

vately operated motor vehicle; the proportion approaches three fourths in urban fringes and in small urban places. Public mass carriers are impor-

[24] Beverley Duncan, "Factors in Work-Residence Separation: Wage and Salary Workers, 1951," *American Sociological Review,* XXI (1956): 48–56.

tant only in the large urban centers. The proportion walking to work in urban areas suggest that they still provide some measure of convenience. But the 11 percent of workers living in rural nonfarm areas who walk to work is difficult to understand without additional information.

As the length and mode of travel to and from work places changed, the general configuration of traffic flows has also been altered. Formerly the flows moved mainly along radial routes, converging on the inner part of the central city in the mornings and dispersing along the same routes again in the late afternoon. These movements have given way increasingly to lateral and circumferential flows. Suburban residents commute to suburban employment destinations. Traffic congestion which was once peculiar to the large city has become common over large sections of metropolitan areas, especially at peak hours. Many suburban areas now experience policing and road maintenance problems comparable to those of the central city. The surviving radial movements involve almost as many blue-collar workers moving outward to suburban industrial establishments as white-collar workers moving inward to employment in the central business district.

Differences in journey-to-work patterns reflect variations in the distribution of available housing. That is most clearly demonstrated in the comparisons of white with non-white workers. Work-trip distances for white workers range from 3 miles for laborers to 7 miles for professional workers. Among non-white workers, those with blue-collar jobs travel farther than those with white-collar jobs.[25] The latter are frequently located in black establishments situated in or nearby Afro-American residential areas. But the blue-collar jobs for blacks are found in white establishments which are often located at fairly long distances from black residences.

The lengthening of the daily trip to work is, among other things, a measure of the adaptive potential of the labor force to possible shifts in the distribution of job opportunities.[26] A working force that travels an average of 5 miles or 30 minutes from home to work place can, should given employment be terminated for any reason, accept alternative employment within that radius while maintaining its original place of residence. Or the principal workers of families can adjust residential choices to that extent in order to allow shorter work trips to supplemental workers in their households.

[25] James O. Wheeler, "Work-Trip Lengths and the Ghetto," *Land Economics,* LIV (1968): 107–12; and Beverley Duncan, *op. cit.,* p. 50.

[26] This is the main thesis of Kate E. Liepman's study on *The Journey to Work: Its Significance for Industrial and Community Life* (New York: Oxford University Press, 1944).

THE NEIGHBORHOOD

The trend toward the removal of household functions from the home to specialized agencies, begun in the nineteenth century,[27] has continued down to the present. Specialists have invaded even the intimate affairs of the family, as represented by homes for the aged, marriage and family counseling agencies, juvenile courts, domestic financial consultants, day nurseries, wedding and party managers, and shopping services, to mention but a few. Every such removal of a function from the home, it will be recalled, creates another destination to be visited. Whereas in 1920 the daily per capita vehicular miles traveled was 1.4, in 1960 the per capita figure for metropolitan streets and roads was 5.6 miles.[28] The members of an average urban household make five or more private automobile trips per day in pursuit of their normal activities, as may be seen in Table 37.

**Table 37. Daily Frequencies of Motor Vehicle Trips
in Selected Urban Areas
(1953–59)**

Urban Area	Year of Survey	Trips per Person	Trips per Dwelling	Persons per Dwelling	Cars per Dwelling
Chicago, Ill.	1956	1.9	6.0	3.1	0.8
Detroit, Mich.	1953	1.8	5.9	3.3	0.9
Washington, D.C.	1955	1.7	5.0	3.0	0.8
Pittsburgh, Pa.	1958	1.6	5.3	3.3	0.9
St. Louis, Mo.	1957	1.9	6.0	3.1	0.9
Houston, Texas	1953	2.2	7.2	3.2	0.9
Kansas City, Mo.	1957	2.2	6.7	3.1	1.0
Phoenix, Ariz.	1957	2.3	6.9	3.0	1.0
Nashville, Tenn.	1959	2.3	7.5	3.3	1.0
Fort Lauderdale, Fla.	1959	1.7	3.6	2.2	0.8
Charlotte, N.C.	1958	2.4	8.1	3.4	1.0
Reno, Nev.	1955	2.5	6.9	2.8	1.1

SOURCE: Compiled from origin and destination traffic studies, by Wilbur Smith and Associates, *Future Highways and Urban Growth* (New Haven, Conn., 1961), p. 65.

From 1940 to 1963 the amount spent on transportation by consumers increased by 190 percent, to almost three times what it had been.[29] A

[27] See Chapter 6. Some tendency toward a reversal of the trend developed with the do-it-yourself industry and the television industry, though these appear not to have altered fundamentally the general movement.

[28] *Automobile Facts and Figures* (Detroit: Automobile Manufacturers Association, 1962), pp. 46–47.

[29] Wilfred Owen, *The Metropolitan Transportation Problem* (Garden City, N.Y.: Doubleday, 1965), p. 237.

great amount of the increased leisure time created by modern technology is being absorbed by daily trips to the many destinations a family must visit.

The territorial spread of destinations regularly visited varies fairly systematically with social-economic status. That is, the higher the income and education of the urban resident, the wider ranging are his activities and the less dependent he is on what is available in the immediate vicinage about his home.[30] There is also a life-cycle influence on the scope of routine circulations. The spread of activities widens with age, narrows during the family rearing phase, expands once more as children grow to maturity, and contracts again after retirement age is reached.

Changes in travel patterns raise interesting questions about the social significance of the residential vicinage in the metropolitan community. When walking was second only to the street railway as a means of getting from point to point, one rarely traveled beyond a half-mile or a ten-minute distance for purposes other than work. The narrow ambit encompassed nearly all of his interests and activities. He usually found there his life-long friends and his marriage partner. The familiarity bred in the close quarters of the immediate locale enabled approval and censure to operate as effective controls on individual behavior. No longer can that be true, except among persons who are unable to utilize the new facilities for movement and communication. Individuals who range far and wide over the metropolitan area need not submit to the limited choices in the vicinage nor to the surveillance of their neighbors.

Proximity of residences is manifestly no assurance of interaction among individuals and families, despite the grouping of households in ever more homogeneous clusters. The greater their similarity, the less have people to say to one another. They are able now as never before to choose their associates and their avocations from an area at least as broad as the metropolitan community.[31] Thus it is not surprising that Caplow and Foreman found in a pilot study of 134 Minneapolis residential localities that the mean interaction rating, measured on a six-point scale, was less than one third (1.47) of the range provided by the scale.[32] In the study of the six metropolitan areas, mentioned earlier, only one third of the suburban residents had any contact with the occupants of adjacent houses; the corresponding proportion in central cities was one fifth.[33]

[30] See Donald L. Foley, "The Use of Local Facilities in a Metropolis," *American Journal of Sociology,* LVI (1950): 238–246, and *Neighbors or Urbanites? The Study of A Rochester Residential District* (University of Rochester, Department of Sociology, mimeographed, 1952).

[31] Cf. Melvin M. Webber, "Culture, Territoriality and the Elastic Mile," *Papers of the Regional Science Association,* XIII (1964): 59–70.

[32] Theodore Caplow and Robert Foreman, "Neighborhood Interaction in a Homogeneous Community," *American Sociological Review,* XV (1950): 360.

[33] Hawley and Zimmer, *op. cit.,* pp. 54–55.

One of the few comparative studies of neighbor activity involving inner city, outer city, and suburb was reported by Sylvia Fava. She observed, through the means of a field survey, the frequency of interchanges between neighbors in small samples residing in Manhattan, Queens, and suburban Nassau. The findings indicated increased incidence of activity at each degree of removal from the inner core of Manhattan, especially when age, sex, marital status, length of residence, nativity, and size of community of childhood residence were controlled.[34] It is unfortunate that some very important factors so far as neighbor behavior is concerned were left uncontrolled: characteristics such as family composition, the employment status of women, family income, and the physical arrangement of housing units. Had the three sample populations been standardized on these characteristics, it is likely that a rather different pattern of frequencies of neighboring would have been observed.

Small though the frequency of interactions among neighbors in contemporary urban areas seems to be, there is actually no standard of what is or should be expected. Moreover, it may well be that occasional and somewhat superficial contacts with neighbors are all that is needed as a complement to the more time-consuming associations with friends and relatives. At least one study has revealed that a modest amount of neighboring is sufficient to assure satisfaction with a place of residence.[35]

The viability of the residential cluster as an associational unit appears to vary inversely with the social and economic level of the occupants much as it does for other kinds of interests. For households in the upper reaches of the status scale the residence place may be simply that and nothing more. The detachment from the locality is set aside, however, during the child-rearing stage of the family life cycle. In that interval parental associations develop about the play patterns of children and last as long as childhood play requires supervision and guidance. Apart from that common interest, a crisis generated by a threat to the value of the residential properties or to the physical well-being of the residents may be required to draw the neighbors into direct interactions with one another. The unity attained in that fashion tends to last no longer than the crisis. Home owners' protective associations are notorious for their short life spans. The middle-class suburb, like the comparable residential area in the large city, possesses few if any primary group mechanisms.[36]

[34] "Contrasts in Neighboring: New York City and a Suburban County," in *The Suburban Community,* ed. by William Dobriner (New York: G. P. Putnam and Son, 1958), pp. 122–31.

[35] John Gulick, Charles E. Bowerman and Kurt W. Back, "Newcomer Acculturation in the City: Attitudes and Participation," in *Urban Growth Dynamics,* ed. by F. Stuart Chapin, Jr., and Shirley F. Weiss (New York: John Wiley and Sons, 1962), p. 341.

[36] Robert Gutman, "Population Mobility in the American Middle Class," in *The Urban Condition,* ed. by Leonard Duhl (New York: Basic Books, 1963), p. 175.

While the residential neighborhood has been waning as a social unit, it has gained importance among city planners as a unit of urban design.[37] The assumption appears to be that, if a residential area is held to a given size, is developed with certain distinctive architectural or design features, and is built about a school or shopping center, the residents will enter into frequent associations and cultivate a relatively intense local life. Thus the social characteristics of the rural small town, as romanticized in the nostalgic literature, can be reproduced in the big, anonymous, and impersonal urban world. All available evidence, however, runs counter to these assumptions, as we have seen. The urban area invites a cosmopolitan rather than a parochial experience. Not all planners, however, have sympathized with the neighborhood concept of urban design. Some regard it as an anachronism, others as a thinly disguised justification of segregation.[38] It is questionable that the small rural town as it actually existed bears a very close resemblance to the image of it that lingers in the minds of its champions.[39] The price paid for its simple and self-sufficient social life was at least a restriction of opportunity and at most excessive conservatism, bigotry, and a narrow view of the universe.

Among members of the lower social-economic levels, to whom the thoughts of planners seldom stray except to contemplate the demolition of their residential quarters, locality serves as a much more effective basis for organized social life. Limited education, ethnic dissimilarity or minority group status, and relative poverty circumscribe the opportunites for participation in the larger community. An active discrimination from the majority group builds higher the walls of isolation. Underprivileged groups are thus turned inward upon themselves. Of necessity they cultivate patterns of behavior and normative standards that enable them to survive in the inhospitable environment. These often take the form of tolerance of illicit occupations and physical assaults against outsiders. High frequencies of arrests for delinquency and crime have prompted a characterization of the residential areas in question as "disorganized." No other term in the language of sociology is as misleading as this; nor is any term more revealing of the biases of the user. The residential areas of the poor and the ethnically different are usually highly organized, though not in the middle-class pattern, as a long series of studies by Thrasher, Wirth, Zorbaugh, Gans, Suttles, and numerous others have

[37] Harlan Bartholomew, "The Neighborhood: Key to Urban Redemption," *Annals American Planning and Civic Association* (1949): 234–56, and C. A. Doxiadis, "The American Greek City and the City of the Present," *Ekistics*, XVIII (1964): 360.

[38] Catherine Bauer (Worster), *Social Questions in Housing and Town Planning* (London: University of London Press, 1952), p. 26 and Reginald Isaacs, "The Neighborhood Theory," *Journal American Institute of Planners*, XIV (1948): 15–23.

[39] See Richard Dewey, "The Neighborhood, Urban Ecology and City Planners," *American Sociological Review*, XV (1950): 502–507.

clearly shown.[40] Organization is evident in the presence of various peer groups and gangs equipped with explicit rules and procedures, in ethnic churches, food stores, bars and other establishments, in communication networks, and in clear understandings of who belongs to the neighborhood and of proper behavior relative to outsiders. That these elements of organization may not be approved by the community at large is beside the point; approval is not a criterion of organization.

Even so, the frequency of informal associations with occupants in adjacent residence units in working class areas is not great.[41] Where kinsmen are present, interactions are confined to relatives. The fact of the matter seems to be that since neighboring seldom involves more than seven or eight families, the probability that the requisite compatibilities will exist between persons in nearby dwelling units is relatively small. There is bound to be unevenness, therefore, in the spacing of associational patterns.

SUMMARY

The reconstitution of urban areas in metropolitan form has involved a general reorientation of the population to distances, locations, and places. Basic to an understanding of modern urban phenomena is the extraordinary reduction of the friction of space brought about by the new means of movement and communication. The enormous increase in the range of location choice must be acknowledged as a prior condition in explanation of almost all differences between urban characteristics of past and present. It has also admitted a large element of randomness into the decision process with the result that explanation has become more difficult.

The large degree of freedom, once enjoyed only in the upper social-economic levels, is rapidly extending into lower strata of the population. Hence blue-collar and low-skilled white-collar workers have joined the suburbanward movement. Selectivity persists, however, especially in respect to family life cycle states. Although occupational selectivity has diminished, the suburbs draw off the top income levels within each occupation. One consequence threatened by this selectivity is that central cities may be left with increasing proportions of poor and insufficiently educated people.

The redistribution of population re-creates in a more open pattern the

[40] Frederick M. Thrasher, *The Gang* (Chicago: University of Chicago Press, 1927), Louis Wirth, *The Ghetto* (Chicago: University of Chicago Press, 1928); Harvey M. Zorbaugh, *The Gold Coast and the Slum* (Chicago: University of Chicago Press, 1929); Herbert J. Gans, *The Urban Villagers* (New York: The Free Press, 1962); Gerald D. Suttles, *The Social Order of the Slum* (Chicago: University of Chicago Press, 1968).

[41] Phillip Fellin and Eugene Litwak, "Neighborhood Cohesion Under Conditions of Mobility," *American Sociological Review*, XXVIII (1963): 366–76.

same kinds of social-economic segregation that have existed in the central city. Indeed, the extent of homogeneity with small areas may be even greater than in the past. But the mere residential congregation of people of similar income and occupational characteristics is no assurance that they will enter into a correspondingly localized social life. On the contrary, their facility for movement, in fact the necessity that they travel frequently and far to secure their daily needs, disperses their interests and leaves little time for neighborhood interaction. An exception occurs during the child-rearing period. Nevertheless, the tendency is for small territorial units to be absorbed and stripped of their identities by the larger universe of activity. The easy mobility of modern man may induce in him an indifference to environmental details. While the area of his vehicular travels expands, the scope of his pedestrian movement contracts. Hence he spends relatively little time in the prolonged association and close observation that familiarity with place demands. Whether this means a transfer of a sense of responsibility to a larger community or simply an abrogation of responsibility is open to debate.

The cosmopolitan life with its emancipation from locality is not available to the entire population of the metropolitan area. At the bottom of the social-economic pyramid are a substantial number of people who live a territorially circumscribed existence. Poverty, discrimination, and alienation confine them to narrow quarters and a partial institutional participation. Local life is organized, not in the manner of the population majority, but in ways that are expedient and workable.

SUPPLEMENTARY READINGS

BOLLENS, JOHN C., and SCHMANDT, HENRY J. *The Metropolis: Its People, Politics, and Economic Life* (New York: Harper and Row, 1970).

ROGERS, ANDREI. "Theories of Intra-Urban Spatial Structure: A Dissenting View," *Land Economics*, XLIII (1967): 108–111.

SMITH, JOEL, and MADDOX, G. L. "Spatial Location and the Use of Selected Facilities in a Middle-Size City," *Social Forces*, XXXVIII (1959): 119–124.

WEBBER, MELVIN, *et al. Explorations into Urban Structure* (Philadelphia: University of Pennsylvania, 1964).

ZIMMER, BASIL, and HAWLEY, AMOS H. "Significance of Membership in Associations in the Central City and in the Fringe Area," *American Journal of Sociology*, LXV (1959): 196–201.

9

Organization in the Metropolitan Community

THE INCREASING SCALE OF SOCIAL UNITS

Metropolitan development, as has been noted in two or three earlier connections, has carried forward a number of trends that were initiated in preceding phases of the urbanization process. Among these, one that is especially important is the increase in the sizes of the units in which men live and work. The trend has proceeded as an involution. That is, it has moved through a differentiation and a regrouping of subdivided functions in new and larger combinations. For some time, extending into the twentieth century, the growth in the sizes of industrial and business firms was of a modest order. It consisted mainly of a multiplication of new extra-familial units engaged in varying degrees of specialized activities. Although the modal unit in the 1920's was small to medium in size, industrial giants were beginning to be more common. In 1929 there were 1,000 firms in the United States with assets of $20 million or more; they employed one of every six workers.[1] At that time half the corporate assets

[1] Thomas C. Cochran, *The American Business System* (New York: Harper Torchbook, 1957), p. 60.

were owned by 200 nonbanking firms.[2] The growth of industrial firm size
was slowed in the 1930's and resumed in the years following World War
II.

Growth in size has resulted from a number of converging developments.
Not the least important of these is the territorial enlargement of urban
systems. Increases in the scope of the market, or, in the case of nonprofit units, in the sizes of potential clienteles, permitted corresponding
increases in the sizes of organized units. The rise of the metropolitan
community attached an expanded local market more firmly to a major
urban center while also affording a more effective penetration of distant
markets by the operating units of the center. It thus became possible to
take advantage of the stream of improvements in technology springing
from centers of cultural change. On the mechanical side the improvements led to more elaborate and more costly equipment. Large volumes
of production are necessary to amortize the capital costs of modern industry. Volume of production, size of producing unit, and scope of the
market are interrelated responses to capital costs. The interaction works
in various ways in different circumstances. New developments in diagnos-
tic equipment have pushed the capital costs of medical practice beyond
the reach of the individual doctor. Hence group practice has replaced
individual practice and the bureaucracy of the hospital has encroached
upon the doctor's freedom to an increasing degree. On the other hand,
the organization of the construction industry in small units devoted to
handicraft methods held that industry in the grip of inertia. Consequently
the use of heavy equipment that has been available and easily adaptable,
such as mechanically powered winches, derricks, and earth moving vehicles, was long delayed. The construction industry has not yet caught
up with the technology available to it.

The impetus to increasing size has been slow to reach into industries
other than manufacturing and transportation. Most of the other sectors
of society, such as commerce, service industries, and nonprofit activities
of all kinds, have been relatively unmechanized until recently. They have
not required capital in amounts comparable to the heavier industries.
And, not having large capital requirements, there have been few economies of scale that might provide an inducement to growth. Mechanization is now rapidly invading these spheres of activity. Numerous clerical,
accounting, and information storage and processing tasks are being absorbed into electronic and other tools.

Not all technological improvements are mechanical, however. As
Cochran has pointed out, the assembly line, which proved so instrumental
in the acceleration of production, was an administrative or organizational

---

[2] Adolph A. Berle and Gardner C. Means, *The Modern Corporation and Private
Property* (New York: Macmillan, 1944), p. 19.

invention. It required no new tools, but merely a rearrangement of the tools currently in use.[3] In a study of the effect of mechanization on the sizes of plants, Baldemus demonstrated that the ways in which tools are employed exerted a significant effect on plant size independently of the nature or amount of mechanization.[4] A distinction between technology and organization is arbitrary. Every feature of organization is a way of accomplishing something, whether it is to use a tool, to assemble the funds necessary for the acquisition of the tool, to manage the personal relationships involved in the use of the tool, or to preserve an environment congenial to the invention and application of tools. Thus the distinction comes down to the difference between the physical tool—the hardware—and the behavior essential to the tool's use—the software.

THE CORPORATE UNIT

Growth of size was enormously facilitated by the adoption of another non-mechanical technique. This was the application of a standard corporate structure to the organization of units. This form of organization, known as the corporation, includes a prescribed set of roles and responsibilities, public accountability, and legal recognition as a unit independent of the persons who carry out its functions. It made possible the mobilization of huge amounts of capital under centralized control. The separation of ownership from control of wealth contributed great flexibility to operations, for it injected a large element of impersonality into procedures and simplified the recruitment of competent personnel. Security is enhanced by, on the one hand, the transfer of risks from individuals to an organization, and, on the other hand, by an unlimited longevity of the organization.[5] The obvious advantages of these several characteristics led to a spread of the corporate form from one sector of society to another. It was applied first, in the 1840's, to public utilities, common carriers, banks, insurance companies, and wherever fixed capital costs were high; it came late to retailing and other service industries where capital costs exist mainly as inventories.[6] Agriculture was also late in adopting the corporate form, though for reasons other than low capital costs. By the

---

[3] *Op. cit.*, p. 39.

[4] W. Baldemus, "Mechanization, Utilization and Size of Plant," *Economic Journal*, LXIII (1953): 66–69.

[5] A difference should be recognized between private and quasi-public corporations. The latter obtains its resources from an investing public. It is this type that prevails in the economic sphere. The private corporation is not open to public investment; its capital resources originate from a family or some other closed group. The private corporation is found mainly in spheres of nonprofit activity. There are, however, numerous variations on both of these types.

[6] Berle and Means, *op. cit.*, p. 17.

1960's the number of corporations in business and industry numbered around one million in the United States alone.

The corporate form has been carried into numerous fields of collective activity beyond business and industry. Municipal governments, churches, educational institutions, hospitals, charitable organizations, *ad hoc* agencies of national governments, and even families have availed themselves of the advantages of incorporation. In a modern developed society corporations have multiplied to such an extent that there are few remaining interstices among them. As one author put it: "There is no longer an unincorporated frontier: corporations everywhere meet and either conflict or coalesce, and consequently, lose their identity and independence. Such a mixing and confusion of corporate forms may be comparable to the breakdown of the village and the drift to the great cities . . ." [7] If one were to attempt to count the corporations in which he is directly and indirectly involved, the number would run quickly into several dozen before he lost track of his count in the labyrinth of overlappings and superimpositions.

There is another and perhaps more compelling cause of the adoption by interrelated organizations of a corporate form. The greater the frequency of interactions and the more extensive the sequences of linkages through which exchanges are transmitted, the more imperative is the possession by all units of similar instrumentalities for communication. Differences in that respect lead to recurring problems of translation from the terms of one instrument to those of another, with costs in time and overhead and risks of possible losses of information. Consequently interacting units tend to acquire similar structures and counterpart functions, they resort to uniform reporting and accounting procedures, and they govern themselves with constitutions and parliamentary rules. The movement toward uniformity of structure leaves no class of units unaffected; nonprofit as well as profit units must submit to the same generalizing influence or invite some degree of isolation from the main flows of information. In other words, a single principle of organization tends to operate in all interrelated human groupings. Whether that is equally true of the system and its subsystems, the whole and the parts, constitutes an important theoretical issue.

Although the corporation is defined and regulated in law, it is not to be understood as a creation of the law. There are other less redundant explanations for the corporation's ubiquitous presence in modern society. It is the answer to a general need for an organization unhampered by the disabilities of the family. In the sociological view a corporate unit is an assemblage of individuals who by virtue of their special and comple-

[7] Scott Buchanan, "The Corporation and the Public," in *The Corporation Take-Over*, ed. by Andrew Hacker (Garden City, N.Y.: Doubleday, 1965), pp. 27–28.

mentary skills are able to perform a given task more efficiently together than they could separately. It is a group the distinctive features of which is a division of labor. In that sense the corporate unit, if not the corporation, antedates its recognition in formal law by a long span of time.

We have spoken before of the movement toward standardization. The rising scale of organization coupled with the spreading adoption of the corporate organization operate as powerful factors in the further standardization of the conditions of individual life. The influence is exerted on many fronts at once. Organizations define the functional niches individuals occupy, make the products they consume, design the services individuals receive, and regulate the terms of their participation in communal and societal affairs. A great proportion of each individual's life is lived in and by means of formally constituted units of organization. The external evidence of that is apparent enough. Internal effects on individual thought and judgment are too ramified for easy summation. One solid bit of evidence on the extent of the penetration of corporate influence lies in the trend with respect to innovations. In 1900 four fifths of all patents were issued to individuals, the rest to corporations. In 1960 the distribution was almost reversed: 62 percent of all patents were awarded to corporations and 38 percent to individuals. The institutionalization of innovation reflects, on the one hand, the decline of self-employment and the absorption of occupations into corporate structures and, on the other hand, the mounting costs of exploration and experimentation which few individuals can sustain.

Needless to say, the organizational changes involved in urban expansion carry both negative and positive effects to the individual. So it is with all major social changes. What is cost and what is benefit are, of course, matters of opinion. Hence the net effect of change is endlessly debatable. It might be proposed for the sake of argument, however, that the removal of the individual from direct participation in the control of organizations through the growth and elaboration of bureaucratic structures and through the increasingly technical nature of operating procedures and problems threatens to deprive him of his sense of personal worth and tends to generate apathy and purposelessness.[8] These symptoms of mental ill-health, assuming they are correctly assessed, might conceivably be aggravated by standardization, which seems to lay a pall of sameness over everything. Individuality is suppressed thereby and creativity is faced with extinction. Diagnoses such as this come from looking too intently at a few aberrant individuals and not noticing the larger scene. For it must be recognized that contemporary individuals enjoy

[8] Victor A. Thompson presents a very interesting analysis of how this malady develops among entrepreneurs in *Modern Organization: A General Theory* (New York: A. A. Knopf, 1961), pp. 138–77

access to a diversity of materials, information, and experiences that is un-
equaled in other times and places. Never before have literature, music,
and art been so easily available to all classes of society. Moreover, individuals can come together with incomparable ease to promote and share
their common interests. Research findings on vertical mobility are in
accord with the abundance of opportunity available, especially in larger
urban areas. They show that, the larger the community in which the
person spent his formative years, the higher is the status of the occupation he is likely to hold. Downward mobility, on the other hand, is more
common in small than in large communities.[9] The effect of urban experience on mobility is similar in European countries to that in the United
States.

VOLUNTARY ASSOCIATIONS

Until the advent of the new freedom in mobility, associations were
formed within residential neighborhoods. They reinforced the individual's
ties to his locality group in addition to serving his particular interests.
With the decline of the neighborhood as an engrossing social unit, however, voluntary associations have been built upon a much broader territorial base. Unfortunately, there are no historical accounts of the emancipation of associational patterns from residential vicinages. But there
are two or three related trends that can be identified. One is an increase
in size of unit, as represented both in the number of members who do
or can congregate for periodic meetings and in the number of units
federated in a country-wide organization. It seems almost axiomatic that
all organizations will tend to grow to the largest size supportable by the
transportation and communication facilities in being.

A second trend has been an increase in the diversity of associations.
Growth of complexity in society has multiplied the number of differences
among people and the opportunities for cultivating special interests. A
perusal of a recent edition of the *Encyclopedia of National Associations*
suggests that there is no trait or interest, however trivial, which cannot
serve as the basis for an association. A third trend is toward the formal-
ization of voluntary associations. Problems of maintaining communications among scattered members, of securing funds for rentals of meeting
places and other incidental needs, and of dealing with various service
agencies call for a division of labor within the association and a regulariza-
tion of procedures. The accumulation of property, funds, and debts soon
argues for the incorporation of the group under existing law to limit the
liability of individual members and to clarify its tax status. Furthermore,

---

[9] Seymour M. Lipset and Reinhard Bendix, *Social Mobility in Industrial Society*
(Berkeley: University of California Press, 1967), pp. 203–19.

formal organization places an association in a much better position to advertise its presence and to open ways of access to sources of interest satisfaction.

Our knowledge of the number of formal associations is limited to observations as of a moment in time. Even so, the data are very instructive. Table 38 indicates that half or more of the household heads in the six

Table 38. Percentage Distribution of Organizational Memberships of Household Heads
(By Size of Metropolitan Area and Type of Place of Residence)

Size of Area and Type of Place	Number of Organizational Memberships					
	Total	None	1	2	3	4 or More
Large areas: Milwaukee and Buffalo						
Central cities	100	70	19	6	2	3
Suburbs	100	60	21	10	4	5
Medium areas: Dayton, O., and Rochester, N.Y.						
Central cities	100	65	19	9	4	3
Suburbs	100	51	22	11	10	6
Small areas: Saginaw, Mich., and Rockford, Ill.						
Central cities	100	61	20	9	4	6
Suburbs	100	62	24	9	3	2

SOURCE: Hawley and Zimmer, *op. cit.,* p. 56.

metropolitan areas belong to no formal organizations, exclusive of labor unions and church-related groups. Although memberships among suburban residents are more frequent than in central city populations in the large and middle-sized areas, they are by no means prevalent. The proportions of nonmembers shown in Table 38 are greater than found in other studies, largely because the data pertain to household heads only, most of whom are males. Where wives are represented as frequently as husbands the proportions of nonmembers vary around 40 percent in both Europe and America.[10] Women are more active joiners than are men,

[10] Gunnar Heckscher, "Pluralist Democracy: The Swedish Experience," *Social Research,* XV (1948): 417–61; Thomas Bottomore, "Social Stratification in Voluntary Associations," in *Social Mobility in Britain,* ed. by David Glass (New York: The Free Press, 1954), p. 354; Morris Axelrod, "Urban Structure and Social Participation, *American Sociological Review,* XXI (1956): 14–18; O. E. Gallagher, "Voluntary Associations in France," *Social Forces,* XXXVI (1957): 154–56; and Charles R. Wright and Herbert Hyman, "Voluntary Association Memberships of American Adults: Evidence from National Sample Surveys, *American Sociological Review,* XXIII (1958): 284–94.

perhaps because they have more leisure time. There is some indication, moreover, that persons who work outside their community of residence are much less active in organized groups than are noncommuters.[11]

If one assumes that the formal organization is an important vehicle for gaining access to sources of community information and for exerting influence in the community, two findings from the various studies are of interest. The first reveals that memberships vary directly with social-economic status. Nonmembers are concentrated in the lowest strata. At that level, people are relatively isolated from what might be a principal means of participation in community affairs. A second finding, however, is that somewhat over one half of the formal associations to which people belong are fraternal and recreational organizations. That is, they are not the kinds of organizations that are normally concerned with civic matters. Thus only 20 to 30 percent of the adults in urban areas are active in associations in which community welfare is or might be of central concern. Most of those are in the upper income and educational classes. The remainder of the population must rely on the mass media for their contact with the community at large. Paradoxically, however, members of upper social-economic categories are apt to be least well informed about local affairs.[12] Because they range more widely over the metropolitan area in the course of their daily lives their interests are dispersed and their attention is diverted. Evidently the organizations they join are metropolitan, regional, and national rather than local in orientation.

For those who are inclined to participate in the community through the instrumentality of the formal association, the relationship of membership frequency with length of residence in the community provides a measure of the rate of assimilation. The one study that deals with this matter reveals that persons with a college education attain a frequency of formal-association membership within two years of arrival in a community that is not equaled by high school graduates until after 10 years of residence. Similarly, white-collar workers are assimilated, by this criterion, some 10 years sooner than are blue-collar workers.[13] The formal association is clearly a means of gaining entrée to active participation in community affairs.[14]

Whether the formal association is a substitute for informal association is a question that has been but briefly investigated. There is some evidence to suggest that members of such groups are much more active in

[11] Alvin H. Schaff, "The Effect of Commuting on Participation in Community Organizations," American Sociological Review, XVII (1952): 215–20.

[12] Gresham M. Sykes, "The Differential Distribution of Community Knowledge," Social Forces, XXIX (1951): 376–82.

[13] Basil Zimmer, "Participation of Migrants in Urban Structures," American Sociological Review, XX (1955): 218–24.

informal relationships than are nonmembers.[15] This seems to say that nonmembership falls mainly among asocial persons. But no such conclusion is supportable without controls on duration of residence and other relevant characteristics.

LIFE STYLES

A great deal has been written about the life styles of modern urban man. Much of it draws a distinction between the ways of living in the suburbs and in the central city. In that literature the suburban life style is held to revolve about an inordinate preoccupation with family concerns, a trait designated by the word "familism." This finds expression, so it is said, in home-centered activities such as child-raising, gardening, do-it-yourself repair and improvement work, informal conviviality with neighbors, and a great consumption of material goods. Familism is manifested at the community level by church attendance, participation in civic affairs, supervision of little leagues for athletic games and other children's organizations, and in a predilection for conformity. All of this, it is said, reflects in suburban residents a revolt against industrialism, an anti-city attitude, and a wish for contact with nature.[16] Elsewhere one finds it asserted that the suburbanward migrant is in pursuit of small town life where he can enjoy participation in town-meeting government and a confrontation with at least facsimiles of frontier problems.[17]

Suburban residents must be surprised to learn that these are their characteristics and their reasons for choice of residence place. They probably are also unprepared to learn that attachment to family is an indication of moral deficiency. In point of fact, the caricature of the suburban resident is sketched from a minimum of data. Even less credible are the intimations that the suburban environment causes the behaviors attributed to the residents. Events that occur together are not necessarily causes of one another. A rising level of education, increasing affluence, growing amounts of leisure time, and suburbanization are all connected, as indeed are all factors in an urban system, but the ties run through numerous intervening variables. Herbert Gans, who takes sharp issue with the suburban myth, reports that his studies disclose only minor changes of behavior

[14] Robert Gutman, "Population Mobility in the American Middle Class," *op. cit.,* p. 175.

[15] Axelrod, *op. cit.,* p. 18.

[16] David Riesman, "The Suburban Dislocation," *Annals of American Academy of Political and Social Science* (1957): 123–46.

[17] Robert C. Woods, *Suburbia: Its People and Their Politics* (Boston: Houghton Mifflin, 1958).

on the part of households relocating in suburban areas and those arise out of having to adapt to a new or different house.[18]

This is not to deny that there are perceptible life style differences in a metropolitan population. The variety is actually great. There are differences in the uses of leisure time, in the kinds and amounts of printed materials read, in consumption habits, in the extent to which legal, medical, and other professional services are used, in organization memberships, in the frequency and distances of travel beyond community limits, and in many other respects. Such differences are a function of social-economic and family characteristics rather than of place of residence. If the correlations of one with the other have seemed to become more pronounced in recent years, it is mainly because urban people have been sorting themselves into more clearly delineated areas of residential homogeneity. These, of course, are to be found within central city boundaries as well as in the outlying or suburban zone.

Nor is there any satisfactory evidence to support a belief that suburban residents are politically more active than residents of central cities. On the contrary, the results of an investigation into the matter found that suburban residents had voting records that were no better than those of central city residents. Moreover, the former were considerably less knowledgeable about who were their governing officials.[19] In that study it was also observed that central city governments attracted more adequately trained persons to their offices than suburban governments were able to do. These findings are consistent with those reported by Gresham Sykes, namely, members of upper social-economic levels are less well informed about local affairs than are persons in lower rankings.[20]

METROPOLITAN INTEGRATION

The metropolitan community is a communication system. That is superficially visible in the periodic movements which daily characterize the functioning of the community. A basic rhythm is apparent in the morning and late afternoon flows of worker traffic. Woven in counterpoint around the main pulsation are various rhythms of lesser amplitudes. These are formed by the movements of children to and from school, of housewives to and from shopping centers, and of service personnel to and from households and other establishments. The complex of coordinated pulsations is dampened at the evening dinner hour and a different rhythm occupies the remainder of the diurnal cycle. The night-time

[18] "Effects of the Move from City to Suburb," in Leonard Duhl, *op. cit.*, 184–98. See also P. Willmott, *Evolution of a Community* (London: Routledge and Kegan Paul, 1963).

[19] Hawley and Zimmer, *op. cit.*, pp. 65–67.

[20] *Op. cit.*

rhythm is a composite of recreational activities, of truck deliveries, of waste removal, and of maintenance services of many kinds. The repetition of the diurnal ebbs and flows is interrupted at the week's end and for two days another and distinctive temporal pattern prevails.

Relatively unexposed to the naked eye is the flux of messages traveling through radio waves, over telephone lines, in the mail, and with the movements of people. Orders to buy and sell, agreements to lend and borrow, contracts, foreclosures, mergers and collusions, arrangements to share leisure time, exchanges of useful and useless information flood the communication channels. The paths of movement of information and of materials enter institutions as inputs, are synthesized and processed, and are fed back as outputs into the communication network. Not unlike the cyclings through institutions, there are input and output flows among metropolitan communities. The communication and transportation network is in a number of respects a delicate fabric of finely woven strands. An interruption of a flow at some one point, through a mechanical breakdown or a failure in the performance of a function, can impair the operation of the entire system. The danger of overloads and of a consequent jamming of channels is ever present. Thus the system and the institutional subsystems develop means for screening irrelevant inputs.[21] But this alone is not enough to insure the smooth working of the system.

There are numerous regulatory mechanisms. Many of those are established in law. Transportation and communication routes and rates are supervised by state and national commissions; banking is subject to regulation by the Federal Reserve System as well as by state agencies; corporations are required to submit to audits and to report their activities to the public; weights and measures, and food, drugs, and various other consumer goods, are regularly inspected. There are other forms of regulation that lie outside the law, but presumably are in accord with it. Professional associations have ethical codes governing the behavior of members and their relations with clients. Similarly, labor unions have devised effective means for managing their internal and external affairs. Better Business Bureaus try to impose ethical practices on merchants and to regularize business hours and other procedures. There are, finally, other control mechanisms that are contrary to law, such as collusive arrangements and intimidations.

Yet there is no institution or set of institutions specifically charged with responsibility for the governance of the metropolitan community.[22] The

[21] See Karl W. Deutsch, "On Social Communication and the Metropolis," in *The Future Metropolis*, ed. by Lloyd Rodwin (New York: George Braziller, 1961), pp. 129–43; and Stanley Milgram, "The Experience of Living in Cities," *Science*, CLXVII (March, 1970): 1461–68.

[22] Norton Long, "The Local Community as an Ecology of Games," *American Journal of Sociology*, LXIV (1958): 255–61.

controls exercised by the various regulative and policing services are fragmentary; they are addressed in each case to limited sectors of the community. No agency concerns itself with the coordination of the specialized control mechanisms. There are also a large number of important segments of the functioning community unattended. Examples include the adaptation of the routines in one institution to those in others, the determination of the timing of industrial activities that affect the entire community, accommodations to peak loads in transportation, traffic, and the use of utilities. Points of interaction such as these seem to be left to controls that operate in market and other system processes. Patterns of dovetailing have been worked out in a piecemeal fashion, through many trials and errors. The extent of the order that prevails and the fineness to which it is tuned is remarkable, therefore.

COMMUNITY POWER

But if there is no formal mechanism for the regulation of the complex operations of a metropolitan system, might there not be an informal mechanism of some kind? Should there not be a centralization of power, formal or informal, sanctioned or clandestine? The nature and locus of power in a community system are issues that have attracted a great deal of scholarly attention since Floyd Hunter's 1953 study *Community Power Structure.*[23] Two widely different approaches to those questions have been proposed. One regards power as a system property; the other treats it as an attribute of individuals who comprise an elite group. The former is the position taken in this volume; the latter occurs mainly in social-psychological analyses of decision-making processes.

Allusions to the conception of power as a system property have appeared in a number of places in preceding chapters. It will be useful, nevertheless, to restate the matter in a more orderly fashion. According to this view, every unit of human organization—family, church, store, industry, community—is an organization of power adapted to the performance of a given activity or set of activities. Through the joining of complementing activities the strengths of a number of individuals are mobilized and raised to a higher level. Power is assembled around the performance of a function and it belongs to the combination of roles and relationships by means of which the function is performed. Thus power is ubiquitous in a system, though it is unevenly distributed among the units performing functions. That is, individuals do not hold power in their own right; it belongs to the functional positions they occupy. In-

[23] Chapel Hill: University of North Carolina Press, 1953.

dividuals acquire power by moving into a functional position and they lose it as they retire from the position.[24]

Function serves as a basis for the mobilization of power in two ways. One is represented in the corporate type of unit. By affecting a closer timing and a more efficient coordination of a diversity of simple functions, the corporate unit forms them into a complex function with a much greater capability than was possible prior to the integration. Such units exercise power internally, i.e., in the conduct of their respective functions, and externally, through influences that unavoidably accompany exchanges with other units. Internal power spills over into the community as externally exerted influence. The latter is manifested in the outcomes of interactions involved in exchanges, in competition among units with similar functions, and in the extent to which the unit is taken into consideration whenever policies are under discussion. In short, external power is contingent on internal power.

A second way in which function serves as a basis for the mobilization of power has been dealt with earlier as the voluntary association. Individuals and units of organization which, because of the functions performed, occupy similar relationships to the community may pool their energies and resources in an organization designed to protect or enhance their positions in the community. Power structures of this type result from threats or challenges to the function that identifies a class of units. Associations of manufacturers, chambers of commerce, labor unions, medical societies, and actors' guilds are illustrative. A social class, when it becomes more than a category in a classification, is another instance of this type of power mobilization.

Power in the second or categorical type of structure is also exerted internally and externally. Its internal strength, however, is contingent in large degree on its external effectiveness. For the categoric unit is called into being by an imbalance of power and it is an attempt to redress the balance. The greater its success in that respect, the greater its internal cohesiveness, the more resources it can command, and the more selective of its membership it can be.

The community, then, is an organization of units which, among other things, engage in an interplay of power. The power interplay is, of course, one of several ways of looking at the strivings of units to pursue their respective functions with a minimum of friction. In the absence of change it might be assumed that the power distribution approaches an equilibrium.

---

[24] For an empirical demonstration of this conception of power see Amos H. Hawley, "Community Power and Urban Renewal Success," *American Journal of Sociology*, LXVIII (1963): 422–31.

Basically, of course, the function of the community—the business in which it is engaged—is the provision of sustenance and other amenities for its members. It is the agency through which a localized population extracts from its environment the things needed or the wherewithal for acquiring the things needed for its day-to-day living. This being the case, the units which maintain the most direct contact with environment, which draw sustenance from it for use by the community at large, occupy a strategic position in the structure of relationships. So vital are their activities that they set the conditions under which all other units must operate. In the self-sufficient agrarian community, the farm household holds the strategic position; in the market-oriented agricultural community that position is occupied by the marketing unit; and in the industrial community the manufacturing unit possesses the same peculiar importance. Such units, therefore, stand at the apex of the power hierarchy whether their members wish it or not. This is because all relationships and functions are contingent on the activities of the basic producing units. But their powers are not absolute. For they cannot function without other units of various kinds. Moreover, their powers may be circumscribed or counterbalanced at any time by the formulation of categoric units which may withhold essential skills or services, or gain monopolies over important conditions. Nevertheless their power positions are unique.

The model of a closed community whose contacts with environment are channeled through one unit or one class of units, to repeat a previously made point, is greatly oversimplified, especially for contemporary situations. In the modern community there are many types of units which have external relations some of which produce supplementary income, additional services, or other contributions to the welfare of the whole. In each such instance the unit in question gains an added ability to affect the conditions essential to the functioning of other units. Its power, in other words, is enhanced thereby. There is also the fact that virtually every unit of the present-day community has or may have external relations; although any given unit may not use the external relationship to bring anything into the community, it may use the relationship to escape, thus exerting power negatively by depriving the community of its labor. A consequence of the existence of manifold external relations is a loose integration of the community, at least in the sense that power is widely diffused and the power differences among units are relatively small. Where this condition prevails, extrinsic power may come to reside in coalitions (categoric units) among basic as well as among other types of units.

The fact that order prevails despite the absence of an official governing authority is to a very large extent a by-product of the functionings of the principal corporate units. These units determine the amount of income that enters the community and hence the level and diversity of ancillary activities that can be supported. Through their starting and stopping times they affect traffic volumes, the burden on police departments for traffic control, and the peaks and valley in utility use loads. The scheduling of activities in the household—the hours of rising in the morning and retiring at night, the timing of meals, the distribution of leisure time—is regulated to a large extent by the rhythm of operation in the employing institution. In a college town the calendar of the college paces all other activities in the town. The routines of the employing institutions also fix the temporal gaps that can be occupied by the functions of other units. Newspapers bring out their morning and afternoon editions before the beginning and at the close of the work day. Retail establishments occupy the intervening time, though they often adapt their peak efforts to the paydays of the employing units. Recreational institutions concentrate their operations in the leisure hours. The influence of the major employing institutions in these respects is less perceptible as size of place increases. For as population size grows larger, the probability that enough people for the support of any given special service will be represented grows as well. In small places community rhythms are very pronounced, but in large places the overall effect of many small pulsations blends into a somewhat arhythmic flow of activity. In the latter instance there can be a fuller and more intensive use of capital installations of all kinds.[25]

Another source of order is found in a number of symbiotic clusters which, deliberately or otherwise, regulate certain spheres of activity. For example, building contractors, realtors, land speculators, lending agencies, municipal planning bodies and the courts have each a special interest in land development and building construction. Through their interactions in that connection they arrive at mutual uderstandings, accommodations, and agreements that have the force of official policy.[26] Likewise, aid to dependent members of the population is regulated by private welfare agencies, schools, courts, service clubs, and federal and state bureaus. Their procedures and interpretations of existing laws develop a body of administrative practices which may or may not accord with the intent of laws. Again, local medical associations, pharmacies, public health agencies, and hospitals rule in matters of health at least to the point of protect-

[25] For a more extensive discussion of temporal organization see Amos H. Hawley, *Human Ecology: A Theory of Community Structure*, ch. 15.

[26] See Philip E. Jacob and James A. Toscano (eds.), *The Integration of Political Communities* (Philadelphia: J. B. Lippincott, 1964), pp. 120–42, and William Form, *op. cit.*

ing their respective interests. Numerous other functional sectors such as these can be identified. Their purviews overlap and interpenetrate to such an extent that they can be highly effective as control subsystems.

The second conception—the social-psychological view—of power regards it as a personal attribute by which certain individuals are able to control the behavior of others, particularly in decision-making processes.[27] Such influential persons comprise an elite which determines, more or less clandestinely, the course of community policies. The research that has followed from this notion has taken several directions. The problem of earliest concern was that of identifying the power figures of the community. This, with many variations, was a procedure that involved (1) determining through survey methods who are persons of notable reputation in a community, (2) using a jury of knowledgeable persons in the community to select the most influential of the reputable citizens, and (3) through direct interview with the persons whose names comprised the narrow list of power figures to ascertain who among them interacts with whom.[28] The labor required to carry out this series of tasks usually exhausted the resources of the researcher with the result that nothing followed the identification of power figures. That is, whether the power clique actually exerted its influence with any effect was not discovered.[29]

A second line of research has proceeded on the assumption that the distribution of power is neither fixed nor monolithic. It has used *a priori* definitions of influential members of a community, e.g., persons who occupy strategic positions, and has moved directly to the task of discovering how they group themselves about different issues. Pluralistic power structures are distinguished from a monolithic structure. Having identified the various cliques, the next step has been to follow the sequence of a decision in the making.[30] The historical account that is compiled in a decision-making study suffers all of the disabilities of any other case study. It is much too concrete and specific to support a generalization and it admits of no observational controls.

A final type of research to be mentioned here is an exploration, through multi-variant analysis, of the relation of community characteristics with

---

[27] "Power," says Terry Clark, "is the potential ability of actors to select, to change, and to attain the goals of a social system." (*Community Structure and Decision Making: Comparative Analysis* [San Francisco: Chandler Publishing Co., 1968], p. 54.)

[28] Floyd Hunter, *op. cit.*; Leonard Blumberg, "The Determination of Local Power Elites," *American Journal of Sociology*, XLIII (1957): 290–96; Delbert C. Miller, "Decision Making Cliques in Community Power Structures," *American Journal of Sociology*, LXIV (1958), 299–310.

[29] One exception is found in William A. Gamson, "Reputation and Resources in Community Politics," in Terry Clark, *op. cit.*, pp. 333–47.

[30] Cf. Benjamin Walter, "Political Decision Making in Arcadia," in Stuart Chapin (ed.), *op. cit.*, pp. 141–87.

the types of power structures.[31] Among the findings of interest from investigations of that kind are indications of a movement away from centralized or monolithic power structures, particularly in the newer urban areas, and in the larger places. Size of place appears to be connected with type of power structure through the variable of diversification in the local economy; pluralism and size both vary with diversification. Research of this kind displays a primary concern with community structure rather than with the testing of a power hypothesis. In any case, the results suggest that power structures are consequents of types of systems rather than of personalities.

Neither the conception of power as a system property or as a personal attribute has been applied to a metropolitan system. They have been treated rather in the context of a particular political unit, usually a municipality. In the former case that limitation has been imposed by the availability of data; in the latter it is inherent in an interest in decision-making, or more specifically, political decison-making. Thus no light of any importance has been shed on the nature or extent of metropolitan integration by either approach. Of the two, however, it is more than likely that the power as a system property approach would prove most fruitful for that purpose.

METROPOLITAN GOVERNMENT

If there is unity and order in the metropolitan community, it is there in spite of rather than because of government. Metropolitan government is approximated in only a few places in the United States; elsewhere metropolitan areas recognized by the U.S. Bureau of the Census held, in 1957, an average of 85 units of local government per area. The average number went up to 96 during the next five years and then declined to 91 by 1967. As may be seen in Table 39, the decrease in the years between 1962 and 1967 was due mainly to school district consolidations. The creation of new special districts failed to make up the loss as it had in previous periods. Municipalities also increase at a rate somewhat slower than usual. It is too early to know whether these changes represent a reversal of a long-term trend. In 1967 the range was from 300 units of local government per area of 1,000,000 or more population to 25 in areas of less than 100,000 population.[32]

The consequences of the coexistence of a multiplicity of governmental

[31] See for example Claire W. Gilbert, "Community Power and Decision Making; A Quantitative Examination of Previous Research," in Terry Clark (ed.), *op. cit.*, pp. 139–54.

[32] U.S. Bureau of the Census, *Census of Governments, 1967*, Vol. 1 (Washington, D.C., 1968), p. 11.

Table 39. Local Governments in 227 Standard Metropolitan Areas

Type of Local Government	1962	1967	Change	
			Number	Percentage
Total	21,817	20,703	−1,114	−5.1
School districts	7,072	5,018	−2,054	−29.0
Special districts	6,153	7,049	896	14.6
Municipalities	4,903	4,977	74	1.5
Townships	3,282	3,255	−27	−0.8
Counties	407	404	−3	−0.7

SOURCE: U.S. Bureau of the Census, "Local Government in Metropolitan Areas," *Census of Government,* 1967, p. 1.

units are numerous. Of primary significance is the fragmentation of the tax base. This impinges most heavily on the central city; not only has it sustained serious losses of population and industry to outlying administrative units, but it contains the major part of the services available in the metropolitan area. Many of the beneficiaries of these services, by residing in suburban jurisdictions, are sheltered from financial responsibility for service costs. Their use of central city streets adds to the street maintenance costs and to the costs for police and traffic controls; the periodic concentration of large numbers of people in the central city increases the risks of fire and therefore of protection costs; and similarly, suburban users of central city services add to the levels of sanitation, health and other expenditures. Hence variations in the operating costs of central city governments have been shown to be more sensitive to the size of the suburban population than to the size of the taxable or central city population.[33] An examination of changes in central city governmental operating costs to changes in successively larger surrounding populations, as in Table 40, reveals that, the more inclusive the aggregate, the closer is the relationship.[34] Noteworthy is the fact that changes in central city population have almost no effect on the level of central city government costs.[35]

[33] Amos H. Hawley, "Metropolitan Population and Municipal Government Expenditures in Central Cities," in *Cities and Society,* ed. by Paul K. Hatt and Albert J. Reiss, Jr. (New York: The Free Press, 1957), pp. 773–82; and Harvey E. Brazer, *City Expenditures in the United States* (Washington, D.C.: National Bureau of Economic Research, 1959).

[34] Cf. Woo Sik Kee, "Suburban Population and Its Implications for Core City Finance," *Land Economics,* XLIII (1967): 202–11.

[35] Table 40 is interesting on another score. It indicates that the effective population aggregate for use in delimiting an urban unit is more closely approximated with each enlargement of territory, at least to metropolitan area boundaries.

**Table 40. Zero-Order Correlation Coefficients Between
Changes of Population of Different Territorial Units
and Central City Government Operating Costs
(1950 to 1960)**

Selected Government Costs	Central City	Urbanized Area	Standard Metropolitan Statistical Area
All government operating costs	–0.10	0.67	0.74
Police department	–0.01	0.28	0.80
Fire department	0.04	0.83	0.86
Highway department	–0.05	0.69	0.74

SOURCE: Computed by John Kasarda, "The Impact of Suburban Population." Unpublished student paper.

The fiscal problem is doubtless similar, though of smaller scale, in many suburban municipalities. A wide dispersion of interest centers and the crisscrossing flows of traffic involve the residents of every unit of local government in the metropolitan area in the use of facilities of other units with, of course, great variations in the intensities of use. Thus far the only locally developed compensatory income is a payroll tax assessed on all persons who work in a city regardless of where they live. That, however, is not permissible in all state constitutions.

SUMMARY

The developing organization of metropolitan areas involves a growth in the scale of the units of organization, a convergence of the structure of units upon a single form, i.e., the corporation, and a multiplication of voluntary associations. The interactions of these trends create a network of relationships so dense and ramified that it cannot be reduced to a simple description. It is among other things a communication system, as prepresented in the regular rhythms of daily movements and the not-so-visible flows of information. The periodicity and other manifestations of order in the operation of the metropolitan system are the more remarkable when it is recognized that there is no governing agency or formally constituted regulatory body.

The metropolitan system may be viewed as a power system as well as a communication network. These are, of course, merely different perspectives toward the same thing. Power is generated in the system and is variously distributed over the system. In general, power is disproportionally concentrated in the units that are most effective in bringing sustenance or wealth into the system. Such units doubtless exert a major controlling effect on the system's operations. This hypothesis has not been empirically demonstrated for metropolitan areas. Another conception of power, which views it as a personal attribute, has inspired a great amount of interesting research. Most of that research, however, has been concerned with either locating powerful figures or with analyzing the process of decision-making. It has not shown that a personal conception of power accounts for the ways in which metropolitan systems, or municipal subsystems, for that matter, operate.

Nor can the orderliness of the metropolitan system be explained in governmental terms. The area is rather fragmented in many governments each of which is autonomous within its jurisdiction. Thus overarching administrative requirements are difficult, if not impossible, to meet, and costs of governmental servces are doubtles higher than need be. Of the costs that are borne it appears that the central city carries more than its share.

SUPPLEMENTARY READINGS

AIKEN, MICHAEL, and MOTT, PAUL E. *The Structure of Community Power* (New York: Random House, 1970).

GOLDSTEIN, SIDNEY (ed.). *The Norristown Study* (Philadelphia: University of Pennsylvania Press, 1961).

GREER, SCOTT. *Metropolitics: A Study of Political Culture* (New York: John Wiley, 1963).

MOORE, WILBUR E. *The Conduct of the Corporation* (New York: Random House, 1962).

MOORE, WILBUR E. *Man, Time and Society* (New York: John Wiley, 1968).

WOOD, ROBERT C. *1400 Governments: The Political Economy of the New York Region* (Cambridge: Harvard University Press, 1961).

10

The Metropolitanization of Society

Not until the last two or three decades has the full significance of urbanization begun to be apparent. Late in the nineteenth century Karl Marx confidently declared, in a statement that aptly illustrates the limitations of historical inference: "The whole economical history of society is summed up in the movement of this separation between town and country." [1] What seemed to be true of the period with which Marx was familiar has proved to be only an early phase of a transformation that has a radically different outcome. Urbanization, far from being merely a process of segregating in a few localities the part of a society's population engaged in non-extractive industries, is rather a comprehensive reorganization of the entire structure of the society leaving no sector or sphere untouched. "Town" and "country" are merged under a single set of institutions and a common set of processes. This assumes, of course, that no permanent obstacles are placed in the way of cultural exchanges and of the application of their fruits to production, transportation, and communication within a society. In this chapter we shall investigate the extent of urbanization of the countryside. In doing so it will be helpful to examine, at the risk of some repetition, a number of the concepts developed in the study of that relationship.

[1] *Capital*, Chicago, 1903, Vol. 1, p. 387.

DOMINANCE

A relatively simple way of characterizing the relationship between the metropolis and the settlement in the territory around it is as one of dominance and subordination.[2] By virtue of its location astride the intersections of major routes of travel and of communications, the metropolis mediates the exchanges between the local region and the larger world. Its key institutions, therefore, are able to determine the conditions under which all other institutions in the domain must operate. That is, through their processing, marketing, and administrative activities, they regulate the amount of wealth that enters the region, they define the kinds of complementary units that are needed, they set the rhythm and the tempo of activity in the entire community, and they influence the types of people who congregate in the area.

The pattern of dominance is made graphic by plotting the gradient [3] describing the territorial distribution of a service emanating from a given center. The choice of a service or indicator of an urban center's influence yields different scales of dominance. High-frequency activities such as daily commuting to work or shopping trips for household necessities are usually held within a 20- to 30-mile radius; for them the gradient is short and steep. Beyond that radius small centers may be effective competitors with larger ones for frequently occurring individual needs. Individual activities that recur fortnightly or monthly and inter-institutional relations, as between wholesalers and retailers or as between bank correspondents, are spread over an area with a radius of as much as 150 miles or more. The influence of the center in these particulars tapers off more gradually as distance is lengthened. Competition for the control of territory on this scale involves only fairly large centers. A third zone of dominance can be delimited by using the export function of a center. The product or products of such activities are usually distributed over an area of interregional scope.[4]

The most ambitious study of dominance that has been undertaken used a somewhat different approach. Instead of employing frequency distributions of metropolitan services by households and other units scattered over hinterlands of metropolitan centers, Donald J. Bogue simply observed the distributions of value added by manufacturing industry per capita and of sales per capita in wholesale, retail, and service establishments by distance

---

[2] R. D. McKenzie, "The Concept of Dominance and World Organization, *American Journal of Sociology*, XXXIII (1927): 28–42.

[3] A gradient is simply a line which indicates the change in one variable associated with increments in another variable, in this instance distance from the central business district of a metropolis.

[4] Hawley, *Human Ecology*, pp. 245–58.

zones about 67 major centers in the United States. A nonrandom or gradient distribution was interpreted as an indication of dominance. His results defined the patterns of dominance for the many centers in each of the four respects.[5]

While the concept of dominance states a general principle of great potential utility, its application in describing the territorial scope of a center's influence oversimplified the realities of territorial organization. Much more is involved than just a unilateral relationship between center and tributary area. This was recognized in Bogue's classification of territorial units within a metropolitan domain as dominants, subdominants, influents, and subinfluents. But the interrelations among these types of units were left undeveloped. Donnell Pappenfort has suggested that the metropolitan community is an abstraction from an ecological field. That is, although it is a clearly definable network of relationships, it does not preempt all of the territory over which those relationships are spread.[6] He observed, for example, that central offices in 23 states administered 335 manufacturing plants located in the state of Illinois, i.e., in the metropolitan area of Chicago. Dominance is clearly a more complex phenomenon than its past uses have revealed. One advance in the direction of refining the conception of territorial organization is represented in what is known as *central place theory*.

CENTRAL PLACE THEORY

According to this theory, as formulated by Walter Christaller [7] and as modified by August Lösch,[8] the greater the number and variety of services provided from a center to a hinterland, the greater is the geometric centrality of its location. But to serve a large area at minimum transport costs, lower-order—i.e., more standardized and more frequently used—services are offered from successively smaller-sized centers nested in groups of sixes, for, according to Lösch, it is only in the shape of hexagons that market areas can efficiently fill an area. Thus urban centers form a numerical and functional hierarchy in a region. The smallest centers, providing the lowest-order functions, are most numerous; the next large size class of centers, only one sixth as numerous, offers all of the lowest-order functions and a selection of somewhat more specialized services;

[5] *The Structure of the Metropolitan Community: A Study of Dominance and Subdominance* (Ann Arbor, Mich.: University of Michigan, 1949).

[6] "The Ecological Field and the Metropolitan Community: Manufacturing and Management," *American Journal of Sociology*, LXIV (1959): 380–85.

[7] *Die zentralen Orte in Süddeutschland* (Jena: Gustave Fischer Verlag, 1933).

[8] *The Economics of Location*. Translated by W. H. Woglom (New Haven: Yale University Press, 1954), pp. 105–34.

at the apex is the regional capital, from which are available all lower-order services and also the most specialized or highest-order services. Now if these centers were situated on a level, undifferentiated plane, they would be arranged so that there would be uniform distances between comparable sized places. An expected pattern of distribution is shown in Table 41, and schematically in Fig. 4.

Table 41. An Expected Pattern of Number, Size, Spacing and Services Offered in a Hierarchy of Central Places

Size of Central Place	Number of Places	Distance Separating Places (km)	Size of Area Served (eq. km)	Average Population in Area Served	Number of Types of Goods and Services Offered
1,000	486	4.0	44	3,500	40
2,000	162	6.9	133	11,000	90
4,000	54	12.0	400	35,000	180
10,000	18	20.7	1,200	100,000	330
30,000	6	36.0	3,600	350,000	600
100,000	2	62.1	10,800	1,000,000	1,000
500,000	1	108.0	32,400	3,500,000	2,000

SOURCE: Adapted from Walter Christaller, *op. cit.*, p. 72.

A number of studies in agricultural areas of America, Western Europe, Australia, India, and elsewhere have provided empirical support to the hypothesis of a nested set of central places.[9] The symmetry in the patterns of city distributions noted in these studies derives from the fact that the central places, i.e., the cities, towns, and villages, are collecting points for the transshipment of agricultural produce and local distributing points for retail, business, and personal services. Their spacing is determined by the distribution of populations engaged in exploiting agricultural resources.

Many urban centers, however, perform functions other than just the collection of produce and the distribution of services. And these other functions have location requirements that are not satisfied at geometrically centered sites. Most manufacturing industries, for example, have a strong transportation orientation; their supplies as well as their markets are un-

[9] J. E. Brush, "The Hierarchy of Central Places in Southwestern Wisconsin," *The Geographical Review*, XLIII (1953): 380–402; J. Körber, "Die zentralörtlichen Berichte im Raume Zwischen dem Rhein und dem Saarland," *Berichte zur Deutschen Landeskunde*, XXV (1960): 69–80; A. E. Smailes, "The Urban Hierarchy in England and Wales," *Geography*, XXIX (1944): 41–51.

For a full review of the literature see Brian J. L. Berry and Allen Pred, *Central Place Studies: A Bibliography of Theory and Applications* (Philadelphia: Regional Science Institute, 1961).

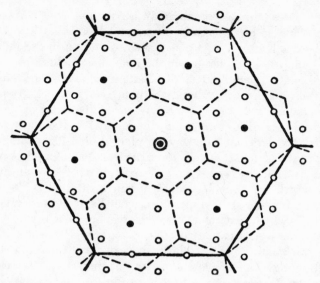

Fig. 4. Schematic representation of central place hierarchy. (After August Lösch, *The Economics of Location* [Stuttgart: Gustav Fischer Verlag, 1954], p. 132. Reproduced with permission.)

evenly scattered over many regions. They are drawn, therefore, to locations at the margins rather than at the centers of geographic regions. It is at the edges of regions that the points of intersection of interregional routes are found. Other functions can only be performed at the sites of resource supplies. This obviously applies to raw-material-producing activities. It pertains also to the locations of vacation industries. There are a number of influences, in short, which distort a central-place tendency so far as to be scarcely recognizable.[10]

The central-place pattern of urban distribution appears to belong to an earlier time or to a less developed stage of territorial organization.[11] In the transition of a region from agricultural settlement, to industrialization, and to metropolitanization, according to Mark and Schwirian, central-place functions cease to be effective as community building activities.[12]

[10] See Chauncey D. Harris and Edward L. Ullman, "The Nature of Cities," *Annals American Academy Political and Social Science,* CCXLII (1945): 7–11.

[11] Such a pattern seems to have occurred during the medieval period in areas of Europe. (See J. C. Russell, "The Metropolitan City Region of the Middle Ages," *Journal of Regional Science,* II [1960]: 55–70.) G. William Skinner describes an unusually symmetrical hierarchy in China, in "Marketing and Social Structure in Rural China, Part I," *Asian Studies,* XXIV (1964): 3–43.

[12] Harold Mark and Kent P. Schwirian, "Ecological Position, Urban Central Place Function, and Community Population Growth," *American Journal of Sociology,* LXXIII (1967): 30–41.

Growth gravitates to metropolitan areas, leaving many outlying towns and villages to wane as local service centers and locations of population increase. The decline of central places seems to begin in the industrialization period and to be accelerated in the later metropolitan phase.

Still, although a symmetrical distribution of towns and cities is not evident within regions or sections, it may appear in a country or in a set of regions taken as a whole. In other words, if the cities of such an area are ranked from small to large and a cumulative percentage distribution is computed, the series of values when plotted on a logarithmic grid will tend to fit a straight line which approximates a 45-degree slope.[13] This log-normal distribution represents an expected pattern in an area all localities of which are fully served by urban institutions. No pockets of rural isolation remain. It is opposed to what has been termed a primate city pattern,[14] which characterizes a great many developing areas. The primate pattern is a situation in which one very large city is found in company with a multitude of villages or very small towns. Urbanization is relatively undeveloped where a pattern of that kind is present. Quite often, however, the primate pattern is an illusion due to the observation of too small an area; were a larger, more inclusive area examined the primate city might fall into a log-normal distribution. We shall return to this topic in a later connection.

A SYSTEM OF URBAN PLACES

Studies of size and spatial distributions of urban centers provide a preliminary insight into their interrelations. In central-place theory a geometrical pattern is taken as presumptive evidence of the directions, content, and even the magnitudes of flows of influence.[15] But it is desirable, where possible, to get beyond a logical argument to an empirical examination of the actual exchanges among urban places. Only then can the outlines of an urban system be revealed in functional terms.

An indirect approach to the determination of intercity relationships was employed in a study of metropolises in southern United States.[16] The

[13] See Rutledge Vining, "On Describing the Structure and Development of Human Population System," *Journal of Farm Economics*, XLI (1959): 922–42.

[14] Mark Jefferson, "The Law of the Primate City," *The Geographical Review*, XXIX (1939): 226–32.

[15] This has been explored with historical data for the United States by Eric Lampard, "The Evolving System of Cities in the United States: Urbanization and Economic Development," in *Issues in Urban Economics*, ed. by Harvey L. Perloff and Lowdon Wingo, Jr. (Baltimore: Johns Hopkins Press, 1968), pp. 81–140.

[16] Rupert B. Vance and Sara Smith Sutker, "Metropolitan Dominance and Integration," in *The Urban South*, ed. by Rupert B. Vance and N. J. Demerath (Chapel Hill: University of North Carolina Press, 1954), ch. 6.

29 cities in the south with 100,000 or more population (1950) were ranked on a composite metropolitan function index which included wholesale sales, business service receipts, number of branch offices, retail sales, bank clearings, and value added by manufacturing industry. On the basis of that index, four degrees of southern metropolitan dominance were identified. As may be seen in Fig. 5, Atlanta and Dallas tower above all others as regional capitals, or second-order metropolises. Houston. New Orleans, Memphis, Louisville, and Birmingham are third-order metropolises. Centers at a fourth level are described as subdominants with metropolitan characteristics. A final level is referred to as subdominants without metropolitan characteristics. The interrelations portrayed in Figure 5 are inferred from rank on the index and from distances from higher-ranking places; no direct data on interrelationships were obtained in the study. Noteworthy is the fact that, while there was a general correlation between the metropolitan function index and population size, there were a number of exceptions. Contrary to central-place theory, size is not an entirely dependable indicator of function performed.

An illustration of inter-metropolitan interaction patterns is presented in Table 42. The matrix represented there is obviously a fragment of a much more extensive network of flows. Nevertheless, it cast some light on types of specialization and of linkages. Intra-regional commodity ex-

Table 42. Commodity Flows and Toll Telephone Calls
(Among Principal Piedmont Cities in North Carolina, 1958)

Freight Origin	Freight Destination (thousands of pounds)				
	Greensboro	Raleigh	Charlotte	Winston-Salem	Durham
Greensboro	—	125.8	230.0	623.8	22.5
Raleigh	191.9	—	96.5	58.3	8.5
Charlotte	138.4	130.5	—	285.3	125.6
Winston-Salem	579.6	100.3	307.4	—	28.4
Durham	255.8	10.1	76.3	8.5	—
Toll Calls Origin	Toll Telephone Call Destination				
Greensboro	—	207	455	466	113
Raleigh	230	—	348	95	437
Charlotte	504	330	—	334	104
Winston-Salem	601	113	402	—	61
Durham	158	534	151	61	—

SOURCE: Adapted from Ralph W. Pfouts, "Patterns of Economic Interaction in the Crescent," in *Urban Growth Dynamics in a Regional Cluster of Cities,* eds. F. Stuart Chapin, Jr. and Shirley F. Weiss (New York: John Wiley & Sons, 1962), pp. 47–54.

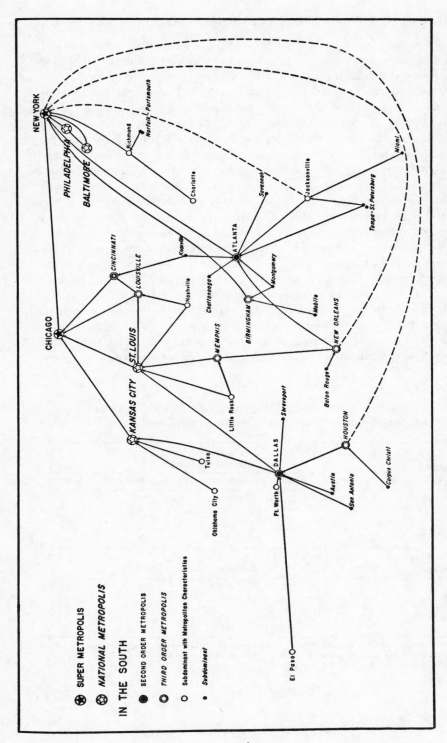

Fig. 5. Orders of metropolitan dominance and major lines of interrelationship in southern United States. (From Rupert B. Vance and Nicholas J. Demerath (eds.), *The Urban South* [Chapel Hill: University of North Carolina Press, 1954], p. 133. Reproduced with permission.)

changes revolve around Greensboro and Winston-Salem primarily. But communications, as measured by telephone calls, center upon Greensboro, Raleigh, and Charlotte. As the state capital Raleigh is the center of po-litical-administrative action. Evidently Charlotte is the principal admin-istrative center for non-political affairs; it is the origin and destination of relatively more telephone calls than of freight shipments. Greensboro ap-pears to be a materials-handling, or wholesale, center for the region.

The concept of a system of cities has been explored on a national level in considerable depth by Otis D. Duncan and his associates.[17] Using data on bank loans and interregional movements of funds, commercial activities, and manufacturing industry involving the 56 metropolitan areas with 300,000 of more population (in 1950), the outlines of a functional hierarchy merged in the study. Coordinating the nation's network of metropolitan areas are five national centers—New York, Chicago, Los An-geles, Philadelphia, and Detroit. These perform their integrative func-tions through the agencies of a number of regional metropolises, such as San Francisco, Minneapolis–St. Paul, Kansas City, Seattle, Portland, At-lanta, Dallas, and Denver. From these centers influences radiate further through lesser metropolitan areas and eventually to smaller cities, towns, and the open country.[18]

The system of urban places, in other words, assumes a hierarchical pattern, but in functional rather than in geometrical terms. Places are functionally ordered without any symmetry in their spatial distribution. Metropolitan areas, the units in the functional hierarchy, are differentiated and linked in sequences ranging from areas specialized in administration on a national scale, through regional to subregional and local areas. Here and there within the areas encompassed in the inter-metropolitan system are small central-place hierarchies, subordinate usually to a nearby met-ropolitan area.

METROPOLITAN CENTRALIZATION

As the inter-metropolitan hierarchy has taken shape an increasing num-ber of aspects of the national society have been gathered into metropolitan areas. In an earlier chapter it was noted that metropolitan areas, in 1970, held in their 10 percent of the land area 72 percent of the total population and had captured close to 100 percent of the increase in population that

[17] *Metropolis and Region* (Baltimore: Johns Hopkins Press, 1960), especially chs. 5, 6 and 11.

[18] Stanley Lieberson has demonstrated the existence of a territorial division of labor in banking. Small banks make local loans while extra-local loans are concen-trated in large banks. There is, moreover, a greater similarity among the borrowers from large banks than among the borrowers from small banks. ("The Division of Labor in Banking," *American Journal of Sociology*, VI [1961]: 491–96.)

occurred in the nation between 1950 and 1960. Figures on population distribution, however, provide the least informative data on metropolitan centralization. In almost all other respects the gravitation to metropolitan areas has proceeded much farther than demographic data indicate.

Manufacturing industry, which was already rather highly concentrated at the start of the present century, has continued to cluster in and around metropolitan centers. Thus, by 1960, as Table 43 shows, nearly three

Table 43. Proportion of Total United States Population and Manufacturing Industry Located in Metropolitan Areas (Constant Criteria)

| Census Year[a] | Population | Manufacturing Industry | | | |
		Plants	Workers	Wages	Value Added[b]
1960	63.4%	71.7%	75.2%	79.3%	80.8%
1940	51.6	69.4	73.9	78.2	75.6
1920	43.6	51.6	66.9	69.8	71.1
1900	31.5	44.5	61.4	65.7	65.7[b]

[a]No manufacturing data pertain to the years 1958, 1939, 1919, and 1899.
[b]No data for value added reported. Figure used is for manufacturing sales.
SOURCE: U.S. Bureau of the Census, *Census of Population,* 1900 through 1960, and *Census of Manufacturing,* 1899, 1919, 1939, and 1958.

quarters of manufacturing plants and workers and four fifths of all wages paid to manufacturing workers and value added by manufacturing processes were found in metropolitan areas. Population has lagged behind the movement of industry. In fact, the recent acceleration of population redistribution appears to represent a belated catching up with the territorial reorganization of industry. Yet it is apparent that the concentration of manufacturing industry has slowed since 1940 in all respects except for value added. Evidently the attraction of metropolitan areas as industrial locations has become increasingly selective of highly productive industries. There is also the possibility that the localized dispersion of industry is spreading it over broader areas than those contained within the arbitrarily drawn boundaries of metropolitan areas—that the areas themselves are becoming more inclusive of adjacent territories.

The metropolitanization of distribution and service industries has been less dramatic, partly because data are available for a much shorter interval of time. Of greater importance, however, is the propensity of the highly consumer-oriented businesses to distribute themselves in close conformity to population distribution. Even so, metropolitan areas have contained disproportionate amounts of wholesale, retail, and service activity as measured by volume of sale (Table 44). That is less pronounced with

Table 44. Proportion of Total U.S. Population and Wholesale,
Retail, and Services Industry in Metropolitan Areas
(Constant Criteria)

Census Year[a]	Population	Wholesale		Retail		Service	
		Establish-ments	Sales	Establish-ments	Sales	Establish-ments	Sales
1960	63.4%	68.7%	85.6%	59.6%	69.2%	64.9%	80.8%
1940	51.6	60.0	85.2	53.2	63.9	61.3	76.4

[a]Industry data pertain to years 1958 and 1939.
SOURCE: U.S. Bureau of the Census, Census of Business, 1939 and 1958.

number of establishments as the measure of activity, particularly in retailing and to some extent in service industry. In other words, metropolitan areas support larger establishments than does nonmetropolitan territory.

Industrial concentration is not the best indicator of metropolitan ascendancy. Manufacturing industry is subject to a great variety of locational influences, variously combined for different types of industries. While the advantages of pools of industrial labor, of market areas, of proximity to ancillary industry, and of bulk carrier transportation facilities lead to a clustering of plants, mixes of these localization factors occur at relatively frequent intervals over broad areas. Advances in automation and further shifts to dependence on chemical and electrical resources will create a still more even distribution of industrial locations. A more revealing evidence of metropolitan preeminence is had therefore in the locations of central offices of manufacturing industry. Administrative headquarters are responsive to a different set of localizing influences. They must be at sites convenient for the coordination of production processes with markets, financial resources, advertising agencies, and a host of technical services. Accordingly, central offices are drawn to the nodal points in communication networks.

The central offices of manufacturing corporations having operating plants in two or more locations are almost exclusively situated within metropolitan areas. Two measures of centralization may be used: one, the number of employees of such corporations and, two, the gross value of plant and equipment they control. Corporate offices of manufacturing concerns located in metropolitan areas have employed over 93 percent of the workers engaged in multiplant corporations. The proportion has increased slightly from 93 percent, in 1947, to 96 percent, in 1960. A somewhat larger concentration of corporate capital, over 96 percent, is found in metropolitan areas. There appears to have been a very slight trend of increase of concentration in that measure as well.

The extent of centralization of corporate administration is considerably greater than is revealed in a simple metropolitan-nonmetropolitan comparison. Well over one quarter of all metropolitan areas have no central offices of multiplant corporations. Most of these are located in southern states, though others are found in the shadows of larger metropolitan areas in other regions. Such areas form the bottom echelon in the intermetropolitan hierarchy. On the other hand, corporate offices located in the New York–northeastern New Jersey metropolitan area administer over one fourth of all employees and invested capital controlled by multiplant manufacturing firms. No less than 85 of the 200 largest industrial corporations maintain their central offices in that one metropolitan area. The five largest areas, those with 3,000,000 or more population, in 1960, provided administrative locations for one half or more of all corporate employees and capital. The number containing central offices for three quarters of corporate activity in manufacturing declined from the 34 largest areas in 1947 to the 18 largest in 1960.[19]

That there is some affinity of corporate offices for places where finances and information are readily accessible is suggested by the fact that the five largest metropolitan areas were also, in 1960, the places of concentration of almost two fifths of the nation's bank deposits and over one fourth of its communication workers. But in both of these respects the five largest areas had lost some ground since 1950. In the 1950–60 decade all metropolitan areas increased their share of the total bank deposits from 75 to 78 percent, and of all communication workers from 69 to 71 percent. In these as in other respects metropolitan functions are being more widely shared.

Metropolitan areas are just as attractive as locations for the central offices of regional and national voluntary associations as for those of industrial corporations. Over 90 percent of the central offices of the 6,300 associations listed in a compendium [20] are so situated, as is shown in Table 45. The New York–northeastern New Jersey area houses one third of the total, and that area together with the Chicago and Washington, D.C., areas accommodate three fifths of all voluntary association headquarters. Concentration of administrative quarters in metropolitan areas is the rule among all types of associations. The largest departure from the rule is found among agricultural associations, but even there over two thirds have chosen metropolitan locations. It is of interest to note that the central offices of religious, educational, welfare, ethnic, health, and labor associa-

---

[19] *Moody's Industrial Manual* (New York: Moody's Investors Service, Inc., 1947 and 1960); and *Mergers and Superconcentration: Acquisitions of 500 Largest Industrial and 50 Largest Merchandising Firms.* Staff Report of the Select Committee on Small Business, House of Representatives, 87th Congress (Washington, D.C., 1962).

[20] *Encyclopedia of Associations* (Detroit: Gale Research Co., 1961).

Table 45. Percentage Distribution of Nationally and Regionally Organized Voluntary Associations That Maintain Central Offices (By Location and by Type, 1959)

Type of Association	Metropolitan Area				Nonmetro- politan	Total	
	New York	Chicago	Washington	Other		Per- centage	Number
Business	38.1	17.3	14.7	26.9	2.9	100.0	2,340
Educational	32.2	7.5	22.5	28.5	9.1	100.0	583
Health	30.6	14.6	8.2	35.9	10.3	100.0	437
Agricultural	6.0	6.6	12.6	42.7	32.0	100.0	334
College fraternal	10.4	7.5	3.9	53.6	24.4	100.0	307
Religious	51.5	9.7	10.0	26.1	2.7	100.0	299
Scientific	23.9	4.8	19.8	42.0	9.5	100.0	293
Welfare	49.2	7.5	13.4	23.8	6.0	100.0	268
Labor	16.1	10.3	29.5	40.0	4.0	100.0	224
Ethnic	59.9	5.4	6.3	25.1	3.2	100.0	222
Governmental	18.9	20.1	36.6	20.0	4.2	100.0	164
Chamber of commerce	49.2	1.5	2.3	24.4	22.7	100.0	132
Athletic	29.7	7.8	3.9	50.0	8.6	100.0	128
Public affairs	53.5	3.1	26.0	16.6	0.8	100.0	127
Fraternal	9.2	11.8	5.9	65.2	7.6	100.0	119
War veteran	16.5	0.9	27.8	43.5	11.3	100.0	115
Hobby	27.0	3.0	5.0	45.0	20.0	100.0	100
Horticultural	11.5	1.1	5.7	60.5	20.7	100.0	87
Other	41.9	4.8	6.4	37.0	9.7	100.0	62
All associations	32.9	11.4	14.6	32.6	8.4	100.0	6,341

SOURCE: Adapted from Stanley Lieberson and Irving L. Allen, Jr., "Location of National Headquarters of Voluntary Associations," *Administrative Science Quarterly*, 8 (1963): 321.

tions exhibit locational preferences comparable to those of business associations.

Information on relocations of voluntary association central offices was assembled for a sample of 190 associations by Lieberson and Allen for the years from 1939 to 1959.[21] The movement during that 20-year period was toward increased metropolitan concentration. The proportion of business associations with central offices in metropolitan areas increased from 94 to 99 percent. The only striking shift in the metropolitan pattern was a growth of the Washington, D.C., area at the expense of the New York–northeastern New Jersey area.

The leadership of the nation has also been gathering in metropolitan areas. In 1940 more than three fifths (62.5 percent) of all professional workers lived in such places. By 1960 the proportion had grown to 72.2 percent. The five largest areas held the same proportion at both dates—slightly less than one fourth of the total. Another, and perhaps a more discriminating, way of identifying leadership in the population is through the listings in the *Who's Who in America* volumes. A 5 percent sample of those lists for each of a series of census years discloses a progressive

21 *Op. cit.*, p. 336.

concentration of *Who's Who* entries in the metropolitan sector and particularly in the very large areas. As may be seen in Table 46, the areas having one million or more population increased their share of distinguished people from 43 percent, in 1920, to approximately 64 percent, in 1960. All other parts of the nation, including metropolitan areas having

Table 46. Percentage Distribution of Persons Listed in
Who's Who in America
(By Size and Type of Place of Residence)

Size and Type of Place	1920	1930	1940	1950	1960
All places	100.0	100.0	100.0	100.0	100.0
Metropolitan areas	75.9	77.2	76.0	79.6	87.1
3,000,000 and over	28.3	29.5	27.4	31.7	41.9
1,000,000–3,000,000	15.0	15.7	16.0	21.0	21.8
500,000–1,000,000	15.0	12.0	13.0	12.1	10.4
250,000– 500,000	8.9	9.9	10.6	7.6	6.7
100,000– 250,000	7.0	8.1	7.8	7.7	6.1
Under 100,000	1.7	2.0	1.1	0.5	0.4
Nonmetropolitan	24.1	22.8	24.0	19.4	12.9

less than one million inhabitants, suffered declines in their proportions of *Who's Who* entries. Whether these findings, viewed in relation to those pertaining to professional workers, mean that some more or less standard metropolitan characteristics are being spread over an enlarging number of areas while a few attributes of key importance continue to be monopolized by a small number of strategically placed areas is a possibility which could bring a hierarchy into still sharper focus.

URBAN INSTITUTIONS IN AGRICULTURE

If we turn to the changes in process in rural areas of advanced nations, we can see the other side of the urbanization coin. As was pointed out early in this volume, agricultural productivity and urbanization are mutually dependent circumstances. The proportion of the population aggregated in urban areas and urban employments is contingent on the productivity of the food-producing industry. Increases in the latter are stimulated by the growth of urban markets for food and other agricultural products. In that interaction the two sectors of society, urban and rural, necessarily become more alike. The particular agents of convergence upon a common organization are market involvement and mechanization.

As the farmer becomes committed to production for a market, the returns from the sale of his products relieve him of having to perform many irksome uneconomic chores. Thus he drifts further into specialization and into a dependence on income from sales for an increasing number of his production requirements and his consumer needs. Soon the market becomes the regulating factor in what, when, and how much he will plant. Attempts to anticipate prices and market demand lead the farmer into a greater use of credit facilities. He borrows for improvement and for expansion of his enterprise. Improvement means cutting costs, or increasing production per unit of cost. Machinery is substituted for labor wherever possible. Mechanization, of course, is uneconomical unless the farm is large enough to afford a fairly intensive use of tools. The growth of farm capital involves the farmer more and more fully in the market and the set of institutions built around the market—credit, transportation, and communication, farm equipment manufacturers, meteorological and various other technical service.

Farming has become a business enterprise much like an urban enterprise and has declined as a family-centered way of life. The successful farmer must be a fiscal expert; indeed, his skills in estimating market trends and in managing his enterprise are at least as important as his ability as an agriculturalist. Consider the following case of the Maine potato farmer:

Mr. Wilson has a ticker-tape in his air-conditioned office at the end of one of several storage houses. Every weekday morning at 10 o'clock he flicks on a switch and a coil of yellow serpentine spins out the prices of Maine potatoes as reported by the New York Mercantile Exchange. Perhaps it is the middle of May and Mr. Wilson has not yet planted anything but the Mercantile is already quoting what buyers will pay for futures from next November through the following April. Mr. Wilson knows pretty well what it will cost him to grow 300 acres of potatoes. He has checked all the current costs: fertilizer, pesticides, machinery, and hired labor. The buyers at the Mercantile have done the same. Fertilizer sales have been checked, government reports on growers' intentions and coop loans have been probed, and some remarks by bankers have not gone unheeded. Mr. Wilson senses that there is going to be overproduction again this year.

The buyers on the Mercantile think so too; they are bidding very close to costs of production. Their bids do not satisfy Mr. Wilson but he must stay in business. Before he plants a single acre he wires his broker to sell two-thirds of his future crop at what amounts to a farm price of $2.80 a barrel. This is approximately the break-even point for a majority of small producers. At this price Mr. Wilson thinks he can net 60 cents, but only because he operates on a big scale. While the price is low it will cover a lot of cash expenses and a big risk is already eliminated.[22]

22 Edward Higbee, *Farms and Farmers in an Urban Age* (New York: Twentieth Century Fund, 1963), pp. 60–61.

This represents the pattern in which American agriculture is rapidly being reshaped. The small, labor-intensive family-operated farm is disappearing. In its place is appearing a large, highly capitalized farm staffed by technically trained agriculturalists, dubbed an agro-business. A small number of the latter is replacing a very large number of the former. The trend for the 1950–60 decade alone is described in Table 47.

Table 47. U.S. Farms and Farm Sales by Productive Size of Farm (1950–59)

Value of Marketed Produce	Farms				Sales			
	Number (000's)		Percentage		Dollars (millions)		Percentage of Market	
	1950	1959	1950	1959	1950	1959	1950	1959
$10,000 and over	484	794	9.0	21.5	11,303	21,860	50.7	71,7
$2,500 to 10,000	1,603	1,270	29.8	34.3	8,268	6,989	37.1	23.0
Under $2,500	3,291	1,637	61.2	44.2	2,340	1,775	12.2	5.3
All farms	5,378	3,701	100.0	100.0	21,911	30,624	100.0	100.0

SOURCE: Adapted from Edward Higbee, *Farms and Farmers in an Urban Area* (New York: Twentieth Century Fund, 1963), Tables 1 and 2, pp. 155 and 156.

Although the number of farms declined by over 30 percent, productivity increased. The reduction has been concentrated largely in the least productive class of farms; at the end of the decade the latter still numbered 44 percent of all farms but produced slightly over 5 percent of the marketed product. By contrast, the most productive farms, which comprised 21 percent of all farms, produced 72 percent of the product reaching the market.

Over most of the economically developed world the sizes of farm populations are in absolute decline and have been for some time. The decline began in Britain in 1871, in France in 1881, and in Japan in 1901.[23] The farm population in the United States passed its peak in 1916. Since then its numbers have shrunk rapidly, especially since 1950. In 1967 there were but 10,875,000 people living on farms, a mere 5.5 percent of the nation's total population.[24] It is entirely probable that this fraction

[23] B. Hoselitz, "Advanced and Underdeveloped Countries: A Study in Development Contrasts," in *The Transfer of Institutions*, ed. by William B. Hamilton (Durham, N.C.: Duke University Press, 1964), p. 34.

[24] U.S. Bureau of the Census, "Farm Population of the United States, 1967," *Current Population Reports* (Washington, D.C., 1969).

will be cut in half during the next decade. Farm productivity per worker is increasing more rapidly than is the total volume of farm output.[25]

Changes in the organization and manpower requirements of agriculture have brought with them a general reduction in the differences between urban and rural styles of life. Widespread ownership of automobiles, telephones, radios, and television sets by rural people have given them as full an access to sources of news and information as urban residents enjoy. Accordingly, the rural population is well informed about national and international events, conscious of style changes, and subject to the consumer habits encouraged by national advertising. The longer travel distances made possible by the automobile have enabled them to bypass the village shopping center to buy directly in larger urban centers. Many villages have declined and disappeared as contacts with cities have multiplied. School consolidations are rapidly replacing the rural district school with modern, well-equipped, and competently staffed schools offering curricula that parallel those provided in city schools. In virtually every sphere of daily life the resident of the open country tends to be deeply involved in interests and activities served by urban-type institutions. Exceptions are found mainly among persons residing on the 44 percent of the farms with annual products valued at less than $2,500. Only there do vestiges of traditional rurality persist.[26]

URBANIZATION AND NATIONAL INTEGRATION

These observations of the growing importance of metropolitan areas in the social and cultural as well as the economic life of the nation invite an interesting contrast between the years prior to 1920 and the present in respect to the ties that bind the nation in a unity. During the regime of the railway, the coastal steamer, and the river boat, intercity and city-hinterland relations were restricted primarily to exchanges of materials and products. Transportation was too slow to encourage the development of a social structure that reached beyond the limits of a rather closely circumscribed locale. Each locality was relatively self-sufficient in all respects save its economic life. Regional and even local differences in interests, thought patterns, modes of speech, and historical orientations

[25] "The most profound of all displacements has been that in agriculture where, in the postwar period, a 5.7 percent annual rate of productivity increase accompanied by only a 1.4 percent increase in farm output has reduced the number of farm owners and workers from 8.2 million in 1947 to 4.8 million in 1964, or 42.3 percent." (H. R. Bowan and G. L. Mangum, *Automation and Economic Progress* [Englewood Cliffs, N.J.: Prentice-Hall, 1966], p. 16.)

[26] For detailed data on the urbanization of the rural population see Glenn V. Fuguitt, "The City and the Countryside," *Rural Sociology*, XXVIII (1963): 246–61.

were fostered in the small scope of experience allowed by the time-consuming means of transportation then in use. National integration could not be more than partial.

But with improved transportation and communication the mechanisms of territorial integration have become increasingly organizational in character. The growth of large-scale organization, operating alike in economic and noneconomic sectors, has spanned distances with many strands of interdependence and has woven a dense network of connections. The numbers of small units of organization in business and industry particularly have stagnated or declined. Mergers, federations, and growth based on competitive superiority have built the enlarged units in which the territorial division of labor is increasingly centralized.

Integration through large-scale organization has further centralized controls over the national society in a few urban areas. Local communities have given up their powers of initiative and decisions as the price, in a sense, of their participating in the larger society. According to one author, the subordination of the nation to the organization concentrated in a small number of metropolitan areas, most of which are located in the northeast, is breeding a new form of sectionalism.[27] That is to say, political alignments are beginning to form in opposition to or support for the northeastern "establishment." Whether historical divisions of the country can be revived despite the manifold interregional dependences remains to be seen. As yet the trend to which reference is made is of much too short a duration to be used as a basis for extrapolations. In any case, integration and centralization are different aspects of the same thing. It may well be that the ideal falls far short of complete or perfect integration, if it is to be achieved only by a corresponding degree of centralization.

GOVERNMENTAL REALIGNMENT

The centralizing tendency involved in the urbanization of an entire society is nowhere better illustrated than in the changing orientations of local governments toward the federal government of the United States. Local jurisdictional boundaries have lost their relevance for many purposes, particularly where metropolitan communities overlay a number of such units. The inability of local governments to resolve fiscal difficulties, attributable at least partly to the reluctance of state governments to attend to urban needs, has encouraged the development of direct relationships with the federal government. State governments are being bypassd in an increasing number of respects. A new federalism, composed not of states

[27] Daniel J. Elazar, "Megalopolis and the New Sectionalism," *The Public Interest* (Spring, 1968): 67–85.

but of cities and metropolitan areas, appears to be developing.[28] The origins of this trend have been traced to the years following the Civil War, but it has become most conspicuous after the 1930's.

The development of federal assistance programs has been occupied increasingly with urban needs. Several congressional enactments during the 1930's established the Federal Housing Administration, provided direct aid to low-rent public housing, and created the Federal National Mortgage Association to insure long-term mortgages for private home construction. In 1947 numerous federal agencies concerned with urban housing and related facilities were combined in the Housing and Home Finance Agency. Two years later a Housing Act put forth the first comprehensive urban renewal program for the clearance and redevelopment of slum lands. The 1949 law was revised in 1954, adding neighborhood rehabilitation and conservation to the renewal program. Urban mass transportation assistance was the subject of legislation in 1965. The following year saw the creation of a cabinet-level Department of Housing and Urban Development. Rent supplements and urban beautification programs were initiated in that year. Again, in 1966, additional legislation inaugurated model cities and metropolitan development programs. By 1967 federal assistance to local governments had grown to almost $15 billion annually, an increase of more than sixfold since 1950.

Through its widening range of programs of direct assistance to local governments, the federal government has added another facet to the organizational structure blanketing the nation. As with other facets of the structure, this one is also urban based. A serious effort is made to restrict the increase of central control. Attempts are made to place the burden of responsibility for participation in programs upon local governments. Still the rules are written, the standards are set, and the resources are controlled by the central authority. It might even be argued that the mere existence of federal programs, together with requirements such as that private industry must be included in local redevelopment planning, actually weaken local units. They relinquish some of their sovereignty with participation in each additional program. An empirical investigation has shown that the probability of joining in a federal program is positively affected by the extent of extralocal integration.[29] It is affected also by the degree of internal integration in urban areas. The more fully mobilized are local communities the more prepared they are to take advantage of new opportunities.

[28] Harry N. Scheiber, *The Conditions of American Federalism: An Historian's View*. A Study Submitted by the Subcommittee on Intergovernmental Relations to the Committee on Governmental Operations, United States Senate (Washington, D.C., 1966).

[29] Herman Turk, "Interorganizational Networks in Urban Society: Initial Perspective and Comparative Research," *American Sociological Review*, XXXV (1970): 1–18.

THE FUTURE OF THE CITY

The urbanization of an entire society raises a question as to whether the city, i.e., the relatively compact urban center, can continue to be useful. Its monopoly of non-agricultural employment has long since disappeared. Similarly it has ceased to be the sole dispenser of high culture. Great music, drama, art, and fine literature are accessible through many other channels. Means of instantaneous communication such as the radio, radiotelephone, television, and satellite have almost eliminated the city as a necessary vehicle for face-to-face exchanges. Kenneth Boulding, who writes in this vein, has pointed out that the value of the city for defense purposes vanished with the perfection of the atom and hydrogen bombs.[30] Indeed, the new weapons have converted the city into a potential trap for hundreds of thousands of people. Having lost most of its reasons for being, it would appear that the city cannot long survive.

But interpretations of current trends such as these, barring the implications of atomic weaponry, are based rather too much on a traditional conception of the city. That, as we have seen, is hardly relevant in the third quarter of the twentieth century. The urban unit is already far along the way toward a much more diffuse spatial pattern. The question, then, is: What is the future of the metropolitan community? Can an early end to the localization of collective life be foreseen? The interpretation would hang upon a near approach to zero of the time and costs of transportation and communication. Until that improbable engineering achievement is at hand, limits to the amounts of outlays for the costs of movement that can be borne by families, firms, and public agencies will remain in force. In fact, as the matrices of interdependence become more ramified it becomes increasingly difficult to stretch the network simultaneously in all directions. It is quite likely that the large urban unit has a greater survival capacity than have smaller ones, for it has much more to offer in the way of special services and opportunities for the pursuit of unique interests.

It seems doubtful, therefore, that urban units will disappear. If anything, the consumption of urban services continues to grow rather than to contract. Still, it seems certain that the territorial scope of urban places will be progressively enlarged over the next fifty years and more. Changes of structure will accompany increases of size. There are already indications that the widening spread of urban places will eventuate in the outer zones' being taken over by industrial districts and residential clusters

[30] "The Death of the City: A Frightened Look at Post-Civilization," in *The Historian and the City*, ed. by Oscar Handlin and John Burchard (Cambridge: The M.I.T. Press, 1966), pp. 142 ff. See also E. A. Gutkind, *The Twilight of Cities* (New York: The Free Press, 1962), pp. 111–19.

of wage-working classes. If so, what is to become of the inner cores of urban places? That they will be abandoned seems most improbable. They will not have lost their advantages of accessibility to the total urban space. One possibility is that core areas might be occupied by the residences of managerial and professional workers together with administrative offices, museums, legitimate theaters, concert halls, and other cultural institutions. Thus, as in other times and places, the working classes would be permitted to shoulder the burden of heavy commuter costs while the well-to-do enjoy easy access to their places of work and recreation. There is also the possibility of great variety in physical patterns among urban places, if only because the reduction of spatial and temporal restraints widens the range of choice and of whim.

SUMMARY

Urbanization in the United States, and to a lesser extent in other Western countries, has taken such possession of the entire country that there is no longer a meaningful distinction between urban and rural. Although differences in the densities at which various segments of the population live may persist for some time and perhaps indefinitely, differences in mode of life are rapidly disappearing. Social-economic rather than place-of-residence differences have become most important in accounting for unequal access to urban institutions and cultural opportunities.

The relationships of urban places with outlying territory have been studied in ways that have become increasingly refined. A simple notion of dominance of large metropolitan centers over surrounding areas provided initial insights into the territorial organization of the national society. A more refined conception appeared in the form of central-place theory, which visualized a geometrically symmetrical hierarchy with reference to sizes of places, spacing of places, and variety of functions performed by different size classes of urban units. But the assumption that urban places are engaged principally in service functions, on which central-place theory rested, is an oversimplification. It ignores the obvious distortion occasioned by various raw-material-extracting and manufacturing industries which pull urban places to eccentric locations. Thus the idea of a functional hierarchy has replaced that of a size and spacing hierarchy. Metropolitan areas tend to be ordered in series from national administrative centers, through regional to local administrative centers, but without anything approaching a neat spatial arrangement.

Centralization of controls in metropolitan areas has been affecting an enlarging number of facets of American society. This is observable in respect to manufacturing and commerce, corporate and voluntary association headquarters, banking, communications, and leadership generally. Although in a number of respects centralization has favored a small number of very large areas, in others there is evidence of a broadening of the participation of metropolitan areas in the administration of society.

National integration is a function largely of metropolitan organization. Originally the means by which that was accomplished was through economic exchanges over the transportation network. That left metropolitan areas and their tributary territories relatively self-sufficient in all other respects. But the growth of large-scale organization in voluntary associations as well as in business and industry has invaded most of the spheres of local self-sufficiency and has tied localities into an interregional system at many points. One of the most recent developments of this kind is the formation of a set of direct links between the federal government and local governments.

SUPPLEMENTARY READINGS

FOLEY, DONALD L. *Controlling London's Growth: Planning the Great Wen, 1940–1960* (Berkeley: University of California Press, 1963).

GREER, SCOTT. *The Emerging City* (New York: The Free Press, 1962).

GUTKIND, E. A. *The Expanding Environment: The End of Cities and the Rise of Communities* (London: Freedom Press, 1953).

VIDICH, ARTHUR J., and BENSMAN, JOSEPH. *Small Town in Mass Society* (Princeton: Princeton University Press, 1958).

WOOLEY, LEONARD. "The Urbanization of Society," *Journal of World History,* IV (1957): 245–257.

11

Metropolitan Problems

It is most unlikely that the momentous changes currently taking place in metropolitan areas could occur without significant repercussions in many phases of collective life. Indeed, metropolitan areas are the locations of some of the most critical problems of the present day. Yet it is interesting to note that a report on cities in the United States, prepared by a government advisory committee and published in 1937, identified thirty-six different categories of urban problems.[1] The list anticipated almost every contemporary problem, in many instances in the form in which it is now being experienced.

But many of the problems for which urban areas are now being held responsible are improperly assigned. The uneven progress of technological change with the social cost it engenders, large-scale movements of population, unequal distribution of a rising level of economic product, the tardy extension of civil rights to minority groups—these are not urban problems in the sense that they are caused by urbanization. They are problems of society as a whole. In the vast redistribution movements that have been in process for a century or more metropolitan areas have fallen heir to most of society's ills. As was shown in the preceding chapter, a modern Western society may be so far urbanized that it is pointless to cling to the old distinction between urban and rural. Nevertheless, it should be recognized that urban areas are not the sources of all pathologies, that many had a long history in rural areas before they were transported to their present locations.

Most social problems arise out of the irregular movement of change

[1] National Resources Committee, *Our Cities: Their Role in the National Economy* (Washington, D.C.: U.S. Government Printing Office, 1937), pp. 55–70.

241

and appear as dislocations in the normal operating relationships of the community or society. Even then the "problem" characterization is apt to be applied only when one or another factor in the situation proves resistant to adjustment. Inadequate resources, barriers to communication, jurisdictional limitations, and various kinds of inertia in organizations can be the sources of resistance. A problem includes both a dislocation and the frictions encountered in its resolution. Thus what constitutes a metropolitan problem varies in different socio-political contexts. There is no reason to believe *a priori* that the metropolitan problems of one country are repeated in all others of comparable levels of development. It is possible, however, that an analysis of the difficulties exprienced in a given country may have more than local interest, mainly for their suggestive value as to how problems arise and how they are constituted. In the investigation of problems that follows no attempt will be made to be exhaustive. A few of the more salient issues will be selected for discussion to illustrate as much as anything else some of the frictions incidental to growth.

TRANSPORTATION

Paradoxical as it may seem, the motor vehicle, which has played such a large part in the development of the metropolitan area, is now regarded in many quarters as the cause of the "metropolitan transportation problem." That there are very serious unanticipated consequences of automobile usage cannot be debated. The 70 million passenger automobiles on United States roads in 1965, representing more than one vehicle for every 2.5 persons in the population, have severely strained the traffic capacities of metropolitan thoroughfares. The volume of traffic has doubled since 1940 and will continue to mount rapidly.[2]

The problem as it is commonly presented is twofold. In the first place, it is contended that traffic congestion on city streets is forcing deconcentration with a resulting loss of land values and rising costs of maintaining and administering municipal services within central cities. Attention is drawn to the "unproductive" uses of land for parking where formerly multistoried buildings stood[3] and to the removal of lands from the tax rolls for the widening of streets and thoroughfares. Every improvement in traffic lanes seems to provoke greater traffic densities and further encouragement to deconcentration of industry and residences.

In the second place, the automobile is viewed as the cause of the de-

[2] Wilfred Owen, *The Metropolitan Transportation Problem* (Garden City, N.Y.: Doubleday, 1966), pp. 29–33.

[3] It is estimated that four or five square feet of parking space must be allowed for each square foot of commercial floor space.

clining fortunes of public transportation services. The volume of passengers carried in public transportation of all forms reached an early peak in the 1920's, subsided during the 1930's, rose again to the highest peak ever attained during the years of World War II, and since then has steadily contracted. Passengers carried declined from over 23 billion, in 1945, to less than 9 billion, in 1960.[4] While transit passenger volume was dropping to two fifths of what it was in 1945, auto passenger traffic was growing to two-and-one-half times its 1945 amount. With this change has gone a shift in the distribution of trips by type. Public carriers are used increasingly for work trips. Shopping, recreation, and trips for miscellaneous other purposes, which once used the off-peak capacities of public carriers, have passed to the private automobile. As the peaks and valleys of public carriers' usage have widened, they have narrowed in respect to automobile usage. In consequence, mass transportation services are in serious financial difficulties in most cities, especially where population growth has subsided to a near zero point, as in New York and Chicago.

The irony in the situation, according to the critics of the motor vehicle's effect on public transportation, is that the customary usage of the motor vehicle is so relatively inefficient. The average passenger load of the private automobile is 1.5 persons. Hence thirteen lanes of highway surface are required to transport as many persons per hour (i.e., 40,000) as a single-track transit line can carry in the same length of time.[5] "The typical (average) capital costs per person trip at peak hour capacity for freeways utilized entirely by automobile is $1,670, while the typical comparable cost for subways is $440 and for rail elevated lines is $140." [6]

Many of the cost and efficiency comparisons between modes of transportation are based on peak-hour traffic levels. Moreover, they are often cast in terms of the absolute maximum capacities of the facility being defended and the minimum or average passenger load of the competing facility. Absolute capacity exceeds realized loads in public carriers by three or four to one. Efficiency losses during peak-load hours vary with the extent to which traffic origins or destinations are concentrated as, for example, in a central business district. But the trend toward deconcentration, already far advanced, relieves traffic congestion as it scatters trip destinations. By the same token, deconcentration makes increasingly dif-

---

[4] Wilfred Owen, *op. cit.*, p. 237.

[5] Mark Reisenberg, *Growth and Change in Metropolitan Areas and Their Relation to Metropolitan Transportation: A Research Summary* (Evanston, Ill.: The Transportation Center at Northwestern University, 1966), p. 14. See also John R. Meyer, "Knocking Down the Straw Men," in *City and Suburb: The Economics of Metropolitan Growth,* ed. by Benjamin Chinitz (Englewood Cliffs, N.J.: Prentice-Hall, 1964), p. 90.

[6] Henry Quimby, "Major Urban Corridor Facilities: A New Concept," *Traffic Quarterly,* XVI (1962): 242–59.

ficult the provision of adequate service by public carriers, with the possible exception of the motor bus. As the spread of urban settlement grows thinner, reliance on the private automobile becomes more imperative. Urban travel flows are assuming a pattern characterized, says the transportation expert John R. Meyer, "more by a large number of relatively uniform, low-level, and criss-crossing trip densities than by very high concentrations in a few corridors emanating like spokes from the center of the city as was previously the case." [7]

The simple fact is that conventional economic considerations are not the guiding principles in the choice of transportation facilities. Flexibility, convenience, and privacy, despite higher trip costs, argue strongly for travel by private automobile. It is also true that the marginal costs of extra miles of automobile use are negligible. Of course, congestion can eliminate some of the major advantages of the automobile. Hence dependence on the motor vehicle for trips in the central cities of metropolitan areas varies inversely with size of area population, as may be seen in Table 48.[8] A

Table 48. Percentage of Work Trips by Selected Means of Travel, Place of Residence, and Size of Metropolitan Area (U.S., 1964)

Size of Metropolitan Area	Private Automobile or Car Pool		Public Transportation	
	Central City	Suburb	Central City	Suburb
Over 1,000,000	48	76	39	12
500,000–1,000,000	68	78	18	6
300,000– 500,000	70	80	15	4
250,000– 300,000	72	76	13	4
200,000– 250,000	72	75	11	3
Under 100,000	76	64	6	3

scarcity of parking space may alone destroy the convenience element for certain kinds of trips. But in general the growing number of trips the members of a family must take each day requires the utmost mobility, which only the automobile can provide.

The frame of reference for much of the concern over the metropolitan transportation problem is the compact city inherited from the nineteenth century. The presumption is that the inheritance must be preserved at

---

[7] *Op. cit.*, p. 89.

[8] Leo Schnore presents data showing fairly close relationships of public transportation usage with size, density and age of cities, in "The Use of Public Transportation in Urban Areas," *Traffic Quarterly*, XVI (1962): 488–98.

the expense, if necessary, of full use of improvements in transportation and communication. This view overlooks the fact that the urban or metropolitan area is essentially a communication system. The amenities it offers vary in direct proportion to the efficiency with which information, goods, and people are able to circulate. Efficiency has fallen short of the potential, but that hardly seems to be adequate grounds for reverting to an obsolescent urban concept. What has been called the transportation problem might with equal appropriateness be termed a problem of outmoded physical structure and of fiscal chaos.

ENVIRONMENTAL POLLUTION

In recent years the urban public has been made aware as never before of some of the consequences of its uses of its immediate physical environment. No other form of human settlement involves so intensive a use of occupied space. Intensity of use imposes undue strains on local water resources, alters climate and surface features, and creates an enormous task of solid and liquid waste disposal. Intensity of use is but one aspect of environmental problems. A second aspect rests with the tools and techniques employed. The fuels consumed in heating buildings and producing power, the rate of consumption and the manner of packaging consumer goods, and the materials used in the construction of streets and buildings exert a marked influence on the urban environment. There is also an organizational dimension, of which more will be said presently.

The maintenance of an abundant and reasonably pure water supply for urban populations has demanded increasing amounts of ingenuity and of financial outlays. Although lakes and streams, which constitute the principal sources of supply, may contain water in abundance, the supply is effectively reduced by the use of the sources for waste disposal. Waterborne sewage and waters contaminated in industrial processes are dumped back into lakes and streams. The reuse of the water for either domestic or industrial purposes requires expensive purification procedures. On the domestic side progress continues to be made, though it is surprisingly late in developing. In 1960, 83 percent of the urban population in the United States were served by sanitary sewers, though only some 63 percent were protected by sewage treatment facilities.[9] Water purification plants, however, are nearly universal in urban areas. But the extensive pollution of supplies adds greatly to the costs of purification and multiplies the hazards of failures in the systems. The success attained in the control of water-

[9] M. D. Hollis, "The Water Pollution Image," *Urbanization, Proceedings: The National Conference on Water Pollution*. U.S. Department of Health, Education and Welfare (Washington, D.C., 1961), pp. 30–40.

carried infections has been remarkable. It may not always be so. A note of warning is sounded by the American Chemical Society in a recent report entitled "Cleaning Our Environment: The Chemical Basis for Action." Very little is known, says the report, about the health effects of the many unidentified chemical compounds now entering municipal water supplies and there is corresponding uncertainty over the ability of water purification plants to deal with the contaminants.[10]

The control of pollution stemming from industrial cyclings of water has much further to go. In part that is because the problems are as diverse as are the industries creating them. But it is also due to the costs involved in carrying out the research needed to analyze the "unidentified chemical compounds" that are being discharged, in developing the appropriate control mechanisms, and in installing them. One estimate of the total costs that will have to be faced by the year 2000 places them at $275 billions for the correction of all kinds of industrial pollution.[11] An additional factor is the relative powerlessness of local governments to enforce conformity to purification standards. Where appropriate powers are available, they may not be exercised for fear that the result will be industrial relocation and still another loss to a city's tax base.

Pollution is not confined to the immediate environs of urban areas. Crops irrigated with contaminated water can be damaged or rendered harmful to health. Industrial pollutants have destroyed game fish and have spoiled beaches and other outdoor recreational resources.[12] The phosphates in detergents and run-off waters carrying lawn fertilizers have led to excessive growth of plant life in ponds and lakes, causing them to lose their attractiveness for boating and swimming. This latter is a reversible process; ponds and lakes can be restored to a nearly original state through concerted action.

Almost as serious is the pollution of the air. In this, too, industry figures prominently, as also do domestic furnaces and power-generating plants. Another major contributor is the motor vehicle. The refuse from combustion in these various energy converters is discharged into the atmosphere as solids, in the form of particles of dust and grit, and as gases such as carbon monoxide, sulfur dioxide, and a variety of nitrogen oxides. The effects of these pollutants on urban population depend a great deal on climate.

Urban areas, however, create distinctive climatic features.[13] The many

[10] *Science*, CLXV (12 September, 1969), pp. 1104–1107.
[11] James J. Hanks and Harold D. Kabe, "Industry Action to Combat Pollution," *Harvard Business Review*, XLIV (1966): 44–62.
[12] "Pollution: A Growing Problem in a Growing Nation," in *Water: The Yearbook of Agriculture, 1955* (Washington, D.C., 1955), p. 637.
[13] William P. Lowry, "The Climate of Cities," *Scientific American*, CCXVII (August, 1967): 15–33.

rocklike surfaces on building walls and street pavements store the sun's heat during the day and give it off slowly at night. Heat storage is augmented by the action of the surfaces as reflectors, directing the rays of the sun into corners and onto walls not directly exposed to the sun. The numerous energy converters concentrated in the city give off vast amounts of heat which add further warmth to the air in and above the city. Moreover, the rapid run-off of rain and melted snow waters reduces the cooling effects of evaporation, thus allowing the air to retain its warmth for longer than would otherwise be possible. One other element of urban climate derives from pollution itself. Particles of dust and ash collect at the top of the column of warm air, and hang in suspension over the city in what is called a "dust dome." Consequently there is a haziness or cloudiness over an urban area that does not exist over open country. The accumulation remains in place as long as there is no wind to carry it away. Most of these characteristics have been found to vary with the size of the urban agglomeration.

Under proper meteorological conditions the cooling of the air at nighttime causes moisture to condense on the particles held in suspension, producing fog. As the fog thickens and descends to ground level it, with the impurities it contains, is recognized as smog. Coincidentally the sulfur dioxide gas may be precipitated as a weak sulfuric acid. The appropriate meteorological conditions—a great deal of sunshine, light winds, little rain, and sheltering effects of nearby mountain ranges—are present in combination in the Los Angeles area.[14] Smog is therefore a frequent occurrence in that locality. In certain seasons of the year similar conditions occur along the northeastern coast of the United States, in London, England, and elsewhere. In the absence of diffusing breezes the ground level atmosphere may be chronically saturated with pollutants.

Although the threat to health of airborne waste matters from combustion has yet to be fully assessed,[15] there is clearly an aesthetic and an economic loss to the communities affected. Offensive odors, soiled clothes, and irritated eyes and skin are discomforting enough. But there is also material damage to the paint on houses, rubber tires, metal products, nylon fabrics and plant life. The annual costs represented in these damages were estimated in one metropolitan area to amount to $20,000 per person.[16]

The control of air pollution seems to present no great technical problems. The costs tend to vary with the standards imposed, however. Some

[14] H. F. Gregor, "Spatial Disharmonies in California Population Growth," *Geographical Review*, LIII (1963): 100–22.

[15] C. Stafford Brandt, "Air Is for More than Breathing," *A Place to Live: The Yearbook of Agriculture, 1963* (Washington, D.C., 1963), p. 128.

[16] *Report of the International Joint Commission (U.S. and Canada) on the Pollution of the Atmosphere in the Detroit River Area* (Washington, D.C., 1960).

controls have even proven profitable; sulfuric acid has been reclaimed
from sulfur dioxide and arsenic has been extracted from the same source.[17]
But control requires cooperation among local units of government within
metropolitan areas. That has been far more difficult to achieve. For in
the competition for industry each administrative unit is reluctant to impose additional expenses upon the firms within its boundaries.

Most proposals for the correction of environmental pollution treat the
problem as a simple matter of man's misbehavior. The complexity that is
recognized lies mainly on the environmental side of the equation. There
is insufficient awareness of the fact that the misbehavior in question is
invariably embedded in a highly ramified system of relationships. Man's
relation to his physical environment has been developed and is maintained
through the organization he has achieved and not by each individual taken
separately. If there is to be any hope of a lasting solution to environmental misuse, it will have to begin in the social structure of the community and society.[18]

URBAN BLIGHT

The physical structure as well as the physical environment of the urban
unit is subject to misuse. This has commonly been referred to by the word
"blight" rather than "pollution." "Blight" is an evaluative term and as
such it is much more difficult of measurement than are water and air pollution.[19] Like them, nevertheless, it is a product of institutional circumstances and processes. A blighted area is one that has lost its attractiveness for all of its former uses; consequently, its buildings and installation
have been allowed to fall into deterioration. There are various factors
that enter into an explanation of how that comes about.

The physical deterioration of an area occurs usually though not necessarily in conjunction with the obsolescence of the structures within it. At
the roots of obsolescence in many instances is speculation in the values of
land. Owners, most of whom live elsewhere, are content to let properties
sink into decay while waiting for a high-intensity use to bid for the land.
In the meantime many owners may receive relatively high rents for buildings that were amortized long ago and that are currently deprived of the
usual repair and maintenance services. Speculation is often misguided,

---

[17] C. Stafford Brandt, *op. cit.*, pp. 122, 126.
[18] See Otis Dudley Duncan, "From Social System to Ecosystem," *Sociological
Enquiry*, XXXI (1961): 140–49.
[19] For a review of the problems of measurement see Coleman Woodbury (ed.),
Urban Redevelopment: Problems and Practices (Chicago: University of Chicago
Press, 1953), pp. 16–54.

however. Some property owners are unrealistic or misinformed about the rate or the direction of change. Hence their aspirations for the values of their holdings will not soon, if ever, be realized.[20] Sometimes that is encouraged by planning agencies that over-zone lands ringing central business districts for commercial uses. In so doing they prematurely depress the residential utility of the lands and raise false hopes among owners.

Another source of influence on the physical deterioration of buildings lies in the agencies that are in the business of lending money for home construction and improvement—banks, building and loan associations, and insurance firms. These agencies have followed policies of "blacklisting" areas of old residential properties or areas upon which deleterious uses are encroaching.[21] The withholding of mortgage monies leaves no alternative in most cases to a continuous neglect of the structures. Thus credit agencies contribute to blight where they might have created enhanced values.

These tendencies are both cause and effect of the centrifugal relocation of erstwhile occupants of blighted areas. Obsolescence, deterioration, and the drying up of sources of funds for remodeling and reclamation lend impetus to the outward movement. That, in turn, accelerates the downward spiral. So far has the process gone in some places that buildings are abandoned by their owners to stand as fire hazards and as shelters for predatory members of the population.[22] In the past there was always a chance that city growth would arrest the blighting process by turning up new clients for uneconomically occupied spaces. But modern forms of intramural transportation have eliminated that prospect. Growth is spread widely over the suburban zone.

While blighted areas offend aesthetic sensibilities, and, too, represent a measure of depletion of a city's tax base, they are a resource of sorts to the urban area at large. New enterprises having little capital can find inexpensive quarters in the outmoded buildings.[23] By that means the community might be regarded as subsidizing innovation and possible enrichment of the economy. Similarly, the old buildings provide cheap meeting places for neighborhood assemblies, theater and dance groups, and other gatherings. One wonders, however, about the value that should be assigned to the constructive uses of old, dilapidated buildings, for there are cost factors in the use of neglected properties such as fire risks and

[20] Collapses of large-scale speculation activities in lands are reported to have occurred in 1819, 1836, 1859, 1873, 1893 and 1929. (M. Mason Gaffary, "Urban Expansion—Will It Ever Stop," *Yearbook of Agriculture,* 1959 [Washington, D.C., 1958], p. 513.)

[21] See Jane Jacobs, *The Life and Death of Great American Cities* (New York: Random House, 1961), ch. 16.

[22] See "When Landlords Walk Away," *Time* (March 16, 1970), pp. 88–90.

[23] Jane Jacobs, *op. cit.,* ch. 10.

hazards to health and welfare.[24] If communities are to subsidize creative activities, it would seem wiser to do so deliberately and with attention to what is needed rather than inadvertently.

SLUM AND GHETTO

One of the principal uses of blighted areas is as housing for the poor and underprivileged. The word "slum" is often applied to such residential areas, especially where the buildings are old, lacking in most modern amenities, and are densely occupied. It is an invidious term that reflects, as Scott Greer has pointed out, middle-class predilections.[25] The social characteristics of the localities subject to the slum label vary between fairly wide extremes. At one pole is an area occupied by a relatively stable, socially integrated, working class population such as is found in many ethnic neighborhoods.[26] At the other extreme is a district of rooming houses, cheap hotels, and tiny apartments the residents of which are so transient that they develop few patterns of mutual aid or collective action of any kind.

Between the two extremes lie the areas housing the great mass of the urban poor. These are found mainly in the interiors of central cities, though rural slums also appear in unincorporated spaces outside of but contiguous to metropolitan centers. The residents are families, for the most part; often they are broken by death or divorce or they are impaired by the incapacity of one of the parents. In a large part of the slum population the income is depressed to three fifths or less of what is needed for a "level of adequate living," i.e., $5,300 to $6,500 per year (*circa* 1960).[27] Inadequate housing is not, of course, the only characteristic of the slum. Congestion, lack of recreational space, and a neglect of neighborhood facilities of every kind appear to be counterparts of defective housing.

Slum conditions are manifestly not conducive to physical and mental health. They do, in fact, embrace disproportionate amounts of delinquency, crimes against the person, and domestic discord. Yet there is no satisfactory evidence that such circumstances cause individual and social disorders.[28] The probability that the problems associated with

[24] The National Association of Home Builders, in *A New Face for America* (1953), contended that slums in cities consume 45 percent of municipal revenues, but contribute only 6 percent of the total property taxes collected. (p. 6)

[25] *Urban Renewal and American Cities* (Indianapolis: Bobbs-Merrill Co., 1965), ch. 2.

[26] See Herbert Gans, *The Urban Villagers*, chs. 1 and 2.

[27] It is estimated in 1958 that an income of $6,000 was required to assure adequate housing. (Alvin L. Schoer, *Slums and Social Security* [Washington, D.C.: Department of Health, Education and Welfare, 1963], p. 98.)

[28] A large part of the literature bearing on this question has been examined by Alvin L. Schoer (*op. cit.*). The state of knowledge is inconclusive.

slums are attributable to their selectivity of residents is at least as great as is the probability that they cause the problem behavior. Certainly poverty, with all of the deprivations for which it is responsible, is a far more important cause of slum problems than are the physical conditions themselves. There is the further influence of minority status which is usually mingled inextricably with poverty. Minority status is often temporary; it is associated with recent migration from depressed rural areas or from foreign origins. In that event, the slum is a point of easiest entry into a strange society and a way station on the path to assimilation. In a generation or two the minority group may disappear, unless it is marked by color.

When the residents of a slum or of any residential area, for that matter, are confined to their quarters by institutionalized practices, whether imposed from within or without, the area tends to be described as a "ghetto." Although in the United States no cultural differences separate black and white sectors of the population and although Negroes may rise to social and economic levels of achievement rivaling those attained by whites, they nevertheless have but a limited choice among residential places. That more often than otherwise turns out to be in areas of advanced obsolescence, if not of outright dilapidation. Three sets of factors have contributed to the blacks' segregation in particular areas within cities. One is the condition of poverty itself. The economically deprived are unable to occupy any but the cheapest rental housing. Second, the movement of whites toward city peripheries and suburbs and their replacement in old residential areas by blacks makes for increasing separation of color groups. The suburbanward movement, though influenced in some localities by influxes of blacks, is basically a response to quite different circumstances. The effect is the same, of course, regardless of the cause.

Institutional practices comprise a third factor. Prominent among such practices have been the activities of land developers and real estate brokers. For example, virtually all real estate subdivisions created in northern urban areas from the early 1920's until the mid-1940's had clauses written into their deeds which prohibited the resale of the residential lots to people of other than Caucasian stock. The "protective covenant," as that clause was designated, was assumed to have the force of a contract. By that means blacks were restricted to old sections of cities. A Supreme Court decision finally, in 1948, declared the "protective covenant" unenforceable.[29] Another institutionalized practice is that of real estate brokers who, under the guise of a "code of ethics," refuse to negotiate sales of property in all-white neighborhoods to members of colored groups. The role of self-appointed custodian of property values has been defended by

[29] *Shelley* v. *Kraemer*, 334 U.S. 1 (1948).

realtors on the basis of a number of questionable assumptions about the determinants of market prices of residential lands and buildings. One of the few competent studies of the effects of non-white entry into white areas dealt with a number of neighborhoods in seven different cities. The principal finding was that non-white invasion was more often associated with price improvement or price stability than with a deterioration of property values. No single pattern of results, however, was found to occur.[30] There is no evidence that studies of that kind have affected the habits of realtors or the ultra-conservative policies of banks and other mortgage-lending institutions.

Thus the ghetto is a slum enclosed by a wall of discrimination. This is manifested in nearly every respect that might be considered. Twice as many of the blacks' houses are overcrowded as are those of whites, and the differential incidence of dilapidation and lack of modern plumbing is about the same.[31] Should the black try to buy a home, he has relatively little access to federally insured mortgages. Hence he must accept short-term mortgages at high interest rates.[32] Neither the education of his parents nor the quality of his segregated schools [33] assure the black child equal opportunity with white children; his performance on national standardized tests is therefore two years below his grade level, whereas the white child is almost a year better than his grade level.[34] Unemployment among blacks is twice as frequent as among whites and it is particularly concentrated in the labor force entry ages of 16 to 20 years.[35] As a consequence of all these disabilities, downward mobility, measured by comparisons of sons' with fathers' occupations, is far more common among Negroes than is upward mobility.[36]

URBANIZATION OF THE BLACK POPULATION

The ghetto notwithstanding, blacks have crowded into cities, largely because they have nowhere else to go. The process of urban concentration has advanced beyond that of the white population. Historically blacks have moved first to cities within the region of initial residence, which is the southeast for the most part, and have later moved to larger

[30] Luigi Laurenti, *Property Values and Race: Studies in Seven Cities* (Berkeley: University of California Press, 1961), p. 47.

[31] U.S. Bureau of the Census, "Social and Economic Conditions of Negroes in the United States," *Current Population Reports*, Series p-23, No. 24 (Washington, D.C., 1967), pp. 33 and 57.

[32] *Ibid.*, p. 58.

[33] *Ibid.*, p. 48.

[34] *Ibid.*, p. 49.

[35] *Ibid.*, pp. 31 ff.

[36] U.S. Department of Health, Education and Welfare, *Toward a Social Report* (Washington, D.C., 1969), p. 24.

urban areas outside of the region of residence, especially to northern urban areas. Ebbs and flows have marked the latter phase of urbanward movement. It began on a large scale in 1916, in response to the labor requirements of the expanded wartime economy of World War I, and subsided with the termination of that war.[37] Although migration into northern metropolitan centers began to increase in the late 1930's, the next great surge came during and particularly after World War II. This most recent phase of black population redistribution has drawn heavily upon southern rural areas, in what amounts to a distress migration of poverty-stricken citizens, as well as upon urban areas of the south. In south, north, and other regions of the country migrations of blacks have focussed on the largest urban centers; the larger the city, the more rapid has been the growth of the black population.[38] Whereas in 1950 12 percent of the population of metropolitan central cities was black, the proportion had increased to 20 percent by 1966. At the latter date 66 percent of the Washington, D.C., population was black, 47 percent of that in Newark, 36 percent in St. Louis, and 34 percent in Detroit. In Atlanta, Memphis, and New Orleans the proportions of blacks exceeded 40 per cent. These proportions are not entirely due to black population growth; they result also from evacuation of central city areas in favor of suburban residences by the white population.

Settlement by blacks in northern cities replaced the foreign-born groups who had preceded them. But unlike the previous residents of those old areas, blacks have tended to remain in them. In Chicago, as O. D. Duncan and Beverley Duncan have shown, the pattern of Negro settlement was established as early as 1920 and remained unchanged through 1950.[39] There is no reason to believe that the experience has been appreciably different in other comparable settings. Expansion from the districts of principal concentration tends to be a laborious process of penetration into adjacent areas. As that has occurred the space vacated by lateral movements is filled anew by later migrants from other cities or rural areas. Occasionally the areas of greatest concentration continue to grow despite losses to adjacent districts.[40] But the areas of major black concentration in the ten central cities of metropolitan areas studied by Karl and Alma Taeuber remained comparatively unaffected by the 1955–60 migrations. Substantial increases occurred, however, in tracts of lesser concentration.[41]

[37] U.S. Department of Labor, *Negro Migration in 1916–17* (Washington, D.C., 1919).

[38] In 1960 58 percent of the blacks residing in northern states east of the Mississippi River lived in the eight largest cities.

[39] *The Negro Population of Chicago: A Study of Residential Succession* (Chicago: University of Chicago Press, 1957), ch. 5.

[40] Duncan and Duncan, *ibid.*, p. 195.

[41] *Negroes in Cities: Residential Segregation and Neighborhood Change* (New York: Atheneum, 1969), pp. 144–50.

The distribution trends during the decade of the 1960's are blurred by incomplete information. In some metropolitan central cities it appears, as shown in Table 49, that concentration was resumed once more. Migration flows may have pushed Afro-American population increases above the supplies of housing available in mixed residential areas. On the other

Table 49. Percentage of All Blacks in Selected Cities Living in Census Tracts
(Grouped According to Proportion Black in 1960 and 1964–66)

City	Year	All Census Tracts	Census Tracts, by Proportion Negro			
			75% or More	50 to 74%	25 to 49%	Under 25%
Cleveland	1960	100	72	16	8	4
	1965	100	80	12	4	4
Phoenix	1960	100	19	36	24	21
	1965	100	18	23	42	17
Buffalo	1960	100	35	47	6	12
	1966	100	69	10	13	8
Louisville	1960	100	57	13	17	13
	1964	100	67	13	10	10
Shreveport	1960	100	79	10	7	4
	1966	100	90	—	6	4
Des Moines	1960	100	—	28	31	41
	1966	100	—	42	19	39
Rochester	1960	100	8	43	17	32
	1964	100	16	45	24	15
Evansville	1960	100	34	27	9	30
	1866	100	59	14	—	27
Raleigh	1960	100	86	—	7	7
	1966	100	88	4	2	6

SOURCE: U.S. Bureau of the Census, "Social and Economic Conditions of Negroes in the United States," 1969, p. 12.

hand, there were indications elsewhere of the beginnings of a suburban movement of Negroes.[42] No doubt this has been made possible to some extent by a general reduction in the amount of poverty. Important gains

[42] U.S. Bureau of the Census, "Trends in Social and Economic Conditions in Metropolitan Areas," *Current Population Reports*, Series p-23, No. 27 (Washington, D.C., 1969), p. 3.

on that score have been realized by blacks as well as by whites, though almost one third of the entire black population, in 1967, still fell below the poverty threshold, as may be seen in Table 50. While the general trend was downward, metropolitan central cities continued to absorb increasing proportions of the impoverished population. Rural poverty

Table 50. Number and Percentage of Population Below the Poverty Threshold[a] (By Color and Type of Place)

Type of Place and Color	Millions		Percentage	
	1967	1959	1967	1959
United States	26.1	39.4	13%	22%
Metropolitan areas	13.2	18.3	10	17
Central cities	8.3	11.3	14	20
White	4.7	7.1	10	15
Black	3.5	4.1	30	43
Suburban rings	4.9	7.0	7	13
White	4.0	5.7	6	11
Black	0.9	1.2	28	52
Outside metropolitan areas	12.9	21.1	19	32
White	9.1	15.9	15	27
Black	3.7	4.9	55	77

[a]The definition of poverty is based on estimated minimum needs of families, taking account of size, number of children, and nonfarm residence. The poverty threshold for a family of four was $3,335 in 1967 and $3,060 in 1959.

SOURCE: U.S. Bureau of the Census, "Trends in Social and Economic Conditions in Metropolitan Areas," p. 52

shifted to metropolitan centers. One fourth of the population of central cities, in 1968, resided in what were designated as poverty areas. But that proportion represents a 21-percent decline since the beginning of the decade. Blacks as well as whites have been deserting the slums of major cities.[43] How much of the scatter can be attributed to the reduction of poverty and how much to other circumstances, such as residential relocations necessitated by urban renewal and a belated enforcement of open housing, is not known.

SUBURBAN–CENTRAL CITY SEPARATION

Suburbs have been attracting to themselves not just the middle and upper classes, but, as noted in an earlier chapter, the more successful or

[43] *Ibid.,* p. 64.

the more fortunate members of all strata in the urban population. Thus it would appear that central cities are being depleted of those elements of the population from which leaders are recruited and which constitute the solid basis of responsible citizenship. They are being replaced by inexperienced and underprivileged people who have fallen heir, as it were, to an obsolescent physical structure. Without trying to exaggerate the cleavage and its consequences, there are a number of real and potential problems worth consideration.

A relocating population tends to take with it or to re-create at the new location the institutions from which it normally obtains its services. In the suburbs, accordingly, appear schools with curriculums designed to meet the expectations of upwardly mobile parents, churches that represent the denominational and liturgical predilections of the residents, and clubs, recreational facilities, and shops that cater to the respective types of people. None of this is new. There was a similar affinity of institutions for special categories or classes of population within built-up urban areas before deconcentration had advanced far along its present course. That tendency persists still in large cities. Thus to speak of the "suburban captivity of the church" [44] is somewhat misleading. There has long been an upper-class residential district captivity of certain churches, and a middle-class residential captivity of certain other churches, and so forth. A stratification of churches has matched the stratification of population. The flight of churches to the suburbs has not really been documented. A Seattle study has shown that fewer than 8 percent of the suburban churches had prior locations within central city boundaries.[45] The tendency has been for old congregations to break up with the turnover of population in an area and for new congregations to form in new locations, suburban or otherwise.

It is true, of course, that population deconcentration has carried wealth and buying power with it. Central cities have found it increasingly difficult to compete for the best among the teachers, preachers, and other institutional personnel. Higher salaries and better facilities and programs are available in the suburbs. But not all suburbs are alike in that regard. As has been pointed out elsewhere, there is great variation among them. Some, those with large industrial properties on their tax rolls, are rich in public monies; others with tax bases composed almost entirely of residential properties, barring a few enclaves of very wealthy residents, are relatively poor. Despite the presence of irregularities, taxable wealth is ac-

[44] Gibson Winter, *The Suburban Captivity of the Churches: An Analysis of Protestant Responsibility in the Expanding Metropolis* (Garden City, N.Y.: Doubleday, 1961).

[45] George Myers, "Patterns of Church Distribution and Movement," *Social Forces*, 40 (1962): 361–62.

cumulating much more rapidly in the suburban zone than it is in central cities.

Furthermore, suburbanization creates a kind of absentee control of central cities and of other parts of metropolitan areas as well. Executives who occupy key policy positions in industry, banking, and business generally tend to live in a few residential suburbs. Nevertheless, their decisions in matters such as plant locations, capital investment, employment and wage levels, and the pricing of products have a critical significance for the welfare of the entire metropolitan community. They affect public outlays for roads and utilities, they influence the amount of police and fire protection required, they have much to do with the rate and direction of population change—in fact, there are few areas of official policy that are not influenced by decisions made in the economic institutions. Yet many of the individuals responsible for those decisions are not directly subject to their effects.

URBAN RENEWAL

Plagued by an accumulation of physical and social problems, none of which promises to yield to an early solution, central cities have turned to the federal government for help. The help sought has been mainly for financial assistance in rebuilding blighted areas. This reflects in part an interpretation of social problems as due to housing deficiencies. But there has also been the hope that a physical renewal of deteriorated sections would restore the depleted tax base directly and indirectly through stimulating private investment in inner city property. Thus what began as federal assistance in the clearance of slums and their replacement with public housing was transformed in the course of experience and political debate to a broader program of urban redevelopment.

The Housing Act of 1949 provided grant funds for surveys and plans, and loans for the acquisition and clearance of lands to be redeveloped. It was required that the redevelopment plan be approved by the local government, that it conform to a general plan for the development of the district as a whole, that there be provisions for the relocation of the displaced residents, and that the purchaser of the project land be required to complete the development as planned in a reasonable period of time. A revision of the Housing Act in 1954 was designed to shift more of the responsibility for urban renewal to local governments and to the private sector. Its principal innovation was insistence that to qualify for federal aid the local community present a "workable program." This concept included (1) a comprehensive plan for the elimination of slums and the redevelopment of formerly slum lands, (2) the relocation of displaced slum dwellers in standard housing, (3) the enforcement of housing codes in order to bring substandard houses up to code standards, and (4) the use of local funds to improve public facilities in renewal areas. That and later revisions reduced the proportion of project funds that must go to housing from nearly 100 to 70 percent.[46] The proportion was further reduced in practice by loose interpretations of the terms of the legislation.

Federal assistance to urban renewal has produced a number of positive effects, many of them intangible, such as enlivening community interest, giving a new emphasis to planning, and liberalizing the principle of eminent domain. Its tangible products are harder to identify.[47] Many existing problems have been aggravated. While the replacement of slum properties with new housing has added to the taxable value in cities, the program has reduced the supply of housing for low-income earners. The new housing is in most cases too expensive for the displaced population. The relocation provision in the "workable program" has been honored more in the breach than in practice. Whether out of negligence or from sheer lack of availability of comparable housing, families displaced from renewal areas have been sorely inconvenienced. In some instances they have been scattered widely over urban areas and far from districts in which their employment and other interests are located. Their expenditures for transportation have been increased, at any rate until adjustment to the new residential areas are made. They have also had to pay more for housing. Table 51 indicates that housing costs after relocation exceeded pre-relocation costs by 7 to 15 percent, depending on the sizes of families. The black population has borne most of the relocation costs, for their areas have been most subject to renewal.

More difficult to assess is the importance of the breakup of neighborhoods and of voluntary associations by land clearances and relocations. No provision is made for the transfer of a social group as a unit.[48] Instead friends and relatives are separated, the clienteles of institutions are dispersed, small businesses are destroyed,[49] and the support and satisfaction derived from an intimate neighborhood life are vitiated. How serious a loss is the destruction of a neighborhood organization can be regarded as arguable. Perhaps it is a small cost in view of the greater enhancement

---

[46] The development of urban renewal legislation is discussed in full by Ashley A. Foard and Hilbert Fefferman, "Federal Urban Renewal Legislation," *Law and Contemporary Problems*, XXV (1960): 635–84.

[47] See the set of papers on this point that have been brought together in *Urban Renewal: The Record and the Controversy*, ed. by James Z. Wilson (Cambridge: M.I.T. Press, 1966), pp. 489–582.

[48] Herbert Gans, "The Human Implications of Current Redevelopment and Relocation Planning," *Journal of the American Institute of Planners*, XXV (1959): 15–26.

[49] Basil Zimmer, *Rebuilding Cities: The Effects of Displacement and Relocation on Small Businesses* (Chicago: Quadrangle Books, 1964), ch. 2.

Table 51. Average Monthly Rental Before and After Relocation
(By Family Size, Nine Cities, 1955–58)

Size of Family	Before Relocation	After Relocation	Difference
2	$30.35	$34.81	$4.46
3	32.35	36.23	3.88
4	34.45	37.96	3.51
5	36.50	39.07	2.57

N = 1,373.
SOURCE: Harry W. Reynolds, "The Human Element in Urban Renewal," *Public Welfare,* 19 (1961): 71.

of the general welfare. There may be some merit, too, in dissolving in-grown enclaves, if doing so forces their residents into a fuller participation in the larger community. Still, the neighborhood might be the only social resource an underprivileged group possesses. The recent "model cities" program has recognized this and is trying to build upon existing neighborhood organizations to improve the physical equipment of residential areas.

A large and increasing proportion of urban renewal funds has been devoted to rebuilding the inner core, especially the central business district. By this means the public is made to subsidize the value of lands owned by a small number of investors. The consequence may be to merely delay a process of dispersion which soon will reassert itself. It may be a waste of public funds to try to perpetuate an outmoded city pattern. But if redevelopment of the inner city restores taxable value, everyone may benefit. The question that needs to be answered is: are the known facts used honestly and objectively to inform policy decisions.

POLITICAL DISUNITY

There are few contemporary urban problems that are not seriously aggravated by the presence in metropolitan areas of a multiplicity of autonomous and semi-autonomous governmental units.[50] It hardly needs to be said at this juncture that local jurisdictional concepts developed in the nineteenth century and before are inappropriate for a society mounted on wheels and equipped with electronic communication devices. The anomaly is compounded where such jurisdictions are juxtaposed in close proximity as in the present metropolitan area.

[50] Morton Grodzins and Edward Banfield hold a diametrically opposed view. (*Government and Housing in Metropolitan Areas* [New York: McGraw-Hill, 1958], p. 156.)

The result is that a great many functions of government can be treated only in a fragmentary way. Health is a case in point. Infections recognize no political boundaries. Likewise, planning is deprived of the scope necessary for effective action. It is either reduced to trivialities within a jurisdiction or faced with the need to create yet another jurisdiction. Transportation can no more be treated as an intramural concern than can health. Polluted streams flow across governmental boundaries and airborne contaminants follow the breezes. Water supplies are drawn from a common source, whether it is a surface source or an underground water table. Independent action addressed to such matters is rarely adequate, and frequently it is contrary to the interests of an adjacent political unit. So it is also in respect to social policy. In order for residential desegregation of races to be effective, for example, it should have joint action by all contiguous governments. Open housing legislation in one suburb, while others preserve their exclusiveness, tends only to develop another ghetto.

There are many precedents for intergovernmental cooperation at the local level. Cities and counties often pool their health facilities; police jurisdictions have been extended over a number of metropolitan areas; and there are joint arrangements for water supply, fire protection, and other services. But these agreements are almost invariably restricted to particular functions. Each unit jealously guards its autonomy. Sometimes the jealousy produces unnecessary costs. When the city of Utica purchased the water company serving its metropolitan area, the surrounding cities and towns were given the option of buying from Utica the water mains and other equipment within their boundaries. Not only did they not take up the option, they secured a law permitting them to tax the capital equipment. Utica could only respond by raising the price of water so that in the end the suburbs were paying more for water than they had previously.[51]

Administrative cumbersomeness is one side of the problem coin; the other side is fiscal fragmentation. As industrial plants, commercial installations, and new housing developments have moved suburbanward, central cities have been progressively isolated from the fiscal resources needed to maintain service levels.[52] This has happened at a time during which the demands on central cities in their roles as metropolitan centers have grown steadily larger. Fiscal embarrassment is not peculiar to the central city, however. There is simply not enough industrial and commercial property, which comprise the most lucrative component in a tax base, to

[51] V. C. Crisafulli, "Economic Development Efforts in the Utica-Rome, New York Area," in *Community Economic Development Efforts: Five Case Studies*, Supplementary Paper No. 18, Committee for Economic Development (New York, 1964), p. 167.

[52] Anthon Downs, "Metropolitan Growth and Future Political Problems," *Land Economics*, XXXVII (1961): 312 ff.

supply all suburban governments with ample tax resources. Thus a common tax base, which taken as a whole might be sufficient for all of a metropolitan area's needs, is so subdivided that only a few local governments are able to adequately finance their capital requirements. Others must be content with low levels of support for schools, police, fire protection, street lighting, street maintenance, recreation, and other necessities of urban life.

Attempts to reduce the administrative confusion and to consolidate fiscal resources have been singularly unsuccessful in the United States. Annexations of adjacent lands by central cities, once an effective means of keeping city boundaries abreast of their spreading populations, is no longer a workable solution in many parts of the country. Although there has been a revival of annexation since World War II, it has been confined mainly to vacant and sparsely occupied lands.[53] Thickly settled territory is easily annexable only in a few southern states where the power of decision has been allowed to remain with the city. There has been no annexation of a sizable incorporated place since the forced annexation of Allegheny to Pittsburgh, in 1915. Incorporation is now often used to anticipate and prevent annexation. Some central cities, such as Milwaukee, Detroit, and Boston, are completely encircled by incorporated municipalities.

Efforts to achieve a fundamental reorganization of government in metropolitan areas have been even less rewarding. In two decades, beginning with 1948, there were over forty attempts to accomplish a merging of governmental units in almost as many metropolitan areas. Many others have been silenced before they reached the referendum stage. Of the two successful ones, that in the metropolitan area of Miami, Florida, has had a struggle for survival lasting for over two decades.[54] Outside of the southern region, experience has been so discouraging that governmental reorganization is no longer considered as a viable solution to service problems.

The resistance to governmental consolidation resides principally in suburban areas, and there it is overwhelming. Thomas Dye and his associates have advanced the proposition that the lack of willingness to enter into jurisdictional agreements and joint authorities is a function of differentiation among populations in reference to per capita income, market value of property, and political party voting. But the findings relative to the hypothesis, investigated in the Philadelphia area, were positive for

[53] *The States and the Metropolitan Problem* (Chicago: The Council of State Governments, 1956), pp. 25–52.

[54] The most notable success occurred not in the United States but in Canada, in the Toronto metropolitan area. There, however, local governments are much less autonomous than they are in the United States. The provincial government could intervene and effect a reorganization of government.

schools only; no relationship was found between differentiation and a willingness to cooperate in the support of other services.[55] A second study attempted to explain the opposition to political integration in terms of life style differences.[56] The findings in this instance, based on survey data from the Nashville metropolitan area, were negative. The author of the study concluded that the demand for urban services exerted an overriding influence in favor of consolidation. A third study, which probed the resistance to consolidation in some depth in six northern areas, confirmed the effect of service deficiencies in fostering a favorable attitude toward governmental reorganization.[57] That study also revealed that resistance rested on a number of suppositions with no foundations in fact. Allegations about the characteristics of officials of the respective local governments were unsupported by knowledge of who the officials were or what offices were involved. Ignorance of local government and a consistent failure to exercise citizenship rights were no barriers to strong convictions on the virtues of autonomous suburban government.

Recently a new factor has been introduced into the debate over governmental reorganization. Where the number of black residents in a central city has been approaching a majority, the issue has become that of preserving the governmental status quo in order to hold a hard-won seat of power. In some southern metropolitan areas blacks have opposed governmental consolidation for that reason. In others blacks have rejected the power argument, for they realize that power might be bought at the cost of deepening municipal poverty.

One of the intriguing contradictions in the behavior of metropolitan people in respect to governmental organization is that, while they cling devoutly to the symbols of local autonomy, they cheerfully give up bits of that autonomy to what have come to be known as "metropolitan authorities." The "authority" is a metropolis-wide special-purpose agency (e.g., for transportation, recreation, water supply, sewage, or other special purpose) voted into being by the local electors and thereafter ruled by an administrative board appointed by and answerable only to the governor of the state. No provisions for recall or referendum are included in the authority's constitution, though it regularly has a share of local real estate tax revenues assigned to it. A single metropolitan area may create four, five, or more "metropolitan authorities," consenting thereby to a piece-by-piece consolidation of administration. These authorities have usually proven to be efficient public agencies, but they do not constitute local governments.

[55] "Differentiation and Cooperation in A Metropolitan Area," *Midwest Journal of Political Science,* VII (1963): 145–55.

[56] Brett W. Hawkins, "Fringe-City Life-Style Distance and Fringe Support of Political Integration," *American Journal of Sociology,* LXXIV (1968): 248–55.

[57] Hawley and Zimmer, *op. cit.,* pp. 65–89.

It is possible that the basic resistance to metropolitan governmental integration lies in a poorly expressed dissatisfaction with large-scale organization. A highly centralized, monolithic organization cannot be immediately responsive to all of the day-to-day operating problems encountered in the administration of scores of different services. Nor can it accommodate direct citizen participation in a very effective manner. The alternative, however, need not be complete disunity. Lying between the two extremes is the possibility of a graduated centralization in what has been called a "poly-centric political system." [58] In this scheme of organization a central government might retain control over broad policy, fiscal matters, interunit relations, and the determination of performance standards, while decision-making responsibility for the ways in which specific services are provided could be delegated to smaller units. In fact, there might be different scales of organization for different services and for different publics. Recreational programs, some aspects of education, certain welfare matters, for example, could be left to local districts to administer within the framework defined by a central administration. Other functions that can be standardized over larger sections, such as street maintenance and lighting, trash collection, and drainage, might be assigned to a unit that embraces a number of local administrative cells. A third class of functions consisting of those that overreach district and section boundaries, as illustrated by planning, transportation, environmental management, police, tax assessment, and collection, could be administered by agencies of a central government.

SUMMARY

It has ceased to be clear where the distinction between urban and non-urban problems falls. That is because the metropolitanization of the nation has made urban areas the repositories of all of society's ills. There are many difficulties that, though their incidence may be high in urban areas, have no necessary connection with urbanism. Crime, family discord, racial discrimination, and poverty are of this order. There are others that are direct outgrowths of urban development. The foregoing paragraphs have surveyed a number of these that have been selected to illustrate the frictions and dislocations which arise in the process of expansion.

Obviously, the form of local government has an important bearing on the kinds of resistances encountered in problem solutions. In the United

[58] Vincent Ostrom, Charles Tiebout, and Robert O. Warren, "The Organization of Government in Metropolitan Areas: A Theoretical Enquiry," *American Political Science Review*, LV (1961): 831.

States with its strong tradition of local autonomy, the disconnection of political from social and economic trends is a critical factor. But in Europe and in other parts of the world where local autonomy is weak or non-existent, the complicating factor in problems of urban growth is of a different character. It may be administrative ineptitude of another kind, it may be budgetary limitations, perhaps it is the speed of change, or maybe it is a combination of these and other elements of resistance. The substantive problems of growth are apt to be very much the same in all areas that have reached comparable stages of urbanization.

SUPPLEMENTARY READINGS

BANFIELD, EDWARD C. *The Unheavenly City* (Boston: Little, Brown & Co., 1968).

CHINITZ, BENJAMIN (ed.). *City and Suburb: The Economics of Metropolitan Growth* (Englewood Cliffs, N.J.: Prentice-Hall, 1964).

CLARK, KENNETH B. *Dark Ghetto: Dilemmas of Social Power* (New York: Harper Torchbook, 1965).

GLAZER, NATHAN, and MOYNIHAN, DANIEL P. *Beyond the Melting Pot* (Cambridge: M.I.T. Press, 1963).

LAVE, L. B., and SESKIN, E. P. "Air Pollution and Health," *Science*, CLXIX (2 August, 1970): 723–732.

POPENOE, DAVID (ed.). *The Urban-Industrial Frontier: Essays on Social Trends and Institutional Goals in Modern Communities* (New Brunswick: Rutgers University Press, 1969).

WILLIAMS, ROBIN. *Strangers Next Door: Ethnic Relations in American Communities* (Englewood Cliffs, N.J.: Prentice-Hall, 1964).

12

Population Growth and Redistribution in Developing Countries

Until quite recent times the course of urbanization as a process of societal transformation has been channeled mainly in the Western world. Peoples elsewhere lingered relatively undisturbed in their traditional, agrarian modes of life. Such societies have not been without urban centers. Scattered at rather wide intervals over the non-Western world were many cities, not a few dating from ancient times. These fall into two broad classes. One is composed of indigenous centers from which the affairs of regions were administered. Some of these were political centers, some were cult centers, others were concentrations of agriculturalists, and still others were market towns. Examples are Bangkok, Ibadan, Kandy, Mandalay, Mecca, Nara, and Timbuctoo. Cities of the second class were formed around the outposts of European empires. They sprang up in the eighteenth and nineteenth centuries as centers for administering the exploitation of native resources and markets. Cape Town, Bombay, Calcutta, Colombo, Jakarta, Rangoon, Hong Kong, and Singapore are representative of this type. Neither one nor the other of the two classes of cities penetrated deeply into the lives of the peoples living about them. They functioned in their respective contexts in very special and limited ways, and while the one was occupied with preserving a status quo the other sought to harness a controlled change to the economic interests lodged in foreign centers of dominance.

Sometimes around mid-twentieth century, however, the pace of change in the societies of the non-Western world, including those of Latin America, was sharply accelerated. The collapse of empires and the removal of foreign-imposed restraints on native peoples, the sudden rise of many new and self-conscious national states, the competition among advanced nations for political and economic alignments in the formerly colonial countries, the increased rates of diffusion of Western culture over the developing world, these and other momentous events created an upheaval unique both in abruptness and in magnitude. The nature of the changes at work are complex and differ in complexity from place to place. But a consistent and highly visible feature of the race for modernization is a rapid growth of cities. The main thrust of urbanization appears, in fact, to have shifted in the present century to the developing nations.

The swarming of population cityward in long-quiescent agrarian areas raises many intriguing questions. What lies beneath the growth of cities? How does the process operate? To what extent does the process parallel that experienced in the West of a century and a half ago? Questions of this character can now be investigated to a far greater degree than was possible a short while ago. The new states, under the tutelage of the United Nations statistical services, are assembling and making available many kinds of information not previously in existence. This is not to say, however, that the data being made available are fully satisfactory. There is actually a great deal of crudeness in the information. It is necessary, therefore, to take up the new opportunity for comparative study of urbanization with a great deal of caution. Where this should be applied will soon become evident. The purpose of this chapter is to examine some of the main currents of change that bear on the process of urbanization. Wherever possible we shall note the similarities and differences with the earlier modernization of the West.

POPULATION INCREASE IN AGRARIAN SOCIETIES

One of the most striking manifestations of change in old agrarian societies is the present rate of population growth. The context in which cumulative increase of numbers began is similar as between nineteenth century and contemporary developing societies. Three quarters or more of the people in each were engaged in agriculture. Poor communications and primitive techniques of cultivation defined a situation, moreover, in which production was addressed primarily to subsistence needs and only secondarily to markets. A labor-intensive agriculture appears to be distinguished by a relatively inflexible population-carrying capacity. Small declines in numbers threaten its labor supply, particularly for peak workload periods, and small increases soon overtax its productivity and reduce per capita consumption. Increases in productivity, other things remaining constant, raise the population-carrying capacity so far as consumption is concerned, but reduce the number of man-hours of labor needed per unit of product. Such was the European experience of two centuries ago. A series of improvements in soil management, in the use of fertilizers, and in seed selection brought about substantial increases in agricultural production at a time when transportation improvements were simplifying the movement of food products in bulk. A result was the initiation of a long-term decline in the death rate, almost one hundred years before significant advances in medical practice occurred.[1] The continuation of birth rates at their high level for another three quarters of a century produced a widening excess of births over deaths and an accelerating rate of growth. The excess numbers of people that arose from the rising rates of natural increase were soon further enlarged by displacements from the land in agricultural districts. The concurrent growth of markets for agricultural products led to extensive forms of cultivation in which capital supplanted workers. The numbers of people available for redistribution grew rapidly in the latter part of the eighteenth and early nineteenth centuries.

In contemporary developing areas growth has also resulted from a widening spread between birth and death rates due to a decline of mortality of the order of 50 percent or more, to around 15 to 20 per 1,000 population, while fertility rates have continued at their traditional levels of around 40 per 1,000. But the causes of reductions in mortality appear to be more complex or at least more debatable than were those operating in the West at an earlier time. Although there have been massive applications of modern sanitary and medical knowledge in many areas of rapid growth, there is still no convincing evidence that such measures have materially influenced mortality rates.[2] On the other hand, death rates have fallen much faster than improvements in the food supply and nutrition would seem to make possible. The United Nations, in its 1965 *Report on the World Social Situation,* was moved to comment: "General improvement in living conditions appears to be no longer a prerequisite for substantial reductions of high morbidity and mortality and, as a consequence, the mortality rate has lost much of its former validity as an index of a country's economic and social well-being." [3] Whatever the causes of recent mortality declines may have been, populations in developing areas today are growing at rates two to four times higher than those of Europe in the preceding century.

[1] T. McKeown and R. G. Brown, "Medical Evidence Relating to English Population Change in the Eighteenth Century."

[2] See Harald Frederiksen, "Determinants and Consequents of Mortality and Fertility Trends," *Public Health Reports,* XXXI (1966): 715–27.

[3] New York; p. 3.

Table 52 compares annual growth rates in developed and developing countries at comparable stages in the modernization process. In contrast to modest growth in the former there is precipitous growth in the latter. The difference is due largely to the speed at which mortality rates declined in each of the two instances. Whereas an annual increase of 1 percent

Table 52. Average Annual Population Growth Rates in Developed Countries, 1815–1870, and Developing Countries, 1945–60

Developed Countries	Growth Rate (1815–1870)	Developing Countries	Growth Rate (c. 1945–60)
Scandinavia	1.09%	Algeria	2.72%
Great Britain	1.11	Ghana	4.98
Belgium	0.85	Tunisia	1.72
Netherlands	0.95	Dominican Republic	3.50
France	0.41	Mexico	2.69
Germany	1.01	Panama	2.94
Switzerland	0.84	Brazil	2.59
Italy	0.68	Chile	1.46
Spain and Portugal	0.79	Colombia	2.23
Poland	1.30	Ceylon	2.84
Russia	0.43	Taiwan	3.12
Austria	0.72	Malaya	2.56
Hungary	0.58	India	1.99
Roumania	1.70	Indonesia	1.52
Balkan Peninsula	0.61	Iraq	3.15
		Pakistan	3.52
		Philippines	3.18
		Turkey	2.93

SOURCE: 1815–1870—B. Hoselitz, "Advanced and Underdeveloped Countries: A Study in Development Contrasts," in W. B. Hamilton, *op. cit.* p. 39; 1945–1960—United Nations, *Urbanization: Development Policies and Planning* (New York, 1968), p. 81.

per year, approximated in nineteenth century Europe, implies a doubling of population in 70 years, a growth rate of 2.5 to 3.0 percent per year can lead to a doubling in 23 to 27 years, or in the span of a generation.

ECONOMIC OPPORTUNITY IN THE RURAL SECTOR

Where upwards of three fourths of the inhabitants of a country are engaged in agriculture, the impact of such high rates of increase is obviously felt mainly, though not exclusively, in the rural sector. In Central America it was estimated that for 1950–60 the number of males reaching working age exceeded the number of job opportunities created by death and retirement by 3 or 4 to 1 in rural areas and by 2 or 3 to 1 in urban areas.[4] Estimates of labor surplus in agriculture in Poland in the years before World War II have been put as high as 5 million.[5] In Pakistan, in 1949–50, disguised unemployment in agriculture, that is, the man-days of labor available above what could be kept fully employed, was estimated at approximately 20 percent of the labor force.[6] Similarly, in South Korea surplus man-days of agricultural labor amounted to 23 percent in 1962, though large seasonal variations were noted.[7] Whether the few days worked during peak periods by such large proportions of underemployed workers adds a positive contribution to the total agricultural product can only be decided by comparing the marginal product to the costs of the workers' maintenance over a full year. No doubt there is a net gain up to a point. Underemployment in excess of that amount, however, must mean that the rural sector is faced with a production deficit.

The consequences of rural congestion are determined partly by the trend in food production but more significantly by developments of opportunities elsewhere in the economy. Increases in food production have, in fact, been occurring, as is shown in the first and second data columns of Table 53. These improvements, however, have done little better than keep pace with population increase, as the second and fourth columns indicate. In half of the countries shown in the table, agricultural output has lagged behind the growth of population. That situation appears to have remained unchanged into 1966.[8] But a dramatic reversal of the trend may have taken place in the years following 1966. New strains of rice, wheat, and other grains are producing yields of as much as 400 percent above those of earlier varieties.[9] Areas that have been food-deficit countries, Pakistan for example, may soon become grain exporters, if new rusts and other parasites do not appear to counteract the capabilities of the improved seeds.[10] As yet no one has estimated how rapidly these agricultural advances will replace traditional practices in old producing areas.

[4] Louis Ducoff, "The Role of Migration in the Demographic Development of Latin America," *Milbank Memorial Fund Quarterly*, XLIII (1956): 206.

[5] M. Phorille, "Development and Rural Over-Population: Some Lessons from Polish Experience," *International Labor Review*, LXXXIX (1964): 227–39.

[6] Islam Murul, "Concepts and Measurement of Unemployment and Under-Employment in Developing Economies," *ibid.*; 240–56.

[7] Yoon-Bock Awh, "Seasonal Variations in Rural Disguised Unemployment and Economic Development," *Land Economics*, XLI (1965): 372–76.

[8] F.A.O., *Production Yearbook*, 1967, Vol. 21 (Rome, 1968), p. 25.

[9] Lester R. Brown, "The Agricultural Revolution in Asia," *Foreign Affairs*, XLVI (July, 1968): 688–98.

[10] The F.A.O. expresses a rather cautious attitude toward prospects for the "miracle" seeds. (*Economic Survey of Asia and the Far East*, 1967 [Rome, 1968], p. 92.)

Table 53. Annual Percentage Change in Farm Production in Selected Underdeveloped Countries

Country	1954–55 to 1962–63		1958–59 to 1962–63	
	Total	Per Capita	Total	Per Capita
Israel	10.1	5.9	8.1	4.4
Mexico	6.2	3.0	2.7	−0.5
Venezuela	4.9	1.3	8.1	4.6
Honduras	4.0	1.0	3.0	0.3
Brazil	4.2	0.9	3.7	0.2
Iran	2.7	0.6	—	−2.5
Taiwan	3.9	0.5	2.8	−0.6
Malaya	3.6	0.5	3.7	0.3
Guatemala	2.8	0.3	3.9	0.7
U.A.R.	2.8	0.3	3.9	0.7
Philippines	3.4	0.2	3.7	0.5
Ceylon	2.7	0.1	5.9	0.3
India	2.2	−0.1	1.9	−0.5
Panama	2.6	−0.1	1.0	1.8
Chile	2.1	−0.3	1.5	−0.8
Pakistan	1.9	−0.3	2.6	0.2
Colombia	11.4	−0.8	0.9	−1.4
Peru	1.9	−0.8	3.6	0.7
Korea	1.9	−0.8	1.1	−1.8
Indonesia	1.0	−1.1	1.4	−0.9
Tunisia	0.9	−1.2	−8.8	−10.2
Ethiopia	0.7	−1.6	1.3	−1.3
Iraq	0.8	−1.3	2.4	1.5
Cuba	−0.4	−2.5	−6.8	−8.9
Algeria	−1.1	−3.2	−1.6	0.3
Median	2.6	−0.1	2.6	−0.5

SOURCE: United Nations, *World Economic Survey,* 1964, pt. II, p. 126.

But a rise in crop production is quite consistent with a decline in employment opportunities in agriculture. The decline may be offset temporarily by the spread of cultivation over formerly unused lands: most of the increases in production shown in Table 53 were obtained in that manner. When the supply of available space is fully occupied no further increase of opportunity from that source is possible. Technical improvements, as represented by the new varieties of seeds, make possible the employment of more man-hours in double and triple cropping. Most, if not all, of that increase can be supplied from the underemployed labor force already engaged in farming. Whether any additional full-time equivalent workers will be needed is a question that only time can answer. To the extent, however, that agricultural improvements require a greater capitalization per acre, they argue for an increasing size of producing unit. At that point absolute displacements from agriculture begin to occur.

Employment opportunities elsewhere in the rural sector of under-developed countries appear to be subject to a more rapid attrition than those in agriculture. In the measure to which industrialization is addressed to consumer goods, locally manufactured products, together with imported commodities, force rural handicrafts into obsolescence.[11] Such a tendency can be expected to become more pronounced as larger proportions of the population are drawn into a cash nexus. The contrast with nineteenth century Europe in this connection is striking. As Table 54 suggests, rural industries were prevalent in Europe; whereas in the developing countries of the present, industry, rural or otherwise, is much less advanced, though the extent of urban population concentration was the same in both times and places.

Furthermore, the early substitutions of factory employment for rural handicrafts take place, not in rural districts, but in urban areas. Not only do urban areas contain the most promising markets for the new consumer goods, they also possess the cost-minimizing external economies, i.e., the financial, professional, maintenance, and numerous lesser services essential to industrial enterprise. The appearance of industry causes these supporting services to be improved and multiplied and that, in turn, enhances the attractive power of the urban area for subsequent additions of industry to the developing economy. An inefficient transportation system contributes further to industrial concentration, as it did in the West during the nineteenth century.

An extreme concentration of industry and complementary urban components in one or a few localities deprives the rural hinterlands of access to small and medium-sized cities and the opportunities they afford. Some of the services industry generates might conceivably develop on the strength of commerce were it not that the scale of commercial activity is also restricted by the primitive state of transportation and communication. Where a small-scale or bazaar-type commerce reigns, the extent of specialization is limited. The merchant, to mention but one example, is the source of credit for his customers, he performs his own accounting and transporting services, he pleads his own case when suit is brought before higher authority, and he has no need for advertising. In these circumstances a system of towns and cities serving an entire country does not develop. There are few bridges, therefore, between rural and urban sectors.

[11] Folke Dovring, "Underemployment in Traditional Agriculture," *Economic Development and Cultural Change,* 15 (1967): 172–73.

Table 54. Percentages of Population in Places of Less than 20,000 Population and Percentages of Workers Employed in Manufacturing (Developed Countries, Nineteenth Century, Developing Countries, Twentieth Century)

Country	Year	Population Less than 20,000	Labor Force in Manufacturing
Developed Countries			
Austria	1890	88	30
France	1856	89	29
Hungary	1900	89	17
Ireland	1851	91	34
Norway	1890	86	22
Portugal	1890	92	19
Sweden	1890	89	22
Switzerland	1888	87	45

Country	Year	Population Less than 20,000	Males Employed in Manufacturing
Developing Countries			
Algeria	1954	82	6
Morocco	1951	73	6
Tunisia	1956	82	7
U.A.R.	1960	84	10
India	1951	88	11
Malaya	1957	77	7
Korea	1957	71	7
Pakistan	1961	88	6
Brazil	1960	72	10
Chile	1952	58	17
Venezuela	1961	53	9

SOURCE: Developed Countries—Bert F. Hoselitz, "The Role of Urbanization in Economic Development: Some International Comparisons," in *India's Urban Future*, ed. Roy Turner (Berkeley: University of California Press, 1961), p. 165.

Developing Countries—United Nations, *Urbanization: Development Policies and Planning*, 1968, p. 84.

PROBLEMS IN POPULATION REDISTRIBUTION

A sustained population growth almost invariably necessitates a redistribution of some part of the total population. That statement is especially true where the composition of economic opportunities is also changing. Rarely does the altered territorial distribution of opportunity correspond to the pattern of settlement. Rapid growth together with a static, if not an actually declining, supply of rural job opportunities creates an accumulating population pressure in the rural sector of a developing country. There are similarities and differences in that respect between earlier and present-day development processes. Rural population surpluses occurred in each of the two situations faster than manpower needs were expanded in urban sectors. Experience suggests that excess population may be an unavoidable feature of the transition from a traditional to a modern economy. Fortunately for European countries, they were able to alleviate transitional problems by "exporting" some of their surplus people to new world areas. Developing countries today do not have that option, for the concept of empty spaces in the world is no longer politically tenable. New nations, therefore, must solve their population problems within their respective boundaries. Accordingly, cities assume the role in the present century that overseas settlements occupied in the preceding one.

Knowledge about internal migration in most countries of the world is very sketchy. Only a few censuses have dealt with the matter and their lack of interest or inexperience in treating it has left much to be desired. According to the 1961 Census of India, approximately 30 percent of the population was living outside the district of birth,[12] but how much of that relocation involved rural-to-urban migration is not reported. The migration question in the 1960 Census of Thailand produced anomalous results. In the U.A.R. the governate of birth question supplies migration data for the two large metropolitan governates—Cairo and Alexandria, but not for other cities. Somewhat more satisfactory is the latest census of Ghana, from which it can be estimated that of the 1,000,000 or more increase of population in urban areas between 1948 and 1960, 300,000 was due to net migration.[13] Apart from censuses, the only other direct source of information on urbanward migration is found in localized studies based on sample surveys. Thus we learn that 80 percent of the family heads in Baghdad were born outside of the city,[14] and that, in 1952, 70 percent of the population of Bombay were born elsewhere.[15] But as with census information, this source of knowledge is much too spotty for general purposes. Nevertheless, there is good reason to believe that large-scale redistributions of populations have been occurring for some time in many developing countries.

[12] Ashish Bose, "Migration Streams in India," *Contributed Papers*, Sidney Conference, International Union for the Scientific Study of Population (1967), pp. 597–606.

[13] J. C. Caldwell, "Determinants of Rural-Urban Migration in Ghana," *Population Studies*, XXII (1968): 361.

[14] D. A. Phillips, "Rural to Urban Migration in Iraq," *Economic Development and Cultural Change*, VII (1959): 405–21.

[15] P. M. Prahbu, "A Study on the Social Effects of Migration," *Social Implications of Industrialization and Urbanization* (Asia), UNESCO (1956), p. 24.

Population transfers are painful and costly processes, though the long-run effect is a net gain to the organization of a society. The departure from the rural village of a supernumerary youth represents a lost investment to the parental household. The sustenance and services he consumes in the period from infancy to 20 years of age add to a fairly large sum, given the level of values that prevails in the peasant situation. We can only guess at what the total might be. It is possible that the costs of child-rearing in a simple society, including food, housing, medical care, clothes, school, and miscellaneous services might come to an average of $75 per year. Interest on that amount, assuming the state of credit that has prevailed in most developing countries, could be of the order of 20 percent per year. Thus the annual cost would rise to $90, or a total of $1,800 for 20 years.[16] But if the interest is compounded over 20 years, as it should be, the cost amounts to $14,000, an extraordinary sum where the per capita income seldom rises above $100 per year. Around age 5 the child might begin to return some value to the household in labor contributions, though in 15 years the worth of his efforts could hardly exceed $500 to $600. The youth's departure from the countryside, then, represents a loss to the rural sector of over 130 man-years of income. He also carries away whatever unique skills and leadership potential he might possess. The loss could be even greater, if he were to remain in the household and be unemployed two thirds to four fifths of the time, because he would continue to consume food and services. On the other hand, the marginal returns from his partial employment might cover the costs of his maintenance. It is unlikely, however, that such returns would be sufficient to amortize the initial investment in him.

There is also a migration of wealth to cities in another form. Where equal inheritance is the rule, as it is in most developing countries, the settlement of peasant estates may necessitate the mortgaging of the property to pay off the absentee heirs. In that event, the property becomes encumbered with a high interest debt. Or the absentee may be content to receive a periodic payment as his share of the productivity of the property. One way or another, wealth that might have been used to improve the farm flows into the city. This, of course, is not the only pattern of estate settlement. Where consanguinity is emphasized, landed property is held in the family, by means of single inheritance or in some other way. In that case it may be the migrant's duty to contribute to the needs of the land and to the main stem of the family: wealth flows from the city to the country.

Age-sex selectivity in migration adds further complications to life in the home area. Urbanward migration streams are composed dispropor-

---

[16] Cf. Ervin J. Long and Peter Dorner, "Excess Farm Population and the Loss of Agricultural Capital," *Land Economics*, XXX (1953): 363–68.

tionally of persons 15 to 30 years of age. Usually, too, the causes operate more persuasively on one sex or the other: in Latin America, females predominate in internal migration; in most of Asia and Africa, migrants are primarily males.[17] The most immediate effects of the resulting imbalance of sexes appear as the interruption or postponement of marriages. Second-order consequences may occur as a discontent and restlessness among the deprived youth. These in turn may lead to further migrations following in the paths of the prior migrants.

In his transfer from rural to urban sectors of the economy, the migrant meets on a personal level one of the major problems of development. His manual skills, such as they may be, are scarcely appropriate to urban occupations. In this the modern-day, rural urban migrant faces a markedly different situation than did his counterpart in Europe of 150 or more years ago. In that earlier instance of modernization a great many skills utilized in urban employments were acquired originally in rural industries. The technological gap between rural and urban industries remained relatively small until industrialization was fairly well advanced. The gap widened rapidly after the middle of the nineteenth century. But then there occurred in the course of rapid economic development a procession of new industries with low skill requirements into which were drawn the waves of rural-to-urban migrants. These new industries provided tutorial experiences which became the ladders of vertical mobility.

In the contemporary developing countries, and in the degree to which they have borrowed Western industrial and institutional lore, the technological gap between rural and urban occupations is too wide to be leaped by migrant peasants.[18] Nor is it likely that, as matters now stand, education in the countryside can narrow that gap in the near future. It helps not at all, of course, to observe, as some have done, that European economies were built on very modest levels of education in their respective populations. Not only were the differentials then small, but there was plenty of time in which to pursue a step-by-step learning process. Ironically, as the technological gap has widened, the time available for effecting a transition may have been sharply reduced by the acceleration of population growth. Still, what was an historical opportunity in the European instance may prove to be an institutional necessity in the new nations' case. In other words, hazardous as it may be, a deliberate slowing of the pace of change might prove necessary. A new technology simply cannot

[17] Sex ratios in the cities of south and east Asian countries range from 111 in Korea to 155 in Ceylon. (United Nations, *The Asian Population Conference,* 1963 [New York, 1964], p. 103.)

[18] Cf. J. J. Habakkuk, "The Historic Experience in the Basic Conditions of Economic Progress," *International Social Science Bulletin,* V (1954): 192; and H. W. Singer, "Problems of Industrialization of Underdeveloped Countries," *ibid.,* 220–21.

be put on as one does a suit of clothes. It is rather built into a system of ancillary behaviors, organizational arrangements, understandings and attitudes, i.e., an institutional structure, that is exceedingly difficult to transport from one context to another. Rural-to-urban migration in developing countries is a movement across cultures as well as across space.

There is, furthermore, much lost motion in migration. Virtually every migration stream has its counterstream. Numerous errors are made in decisions to migrate, especially where communication is conducted by word of mouth. Hence many who journey to the city find that, for reasons of misinformation or personal unsuitability, they are unable to adapt to city life. They pass into the rural backflow. There are also others in the return stream, persons who are temporarily out of work or who are simply taking a vacation. These different classes of return migrants are not readily distinguishable in practice, if only because the outcomes of returns are impossible to forecast.

It is seldom feasible for the returnee to take up again the life he left when he chose the city. If his initial departure created a gap in village organization, that was doubtless long since filled by one of the many available youths. Moreover, he may find himself a burden on his family, which already has too many mouths to feed. There are limits to the capacity of the rural village to serve as a cushion to economic and other forms of distress in the city.[19] There is the further probability that the returning migrant will prove to be a disruptive agent. He brings strange and challenging ideas into the traditional order of village life. And, having tasted freedom from local restraints, the migrant cannot easily submit again to the rule of village authority.

In view of irreversible alterations such as these, the migrant who failed in his first attempt to find a place in the city may try once more. Successful establishment in the city may come only after several returns to the village of origin. The break with the past is not easy, and the village, for all its inadequacies, is a refuge. Thus, instead of a simple migration stream from rural district to city, there tends to be a flux of movements formed by migrants passing repeatedly back and forth. Shuttling movements, common in rural to urban migrations in western nations, appear to be one of the mechanisms by which a transition to urban life is affected. They also impose a heavy drain on the traveler's slender resources. Little is known about how costs regulate migration flows or how costs compare with the gains realized.

[19] For a discussion of the changing importance of the rural sector in this respect see Kenneth H. Parson, "Poverty as an Issue in Development Policy: A Comparison of the United States and Underdeveloped Countries," *Land Economics,* XLV (1969): 52–65.

URBAN GROWTH

The measurement of urban population increase is more subject to error in the case of developing areas than it is elsewhere. Definitions are more varied and reporting is more erratic. There is also less reason to believe that aggregates of a given size or that growth increments of a given amount have even roughly similar social and economic correlates. As has been pointed out before, aggregation does not always mean urbanization. A simple, though arbitrary, solution to some of these difficulties is to deal only with places of 100,000 or more population. This common procedure has the advantage of the places' being fairly consistently reported. It is not always clear, however, how such units are bounded.[20] On the other hand, the arbitrary size limitation leaves out of account all of the urbanization embodied in smaller-sized places. The omission has implications for comparative statements that will be discussed later. One further difficulty, not peculiar to developing areas but harder to rectify in the data for such countries, is the change of population that occurs through reclassification. That may result from a government's decision to designate as a city a place that formerly had not been so defined. Or, as smaller places grow to larger size, many cross the minimum class limit adopted for observation purposes with the result that their entire sizes enter into the measured growth for a given interval of time. Some of the very high growth rates in places of 100,000 or more people that are reported in standard sources seem to include substantial amounts of reclassified population.[21]

Population increases in cities of 100,000 or more inhabitants, in a sample of developing and developed countries grouped by average per capita income, are shown in Table 55. So far as possible changes due to reclassification have been excluded from the measures shown. The data in the table need to be read with care. A comparison of the first two rows indicates that both total population and urban population vary inversely with average per capita income: the poorer the country, the higher the growth rate.[22] The poorer the country, furthermore, the larger is the differential between urban growth and total country growth. Why this should be true is not apparent on the surface. It is perhaps partly an artifact of the definition. That is, in high per capita income or advanced nations urban growth in recent years has accrued mainly to middle-sized

[20] The populations of capital cities regardless of size are also reported. Data on places of 20,000 or 100,000 are aggregated and reported as a lump sum.

[21] Cf. United Nations, *Urbanization: Development Policies and Planning* (New York, 1968), p. 81.

[22] See also P. M. Hauser (ed.), *Urbanization in Latin America* (UNESCO, 1969), pp. 93–100.

and smaller cities and to metropolitan territory surrounding large cities, while in under-developed nations a small number of large cities may be responsible for most of the urban population increase.[23] But line three taken in conjunction with line two indicates that, the smaller the proportion of the total population in places of 100,000 or more, the more rapid has been the growth of such places. This, it should be noted, cannot be attributed to differences in the sizes of base populations. The low per capita income classes contain the world's largest countries. In any case, it is clear that population concentration has been racing ahead of general growth in the least-developed nations.

It is possible that relatively small changes in the social-economic structure of societies have disproportionately large effects on the distributions of their populations. It seems unlikely, in view of the data in the last six rows of Table 55, that rapid urban population growth can be explained by modernization. Instead the contrary appears to be the operating principle: advances in modernization are associated with lowered rates of urban population increase. Noteworthy are the strong inverse relationships between urban growth rates and measures of communication development. Evidently people move city-ward on the strength of very occasional, and perhaps meager, flows of information. It must be acknowledged, of course, that cross-sectional data are less than satisfactory for the purpose at hand. Areas at different stages of development may have had quite different growth histories. But there are no usable time series data that can be brought to bear on the problem.

A second aspect of urban development has to do with its configuration. An earlier distinction between "primate" and hierarchical city patterns will be recalled. The former is presumably representative of undeveloped countries, which are very poorly served by urban institutions. The hierarchical pattern, on the other hand, would appear to be constituted to deliver urban services to all localities within a national territory. It seems to belong to developed countries. Thus one might expect that modernization or development would involve a transition from a "primate" to a hierarchical pattern.

Whether there is actually a systematic relationship between the existence of a hierarchy of cities and the extent of economic development in an area has not yet been ascertained. The one study that dealt with the question yielded negative results.[24] While in many under-developed countries, as reported in that study, the expected "primate" pattern is

[23] There is evidence that in the decade since 1960 rapid growth rates have shifted from the very large cities to cities of less than 100,000 population. See Kingsley Davis, *World Urbanization, 1950–1970,* Vol. I, *Basic Data for Cities, Countries and Regions* (Berkeley: University of California Press, 1969), pp. 141 ff.

[24] Brian J. L. Berry, "City Size Distribution and Economic Development," *Economic Development and Cultural Change,* IX (1961): 573–58.

present, in others, such as India, Korea, China and Brazil, a seemingly mature hierarchical pattern is found. On the other hand, many of the smaller European countries exhibit a "primate" city size distribution. Interesting as these findings are, it is not clear what they mean. In the first place, as we have seen, the definition of city is unstandardized. Irregularities in that connection are particularly great in the non-Western parts of the world. A second difficulty lies in the fact that not all nations are economic universes in the same degree. In Europe city-building forces operate over broad economic regions rather than within political boundaries. But in many developing countries those forces have not yet taken possession of the space embraced by political boundaries.[25] The study referred to also suffers from having had to use cross-sectional data.

OVER-URBANIZATION

The data in Table 55 suggest that there might be a large amount of premature concentration of population in cities. This possibility finds further support in the huge settlements of squatters attached to the peripheries of many cities in Asia, Africa, and Latin America. "Over one-third of the population of Mexico City, 1.5 million people, live in the *colonias proletarias* . . . ; nearly half of Ankara's population of 1.5 million in the *gecekondu* districts—the squatter settlements whose name describes a house built over-night; the area of the *villes extra-coutumières* of Leopold-ville is greater than that of the city itself." [26] These great peripheral slums are the creations of floods of migrants from rural areas who for want of any alternative have gravitated to a major city in the hope of employment.[27] Among them unemployment and underemployment are assumed to be widespread. Underemployment is an elusive concept that has yet to be

[25] Kingsley Davis has computed a four-city index of primacy for every country having four or more cities of at least 100,000 population. The index is the population of the largest city divided by the combined populations of the next three cities (*op. cit.*, pp. 242–46).

[26] John C. Turner, "Uncontrolled Urban Settlements: Problems and Policies," in *The City in Newly Developing Countries,* ed. by Gerald Breese (Englewood Cliffs, N.J.: Prentice-Hall, 1969), p. 189.

[27] Robert L. Heilbroner writes: "In Java, where population density has reached the fantastic figure of 1,100 per square mile, five hundred families a day move into Jakarta from the surrounding fields. Two hundred and fifty families a day move into Bangkok and Rangoon" (*The Great Ascent: The Struggle for Economic Development in Our Time* [New York: Harper Torchbooks, 1963], pp. 56–57). See also P. M. Hauser, "The Social, Economic and Technological Problems of Rapid Urbanization," in *Industrializaton and Society,* ed. by B. F. Hoselitz and W. E. Moore (UNESCO, 1963), p. 203; Guy Hunter, *The Best of Both Worlds* (New York: Oxford University Press, 1967), pp. 36–37; D. G. Phillips, *op. cit.,* pp. 405–21; Kingsley Davis, "Urbanization and the Development of Pre-Industrial Areas," *Economic Development and Cultural Change,* III (1954): 6–26.

Table 55. Measures of Population Change and of Selected Economic and Social Characteristics
(In a Sample of Countries, by Average Annual Per Capita Income)

Measures of Population Change and of Economic and Social Conditions	Countries Grouped by Annual Per Capita Income (dollars)				
	Under 125[a]	125–249[b]	250–374[c]	375–799[d]	800 and Over[e]
Average annual growth of total population, 1950–60, per cent	2.2	2.9	2.6	1.6	1.4
Average annual growth of cities 100,000 and over, 1952–62, per cent	3.8	4.4	2.6	2.2	0.9
Per cent total population in cities 100,000 and over, 1956	8.5	13.2	16.1	28.4	26.0
Proportion economically active population in primary industries	69	64	50	31	19
Average daily caloric output per capita of agriculture	2,153	2,373	2,600	2,862	2,073
Manufactures as per cent of gross domestic product	11	14	18	21	15
Communications: per 1,000 population					
Mail delivered	8	22	28	47	258
Phones in use	2	13	29	49	283
Newspapers printed	23	27	97	140	322

[a]Burma, Ceylon, India, Indonesia, Kenya, Korea, Leopoldville (Congo), Pakistan, Peru, Taiwan, Tanganyika, Thailand, U.A.R.
[b]Algeria, Brazil, Colombia, Ecuador, El Salvador, Honduras, Morocco, Philippines, Rhodesia, Tunisia Turkey.
[c]Costa Rica, Cyprus, Greece, Jamaica, Lebanon, Mexico, Panama, South Africa.
[d]Argentina, Chile, Ireland, Israel, Puerto Rico, Trinidad and Tobago, Venezuela.
[e]Belgium, Canada, Denmark, France, Netherlands, Norway, United Kingdom, United States, West Germany.
SOURCE: Sample obtained from United Nations, *World Economic Survey*, 1961 (New York, 1962) pp. 17–18.

satisfactorily measured; it is particularly hard to locate where job sharing, unpaid family help, and reimbursement in kind are prevalent. In the absence of an acceptable measure, references are made to apparently overcrowded service industries. In the mid-1950's, for example, the reported proportions of male labor forces in administrative and personal services exceeded 50 percent in Colombo, 40 percent in Rangoon, and 27 percent in Bangkok, Taipei, Manila, and Bombay.[28] These figures do not include peddlers, streets solicitors and entertainers, and hangers-on of various kinds.

Use of the term "over-urbanization" has been severely criticized. The main objection has pertained to the way in which it has been measured, though there have also been unsupported assertions that the level of living

[28] United Nations, *The Population of Southeast Asia (Including Ceylon and China: Taiwan), 1950–1980*, Report III, *Future Population Estimates by Sex and Age* (New York, 1958), p. 47.

is higher among migrants to cities than among rural non-migrants.[29] It must be granted that the term is unfortunate in some respects. Whether, for example, the number of people in cities is more or less excessive than the number in rural areas of countries where rapid redistribution has been occurring is an empirical question that has not been investigated. It could be argued, too, that many developing countries are under-urbanized. That is, they have many fewer cities than are needed to provide adequately for modern services and cultural opportunities. Still, there remains the probability that cities have been receiving population faster than they are able to assimilate newcomers into their institutional structures. In this sense "over-urbanization" is a tenable hypothesis.

The hypothesis is not entirely an idle one. There is much that needs to be learned about the mechanics of rural-to-urban migration in the context of modernization. The "push" in the rural sector is easy enough to comprehend.[30] But, if there must also be a "pull" to give direction and timing to a migration stream, in what form does that arise in the burgeoning city? Is the "pull" an illusion fostered by misinformation and the glitter of novelty?[31] Is there a measurable migration overload for each given amount of opportunity at a destination? What is the interaction between available job opportunities and migration flows? Answers to questions such as these will go far toward illuminating the process of urban population growth.

In any case, there is nothing new about excessive population in cities in periods of rapid change. It occurred repeatedly in Europe from the fifteenth century onward. According to Fredrick Nussbaum:

In the fifteenth century a contemporary estimated the number of beggars in Paris at 80,000; in 1634, another set their number at one-fourth of the city's population. In the provinces, conditions were equally bad. In 1482, Troyes numbered 3,000 beggars in a population of 15,000. In 1678, Amiens had from 5,000 to 6,000 laborers who depended on alms. The bishop of Montauban wrote in 1694: "We find six or seven dead at the gate of the town almost every day, and in my diocese of 750 parishes about 450 die every day from the lack of food." In the German ecclesiastical states in the eighteenth century it was

[29] N. V. Sovani, "The Analysis of 'Over-Urbanization,'" *Economic Development and Cultural Change*, XII (1964): 113–22; David Kamerschen, "Further Analysis of Over-Urbanization," *ibid.*, XVII (1969): 235–53.

[30] Sovani reports a study of three rural districts in India in which questions concerning planned or potential migration were asked. Of 23,090 respondent households, 4,079 families declared that one or more of their numbers was a potential permanent migrant to a city. More than half of the potential migrants were members of farm households and of those most occupied very small farms. Sovani thinks that 17 percent of the families with members poised for migration at a given moment in time is a small proportion. To the present author it seems quite large. ("Potential Out-Migrants and Removable Surplus Population in Three Districts of Arissa [India]," *International Population Conference, Vienna, 1959* [Vienna, 1959], pp. 703–709.)

[31] P. M. Hauser, *op. cit.*, p. 210.

estimated that in each thousand of population there were fifty clergy and 260 beggars. Cologne had 20,000 beggars in a population of 60,000.[32]

English cities were inundated with floods of displaced agriculturalists in the nineteenth century. Charles Booth estimated the number of impoverished persons in London, in 1888, at 25 percent of the population.[33] In many occupations, emigration societies were formed to subsidize and assist migration to overseas destinations, as was noted in an earlier chapter.

THE FUTURE OF URBANIZATION IN DEVELOPING AREAS

It would be a mistake, of course, to regard population increase and urban growth as cause and effect. Events of the magnitude on which these trends have been mounted in new nations cannot be so simply explained. Each is rather a consequence of a multifaceted third factor known as industrialization. By this term is meant a direct and increasing involvement in the industrial culture projected over the world from Western nations.

While urban centers may exist in some independence of industrialization, as was the case in ancient and medieval times, industrialization can have little if any independence of cities. The economies of large-scale production presuppose the various complementary services and the quick communications that only urban areas can supply. Those requisites depend in turn on the markets represented by large aggregates of consumers who earn their livings from non-agricultural activities. There is a mutually stimulating interaction between industrialization and urbanization.[34]

There is also an interactive relationship between population increase and industrialization. The first beginnings of industrialization, as represented in the advances of scientific knowledge and its application to the generation of mechanical power and the fashioning of mechanical tools, release the forces of population increase. Thereafter population increase can be a stimulant to industrial development, through the increased labor supply of young, adaptable workers and the enlarged numbers of consumers of industrial products it creates. If, however, population growth is too rapid, it can dampen the progress of industrialization by diverting investment capital from industry to consumer services.[35]

[32] A History of Economic Institutions of Modern Europe (New York: F. S. Crofts, 1933), pp. 108–109.

[33] Charles Booth on the City, ed. by Harold Pfautz (Chicago: University of Chicago Press, 1967), p. 184.

[34] See Benjamin Higgins, "The City and Economic Development," in The Urban Explosion in Latin America, ed. by Glenn H. Beyer (Ithaca: Cornell University Press, 1967), pp. 117 ff.

[35] R. T. F. King, "Population, Food Supplies and Economic Growth," in Population and Food Supply, ed. by Sir Joseph Hutchinson (Cambridge: The University Press, 1969), pp. 44–45.

A country industrializing under modern conditions is faced with a serious dilemma. It must try to remove enough people from agriculture to permit a reorganization of that industry on a more efficient and productive basis while at the same time generating the non-agricultural job opportunities needed to absorb the displaced agriculturalists. To direct and regulate a neatly timed changeover of this kind is a task of herculean proportions. The requisite administrative skills, moreover, are so scarce as to be all but nonexistent. Consequently the processes involved in the transition operate perforce with a large element of spontaneity guiding them. Most of the content of this chapter has dealt with the dislocations and frictions that commonly occur in the course of modernization. There is one line of thought which contends that there can be no simultaneous and balanced reorganization of agriculture and development of industry. It argues that the agricultural sector and its population must be held in subordination to the urban-industrial sector—that the former must submit to having its surplus product taxed away to form the capital needed for the growth of the latter. The forcibly extracted loan is repaid at a later time when the urban-industrial sector is firmly established and able to create its own capital.[36] Rapid population growth, however, threatens to defeat the capital accumulation process, for the increasing numbers of people consume the surplus product of the agricultural sector. Industrialization, therefore, may be slowed and conceivably stopped altogether.

A counterargument questions the effect of population growth on development. After showing that historically there has been no consistent relation between the two processes, Simon Kuznets declares that there are economic advantages in backwardness that could be exploited were the local institutions sufficiently flexible.[37] The large pools of cheap labor, for example, could be employed in lightly capitalized industries as was done in the Japanese and more recently in the Hong Kong economies. Such opportunities are often not perceived, and when perceived are too infrequently grasped. The institutional rigidities that are most critical are those that are gathered about the governmental process, largely because governments have had to take a major share of the responsibility for economic development in new nations. The persistence of parochial loyalties, the ritualized deference to seniority, a preoccupation with form rather than substance, a competition for bureaucratic prerogatives, these and other irrelevancies render governments inefficient in action. What is true of governing institutions is no less true of other institutions in the society. The point is, however, that so long as impediments such as these exist

[36] Nathan Keyfitz, "The Political-Economic Aspects of Urbanization in South and Southeast Asia," in *The Study of Urbanization*, ed. by P. M. Hauser and Leo F. Schnore, p. 304.

[37] "Population and Economic Growth," *Proceedings of the American Philosoyhical Society*, CXI (1967): 190 ff.

(which incidentally are often mingled with partially assimilated borrowings from abroad), the problems of economic growth cannot be charged exclusively to population increase.

In any case, the overgrown city in the developing country is in a favorable position for the facilitation of modernization and economic growth. It has concentrated enormous manpower resources within a radius of manageable accessibility. The external economies required by business and industry are monopolized by the city, as are the repositories of the nation's capital resources. Standing as it does at the crossroads of intra- and interregional lines of communication, the city is exposed to cultural diffusions from abroad and is thus a locus of innovation. It either has, or is well placed for, the cultivation of cultural institutions that foster technical and liberal educations. In all of these respects the city of the contemporary developing area, as did cities in earlier occasions of development, has assembled most of the advantages of proximity. It will do that more fully and more efficiently, of course, as capital is applied to the improvement of its internal transportation and communication facilities.

But urbanization and population redistribution will have to be carried much further than their present point of progress. Some idea of the amount of population that may have to be reallocated can be gained from a simple speculation. Kingsley Davis has suggested that not less than 50 percent of the employed population must be engaged in non-agricultural occupations for a country to be judged to have advanced beyond the agrarian stage.[38] Let us accept that arbitrary figure as the minimum required in cities of 20,000 or more inhabitants in order for a country to be safely past the takeoff point in its modernization. On that basis India would need to relocate some 170 millions of people, or 38 percent of its total 1961 population. Corresponding proportions in other countries are 47 percent in Tanganyika, 42 percent in Pakistan, 41 percent in Indonesia and Rhodesia, and 40 percent in Burma. On the whole, 35 percent of the population of the under-developed part of the world would have to move from rural to urban areas. But if development objectives are kept in mind, all future natural increase will also have to be concentrated in cities.

Were such a transfer of population to lead to the emergence of a network of cities, numerous benefits would accrue to a society in process of development. First, it would reduce the gap between rural and urban sectors and thereby simplify all sorts of movements between the two. The dissolution of rural isolation would equalize opportunity over the entire population and would make for a more responsive citizenry. Second, the proximity of urban centers to rural residents would bring supplementary sources of income within reach of farm families. A closer dovetailing of

[38] "Population and the Further Spread of Industrial Society," *Proceedings of the American Philosophical Society*, XCV (1951): 8.

farm and nonfarm occupations permits a more efficient use of manpower. Third, a widespread distribution of urban centers places markets for agricultural products closer to producing areas. The farmers could then sell their produce to competitive bidders rather than dumping it in glutted markets as they usually have to do. An extensive system of cities, fourth, would permit a more complete and equitable distribution of governmental services. At the same time it would foster the conversion of the entire population into a domestic market for the support of industry. Regions and districts would thus be drawn into an integrated social, political, and economic system.

<h2 style="text-align:center">URBANIZATION AND THE
DECELERATION OF POPULATION INCREASE</h2>

The great growth of urban population, it has been said, has been due to rather abrupt declines in mortality rates while fertility rates have continued at their traditionally high levels. Population growth accelerated therefore, and large proportions of the increases in numbers of people moved to urban destinations in the search for employment. There is now the question of whether urbanization will have a decelerating effect on population growth rates. In other words, will developing areas repeat the experience of the West? In the modernization of the latter, urbanization and the decline of the birth rate went hand in hand. Was that simply a coincidence, or is there a causal relationship between the two classes of events? What—in the present state of knowledge—appears to regulate the level of fertility rates?

Three factors, all structural in character, are of central importance in any consideration of changes in fertility rates. The first of these is the level of mortality. Under conditions approximating equilibrium of a group with its environment, mortality and fertility tend to be equal. Fertility is controlled so as to affect a replacement of numbers lost in mortality. The controlling mechanisms are usually folk practices of various kinds, such as rules concerning whom and when people may marry, the remarriageability of widows, abstinence during lactation, abortion, and so forth. Migration and colonization are used to supplement fertility controls. But when an equilibrium is disrupted with the result that the mortality rates decline, the fertility rates tend to behave accordingly. Thus mortality and fertility are positively correlated. There is, however, a lag in the response of fertility rates to changes in mortality. The former is more sensitive to variations in environmental conditions than is the latter. Time lags of as long as 100 years have been recorded. It is not entirely clear how the relationship between fertility and mortality is maintained or restored. Two researchers who have studied the problem rather extensively declare that modest reductions in mortality are not accompanied by fertility declines because parents are uncertain about the permanence of the change and the prospects for survival of their offspring. Proportional fertility declines can be expected only with very substantial declines in death rates.[39] But there is a second structural factor that should be considered.

Where the family or the household is the major producing unit, as it is in agrarian societies, it obtains its labor supply through reproduction, though various kinship equivalents may be used when reproduction fails. For that reason there is an economic and therefore a moral imperative to produce children. From an early age the child has a role to fill as an unpaid worker in the household economy. He is also security for the parents in their old age. The importance of children changes, however, as the household loses its producing function and its members become involved in wage employment and a cash nexus. Children may for a time continue to be useful as means of supplementing family income and as aids to parents in their retirement. Eventually those utilities disappear also. Children cease to be necessities and become matters of choice, not unlike other consumer goods.

As a general statement, then, it may be said that fertility rates vary directly with mortality rates and inversely with the extent to which the household is engaged directly or indirectly in market processes. The joint effects of these two influences are not immediate. Nor is the mere transfer of residence to an urban area a sufficient indication that the influences are fully operative. Some families continue as producing units after having settled in a city; they ply their rural crafts or operate retail shops as family enterprises. Others that possess no craft skills or lack capital for any kind of independent venture are unable to function as units. The difference between families with and without producing functions may account for some of the inconsistency observed in the relation of fertility rates to urbanization in developing countries. As Robinson has shown, it does not follow that urban populations invariably have lower fertility ratios than rural populations. That divergence from the expected pattern has diminished over time, as one might anticipate, and some of it is removed when the effects of variations in infant mortality and the proportions of women married are controlled.[40] But there remains a residual difference that is unexplained. Much of that may be due to differences in family type. Families that persist as operating economic units find children useful in their enterprises, if not as imperative as they were in the

[39] David Heer and Dean O. Smith, "Mortality Level, Desired Family Size and Population Increase," *Demography*, V (1968): 104–27.

[40] Warren C. Robinson, "Urbanization and Fertility: The Non-Western Experience," *Milbank Memorial Fund Quarterly*, XLI (1963): 291–308. See also David Heer, "Economic Development and Fertility," *Demography*, III (1966): 423–44.

rural setting. The head of the household and his wife may therefore be relatively indifferent toward family limitation opportunities.[41] On the other hand, in families that operate essentially as consuming units there is no economic role for children. Hence they, other things equal, might turn more quickly to family planning practices.

Although mortality decline and household reconstitution might have occurred, fertility may continue at a relatively high rate nevertheless. Unless some alternative means for providing security to parents in their old ages is found, the incentive to have numerous offspring remains strong. This is the third factor mentioned earlier. In other words, there must be enough disposable income left to the wage worker after all necessary expenses are paid to permit him to accumulate a fairly substantial amount of savings. His savings may either be in the form of a private bank account or other private investment, or they may accrue in the reserves of a publicly operated social security system.

Urbanization, in short, does not lead to an immediate reduction of the rate of population growth. Even after the family is separated from its customary functions there is a lapse of time while the married couple is grasping the implications of the change and acquiring knowledge of how to apply modern controls. Usually these awakenings come in the second generation of city life. They are delayed further by illiteracy, poverty, and relative isolation from the mainstream of city life. In time the influences of urban life manifest themselves in reduced fertility rates and a declining rate of population increase ensues.

SUMMARY

Cities are not new in the old, agrarian areas of the world. Indeed, some of the world's oldest cities are to be found there. But they have been held to relatively limited importance by primitive technologies and subsistence economies. Around mid-twentieth century, however, the full force of change was unleashed by political events in the West. Urban population growth in non-Western and Latin American countries—the so-called developing areas—accelerated rapidly after 1945. Currently cities in developing areas are growing at faster rates than are cities anywhere else in the world and at rates that rival those in the West of the nineteenth century.

Changes have had their greatest impact on population. Sharp declines in mortality rates while fertility rates have remained constant and high resulted in rapid rates of population increase. The immediate conse-

[41] See A. J. Jaffee and K. Azumi, "The Birth Rate and Cottage Industries in Underdeveloped Countries," *Economic Development and Cultural Change,* IX (1960): 52–63.

quence has been a crowding of people on the land, for 70 percent or more of the population are engaged in agriculture. Economic opportunities have been unable to keep pace with population growth largely because a subsistence agriculture has limited capacity for expansion. Population can only spread into unused lands until they are fully occupied. Increases in food production have occurred, though in most developing countries such increases have fallen behind population growth. Where production increases resulted from higher levels of capitalization there tends to be a displacement of farm workers. Thus rural unemployment or underemployment stems from absolute increases in the number of people and from declines in job opportunities on farms. Of importance among the latter is the obsolescence of rural handicrafts. New consumer goods industries and imported products tend to eliminate traditional products and the skills by which they were produced.

Population redistribution thus becomes imperative. Since there are no appreciable opportunities abroad, cities must serve the purpose in developing areas that overseas destinations served for the West during the eighteenth and nineteenth centuries. Although out-movement from congested rural areas provides relief to population pressures, there are also substantial costs. Lost is the investment in the nurturing and training of migrant youth. There tends also to be a relocation of wealth where there are estates to be settled. At the receiving end of the rural-urban migration streams, cities are confronted with large and increasing numbers of inadequately trained youth. Rural skills are inappropriate for modern industrial needs. The technological gap is too great to be leaped by the peasant in a short period of time. There is much more to be learned than just the uses of new tools; the implements involve an altogether different institutional setting and related patterns of behavior.

Frustrations for the migrant are numerous—long waits for employment, strange job assignments, ignorance of urban ways, and a general irrelevance of most of his traditional culture. Return migrations are therefore common. Seldom is that a solution to the migrant's problem, for his place in the village has usually been filled by another youth. Moreover, his emancipation from village authority is apt to be looked upon as a threat to village stability. So he turns once again to the city, and perhaps comes once or twice more to the village. Shuttle movements of that nature consume his slender savings and add to the costs of population redistribution.

Although descriptive data are of poor quality, it appears from those that are available that city growth in developing areas has been proceeding much faster than the increase of employment opportunities warrants. Population growth in large cities is most rapid in the poorest countries and where modernization is least advanced. Evidence of premature concentration of population in cities occurs also in the presence of large settlements of squatters attached to many city peripheries, and in the crowd-ing of workers in marginal occupations. These observations have given rise to the use of the term "overurbanization" to characterize urban growth in developing areas. If the term means no more than that there are more people than can be effectively accommodated in the social-economic sys-tem, it is acceptable. Even so, there is a measurement problem still to be disposed of. But in the respect in which the term is applicable there have been many precedents in cities of Europe a century or more earlier.

In one sense, at least, it seems that many developing countries might be under-urbanized. They lack a full size range and a fairly even terri-torial distribution of cities. Hence many localities are not reached by urban-type services and a wide social gap exists between rural and urban sectors. Doubtlessly, too, industrialization is slowed by the uneven dis-tribution of external economies. One argument holds that rapid popula-tion increase impedes the accumulation of capital required for industriali-zation inasmuch as increasing numbers consume the surplus product. But another line of reasoning points out that a major barrier to industrializa-tion is the presence not so much of too many people but of numerous in-stitutional rigidities. But the progress of urbanization, distorted though it may be, has already contributed to the facilitation of industrialization. The process needs to advance much further, however. As a rough indi-cation of how much additional urbanization is needed, another 35 to 47 percent of all existing population plus all subsequent natural increase should be relocated from rural to urban areas.

The deceleration of population growth does not follow automatically upon the heels of urban concentration. Declines in fertility are functions of major structural changes: fertility rates vary directly with mortality rates and inversely with the extent of the involvement of individuals and households in a cash nexus. The latter is delayed by the persistence of the transplanted household as a producing unit.

SUPPLEMENTARY READINGS

GULICK, JOHN. *Tripoli: A Modern Arab City.* (Cambridge: Harvard Univer-sity Press, 1967).

HANCE, WILLIAM A. "The Economic Location and the Functions of Tropical African Cities," *Human Organization,* XIX (1960): 135–136.

HIGGINS, BENJAMIN. "Economic Development of Underdeveloped Areas," *Land Economics,* XXXI (1955): 179–195.

PEATTIE, LISA. *A View from the Barrio* (Ann Arbor: University of Michigan Press, 1968).

SCHMITT, ROBERT. "Urbanization in French Polynesia," *Land Economics,* XXXVIII (1962): 71–75.

SMOCK, DAVID R. "Cultural and Attitudinal Factors Affecting Agricultural De-velopment in Eastern Nigeria," *Economic Development and Cultural Change,* XVIII (1969): 110–124.

13

The Urbanization Process in Developing Countries

Having looked at urbanization in developing countries as an aggregation process, it is now appropriate to examine the phenomenon as a social and economic transformation. This involves one more directly than has been necessary heretofore in a consideration of the meaning of cultural differences. Since it is a common tendency to translate cultural differences into value differences, special attention must be given to the effects of these subtle manifestations of culture on the urbanization process.

There are two major objectives in this chapter. One is to trace as fully as possible the process by which urban organization takes form in developing countries. The other is to try to answer the question: To what extent is it proper to speak of a single urbanization process that is reiterated in different times and places?[1] Or are there as many urbanization processes—if one may entertain a *non sequitur*—as there are cultures?

We have seen that large-scale city growth has been initiated repeatedly in many different cultural circumstances. In the early phase Anglo-Saxon, Scandinavian, Teutonic, Latin, and Slavic peoples successively submitted to massive redistributions and concentrations of their numbers. The same tendency subsequently affected the even more diverse peoples of Asia,

[1] This question has been investigated inconclusively in the geographical literature by Norton S. Ginsburg, "Urban Geography and Non-Western Areas," P. M. Hauser and Leo F. Schnore, *op. cit.*, pp. 311–46.

Africa, and Latin America. Although the 130-odd nations in the present-day world are spread across the full spectrum of cultural variation, virtually none has been immune to the forces making for city growth.

But population aggregation indicates only that a basic change is occurring. The nature of the change is obscure, unless further evidence is adduced. In some instances the change may be principally demographic in character; that is, alterations of birth-death ratios result in setting afoot migration streams even though no significant changes in the composition or the distribution of activities have taken place.[2] As Janet Abu-Lughod has observed, in Egypt, recent increases in places of 20,000 or more population may be due largely to a widening deficit of deaths relative to births in large, densely settled, agricultural villages.[3] Apparently the rapid growth of Yoruba towns in the past decade has resulted from a similar demographic shift.[4] There are other instances, however, in which population concentration is associated with profound changes at work in the constitutions of the societies concerned. Rare is the case among developing areas today in which both kinds of change are not involved. The relative importance of each varies, of course, from place to place.

It is to the nature of the transformation that we should now turn. Various approaches to the phenomenon have been employed. Before turning to these several conceptualizations we should note that most of what can be said about urbanization in developing countries pertains to the city proper; very few data are available on the extension of urban influence over the hinterlands of urban centers. That is an unfortunate limitation. Still, the city affords maximum observability of many of the structural features of an urban system. Most of the dislocations and accommodations incidental to major social and economic changes are also vividly portrayed in the core of an unfolding urban organization.

THREE HYPOTHESES

At least three hypotheses purporting to describe the urbanization process are more or less explicit in the literature on comparative urban studies. The first of these argues that all occasions of urbanization repeat a particular series of events—that there is a unilinear continuum from a folk to an urban form of organization. The second holds that urbanization advances along parallel lines of change, each of which tends to culminate

---

[2] Kingsley Davis, "Urbanization of Human Population," *Scientific American,* CCXIII (1965): 41–53.

[3] "Urbanization in Egypt: Present State and Future Prospects," *Economic Development and Cultural Change,* XIII (1965): 314.

[4] A. L. Mabogunje, *Yoruba Towns* (Ibadan, Nigeria: Ibadan University Press, 1962), pp. 19–20.

in a relatively unique outcome. The third hypothesis contends that the several lines of development necessarily tend to converge upon a single pattern. Let us examine these propositions briefly before turning to the empirical materials that bear on the question.

The concept of a universal folk-urban continuum has been widely discussed in sociological and anthropological writings. Representatives of the two disciplines have come to this proposition from rather different assumptions. Louis Wirth, who was responsible for the sociological formulation of the hypothesis, cast it in demographic terms. He reasoned that increases in population size, density, and heterogeneity led to correspondingly more transitory, anonymous, formalized, and specialized interrelationships, i.e., to a more urbanized way of life.[5] The anthropologist, Robert Redfield, adopted a diffusionist approach. According to Redfield, the transformation of an isolated folk community into an urban society occurs through a transmission of influences from the latter resulting in cultural heterogeneity, disorganization, secularization, and individuation in the former. Thus communities can be arrayed in a spatial-cultural sequence which represents the extent to which they have been affected by diffusion emanating from an urban center.[6]

Among the various criticisms leveled at the idea of a single folk-urban continuum, one that has figured most prominently has dealt with the limitations inherent in a dichotomy.[7] This is somewhat specious, however. So preoccupied have critics been with the polar concepts *folk* and *urban* that they have all but ignored the curve of variation linking the two ends of the process. Yet in at least one respect their criticism seems justified. That is, *folk* is undoubtedly an overly abstract concept; the differences concealed in the term may be more significant than the similarities it purports to represent. Furthermore, the assumed linearity in the covariation among the variables encompassed in communities and societies is questionable.[8] In short, it appears that the single continuum proposal unduly simplifies a complex problem. For that reason we shall set it aside.

Hypotheses two and three both contend that change in culturally differentiated societies proceeds along diverse continua. Multilinearity is just as tenable a position to hold with reference to short-run change as

[5] "Urbanism as a Way of Life." *American Journal of Sociology*, XLIV (1938): 1:24.

[6] *The Folk Culture of Yucatán* (Chicago: The University of Chicago Press, 1941), pp. 344 ff. It should be recognized that, though the folk-urban continuum has been interpreted as a unilinear process, it need not be so restricted. The concept is applicable also to a multilinear convergence hypothesis of development.

[7] Oscar Lewis and Philip M. Hauser, "The Folk-Urban Ideal Types," in P. M. Hauser and Leo F. Schnore, *op. cit.*, pp. 491–517.

[8] See Horace Miner, "The Folk-Urban Continuum," *American Sociological Review*, XVII (1952): 529–37.

it is in regard to long-run or evolutionary change.[9] Widely scattered societies existing in varying degrees of isolation from one another would necessarily embark upon careers of change from various points of departure. Differences in culture, in physical environment, and in intersocietal relationships make for a variety of contexts each with somewhat unique facilitating and frictional conditions. And the nature of the agglomerations found over such a range of differences may be as varied as the mercantile towns of eighteenth century Europe, the cult centers of southeast Asia, and the lineage aggregates of agriculturalists occupying walled compounds in West Africa.[10] Not only were there differences of internal organization, there was also a diversity of external conditions at the time of entry of each society upon a course of urbanization. Colonial policies and practices, the mechanization of technology, the efficiency of transportation and communication facilities, the character of world markets, and the patterns of national political alignments have altered radically over the past two centuries and more. It would be strange indeed if, in view of so great a variety of experiences and circumstances, urbanization followed an identical path in every society.

So much for the similarity between the two propositions. Beyond that they differ markedly. The one argues for a parallelism among urbanization processes, the other for a convergence. The case for the former rests primarily on the existence of unique and widely divergent value systems among various societies. William Kolb declares that the Western predilection for sacrificing immediate gratifications for later ends, for a readiness of individuals to interact with one another in sharply delimited roles, and for emphasizing performance as a prime criterion in the distribution of rewards has no counterparts in traditional societies.[11] Hauser offers a more extensive list of values that distinguish under-developed peoples, including an emphasis on spiritual ends, a stress on an afterlife, a preference for traditional patterns of thought and action, rigid definitions of roles, parochialism of groups, familistic orientations, a deference to age and seniority, allocations of large amounts of life space to ceremonial and ritualistic activities, and an inclination to hoard wealth in unproductive investments.[12] Thus he is led to conclude that "the patterns of urbanization in the under-developed nations have not followed the Western

[9] Cf. Julian Steward, "Introduction," *Irrigation Civilizations: A Comparative Study.* Social Science Monographs. Pan-American Union (Washington, D.C., 1965), pp. 1 ff.

[10] Gideon Sjoberg contends, contrariwise, "that in their structure, or form, pre-industrial cities—whether in medieval Europe, traditional China, India or elsewhere—resemble one another closely . . ." (*op. cit.*, pp. 4–5).

[11] "The Social Structure and Functions of Cities," *Economic Development and Cultural Change,* III (1954): 30–46.

[12] "Cultural and Personal Obstacles to Economic Development in the Less Developed Areas," *Human Organization,* XVIII (1959): 82.

lines, and are not likely to do so in the future." [13] Whether these authors have accurately identified significant differences in values or have merely reported impressions casually arrived at need not be argued at the moment.

The case for the convergence hypothesis lies in the implications of the growth and ramification of regional interdependences. It assumes that increasing participation by initially differentiated societies in a common technology, common markets, and a common universe of discourse exerts a powerful generalizing and standardizing influence. Social units that engage frequently and regularly in mutual exchanges tend to acquire counterpart functions and matching structures,[14] for to do otherwise impedes communications, raises the costs of exchanges, and preserves inequality of opportunity. This is not to say, as Wilbert Moore alleges, that the convergence hypothesis implies that there is a "stable destination." [15] It proposes rather that different lines of development will become increasingly similar as they become less separate.

Furthermore, the convergence hypothesis calls into question the notion of the immutability of values. They can be modified, worked into different combinations, or even replaced by newly emergent values.[16] To assume otherwise is to impute a much greater rigidity to a construct than is possessed by the reality from which it is inferred. Alex Inkeles has demonstrated the existence of a remarkable agreement among the values of persons of comparable ranks in a number of Western societies at mid-twentieth century.[17] The dynamics of culture change in the West have certainly narrowed the range of differences among societies. If so, there is no reason why a similar result could not be repeated elsewhere if and when appropriate conditions are present.[18]

Of the two hypotheses, multilinear parallelism and multilinear con-

[13] "The Social, Economic and Technological Problems of Rapid Urbanization," in *Industrialization and Society*, ed. by Bert Hoselitz and W. E. Moore (UNESCO: Mouton, 1963), p. 214. See also William B. Hamilton (ed.), *The Transfer of Institutions*, p. 53.

[14] *Social Change* (Englewood Cliffs, N.J.: Prentice-Hall, 1963), p. 112.

[15] Frank Young and Ruth Young prefer to regard this as a uni-dimensional movement toward "greater articulation with what may be called the emerging urban-industrial structure" ("The Sequence and Direction of Community Growth: A Cross-Cultural Generalization," *Rural Sociology*, XXVII [1962]: 374–86).

[16] Robert Redfield and Milton Singer are brought somewhat reluctantly to this conclusion in their analysis of "generative" transformations which occur in the late stages of urbanization. ("The Cultural Role of Cities," *Economic Development and Cultural Change*, III [1954], 53–73.)

[17] "Industrial Man: The Relation of Status to Experience, Perception and Value," *American Journal of Sociology*, LXVI (1960): 1–31.

[18] This view is shared by many others, such as John Friedmann, "Cities in Social Transformation," *Comparative Studies in Society and History*, IV (1961–62): 87, 102; Leonard Reismann, *The Urban Process* (New York: The Free Press, 1964), pp. 158, 167; and Daniel Lerner, "Comparative Analyses of Processes of Modernization," in *The City in Modern Africa*, ed. by Horace Miner (New York: Praeger, 1967), p. 22.

vergence, the latter seems much the more reasonable. But rather than argue this further on logical grounds, let us examine the available evidence pertaining to urban development in as wide an assortment of cultures as possible. There is one important difficulty involved in this procedure. In few if any places in the non-Western world has urbanization advanced to the same stage as that attained in the West. Hence actual convergences cannot be conclusively demonstrated. It is possible, however, to observe urban characteristics cross-historically, that is, at roughly comparable stages, as well as cross-culturally, and to note the similarities and differences. Comparisons of this sort will cast light on how peculiar values and value systems influence urban trends in various countries.

PHYSICAL STRUCTURE

A convenient starting point in a comparative study of urbanization is the physical structure of the city. Human activity redesigns the immediate natural environment to conform to its patterns. The network of streets and lanes, the allocations of spaces to uses, and the types and sizes of buildings that house the various uses are together an overt expression of the total concert of behavior which constitutes a community. The amount of detail in any such pattern far exceeds what can be considered here, of course. It will be sufficient for present purposes to consider four of the more salient properties of urban pattern.

An obvious structural feature of the city in the early phase of city formation—one which under certain conditions may persist into much later phases of the process—is its very dense and compact form. Streets are narrow and buildings fill all of the spaces separating streets. Although multi-storied buildings seldom rise above two or three floors, densities may reach 10,000 and more persons per square mile.[19] High densities prevail over the built-up areas, exhibiting no visible tendency to decline with distance from an inner locus to the edge of the city. Consequently the break between city and country is usually a sharp one. Suburbs appear, not as gradual penetrations of the hinterland by the city, but as detached agglomerations that resemble the parent city in their physical aspects.

High densities are sometimes explained in value terms. People congregate in dense aggregates, says Sjoberg, because the persistence of a feudal tradition confers high status upon residence in a city.[20] But it is

[19] Peking in the first decades of the present century is reported to have had an average density of 34,000 persons per square mile. See Y. F. Tuan, "A Preface to Chinese Cities," in *Urbanization and Its Problems,* ed. by R. P. Beckinsale and J. M. Houston (Oxford: Blackwell, 1968), pp. 245

[20] "Cities in Developing and in Industrial Society," in P. M. Hauser and Leo F. Schnore, *op. cit.,* p. 230.

difficult to accept the suggestion that status in and of itself has so over-powering an attraction that it can overcome the many discomforts of ex-tremé congestion, particularly for erstwhile peasant people long accus-tomed to open spaces. Such people are used to carrying on a large part of their domestic lives in full view of their neighbors and they continue to do that after moving to cities, especially in tropical areas. Privacy is a luxury that few can afford. Still, to live elbow-to-elbow day in and day out, with insufficient space for even the normal round of activities, would seem to have familiarity with inconvenience as its only support in past experience. If a value interpretation is at all applicable, it may have to acknowledge a displacement in the city of old values by a new one, namely, accessibility. The developing city, in the West of one hundred and more years ago as well as in new nations of the contemporary period, is a pedestrian city. In the former, efficient means for intramural move-ment had not yet appeared; in the latter neither personal incomes nor consumer credit facilities are adequate for a wide diffusion of the auto-mobile and the telephone. Nevertheless, the ramified interdependences of urban life put a premium on accessibility, even at the cost of serious insanitation and of offense to aesthetic sensibilities.[21]

A second element of structure common in premodern cities is a seg-mentation of population by tribe, caste, lineage, or previous place of resi-dence. The city appears as a mosaic of residential quarters or enclaves. Nineteenth century Peking is described by Koningsberger as a "loose grid, stuffed as it were with dozens of villages." [22] The seven quarters of mod-ern Timbuctoo are set apart by tribal and ethnic differences.[23] In the Yoruba towns patrilineage groups occupy separate compounds.[24] Caste in India forms the basis of residential groupings. This immemorial tend-ency is sustained by any form of association that proves useful in dealing with the exigencies of life in a strange and inhospitable place. It was just as common in the medieval European town where neither tribe nor caste constituted the basis of social units.[25] Migrants from a given village or district congregated in a narrow section of the town and there sought to

[21] Before concluding that, in view of such costs, high densities are "dysfunctional," as Daniel Lerner contends, careful consideration should be given to the options. A cost-benefit analysis might lead to a different conclusion. (See William B. Hamilton, op. cit., p. 16.)

[22] Hans Koningsberger, Love and Hate in China (New York: McGraw-Hill, 1966), p. 5.

[23] Horace Miner, The Primitive City of Timbuctoo (Princeton, N.J.: Princeton University Press, 1953), pp. 36 ff.

[24] P. C. Lloyd, "The Yoruba Town Today," Sociological Review, n.s., VII (1959): 45–46.

[25] Enumerations of quarters in medieval cities of the Near East list about seventy in Damascus, fifty or more in Aleppo, thirty-seven in Cairo, and some fifty in Jeru-salem. (I. Marvin Lapidus, Muslim Cities in the Later Middle Ages [Cambridge: Harvard University Press, 1967], p. 85.)

re-create a familiar pattern of life. Not until late in the nineteenth century did the cellular aspect begin to fade from the Western city.[26] The residential enclave, of course, is not to be understood simply as a response to the need for a refuge from abrasive experiences. While it serves that purpose, its origins lie mainly in a primitive state of local transportation and communication, as pointed out in an earlier chapter.[27] Without fairly efficient means of moving about, a large aggregate cannot attain more than a rudimentary integration.

A third physical feature is actually a corollary of the mosaic or cellular settlement pattern. That aspect is an absence of any marked concentration of specialized functions such as is represented, for example, in a central business district. The same circumstance that seals off residential enclaves makes a great degree of centralization impractical. Specialization is not highly developed in the early stages of industrialization, and most special functions, particularly those that cater to daily needs, are scattered more or less uniformly over the settled area. This does not apply to the very intensely specialized activities, e.g., money lending, silver-smithing, importing of exotic products. These are usually clustered by type within enclaves for the most part. The lack of a concentration of specialized activities at a central point does not mean that there are no focal points or interest centers in a preindustrial city. There is usually more than one, in fact, depending on the breadth of the thickly settled area. Interest centers, however, are commonly formed by the location of a ruler's palace, a major temple, or a gate through which pass communications with the outside world. Periodic markets and festive celebrations may also be held at such sites.

Still another characteristic of the emergent urban center is the gradient distribution of residential areas. Residential quarters are arranged with reference to a principal locus of interest, such as the palace of a ruling household or a religious edifice, in order of decreasing power and prestige of the occupants with distance away from the center of interest. In some instances, as in the Japanese castle town [28] or the Latin American agrarian center,[29] a gradient distribution of residences by rank was the product of a deliberate plan. Elsewhere its origin appears to lie in the uneven preemptive powers of the various social strata. Whatever may have been its history, the tendency is manifested in a great many cities of developing

[26] Cf. Paul Chatelain, "Quartiers historiques et centre ville: l'exemple du quartier du Marais," *Urban Core and Inner City*, Proceedings of the International Study Week, 11–17 September, 1966 (Leiden, The Netherlands: E. J. Brill, 1967), pp. 340–55.

[27] See Chapter 5.

[28] John Hall, "The Castle Town and Japan's Modern Urbanization," *The Far Eastern Quarterly*, XV (1955): 48 ff.

[29] See Lee F. Schnore's excellent review of the literature on this matter in P. M. Hauser and Leo F. Schnore, *op. cit.*, pp. 347–98.

areas.[30] By one means or another the lower classes are pushed outward toward the periphery while the interiors are occupied by public buildings and the homes of the upper classes. Public housing to replace cleared slums is built usually on the edge of a city where land is relatively cheap. Prestige gradients are much less in evidence in very large agglomerations; they can be detected in the near vicinities of focal points, but at distances of a mile or more removed they are blurred and equivocal.

These several elements of a pattern—compactness, residential segregation of traditionally defined groups, absence of functional centralization, and residential enclaves arrayed over distance from a focal point by rank of groups—are not peculiar to any time or place. They are products of a particular transportation and communication regime. They belong to the pedestrian city. Hence, regardless of its cultural setting and of the values that may be current, urbanization is invariably shaped by the frictions of space inherent in the means of locomotion in use at the time. The more primitive the means of movement over space, the fewer are the degrees of freedom available in the shaping of an organized group's settlement pattern.

THE RESIDENTIAL QUARTER AS A SOCIAL UNIT

The cellular structure of the city is reinforced by the flows of migrants from the rural countryside. The point of entry into the city is the residential quarter peopled by the migrant's kinsmen or fellow tribesmen. The quarter is the urban counterpart of the rural village.[31] In it are reproduced, as faithfully as urban conditions permit, the traditional institutions and customs of the kin or ethnic group, e.g., a local market with bargaining as a means of price setting,[32] a church or temple, village associations, and festive rites. In the enclave the migrant is greeted by friends who induct him into the transplanted mutual aid patterns and assist him in his search for work. They teach him the ways of the city so far as they are able.

There are many lessons to be learned by the newcomer, for the social gap between rural and urban can be as large as the technological gap. Actually, much of what separates the two turns out to be differences of

[30] John C. Brush, "The Morphology of Indian Cities," in *India's Urban Future,* ed. by Roy Turner (Berkeley: University of California Press, 1962), pp. 60–65.

[31] UNESCO, *Social Implications of Industrialization and Urbanization in Africa South of the Sahara* (Paris, 1956); "Demographic Aspects of Urbanization in the ECAFE Region": *Urbanization in Asia and the Far East* (Calcutta, 1957); Janet Abu-Lughod, "Migrant Adjustment to City Life; The Egyptian Case," *American Journal of Sociology,* LXVII (1961): 25.

[32] Gideon Sjoberg, "The Preindustrial City," *American Journal of Sociology,* LX (1955): 438–45.

degrees rather than of kind and differences in procedures by which familiar objectives are pursued. For example, the migrant is unprepared for the sharpness of the distinction between the work group and the social group. Nor is he able to adjust immediately to what seems to him a calculated neglect of his personal characteristics. He is trained to a discipline, but not one composed so entirely of standardized behaviors, of roundabout means to ends, and of contractual arrangements as binding among strangers as among kinsmen. These contrasts are troublesome enough without their being exaggerated as has often been done by Western observers. For example, Polanyi's assertion that market systems were nowhere known until the end of feudalism in Western Europe is a case in point.[33] Bascom finds historical evidence of fairly sophisticated market behavior in the early African city.[34] Just as questionable is the allegation that in the under-developed world spiritual values take precedence over material interests. This view, according to Agit Dasgupta, has been as harmful to India's economic development as it false.[35] It is more than likely that every people is as materialistic as the productivity of its economy permits it to be.

If, out of frustration with the new demands urban life imposes upon him, the urban migrant returns to his home village, it does not necessarily mean that he has a deep emotional attachment for the land.[36] There is no way of knowing whether rural attachments are stronger in one time or place than in another without at least standardizing the comparison with reference to land tenure practices, stability of employment in the cities, urban-rural differences in income and opportunity, and other relevant factors. Occasions arise, as in the Rhodesian city, where the native has no choice other than to retain his foothold in the land. He is brought to the city on a short-term work contract and upon its termination he finds himself excluded from the city's institutions.[37] The Yoruba town-dweller, on the other hand, is an absentee farmer; he and his lineage group derive

[33] Karl Polanyi, *The Great Transformation* (Boston: The Beacon Press, 1957), p. 54.

[34] W. Bascom, "Urbanism as a Traditional African Pattern," *Sociological Review*, n.s., VII (1959): 41.

[35] "India's Cultural Values and Economic Development: A Comment," *Economic Development and Cultural Change*, XIII (1964): 100–102. See also Milton Singer, "Cultural Values in India's Economic Development," *Annals of the American Academy of Political and Social Science*, CCCV (1956): 81–91.

[36] Richard D. Lambert, "The Impact of Urban Society on Village Life," in Roy Turner, *op. cit.*, pp. 135–36; Horace Miner and George DeVos, *Oasis and Casbah: Algerian Culture and Personality Change* (Ann Arbor: University of Michigan Press, 1960), pp. 27–29; R. B. Textor, *From Peasant to Pedicab Driver:* Cultural Report Series No. 9, Yale University Southeast Asian Studies (New Haven, 1961); D. J. Bogue and K. C. Zachariah, "Urbanization and Migration in India," in Roy Turner, *op. cit.*, p. 45; Doris A. Phillips, *op. cit.*; and J. C. Caldwell, *op. cit.*

[37] William J. Barber, "Urbanization and Economic Growth: The Cases of Two White Settler Territories," in *City in Modern Africa*, ed. by Horace Miner, p. 100.

their economic and their political power from the lands they own.[38] His feeling for the land may be not unlike that of a merchant for his investment capital. Between these extremes occur the majority of the cases in which sentiment for the land is dulled by the lack of rural opportunity.

Social solidarity within the residential enclave, however, tends to be an unstable balance of divisive and cohesive forces. On the other hand, the mutual obligations in which individuals have traditionally been bound to one another are found to have a limited relevance in the city. They are apt to grow more tenuous with the passing of time and are easily converted into mutual exploitation. In India, for example, the caste enclave is often ruled by a labor contractor. Having gained control of an industrial occupation, he determines who may work, how much he will earn and, in effect, whether he can remain as a resident of the enclave.[39] The parallel with the role of the *padrone* in the immigrant colonies of southeastern Europeans in American cities of the past century is a striking one.[40] Cityward migration, with or without the mediation of a labor contractor, tends to select the malcontent and misfit, as well as the vigorous and enterprising, members of village communities. Speaking of the migration to Bamako, in Mali, Claude Meillassoux declares: "People do not come to town merely to reconstruct village institutions. Young men are trying to free themselves from patriarchal rule and sexual restraints." [41] The submission of such people to group values in the city doubtless contains a large element of opportunism. Potential turbulence is also implicit in the radically distorted sex and age compositions that usually exist in places of rapid in-migration. The absence of elders, of family responsibilities, and of normal mating opportunities deprives the urban enclave of many of the common informal controls found in communities.

On the other hand, there are various and potent strains toward cohesiveness in the urban assemblage of persons with common backgrounds. These derive their strengths, for the most part, from the force of external influences. A multiethnic situation, such as exists in great diversity in most cities of Africa south of the Sahara,[42] generates numerous occasions for intergroup challenges and rivalries, not to mention the possibility of

---

38 P. C. Lloyd, *op. cit.*, p. 61.

39 Walter Phillips, "Technological Levels and Labor Resistance to Change," *Economic Development and Cultural Change*, XI (1963): 264.

40 John S. MacDonald and Leatrice D. MacDonald, "Chain Migration, Ethnic Neighborhood and Social Networks," *The Milbank Memorial Fund Quarterly*, XLII (1964): 86–88.

41 *Urbanization of an African Community: Voluntary Associations in Bamako* (Seattle: University of Washington Press, 1968), p. 75.

42 William J. Hanna and Judith L. Hanna, "The Political Structure of Urban-Centered African Communities," in *The City in Modern Africa*, ed. by Horace Miner, p. 155. See also UNESCO, *Social Implications of Industrialization and Urbanization in Africa South of the Sahara*, pp. 568–72.

the revival of old enmities. Competition for space, for employment, and for other preferments is interpreted, correctly or otherwise, in ethnic terms. Hence the members of identifiable groups draw together in mutual support and turn to their respective pasts for the symbols of group legitimacy. So turned in upon itself may be the residence group that some people, notably women, never venture beyond the boundaries of the enclave.[43] Cohesiveness of this kind, where repeated in each of many lineage or tribal groups, obviously militates against the development of common loyalties. If there is a set of values to which all groups are responsive, it tends to be that of an alien group whose superior knowledge and capital resources enable it to control the economy.[44]

VOLUNTARY ASSOCIATIONS

The unity of the residential quarter tends to be enhanced by the reestablishment there of traditional associations. Initially these may be reconstituted in reaction to the frustration of city life or as defenses against real or imagined threats from competing ethnic groups. But recreated associations cannot survive long on conflict alone. Sooner or later they must come to terms with the city; they must acquire a positive utility for their members.[45] Metamorphoses of that kind are occurring in many different places. In the Indian cities the castes are developing credit facilities, employment services, and educational aids for their members.[46] The landholding lineage group in the Nigerian city has adopted many of the fiscal and management procedures employed in a modern agricultural cooperative.[47] In the *barriadas* and *favelas* of Latin America the transplanted village associations have equipped themselves to deal with the legal problems of squatting on urban land and have found means to gain representation in municipal affairs.[48]

How durable these modified versions of traditional groups will prove to be is a conjectural matter. They clearly fill a vacuum formed by the

[43] Marshall B. Clinard and B. Chaterjee, "Urban Community Development in India: The Delhi Pilot Project," in Roy Turner, *op. cit.*, p. 91.

[44] Leo Kuper, "Structural Discontinuities in African Towns, Some Aspects of Racial Pluralisms," in *The City in Modern Africa*, ed. by Horace Miner (New York: Praeger, 1967), p. 128.

[45] Peter Marris, "Motives and Methods: Reflections on a Study in Lagos," in Horace Miner, *op. cit.*, p. 52. See also Peter Suzuki, "Village Solidarity Among Turkish Peasants Undergoing Urbanization," *Science*, CXXXII (1962): 891; and P. C. Lloyd, *Africa in Social Change* (Hammondworth: Penguin Books, Ltd., 1967), pp. 143–213.

[46] Bernard Cohen, "Changing Traditions of a Low Caste," *Journal of American Folklore*, LXXI (1958): 413–21; and Lloyd and Suzanne Rudolph, "The Political Role of India's Caste Associations," *Pacific Affairs*, XXXIII (1960): 5–22.

[47] P. C. Lloyd, *op. cit.*, p. 61; and W. Bascom, *op. cit.*, p. 41.

[48] P. M. Hauser (ed.), *Urbanization in Latin America*, pp. 174 ff. and 191 ff.

absence of alternative structures.[49] Their persistence may be contingent
on the same circumstance. It is also possible, of course, that some of
them will become parts of the city's permanent social structure, which is
itself in a formative stage in most instances. As their members scatter
over the city and as needs change, the surviving associations will lose
their spatial and even some of their sectarian identification.[50] Shanti
Tangu believes that, should that not happen, the Indian city "will merely
duplicate village society on a larger scale." [51] But new associations that
cross ethnic lines, such as political parties and labor unions, are appearing
with increasing frequency in cities of developing areas. They are, however, mobilized largely by personal leadership and they draw their main
support from ethnic, lineage, or tribal followings.

No doubt the probability that the individual's horizons of interest and
his range of activity will be broadened is increased by the growth of
community-wide associations. Yet his access to the opportunities offered
in the city is bound to be limited as long as he is confined to intermittent
employment in unstable and marginal enterprises and to a correspondingly meager income. Without security the migrant is apt to regard himself as merely a sojourner and to cling tenaciously to his rural ties.

THE CHANGING FAMILY

What happens to the traditional family form in the urban context depends in no small degree on how it enters into the urban economy. If it
reestablishes itself as a producing unit, as it might do were it previously
engaged in a rural industry other than agriculture, it may preserve its
extended pattern in which sons with their wives and children remain in
the parental home or compound and under the patriarch's authority. The
household enterprise depends upon family members for its labor supply
and, in turn, provides each the security of a contributing role, at least
until its function is discovered to be uneconomic. In Nigeria the extended
family promotes entrepreneurship, by apprenticing a young member to
an experienced enterpreneur, and supplies the capital for a family-run
firm. Thus industrialization is founded in part on the family system.
But the more successful the firm, the larger is the number of dependents

[49] Lucian Pye has noted that the rapid influx of refugees into Rangoon outstripped
the development of appropriate control mechanisms, resulting in a reversion to traditional forms of control. The headmen in squatters' settlements were made responsible
to civil authorities (*Politics, Personality and Nation-Building: Burma's Search for
Identity* [New Haven: Yale University Press, 1962], p. 92).

[50] This appears to happen in even so primitive a town as Bamako, Mali. (Claude
Meillanssoux, *op. cit.*, p. 76).

[51] "Urbanization, Political Stability and Economic Growth," in Roy Turner, *op.
cit.*, p. 207.

the entrepreneur is required to support. Hence firms are kept small by the dissipation of earnings that might have gone into capital expansion. Economies of scale are lost thereby.[52]

Where, however, the family upon entering the city ceases to be a producing unit there is no longer a need for a large multiworker household dominated by a male parent. Consequently, although there may be strenuous efforts to preserve it, the extended family household tends to break up under the pressures of housing costs and availability, on the one hand, and the accessibility requirements attached to different occupations, on the other.[53] The kinship group survives, nevertheless, as a viable mutual aid association. It does so in the Western city as well, though there have been no antecedents in an extended family form.

The dissolution of the extended family is hastened as members acquire employment in salary- or wage-paying occupations. In Ibadan, for example, educated white-collar workers, employed largely in government positions, have deserted the compounds to lead nuclear family lives in widely dispersed residential areas.[54] Unlike the mass of the population, their marriage practices are exogamous and monogamous. Husbands depart further from tradition by assisting with the care and training of children, by applying verbal rather than physical punishments to childish misbehaviors, and by taking meals with their families. The family-life style of the white-collar group converges upon the European pattern. While such behavioral adaptations may be thought to represent extreme instances, there are other signs that similar tendencies are appearing in other sectors of city populations. Wherever there is occupational diversification and even small advances in education there are indications of dissolution of the residential enclaves. In Stanleyville,[55] Freetown,[56] and other African cities, cultural differences are giving way to a set of standard norms.[57] Everywhere urbanization erodes ethnic differences.

There are costs involved in the decline of the extended family. The

[52] E. Wayne Nafziger, "The Effect of the Nigerian Extended Family on Entrepreneurial Activity," *Economic Development and Cultural Change,* XVIII (1969): 25–33.

[53] There is some disagreement in this respect among observers of changes at work in the urban center. Most of the contention, however, seems to rest on differences of definition. The problem of definition is very nicely described by Richard D. Lambert (*op. cit.,* pp. 125–27).

[54] Robert LeVine, Nancy H. Klein and Constance R. Owens, "Father-Child Relationships and Changing Life-Styles in Ibadan, Nigeria," in *The City in Modern Africa,* ed. by Horace Miner, pp. 215–55.

[55] UNESCO, *Social Implications of Urbanization and Industrialization in Africa South of the Sahara,* pp. 688 ff.

[56] Michael Banton, "Social Alignment and Identity in a West African City," in *Urbanization and Migration in West Africa,* ed. by Hilda Kuper (Berkeley: University of California Press, 1965), pp. 131–48.

[57] R. Clignet, "Urbanization and Family Structure in the Ivory Coast," *Comparative Studies in Society and History,* VIII (1965–66): 385–401.

individual is deprived of an important source of emotional support and the community loses one of its principal agencies of social control. Yet the gains may equal if not exceed the losses. For in a strongly family-oriented society there is an indifference toward the well-being of the community at large. Welfare is a family concern almost exclusively; the family may lend assistance to kinsmen and to a few clients, domestic servants, and their dependents for the most part, but to all others it turns a deaf ear. The preferential treatment of kinsmen, moreover, corrupts politics and introduces inefficiency into business enterprise. In short, the development of interdependence in all its forms is restricted by the persistence of parochial institutions such as the extended family. The rise and spread of a sense of civic responsibility in both private and public life presupposes a secularization of relationships.

THE MIDDLE CLASS

One of the major proponents of secularization in society is the middle class, the class of people who derive their sustenance from wage and salary employment in business, government, and professional occupations. The middle class supplies the driving force for the creation and improvement of civil institutions which attend to welfare needs and provides the paths for social mobility. In developing countries middle classes, though they are emerging and growing, are still numerically small. The proportions of population that might be so classified, as reported by the United Nations, averages no more than 26 percent in two thirds of the countries, and not more than 42 percent in the remaining third.[58] These figures are to be compared with proportions ranging from 60 to 85 percent in developed countries. In Latin America, as seen in Table 56, the proportions forming middle classes are considerably smaller than 26 percent in all but one of the fifteen countries.

It has been observed that middle classes, small though they are, have their effectiveness increased by virtue of the primate city pattern of urban development.[59] Under those conditions the middle class is concentrated in close proximity to the seat of government and can thus exercise a maximum influence for social improvements. By the same token, however, most of the effects are apt to be localized in the primate city. To that extent the rest of the country lingers in an undeveloped state. One of the persistent difficulties in countries with primate cities is the refusal of middle-class members to live anywhere beyond the environs of the metropolis.

[58] United Nations, *Urbanization: Development Policies and Planning*, p. 23.
[59] S. Lipset and A. E. Solari, *Elites in Latin America* (New York: Oxford University Press, 1967), pp. 61–93.

Table 56. Percentage Distribution of the Economically Active Population (By Occupational Class, and Country, Latin America, ca. 1950)

Country	All Workers	Urban Sector			Rural Sector		
		Total	Middle Class[a]	Working Class	Total	Landowners and Small Farmers[b]	Peons
Argentina	100	73	28	45	27	8	19
Chile	100	71	21	50	29	1	28
Venezuela	100	61	16	45	39	2	37
Cuba	100	59	21	38	41	—	41
Ecuador	100	48	10	38	52	1	51
Panama	100	46	15	31	54	1	53
Costa Rica	100	45	14	31	55	8	47
Paraguay	100	45	12	33	55	2	53
Colombia	100	44	12	32	56	10	46
Brazil	100	37	13	24	63	2	61
Guatemala	100	37	6	31	63	2	61
El Salvador	100	36	9	27	64	2	62
Bolivia	100	27	7	20	73	1	72
Honduras	100	16	4	12	84	—	84
Haiti	100	14	2	12	86	1	85

[a]Includes entrepreneurs, professions, technical and managerial personnel, white collar workers.
[b]Includes only farmers who employ hired laborers.
SOURCE: Adapted from Glenn H. Beyer (ed.), *The Urban Explosion in Latin America*, p. 237.
Copyright © 1967 by Cornell University Press. Used by permission of the Cornell University Press.

The effectiveness of the middle class is also conditioned by its composition. In the development of the West the middle class sprang from commerce and industry, and it grew rapidly with the expansion of economies. Because of its origins it acquired great power in its respective society. In contrast, as Hoselitz has pointed out, the middle class in developing countries is founded on advanced education and government employment.[60] Neither of those circumstances is associated with economic power. Furthermore, the class is subservient to the elite which controls the government bureaucracy. A middle class so constituted can hardly be as aggressive or as creative as one based on entrepreneurial achievement.

[60] William B. Hamilton, *op. cit.*, pp. 45–66. See also *Development of a Middle Class in Tropical and Sub-Tropical Countries*, International Institute of Differing Civilizations, 29th Session (Brussels, 1956), p. 451, and Hans Dieter-Evers, "The Formation of a Social Class Structure: Urbanization, Bureaucratization and Social Mobility," *American Sociological Review*, XXXI (1966): 430–38.

THE CITY AS AN ORGANIZED UNIT

In areas undergoing rapid change from traditionalism to modernization the city is usually unprepared both physically and organizationally to deal with the great burdens thrust upon it. Its low-cost housing resources are quickly crowded to the point of danger to health and welfare, and beyond. Growth overflows into teeming squatter settlements of flimsy shacks without water and sewage facilities. Housing codes, inspection services, and preventive medical measures are either nonexistent or unattended by adequate enforcement provisions. Police, fire, sanitation, and other municipal agencies are usually understaffed and inexperienced. They may also be racked by corruption and immobilized in bureaucratic inertia. Welfare services, if they exist at all, are supplied by a few feeble private agencies. School facilities, at their best in the large city, are even there deficient in capacity and quality of program. The fact that cities in developing areas generally are adjuncts of their central governments means that they have very little latitude for the exercise of initiative.

The scale of organized activity of all kinds, economic as well as social, is kept small and localized by the almost total reliance by most people on walking as the means of getting about. Home and work place are one and the same for a large part of the labor force. Markets for many crafts and shops are no more extensive than the residential quarter in which they are located. Where the cellular pattern is found the circulation of information is slow and uncertain, the labor market is fragmented, and municipal administration is impaired by physical and social cleavages. The combined effect of such disabilities is to hold the city's contribution to modernization and economic development far below its potential.

THE CITY IN TRANSITION

But change is ubiquitous in the developing-area city. The transition from traditional to modern phases gives rise to a marked duality of structure. There is, as has been pointed out, an old pattern formed of a congeries of cell-like compartments in which the great mass of the population pursues a life half-village and half-urban in character. Superimposed upon the cellular structure is a newer pattern consisting of a thin overlay of modern urban organization embracing the interests and activities of a small cosmopolitan segment of the population. In the former the daily round revolves closely about the home and neighborhood. But in the latter individuals routinely commute from widely scattered residences to specialized business, administrative, and recreation districts. The institutions concentrated in these specialized districts are almost as foreign to the erstwhile peasants in the residential quarters as are those of distant countries. It is as though there were two cities occupying a common site.

As change progresses, the newer sector grows steadily at the expense of the older. That is, the network of relationships thickens and spreads, invading the enclaves and dispersing their activities. The pace at which the latter is absorbed into the former is measured by improvements in transportation and communication facilities and by increases in the volume of their use. Those measurements reflect more fundamental shifts, including a rising level of literacy, an increasing reliance on monetary income, and a spreading participation in modern institutions. In other words, there is a developing social and economic system in which is integrated an increasing proportion of the city's residents.

Where colonialism has been an influence the emergence of the newer urban pattern may assume various forms. The British, for example, often created a concentration of Western administrative and mercantile institutions at some distance removed from native markets, usually at points of easy access to interregional transport routes.[61] The French, on the other hand, adapted themselves to local circumstances. In Algeria, from which the preceding Turkish administration had disappeared entirely, the French redesigned the cities in their own patterns. But in Tunis and Morocco, where local authority had been preserved, the cities were left as they had been found and the French contented themselves with building new residential quarters at the peripheries.[62] Such influences tended to shift the centers of gravity of urban growth toward the loci of foreign activity.

A redistribution and regrouping of population and of land uses accompanies the integration of the urban center. Its structure is, in a sense, turned inside out. In a process of centralization many small retail and service units are replaced by a smaller number of larger units which concentrate their operations at strategic locations in a core district. Growth of a central business district threatens adjacent residential properties with obsolescence, though the walled compound so prevalent in Asiatic cities delays that effect much longer than would be the case in its absence. Eventually the encroachment of noise and dirt-producing activities, together with improved commutation facilities, induces members of the elite and of the middle class to move to peripheral locations. They desert ethnic and provincial enclaves to form income and status residential groupings in the outer zones. Some of the residential properties vacated in this way are appropriated by other uses and some are converted to more intensive residential occupance. Relocation of low-income residential areas,

[61] Noel P. Gist, "The Ecology of Bangalore, India: An East-West Comparison," *Social Forces*, XXXV (1957): 357–58.

[62] R. LeTourneau, "Social Change in the Muslim Cities in North Africa," *American Journal of Sociology*, LX (1955): 527–35.

however, is more a relative than it is an absolute shift; that is, established low-income areas are engulfed by the expanding city. The general effect of the various movements and positional alterations is to bring about a reversal in the residential distribution from the older inverse relationship of class status with distance from an inner point to approximate the direct pattern more common in the Western city. The introduction of the railway, which inaugurated the transition, produced a very pronounced centralizing effect.[63] That effect was carried further with the development of intracity, mass transportation facilities. The consequences have been observed in Mexico City and elsewhere in Mexico,[64] in Bogotá,[65] in Bangalore, India,[66] and even in Yoruba towns.[67] But the pattern that is emerging in cities of developing areas belongs to a transportation stage that is rapidly being left behind in Western cities. The universal distribution of the automobile, telephone, and other forms of instantaneous communication is fashioning a new city pattern the shape of which is not yet clearly visible.

There is a proposition implicit here that warrants closer scrutiny. It is that cities repeat a growth pattern in the degree to which they pass through a given sequence of transportation changes. This might appear to place an excessive emphasis on distances, locations, and configurations in space. But a city is a city only so far as it constitutes a communications system. And the types and the scales of units of organization comprising a city's structure are affected to a very considerable extent by the ease with which people can assemble for collective action. What is not so clear is how dependent each step along a course of change is upon preceding steps. Although it might be possible to skip a transportation stage by mobilizing enough capital to install the advanced equipment involved two stages removed, there are numerous supporting elements that are accumulated much more slowly and perhaps only in logical order, such as comprehension of the necessary technical lore, skill in applying the knowledge in maintenance service, familiarity with appropriate forms of organization, management competence, and the like. Tools can be moved about with very little difficulty, but the behavioral frameworks essential to their use are much harder to transfer from one context to

[63] R. D. McKenzie, "The Concept of Dominance and World Organization," p. 31. *American Journal of Sociology,* XXXIII (1927): 28–42.

[64] Norman Hayner, "Mexico City: Its Growth and Configuration," *American Journal of Sociology,* L (1945): 295–304; and Fernando Penalosa, "Ecological Organization of the Transitional City: Some Mexican Evidence," *Social Forces,* XLVI (1967): 221–28.

[65] Peter W. Amato, "Population Densities, Land Values, and Socio-Economic Class in Bogotá, Colombia," *Land Economics,* XLV (1969): 66–73.

[66] K. N. Venkatarayappa, "Urban Land Value and Land Utilization Trends in India," *Sociological Bulletin* (Bombay), IX (1960): 34–47.

[67] A. L. Mabogunje, *op. cit.,* p. 17.

another. The problem at issue is manifestly much broader than city development; it is a question of critical importance in all instances of social change, particularly when intervention is to be attempted.

It may be a Western habit of mind that leads one to seek a logical order in cultural and organizational change. Clearly, acculturation is not a smooth transition with no discontinuities or ambiguities. Apparently it comes easiest to those modes of behavior that involve individuals in the fewest, the most indirect, or the most transitory interpersonal relationships. These turn out to be the use of tools and the adoption of formalized behaviors, and they are often superimposed upon traditional patterns of action. The Japanese male, who wears Western dress on the city streets, changes to the long-familiar *ukada* upon retiring to his household at the end of the working day. The southeast Asian artisan listens to the advice of the Western technical expert and then consults the spirit world for a propitious time at which to put the advice into effect. Eventually many such survivals of old ways disappear, as has been happening rapidly in Japan in recent years in respect to the subordination of women.[68] It may be true that the attenuation of traditional practices is accompanied by internal tensions, as Miner and DeVos concluded from their study of personality changes incidental to urbanization.[69] The reconciliation of contrasting behaviors can be a frustrating task; but again it may not be. It does not follow that the juxtaposition of seemingly incompatible elements is always productive of tensions and disorders. Man has the happy facility of being able to live quite comfortably with inconsistencies in his culture. Traditional and modern cultures are neither pure, as Gusfield has pointed out, nor without many idiosyncrasies.[70]

URBAN EXPANSION

The metamorphosis of the city pattern from one resembling a cluster of cells to an integrated or organic-like system is symptomatic of a changing relationship to the hinterland. In the first instance center-hinterland relationships are few; they may consist largely of the extraction of food and raw materials from the countryside, in exchange for which military protection and internal order are provided. In most other respects outlying areas exist in isolation from urban centers and from one another.

[68] R. P. Dore, *City Life in Japan: A Study of a Tokyo Ward* (Berkeley: University of California Press, 1958), pp. 157 ff.; and Robert J. Smith, "Pre-Industrial Urbanism in Japan: A Consideration of Multiple Traditions in a Feudal Society," *Economic Development and Cultural Change*, IX (1960): 241–54.

[69] "Algerian Culture and Personality in Change," *Sociometry*, XXI (1958): 255–58.

[70] See Joseph R. Gusfield, "Tradition and Modernity: Misplaced Polarities in the Study of Social Change," *American Journal of Sociology*, LXXII (1967): 351–62.

Linking roads are widely spaced and poorly maintained, transportation time and costs are high, markets are undeveloped, there is little money in circulation, and the hinterland population is preoccupied with an agricultural economy concerned primarily with subsistence. Politically the situation is not unlike an Italian city-state of the Renaissance. It consists, that is, of a large, loosely organized aggregation of consumers holding in peonage the population of an extensive tributary area. Since the relations between center and surounding area are limited in number, no very elaborate division of labor and administrative organization at the center are needed.

Thus it follows that as urban-hinterland relationships multiply and diversify, the organization at the center must be developed so that it can service and coordinate as well as conduct the enlarging network of exchanges. Growth in scale, it will be recalled, necessitates a change in form, i.e., a development of organization, if the expanding unit is not to lapse again into semi-independent localities. The spread of a territorial division of labor and the rise of the city or cities as effective integrating and administrative mechanisms advance interactively with improvements in transportation and communication. Urban organization moves out along radiating routes, leaving interstitial zones relatively untouched at first. Subsequently lateral extensions penetrate the spaces between radial routes, bringing those localities into the system. Given a transportation network, marketing, credit, retail, educational, health, and other institutionalized services must then be reproduced at frequent intervals over the hinterland territories. For reasons of efficiency the various institutions are clustered here and there, forming the nuclei of growing towns and cities. This complex apparatus of urbanization is sometimes described as social overhead, for it serves a purpose similar to that served by industrial overhead.

Discussions of economic development often treat the two kinds of overhead as competitors for a fixed capital fund. The implication suggested is that if social overhead is enlarged economic growth will languish, or if industrial overhead attracts investment funds the facilities for training and serving a qualified labor supply will be neglected. The distinction, however, implies a greater exclusiveness than is actually involved. Social overhead is a vital external economy for industry. Industry depends on the same transportation and communication system used by the consuming public; schools are essential for the education of the young who will fill industrial as well as other positions; and a labor force must be fed, kept healthy, and have its other needs supplied. Financial, legal, and other professional services are used by the public jointly with industry.

Urbanization in a developing area, in the contemporary as well as in the nineteenth century period, is a process of bringing a multiregional territory under a single organization integrated and administered from a set of urban centers. Empirical descriptions of how that comes about have not been produced. The detailed information needed for such a purpose is not to be had. An interesting study, though cross-sectional in design and forced to use countries as units rather than regions or districts within countries, throws light on the interactions among the relevant parameters. With data for forty-one countries, the authors discovered fairly close correlations between the percentage of population in metropolitan areas, industrial diversification, technological development, and the territorial dispersion of the sources of consumer goods imported.[71] It would be surprising, of course, were the findings different from those reported. While the four factors may be set apart for analytical purposes, they are in fact different aspects of the same thing. In this regard what is true on an international scale should be true also intra-nationally.

Intercorrelations among a number of urban indicators in a sample of countries are shown in Table 57. The first row is interesting because it involves correlations with the proportion of country populations concentrated in places of 20,000 or more inhabitants. As that proportion rises so do all of the measures of urban organization—industrialization, health, education, and communication. Particularly noteworthy are the very close relationships between energy consumption and per capita income with letter mail. Evidently the actual amount of correspondence exchanged is more important than the level of literacy so far as economic development is concerned. It should be recognized, however, that while the coefficients are relatively high, they leave ample room in all but three or four cases for a considerable amount of deviation; only where the coefficient is above .71 does a given indicator account for 50 percent or more of the variation in a correlated indicator.

THE CONVERGENCE HYPOTHESIS RECONSIDERED: A SUMMARY

The recurrence of the phenomenon of population concentration in urban areas in so many different times and places can hardly be regarded as a series of fortuities. On the contrary, it points to the operation of a cumulative process in which the regions and nations of the world are being absorbed into an expanding world ecumene. As one society after another has yielded to the superior economic and political power of an industrialized market economy, it has been thrust along a path toward a drastic internal reorganization. For it could not remain in its traditional

[71] Jack P. Gibbs and Walter T. Martin, "Urbanization, Technology and the Division of Labor: International Patterns," *American Sociological Review*, XXVII (1962): 666–77. See also Walter T. Martin, "Urbanization and National Power to Requisition Resources," *Pacific Sociological Review*, V (1962): 93–97.

Table 57. Zero Order Correlations Between Selected Indicators of Modernization
(36 Countries, Ca. 1960)

Variable	Per Cent Urban	Males in Non-agricultural Employ-ment	Life Expectancy	School Enroll-ment	Newspaper Circula-tion	Literacy Ratio	Energy Consump-tion	Letter Mail	Income per Capita	Infant Mortality
Per cent urban	—	.85	.72	.70	.69	.65	.62	.57	.56	-.52
Males in nonagriculture	—	—	.82	.82	.80	.74	.73	.71	.71	-.62
Life expectancy	—	—	—	.83	.77	.78	.60	.58	.61	-.82
School enrollment	—	—	—	—	.69	.75	.70	.64	.70	-.73
Newspaper circulation	—	—	—	—	—	.57	.70	.71	.68	-.66
Literacy ratio	—	—	—	—	—	—	.62	.57	.45	-.34
Energy consumption	—	—	—	—	—	—	—	.93	.97	-.53
Letter mail	—	—	—	—	—	—	—	—	.92	-.55
Income per capita	—	—	—	—	—	—	—	—	—	-.53
Infant mortality	—	—	—	—	—	—	—	—	—	—

SOURCE: United Nations, *Urbanization: Development Policies and Planning*, 1968, p. 30.

pattern and at the same time participate in a highly rationalized network of interregional relationships. Participation in the world economy has demanded of every society the adoption of a new technological regime, a reorientation to resources, a fundamental reconstitution and realignment of social units, and a broad-scale redistribution of its population. Urbanization is a more or less localized manifestation of this regionwide or multiregional transformation.

Still, it is not possible in the current state of progress of urbanization in developing nations to arrive at a definitive conclusion concerning its eventual outcome. This problem, it will be recalled, was anticipated. Nevertheless, the evidence that has been assembled lends very strong presumptive support to the convergence hypothesis. Although urbanization begins in very different cultural contexts, in each instance the trend soon begins to reproduce phases and patterns that have occurred in other times and places. The convergence tendency penetrates surface features, such as spatial arrangements—though even those are not as arbitrary as an uncritical view might lead one to suspect, to affect family structure, types of voluntary associations and interpersonal relations of virtually every kind. Indeed, if one may be permitted a rather self-evident observation, it is only because that is the case that we are able to refer to a single process, i.e., urbanization, rather than to a multiplicity of processes.

Obviously, convergence does not imply identity in all respects and in minute detail. Urbanization has not stamped all urban places within developed countries in a single mold. There are innumerable qualitative differences that reflect various locational circumstances, peculiarities of growth experience, administrative eccentricities, and other unique events. Moreover, it is in the nature of a territorial division of labor that urban areas should be unique in their producing functions and similar in their distribution, communication, and administrative functions. Movement toward similarity in the latter respect has advanced as the lines of interdependence have been more tightly drawn. That process is not yet finished. Needless to say, the development of a worldwide division of labor embracing the under-developed as well as the developed nations has far to go before exerting an effect on urban places comparable to that observable in Western countries.

But a great many other characteristics, directly or indirectly associated with production practices, are also brought forward from the past. These appear in many forms. Some may have a transitory utility, such as the village council means of self-help. Others—nepotistic employment policies and animistic beliefs, for example—are obstructive. Still others, notably art forms and handicrafts, prove to be decorative. Even after many such survivals of a traditional life are erased in the acculturation process, numerous subtle traces of the past may persist to shape the imagery and color the moral predilections of current generations. Whether all differences can be eliminated is uncertain. The question, however, calls attention to a problem that is inherent in comparative study; namely, how much difference can be accepted in a judgment of similarity as between forms of behavior or institutions? One answer might be that similarity exists in the measure to which the practices in use in one society are substitutable for those observed in another society. No doubt the relative weight to be assigned to indications of similarity increases with the number of respects in which interchangeability is feasible.

It has been sugested, however, that there is no necessary dependence of a function on a particular institutional structure.[72] New functions acquired in the modernization process can be fitted to traditional structures. Feldman and Moore point to instances in which kinship systems operate as corporate units in the modern sense, such as was observed in Nigeria, in which recruitment to industrial employment is by the old method of ascription, and in which group restraints on the transfer of rights to property remain in force in urban settings.[73] Clifford Geertz is inclined to subscribe to the same view. Although his data indicate that developments in the organization of business activity stemming from, on the one hand, a bazaar-type entrepreneurship in Java and, on the other hand, from aristocratic business ventures in Bali, are tending to converge upon the pattern of the Western firm, he concludes that "a modern economic system may be compatible with a wider range of non-economic cultural patterns and social structures than has often been thought." [74]

Most of the examples of the adaptation of traditional institutions to modern industrial functions are glimpses as of a moment in time; the changes in question have not yet run their courses. But it is conceivable that mixes of traditional structures and modern functions can persist as long as the societies remain insular. If and when they become linked to the world economy, and in the degree to which they are caught up in interregional exchanges, it would seem unlikely that indigenous structures could long survive, except in ceremonial ways. The exigencies of communication would soon impose requirements for standardization. There may be no end to cultural inconsistencies in minor matters, especially in those that are of no more than local concern; but, in those connections in which different systems meet and interact, it is doubtful that there is much tolerance for structural divergences.

It is at the point of explaining persistencies that values are most often

---

[72] Cf. C. E. Black, *The Dynamics of Modernization: A Study in Comparative History* (New York: Harper Torchbook, 1967), pp. 46–49.

[73] "Industrialization and Industrialism: Convergence and Differentiation," *Transactions of the Fifth World Congress of Sociology,* Vol. II (International Sociological Society, 1962), p. 156.

[74] *Peddlers and Princes: Social Development and Economic Change in Two Indonesian Towns* (Chicago: University of Chicago Press, 1963), p. 127.

called into use. Why this should be is not clear, for there is no time dimension implied in the value concept. Nor does it seem likely that anyone would care to argue that all things which persist are classifiable as values. As a matter of fact, the inertia in behavior is much more readily understood as due in part to the lack of knowledge about or skill in the use of alternative ways of acting and in part to the interlocking relationships among behavior patterns.[75]

In many respects it is unfortunate that facilitating and inhibiting factors in social change have been characterized as values. Useful as the term may be in humanistic discourse, in social science it obscures more than it reveals. Value is variously used to refer to ends, to conditions, to motives, and to the attitudes toward one or more of these. Ethel Albert's definition of values as the criteria by which behavior is judged is one of the clearest to be found in the literature.[76] But a criterion is not simply a state of mind or a phonetic utterance. To have effect it must be manifested in behavior. Thus a criterion is an act evoked by another act and which is supportive, redirective, or repressive of the other act. All conduct is interactive and therefore is evaluative; conversely, all values are translatable as conduct. The fact that behaviors have verbal counterparts should not be allowed to confuse the issue. At most the difference between values and behavior is a difference in the abstractions observers choose to employ. Seen in this light urbanization is, among other things, a process of changing values.

SUPPLEMENTARY READINGS

Breese, Gerald (ed.). *The City in Newly Developing Countries* (Englewood Cliffs, N.J.: Prentice-Hall, 1969).

Cohen, Abner. *Custom and Politics in Urban Africa: A Study of Hausa Migrants in Yoruba Towns* (Berkeley: University of California Press, 1969).

Davis, Kingsley, and Casis, Ana. "Urbanization in Latin America," *Milbank Memorial Fund Quarterly*, XXIV (1946).

Johnson, John J. (ed.). *Continuity and Change in Latin America* (Stanford: Stanford University Press, 1964.

Little, Kenneth. "The Role of Voluntary Associations in West African Urbanization," *African Affairs*, LIX (1957): 579–596.

Plotnicov, Leonard. *Strangers to the City: Urban Man in Jos, Nigeria* (Pittsburgh: University of Pittsburgh Press, 1967).

[75] For a perceptive examination of the explanatory utility of values see John H. Kunkel, "Values and Behavior in Economic Development," *Economic Development and Cultural Change*, XIII (1965): 257–77.

[76] "Value Systems," *International Encyclopedia of the Social Sciences* (New York: Macmillan and The Free Press, 1968), vol. 16, p. 286. Raymond Firth has the following to say: "Of course we must guard against reifying values, much as we should avoid reifying social structure. Our statements about values are inferences from observations of behavior. Our use of the term 'value' is a way of talking about behavior" (*Essays on Social Organization and Values* [London: Athlone Press, 1964], pp. 208–209).

14

Urbanization and a
Theory of Change

A great deal has been said in the preceding chapters that has to do with general aspects of change. These scattered observations and propositions are brought together in this final chapter as a step toward the formulation of a comprehensive theory of change. The tentative nature of this effort must be emphasized at the outset. While the attempt will undoubtedly fall short of achieving a resolution of this most difficult problem in social theory, it should bring some measure of order into what is known and in so doing it should expose gaps in the state of the art and areas where research is needed. Some such attempt seems to be indicated in a work of this kind, for urbanization is above all a process of change. It is social change in the fullest and most inclusive sense of the word.

In approaching this task one is led to speculate on what should be the objectives of a theory of change—to what kinds of questions should it propose answers. There is no better way to discover the dimensions of the problem. As a minimum requirement it seems that such a theory should address itself to the following questions: What is the nature of change? How is it to be observed, i.e., what is the unit in which change is to be observed and what are the indicators of change? Where and under what conditions does it occur? How predictable is change? Are there points where change characteristically impinges upon or enters a unit? How are its effects transmitted through the unit? What are its repercussions and its interaction effects? Does it have a determinable duration? There are many more questions of importance that could be probed, but these are a fair sample of what is encountered in an attempt to deal comprehensively with the matter. Something has been said in preceding discussions about most of the issues. At the risk of seeming overly abstract we shall repeat without belaboring the points here.

THE MEANING OF CHANGE

The study of change of the kind represented in urbanization requires that one deal with a system as a whole. This necessity immediately narrows the range of concern in some respects while leaving it very broad in other respects. A focus of attention upon a system permits many exclusions. Modifications of individual behavior, the improvements of a family's fortunes, or the contraction of an institution's budget are not in themselves of interest in a study of system change. There are also various kinds of losses and replacements that fall outside the definition; families come and go, firms fail and others appear in their places, generations succeed one another in endless progression without any measurable effect on a system. Finally, there are numerous rhythmic variations, such as day and night pulsations of activity in a community, the ebbs and flows of population in its daily rounds, the intake of materials by a community and the output of products—these and other oscillations are the means by which stability is maintained.

It is important to recognize, moreover, that a social system is a loosely knit fabric of relationships. In consequence there is a certain amount of independent variability among the interdependent parts. But flexibility of this nature should not be mistaken for changeability.[1] On the contrary, it is just that flexibility which enables a structure of relationships to withstand random shifts and pressures. Too great a rigidity would subject a system to a continuous risk of destruction in an unstable environment.

At first glance the task of observing change in an entity as multifarious and as complex as a social system seems too formidable for an individual's powers of observation. But what has just been said simplifies the matter a great deal. System change may be defined as the removal or the addition, the contraction or enlargement, or the realignment of one or more functions. Simple as this may seem on the surface, such events have profound repercussions. They affect extensive networks of relationships, alter the rhythm of system operations, modify the number and kind of people needed, shift resource requirements, and produce reverberations in nearly every part of a system. Some of these consequences are much more visible as manifestations of change than are the fundamental shifts

---

[1] See Wilbert E. Moore, *Social Change* (Englewood Cliffs, N.J.: Prentice-Hall, 1963), p. 16.

themselves. One of the most sensitive of all categories of indicators of change, for example, are those of a demographic character. Variations in the number of people or alterations in the rates of birth, death, or migration, when permanent, are incontrovertible evidence that something of basic importance has happened, though they do not indicate the nature of the change.

System change, then, tends to move in either of two directions—toward contraction and increasing simplicity, or toward expansion and complexity. Whether there is a third possibility in which some functions are simply substituted for others without the occurrence of either contraction or expansion of the system is uncertain. This question might better be left to empirical determination. With a few notable exceptions,[2] most occasions of contractions result from expansions in other systems. An expanding system tends to encroach upon systems in adjacent areas. If successful, it usurps functions and eventually may either obliterate the neighboring system or reduce it to the status of a subordinate part, a subsystem, in the expanding unit. This volume has been concerned mainly with expansion, which might also be described as cumulative change or growth. The concentration of attention upon one kind of change is justified partly because urbanization is defined as such change, and partly because expansion appears to be the more general form of social change.

The remarks on the possibility of system contraction call to mind a second characteristic of change that is closely related to the first one mentioned. Not only is change a nonrepetitive alteration, it is also irreversible. It is a modification that cannot be undone. New properties are acquired in the process of alteration with the result that it is impossible to restore a thing to its original state. What has been changed might be returned to a primitive condition but not to the original condition. Nor can retrogression retrace the sequence of steps followed in a prior development. Thus, once a system is launched on the course of urbanization, there is no turning back. The process may be arrested or turned in the direction of contraction, but there is no possibility of a complete reversion to an earlier state of affairs.[3]

In order to pose the problem of system change it will be helpful to recall some of the remarks made in Chapter 1. It was there observed that

[2] Among these the most common case is that in which a group, through continuous and unchanging use of its natural resources, so modifies their character or exhausts their supply, that it can no longer sustain a customary mode of life in its area. If the group remains in the area it may have to submit to a retrogression to a more primitive level of organization. If it leaves the area, it will have to reorganize in adaptation to a different set of life conditions.

[3] Emmanual G. Mesthene refers to this property of change as its "one-wayness." Once an innovation is admitted to a system there is no way of avoiding a series of consequences ("How Technology Will Shape the Future," *Science*, CLXI [12 July 1968], p. 136).

a social system is an organization by means of which a population maintains itself in a definable area. Organization, population, and territory are essential components in any life situation. To these three should be added an environmental niche or position in a social field. The latter includes such relationships with other organized populations as the social system in question regularly sustains. Now, in the absence of any disturbances a population tends to fill all of the territory it can monopolize with the organization it possesses. An approximation to equilibrium develops: there is no unused space, all manpower requirements are supplied by the population, all parts of the organization are fully complementary, and the exchanges with neighboring systems regularly provide what is not available within the immediate habitat.[4] Under these·conditions no one of the several components can be significantly altered without changing the others correspondingly. How then does change occur?

THE CHANGE PROCESS

The closed circle formed by organization, population, territory, and position in a social field is broken mainly, if not exclusively, by an intrusion from the outside. This may come from either the natural or the social environment. Noncyclical events in the natural environment, such as volcanic eruptions, the shifting of its course by a river, or the silting of a harbor, break the close connections among the four components of the life situation. Adaptations will have to be reestablished on a different basis, or the group may have to begin life afresh in a new location. From such an experience nothing new is gained, however; the natural environment is no creator of innovations. Cumulative changes do not result from upheavals in the physical world.

The impetus to cumulative change is supplied from the social environment. It appears as a cultural input of some kind, brought to a given social system by an invader, a trader, or by a mechanical means of communication. Diffusion, the anthropological term for the communication of culture from one group to another, is an indispensable factor in the genesis of ideas. New ways of doing or of thinking about things when joined with familiar practices or ideas tend to give rise to novel syntheses, i.e., inventions. The new idea may supply a missing element of vital importance to a potential invention or it may operate catalytically by providing a middle term in the reasoning that integrates two or more existing concepts. Diffusion contributes the wherewithal for the growth of organ-

[4] The equilibrium notion is introduced here solely to simplify the discussion, not to imply an actual state of affairs. It should call to mind a situation in which all changes introduced at a previous moment have run their courses and the mutual adjustments among the components have been brought to maturity.

ization. When diffusion ceases the rate of invention subsides, for eventually the members of a system use up the possibilities of combination among the elements of information in their possession.

It will be noted that the term *ideas* is here used in preference to *technology*. The latter term is too closely identified with physical tools and the manipulation of physical tools to be satisfactory when what is under consideration is really the instrumental aspect of behavior. There are many forms of behavior that have instrumental significance but that are not recognized as tools. Unfortunately, our habits of language have led us to a spurious distinction. A tool, needless to say, has no inherent motive power; it has to be pushed around by man. It embodies a practice or, more abstractly, an idea. But it can be an aid to behavior only for those who know the practice and have mastered the skill. Culture, on the other hand, is the general term for technology, practices, and the like. Culture and organization are used here as different perspectives on the same thing. Culture is organization dissected and sorted according to a classificatory scheme. Organization is culture assembled in workable combinations and operating as a functioning entity. In diffusion, organization is transposed as culture when pieces of the former are detached or copied and are transported from one place to another. The pieces are transposed once again from culture to organization when they are assimilated to a social system.

The greater the exposure of a social system to other social systems the greater is the probability of its receiving cultural inputs and, therefore, that cumulative change will occur. Exposure to such influences is maximal at the points of intersection of routes of travel and communication. It varies, too, with the amount of traffic passing over intersecting routes. Accordingly, social systems so situated are much more susceptible to change than are those located at distances removed from route intersections. Cities, because of their need to be supplied from the countrysides with food and other materials, invariably occupy sites at which two or more avenues of travel converge. Hence change usually begins first and proceeds most rapidly in urban centers. They differ in this respect, of course, with the number and the importance of the routes represented. The comparative accessibility of locations, however, may be altered over time; river courses are modified, harbors fill with silt, and technical improvements open new routes or shift the importance of old ones. When events such as these occur, the incidence of change shifts among locations; some localities sink into stagnation while others are stirred to growth.

At what point or points in its structure innovations normally enter a system depends on the extent of its integration. In relatively closed systems, those that are tightly integrated, inputs from foreign cultures usually enter through the functionaries who occupy the apex of the local hierarchy. These "gate-keepers" control the relations of the system with the external world. But they are as likely to turn aside disturbing ideas as they are to admit them: despots have almost always exercised a censorship over what is brought into their domains. Where, however, the system is only partially integrated, which is commonly the case, new elements may enter at many different points or through many different functions. An open system, and in the degree to which it is open, tolerates the movements into and out of the territory of many kinds of travelers and news gatherers. Of these the most ubiquitous through history is the trader. Because novelty is his business the trader is an inveterate carrier of ideas.[5] Immigrants have also been important transporters of knowledge and skills, especially in the period before the physical separation of communication from transportation. Other classes of travelers have performed in the same way in different times and places. Yet in all probability the most effective bearer of innovation is he whose functional position enables him to introduce the acquisition into the system.

Much of what is transmitted along the lines of communication is of questionable utility for a receiving system. Some of it is trivial. Gossip, anecdotes, and unconnected bits of information add nothing of consequence to an organization. Other acquisitions may be premature. Techniques for manufacturing tractors have no more utility for a group practicing slash-and-burn agriculture than has the digging stick for a society that possesses the tractor. What can be borrowed depends to a considerable extent on the level of development of the system at the receiving end, or, as has been said, on the size of the culture base already acquired. A simple society has neither the cultural repertory nor the manpower needed for the assimilation of complicated techniques. Although, as a general rule, material items can be transferred with greater ease than nonmaterial traits, many of the former presuppose so much in the way of skills and related knowledge that they can be effectively moved only between systems of comparable levels of development.

The importance of any given innovation for growth is determined in some degree by the circumstances that prevail. In general, however, growth is facilitated by acquisitions that (1) raise the level of productivity of the economy and (2) reduce the time and cost of mobility. In some respects these different classes of techniques have the same effects. Increases of productivity enlarge the surplus product available for the

[5] From his studies of peasant societies Sidney W. Mintz concluded that the productive sector of society is more conservative, unexpansive, and bound by tradition, while the distributive sector is more open to change, more willing to take risks, and more resilient. ("Internal Market Systems as Mechanisms of Social Articulation," *Intermediate Societies, Social Mobility and Communication*, ed. by V. F. Ray. Proceedings of the 1959 Annual Spring Meeting of the American Ethnological Society [Seattle: University of Washington Press, 1959], p. 21).

support of more people doing a greater variety of activities and capable of receiving and making use of a greater diversity of cultural acquisitions. The surplus product may also be used to pay the costs of more frequent and more far ranging movements by members of the population. Thus the area controlled can be expanded and the resource base of the economy enriched thereby. On the other hand, techniques for reducing the time and cost of mobility may start a roundabout process of increasing the amount of product, if not of productivity. The enlargement of the accessible area adds to the resource base and to the size of the population. It speeds exchanges of all kinds and by that means advances the possibilities of specialization and the extent of the division of labor. More efficient movement capabilities also increase the frequency of contacts with alien peoples.

Chance figures prominently in what is available for the borrowing at points of route convergences. For that reason alone the prediction of change is all but impossible. There is the further problem of anticipating what combinations of the new information with existing knowledge will be made. The advance of learning has made possible fairly accurate estimations of the probable frequency with which innovations will appear at a given place. It has not removed the difficulty of forecasting the quality of innovations and the temporal order in which innovations of given kinds might be expected to occur. Even more resistant to learning is the skill needed to correctly infer the subsidiary effects of innovation, which are often more important than the immediate applications.

The information that enters a system may be assimilated immediately or it may be "stored" for possible later use. That which passes directly into application does so through affecting existing functions in one way or another. Some of it may bear on the ways in which particular occupations are conducted, that is, it may constitute new or improved techniques. If so, the occupation is altered in the materials it uses, its relations with other occupations, the efficiency of its performance, or various combinations of these results. Or the innovation may result in the splitting of a new specialty from an old relatively unspecialized occupation. Weaving, casting metal, teaching, and administering a government have been subdivided again and again by succeeding innovations. Specialization appears to move from sector (e.g., extractive to non-extractive), to industry, to skill, to task in ever finer parings from an original bundle of activity. Still another way an innovation may directly modify a system is through bringing about new combinations of preexisting functions. The appearance of the extra-familial producing unit was at first a recombination of functions that had been present for some time. Every further advance in institutional specialization constitutes another combination of old occupations.

Functional modifications disrupt a network of relationships among functionaries and require realignments of interdependences. A change in the way a function is performed causes some ancillary functions to be cut off and isolated from the system while others may gain a new importance. Whalers, harness-makers, glass-blowers, and hod-carriers have been supplanted by oil drillers, automobile workers, machine tenders, and lift operators. The effects spread over geographic districts from which materials were formerly obtained or in which the obsolescent occupations were concentrated. They disturb the relations among age groups, inasmuch as old occupations belong usually to old workers and new ones are taken up by young people. Where a new specialty is split off from a preexisting occupation the remaining part itself becomes more specialized. Both the new and the remnant of the old are momentarily disoriented by the separation and loss of mutual support. They must work out appropriate relationships with other functions. Increases in productivity start searches for larger markets with implications for further expansion of the system.

In considering the movement of the effects of functional modifications, it is helpful to think of a system as composed of a number of series or chains of functions, each with two, three or more links, fanning out from a small number of coordinators or administrative headquarters. A difference between simple and complex systems is found in the number and the lengths of the series. In complex systems functional chains are also cross-linked at numerous points by mediating and service functions. There are also shorter, subordinate chains of functions taking off from functions variously located in the major series. Change passes along a functional chain, moving from link to link, forging new links at some points, and altering old links so that they must be readjusted in their relationships to one another. Change moves laterally in a system through the cross-linking functions. Sometimes a strong resistance in a certain function will be responsible for the lateral spread. Cumulative change lengthens functional series, multiplies the number of cross-linking functions, and starts new series of functions.

Were it not for the devious courses often pursued by the effects of innovations moving through a system, the time required for a change to be completed could be estimated by the number of links in a functional sequence. Whatever its path, system change is spread over time. It involves a protracted series of alterations and not merely the introduction of an innovation. More often than not the observer comes upon change in midpassage and is unable to witness the entire flow of events. This common experience is largely responsible for the prevalence of the limited notion of change as a difference between before and after states.

A recent attempt to measure the time involved in the culmination of change processes is shown in Table 58. "Incubation Period" in the table is the lapsed time between the establishment of the technical feasibility of an innovation and the date of the decision to prepare the product for market distribution. From that date to the actual appearance of the product on the market is the period of "Commercial Development." Rather

Table 58. Years Required for Development of Selected Technological Innovations

Technological Innovation	Date of Commercial Introduction	Lapsed Time (years)		
		Incubation Period	Commercial Development	Total Time
Aluminum	1892	15	6	21
Motor vehicle	1894	7	4	11
Synthetic resins	1910	12	3	15
Air transportation	1911	18	8	26
Electronic vacuum tube	1920	4	6	10
Radio broadcasting	1922	11	9	20
Frozen foods	1925	2	9	11
Vitamins	1937	20	11	31
Synthetic fibers	1939	26	3	29
Synthetic rubber	1940	22	11	33
Antibiotics	1940	49	1	50
Television broadcasting	1945	6	12	18
Titanium	1950	11	14	25
Electronic computers	1950	17	6	23
Semiconductors	1951	7	3	10
Nuclear power generation	1957	31	3	34
Freeze-dried foods	1961	23	6	29
Integrated circuits	1961	6	3	9
Synthetic leather	1964	13	14	27

SOURCE: Adapted from *The Employment Impact of Technological Change,* Appendix Vol. II, *Technology and the American Economy.* Studies Prepared by the National Commission on Technology, Automation and Economic Progress (Washington, D.C., 1966), Tables 1 and 2.

large variations in developmental times are apparent. The average time from the beginning of incubation to the end of commercial development period has declined from 37 years, for innovations introduced in 1890–1919, to 14 years, for those that appeared in 1945–64. Most of the reduction occurred in the "incubation period"; the length of that period was cut from 30 to 9 years. It should be noted that these time estimates measure just two segments of the entire period of change. For example, aluminum, having been successfully put on the market, was then at the threshold of its last phase—of absorption—in which it replaces other metals in a widening assortment of uses. This phase has not yet been concluded.

As specialization advances, interdependences become more compelling as well as more manifold. The free flow of communications and of exchanges of all kinds becomes indispensable. There is thus a pronounced tendency to remove obstacles and frictions from the channels of interaction. This is expressed in a movement toward standardization and interchangeability of parts. It is also evident in a marked drift toward isomorphism in the subsystems. That is, all units, subject to size limitations, tend to acquire similar structures and procedures; their complements of officers, line and staff arrangements, accounting methods, and the like, converge upon a central tendency. This convergence, as was argued in Chapter 13, operates among systems, as it does among the parts of a given system, in direct relation to the frequency and the importance of their interactions.

Information that has no immediate applicability may be stored. In the absence of writing and record keeping, information can be stored only in the memories of members of a population. The amount of information that can be retained in that way is limited by population size and, of course, by the memory capacities of human beings. But where writing and record keeping are practiced, the amount of information that can be accumulated for later use is limited only by the resources that are devoted to storage facilities. Whatever the means of preservation, when the information is eventually brought into use it has effects on the system of the kinds already described.

OBSTACLES TO CHANGE

The progress of change in a system can be impeded by various circumstances. Quite often change is delayed by the absence of a necessary element. It was noted in Chapter 4 that technical change in eighteenth century England moved by stops and starts: development of mining was blocked by lack of a device for dealing with flood waters in the mines; in ironmaking it was a shortage of suitable fuel; the textile industry was retarded by inefficient techniques for producing yarn. Or sometimes a technical change cannot go forward for want of an appropriate organization. That was illustrated in Chapter 3 in connection with the application of the moldboard plow to the heavy soils of European river valleys. Use of that tool required of farmers that they pool their resources and devise a means of regulating responsibilities and practices. Eventually the village council arose to meet the need for collective action. A lack of credit and marketing institutions presents a very similar problem over much of the under-developed world. There also, as in the United States in the early nineteenth century, industrial development is slowed by an absence of skilled labor. A very common deficiency standing in the path of change is inadequate transportation and communication. Sometimes that appears as a confusion in the terms of discourse—language, weights, and measures, coinage; not infrequently it lies in a lack of consensus over procedures; but very generally the critical element missing is the set of tools for movement over space—roads, carriers, telephone lines, and the like. Whatever the communication impediment, it limits the scope of the market, deprives units of the economies of scale, and thus interferes with the adoption of innovations and the rise of new specialties.

Another class of frictions in change is composed of what may be called structural persistences. These, too, are of many kinds. The entrenchment of old elites with their archaic notions has proven a formidable barrier to change. A classic case, dealt with in Chapter 3, is represented by the aristocracy of the medieval town, Eisenstadt finds a parallel in China where modernization was long delayed by the monopoly in a single elite of control over economic, political, and religious institutions.[6] Or, again, the village council, which proved so effective in the application of a useful tool at one stage of development, became an obstacle to innovation in a later phase. Similarly, family traditions stand in the way of change in traditional societies. The practice of successive subdivision of property at inheritance eventually reduces agricultural units to sizes that are too small to accommodate some innovations.[7] Nepotism, by starving a firm of capital, can hold urban enterprises to sizes too small to function economically, as the Nigerian experience with the family firm illustrates (Chapter 13). The apprenticeship system, it was seen, lingered on in English society beyond the disappearance of its usefulness to unduly complicate an otherwise simple process of labor recruitment.

The great inertia in social structure was demonstrated on a much larger scale in the rebuilding of cities that were extensively damaged in areal bombings during World War II. In many cases destruction embraced more than 60 percent of the built-up space and was most thorough in the oldest and densest sections. There was thus a unique opportunity in each instance to rebuild in accordance with the most up-to-date and efficient designs. Yet, although serious attempts were made to take advantage of the unusual opportunity, most of the cities were restored in very much the same patterns that existed before the war. What were not destroyed in the bombings were the sets of claims to the lands—the private ownerships of home and business sites, the public transportation rights-of-way, and the spaces for parks and other public uses. Many of these institutionalized rights could have been removed had there been time for

---

[6] "Transformation of Social, Political and Cultural Orders in Modernization," *American Sociological Review*, XXX (1965): 659–73.

[7] H. J. Habakkuk, "Inheritance Rules and Economic Change," *op. cit.*

lengthy litigation. Since there was not, new buildings arose on the old sites before plans could be drawn and controls put into effect.[8]

There are also deterrents to change of a more dynamic kind. These appear mainly as vested interest groups rising in opposition to an impending loss or radical modification of their functions. Industrial history is replete with such occasions. An extreme instance is that created by the Luddites in the early nineteenth century. These were workers who banded together to destroy the machinery which was threatening to eliminate their employment. The more recent "feather-bedding" provisions in craft union work agreements, whereby the amount of work done per unit of time is restricted, were designed to offset increases in efficiency resulting from technical change. Every occupational category is inclined to resort to organized efforts to protect itself from unwanted changes in its function. Whether the proposed changes are mechanical or administrative makes little difference. We have seen how small-town retailers opposed the introduction of mail-order merchandising, which was nothing more than an administrative innovation (Chapter 6).

Enough has been said to indicate the variety of discontinuities that occur in change. In a sense, together these offer a view from the negative side of the progressive nature of system change. A social system cannot change simultaneously in all of its parts. It is neither perfectly integrated nor are its internal communications instantaneous. The more complex the system, the more devious are the paths and the longer are the lapsed times in the consummation of change.

POPULATION AND CHANGE

As stated in an early chapter, population is a necessary condition for organization and, therefore, population change is a necessary condition for organization change. By that is meant that there is a given size and composition of population for every type or extent of organization. There must be enough people to staff the various functions and enough new members maturing to responsible ages to replace those dying and becoming disabled. Organization growth requires an increase of people sufficient to man the added functions.

To assert that population is necessary, however, is not to declare that it is a sufficient cause of organization. There is a great deal of contrary

[8] F. Ikle, "The Effects of War Destruction upon the Ecology of Cities," *Social Forces*, XXIX (1951): 313–91; Amos H. Hawley, "Land Value Patterns in Okayama, Japan, 1940–52," *American Journal of Sociology*, LX (1955): 487–93; and L. Grebner, "Continuity in the Rebuilding of Bombed Cities in Eastern Europe," *American Journal of Sociology*, LXI (1956): 463–69.

evidence and none in support of Herbert Spencer's contention that increase of numbers is the driving force behind differentiation and the progress of a division of labor.[9] Population increase over and above what is needed to keep pace with organization change may generate opportunities for further elaborations of structure or create problems that can only be resolved by improvements of organization. But there is nothing imperative about these consequences. Their failure to materialize has often in the past resulted in an elimination of excess numbers of people through a rise in mortality or emigration. Population is a passive factor in change.

The causal issue aside, there is still a question of the nature of the co-variation of organization and population. The relationship is manifestly a close one. In fact, the two factors are sometimes described as endogenous to a system, which is to say that they are separable only in abstraction. Yet dislocations do occur.[10] That is because change operates differently in each case. In the one it proceeds through biological mechanisms, in the other through communication. Population change begins with disturbances of the birth-death ratio from which follow shifts in age composition. Distortions in age composition remain in the population for two or three generations, though the source of the initial disturbance may have been of very short duration. Population and organization each possess some capacity for independent variability, but the tolerable ranges are as yet unmeasured. It is possible that the range of variability is widened as social systems advance from simple to complex forms. These are problems that have yet to be investigated.

Still, the relationship appears not to be governed by any rule of proportionality. That is, increases in organizational complexity seem not to be matched by corresponding increases in population. It was earlier noted (Chapter 6) that increases in functional differentiation produce other miscellaneous differentia at a faster rate. Thus, while for every increase in the number of tasks to be performed there may have to be an equal increase in the number of people, increases in the numbers of non-sustenance activities and roles do not require equal-sized increases in population.[11] The difference is due at least in part to the fact that the division of labor role tends to be too time-consuming to permit more than one to a person, whereas most other roles make lesser time demands so that two or more may be held by each person. Hence the total number

[9] *The Principles of Sociology* (New York: Appleton-Century-Crofts, 1929), vol. I, p. 471.

[10] Amos H. Hawley, "Population and Society: An Essay on Growth," in *Fertility and Family Planning: A World View*, ed. by S. J. Behrman, Leslie Corsa, Jr., and Ronald Freedman (Ann Arbor: University of Michigan Press, 1969), pp. 189–212.

[11] See Raoul Naroll, "A Preliminary Index of Social Development," *American Anthropologist*, LVIII (1956): 687–715, and Robert Carneiro, "On the Relationship Between Size of Population and Complexity of Social Organization," *Southwestern Journal of Anthropology*, XXIII (1967): 234–42.

of activities and subsystems comprising them may rise at a more rapid rate than population increase.

In point of fact the work sector of a social system seems to be subject to a similar tendency toward nonproportionality in growth. This can be illustrated by comparing the energy generated and presumably the work done under varying conditions. When a worker himself produces all of the energy his task consumes, his labor power is equivalent to roughly one twelfth of one horsepower unit. But where the worker is assisted with modern techniques and organization the energy produced is approximately seventeen horsepower units per worker.[12] The difference is of the order of 1 to 204; or 204 primitive workers would be required to do the work of one worker in an industrialized society. Obviously, therefore, there is an organizational equivalent of population acquired in the development of a social system. Some of that is built into the tools that are created and some lies in the structuring of relationships.

The lack of proportionality notwithstanding, there is still a linear relationship between the number of people and the complexity of a system. Increases in the latter require increases in the former, though the required population increments grow relatively smaller. But the relationship also becomes progressively more difficult to analyze into its components. Superficially, for example, it seems that with computerized information-storage and retrieval systems a small number of people can serve the memory function for a vast population. Upon more careful consideration one is reminded that very large numbers of people are needed to produce, maintain, and administer the use of such elaborate equipment, to say nothing of the producers of the information in volume sufficient to justify its use. The labor invested in almost any other so-called labor-saving device is likewise enormous and virtually impossible to measure, for the chain of contributions reaches through many links extending back to the mines and quarries.

TERRITORY AND CHANGE

An advance in the complexity of a social system usually involves an expansion of the territory under its control, but not always for the same reasons. More territory is commonly needed to provide adequate living space for the enlarged population and sometimes to ensure an increased food supply. The latter, however, might conceivably be obtained through an intensification of cultivation. Another and more important advantage of an enlargement of territory is that it affords a greater range of choice. It allows a substitution of more productive for less productive lands. It

[12] W. S. and E. S. Woytinsky, *World Population and Production: Trends and Outlook* (New York: The Twentieth Century Fund, 1953), pp. 924–25.

may also provide an increased variety of food objects. The broadened range of possibilities applies also to nonfood resources. The acquisition of new techniques in the diffusion process means that a wider assortment of materials will be used in the future. Resource deposits must therefore be found. The probability of resource diversification varies with area.

Territorial expansion is seldom a matter simply of stretching a system over unoccupied adjacent lands. Not since the prehistoric period have there been vacant lands in any considerable quantity. Expansion is rather a process of either displacing the original occupants so that a system can be extended through the spread of new settlement, or of absorbing the initial occupants into the growing system. In either case, land uses are reconstituted to bring them into appropriate relationships with the activities at the center of expansion. The reorganization of the uses of the enlarged territory proceeds through centrifugal and centripetal processes. Certain kinds of specialists move out to the periphery to locate and develop new resources, to build transportation and communication lines, and to service the outlying settlements. Other specialists are drawn into the center where special clienteles and various external economies are present in suitable combinations. Administrative functions are also consolidated and enlarged in the centripetal process. The two movements play a large part in the changing form that must accompany increasing size.

Increases in population and in the scope of territory to which access has been gained not only provide the necessary manpower and raw materials for system growth, they contribute to growth in other ways. As enlargements of the "markets" for various products and services they permit further advances in specialization. For even though the skills required in a special function may be known, they cannot be cultivated or practiced without a sufficient demand for the product. Increases in the scope of the market also make possible increases in the sizes of units of organization or subsystems. Larger units can employ more capital and can absorb and put to use more technical acquisitions.[13] The rate of growth may be accelerated therefore. Increased sizes of units represent higher degrees of centralization and an extension of the hierarchical structure of the system. These tendencies are not confined to commerce and industry; they are just as characteristic of educational, governmental, religious, and avocational institutions. As stated in an earlier connection, every unit of organization tends to grow to the maximum size possible under the prevailing conditions of transportation and communication.

This tendency can be offset, however, by various circumstances. The productivity of the unit, for example, may not be sufficient to enable it to take full advantage of the scope of the market. Productivity, moreover,

[13] E. Mansfield, "The Speed of Response of Firms to New Techniques," *Quarterly Journal of Economics* (1963).

will certainly affect its competitive position vis-à-vis other similar units. Thus the presence of many competing units may restrict all to a size below a possible maximum. Again, although productive capacity may be adequate for the support of large size, the internal administrative organization may be too undeveloped to assure coherence among the parts of units should they tend to rise above a modest size.

Sooner or later an expanding urban system encounters limits to its further growth. These may be either intrinsic or extrinsic in character. The principal internal limitation, alluded to in the preceding paragraph, arises when the physical and organizational instruments of transportation and communication receive no further improvements. In that event there can be no more increases in population size or territorial spread without sharply increasing costs of communication, including, of course, that involved in administration. As such costs tend to exceed the advantages gained from increased size equilibrium conditions begin to appear in the systems. Population controls come into play and there is a return to scale.

The extrinsic limitations to expansion develop in various ways. Where growth has been proceeding from two or more centers, the boundaries of one can become a barrier to the extension of the other. Boundaries of that kind are never clear lines; they are rather zones of overlap and contention between adjoining systems. Thus each system tends to carve out a domain of its own. That, however, might be but preliminary to a final stage. A continuation of interaction between systems leads them to cultivate their respective location advantages and specialization and ultimately to establish relations of superordination and subordination. In the end a hierarchical system, in which each urban complex is reduced to a sub-system, envelops the entire territory.

It might seem that the political boundary of a sovereign state would serve as an effective limit to the expansion of an urban system. Such is not necessarily the case in the modern era. Urban centers do not rule their territories; they only coordinate and administer the activities scattered over them. Transportation and communication lines may convey exchanges of materials and information across political boundaries as well as within them. Of course the boundary may mark off linguistic, monetary, and legal universes and it can be used further to impede exchanges by means of tariffs, import quotas, visa requirements, and the like. Nevertheless, there are numerous instances in which urban influences reach across a political boundary to attach foreign area to a hinterland. The extent of urban development in a small country such as Belgium, the Netherlands, or Switzerland can greatly exceed what the scope of the respective national territory would seem to warrant. Trade and other exchanges may be regarded as ways of pooling manpower and other resources and of raising the power of organization.

This calls attention to a serious measurement problem. It is exceedingly difficult to draw accurately the boundaries of highly developed urban systems, whether one is dealing with an individual metropolitan area or a nested set of metropolitan areas. Neither the effective population nor the totality of the organization of the system is fully embraced by any official boundary. And any boundary cast in terms of functional relationships can be no better than an approximation. Consequently, attempts to investigate the quantitative relationship between size of population and characteristics of organization in modern urban areas are subject to a fairly large error.

CHANGE AS EVOLUTION

Urbanization or system change is evolutionary. That is, it is a movement from simple to more complex forms of organization. This is what the word "expansion" is intended to convey. Lest there be any misconception, it should be said that the idea of evolution belongs to no particular subject matter or class of phenomena, biology not excepted. The term refers only to a kind of change, a kind that might occur in many categories of things. Nor is the concept restricted to changes measurable exclusively on a geological time scale. Again, the rate of change is peculiar to the phenomenon, not to the concept. Developments spread over a year, a century, or an eon are equally amenable to the descriptive term "evolution."

More difficult to deal with is the notion of stages that has become identified with evolutionary thought. Although they are not responsible for that concept, social scientists have contributed to its wide dissemination. Much of their early thinking used organic evolution as a model with the result that temporal sequences were frequently subdivided by stages. The idea is firmly implanted in various conceptions of change that are still current. The cyclical hypothesis holds that change alternates with equilibrium and that each equilibrium constitutes a stage in an on-going process. The dissolution of equilibrium releases change which culminates in another equilibrium or stage. Succession is the name for a conception of change that combines several cycles in a series culminating in a climax phase at which equilibrium prevails. Thus a residential area or an entire community may evolve in a succession-like manner.[14] Another use of the change-by-stage idea is found in the logistic curve model that is applied to population growth. The increase of numbers, other things constant, is assumed to proceed at first slowly, then rapidly, and

[14] R. E. Park, "Succession: An Ecological Concept," *op. cit.*

finally to subside as size approaches a point at which the resource-carrying capacity is saturated.[15]

The use of stages to mark off segments of change has its principal justification in methodological utility. It is convenient to be able to break through a great mass of information and to highlight what a scholar deems important by reference to a set of benchmark categories. Thus one can arrange his data around a set of temporal designations such as no-madic hunting, settled hunting and food gathering, horticultural village, agricultural-state, and industrial urban societies,[16] or as village, town, urban, and metropolitan systems.[17] Trouble is apt to arise, however, when the scholar forgets what he has done and comes to regard his distinctions as real. But this danger is contingent on how change actually proceeds. No doubt in earlier times, when communications were slow and uncertain, cumulative change in social systems was episodic. Important innovations occurred infrequently and after each such acquisition there were long periods during which a system could recapture stability before the next significant innovation appeared.[18] Under such conditions the use of stages may be a fairly accurate representation of the way change pro-ceeded. There might still be some room for debate, however, over which stages are noteworthy. But as communications have been improved the flow of information has become continuous. System change has tended to lose its cyclical character and has approached a continuous movement. In these new circumstances it is still permissible to employ the stage con-cept provided the purely heuristic purpose of the concept is kept in the foreground of attention.

A question of importance in the study of urbanization across cultures and historic periods is whether in each different setting the process re-peats the same sequence of events. Can a society in transition from an agrarian to an urban-industrial urbanization leap directly to a mechani-cally powered industrial economy without having first accumulated ex-periences in handicraft industry? Is it possible to install in a newly urbanizing society a full set of modern social and political institutions without a prior period of apprenticeship in which leaders are trained and clienteles are cultivated? Is there a necessary logic in the order with

[15] Raymond Pearl, *The Biology of Population Growth* (New York: A. A. Knopf, 1930), chs. 1 and 2.

[16] Walter Goldschmidt, *Man's Way: A Preface to the Understanding of Human Society* (New York: Holt, Rinehart and Winston, 1959), pp. 183 ff.

[17] Adapted from N. S. B. Gras (*op. cit.*), who spoke of village, town, and metro-politan economies.

[18] Margaret Hodgen claims to have assembled evidence to show that in England during the 900 years from A.D. 1000 to 1899 only 2,407 or 18 percent, of the 12,849 parishes she studied, ever experienced an innovation, defined as a new occupational specialization (*Change and History*, The Viking Fund in Anthropology, No. 18 [New York, 1952]).

which the urbanization process unfolds? That such may be the case is suggested by the numerous instances in which developing societies have failed to accomplish a significant change for lack of sufficient preliminary experience of necessary supporting institutions. Still, there may be ways of circumventing some of the steps taken in the modernization of the West. That earlier experience may not, in fact, define a logic of development. The natural progression from simple to complex forms, if indeed such a generalization is feasible, may lie somewhere between the patterns of change of Western nations and those now occurring in new nations.

That there is a particular pattern or direction in system change, as might be implied in the term "development," is seriously questioned by Robert Nisbet. Such a notion, he says, is wholly subjective; it belongs to a misleading, albeit ancient, metaphor which applies the model of organic growth to social units.[19] Given the assumptions that (1) significant change is of external origin and (2) the occurrence of change-producing events is unpredictable, it follows in Nisbet's judgment that social change is discontinuous and without direction. Tenable though the two assumptions are, they do not necessarily support the conclusion, at least not in the absence of other premises. If, for instance, we add the assumption that what is already present in a system is selective of what is admitted from the environment, a somewhat different conclusion is reached. It is then reasonable to expect that change might proceed with direction. The direction, however, need not be regarded as rigid. The conception could allow for frequent deviations from a trend line; some importations could prove to be incompatible and, after a trial-and-error period, would be eliminated; others that were momentarily useless might be shunted aside and retained in repositories.

SUMMARY

Instead of the usual summary it might be more useful to consider a condensation of information, as shown in Table 59. The content of the table is intended to be no more than illustrative. The columns are headed by the four successively larger territorial systems mentioned earlier. All that follows in the columns below is by way of definition of village, town, urban and metropolitan systems. Much of the definitional material is approximate, of course. Nor is it implied that the differences in characteristics are affected by leaps from stage to stage; the stages should be thought of as a set of points arbitrarily identified on a continuum.

Transportation is the critical factor in the determination of scope. In that a distinction must be made between intramural and extramural. The

---

[19] *Social Change and History: Aspects of the Western Theory of Development* (London and New York: Oxford University Press, 1969), pp. 284 ff.

Table 59. Scope and Characteristics of Territorial Systems

System Characteristic	Village	Town	Urban	Metropolitan
Transportation and Communication				
Intra-mural	Pedestrian	Pedestrian, animal	Pedestrian street rail	Motor vehicle, telephone
Extra-mural	Pedestrian	Horsecart, barge, sailing ship	Horse & wagon, steam railway, telegraph	Motor vehicle, railway, airway, radio, television
Radial extent of exchanges				
Daily frequency	3–5 mis.	3–8 mis.	8–12 mis.	25–50 mis.
Weekly frequency	3–5 mis.	10–20 mis.	25–150 mis.	50–1000± mis.
Size of population in largest nucleus	250±	1,000 – 15,000	15,000 – 100,000	250,000 and over
No. of territorial units subordinate to largest unit	None	Few	Many	Many
Proportion of population in non-farm residence aggregations	2% ±	15–25%	35–45%	55–80%
Proportion of labor force engaged in primary industry	98% ±	65–80%	35–50%	4–20%
Sources of energy	Animal, including human	Animal, water, wind	Fossil fuels	Fossil fuels, electricity, nuclear fission
Energy produced per worker	$\frac{1}{12}$ hp.	$\frac{1}{4}$ hp.	2 hp.	17 hp.
Productivity per worker (relative value)	1	3	24	204
Work unit: Type	Family, kin group	Family, guild	Extra-familial shop and factory	Multi-plant corporation and chain organization
Size: Number of persons	3–5	3–10	6–50	20–50,000 ±
Differentiation: Basis	Sector	Industry	Skill	Task
No. of functions linked in sequences	2–3	3–4	4–6	6 or more
Integration: Mechanism	Barter and gift giving	Specialized trader and political elite	Business enterprise, political institution	Business enterprise, political institution, large-scale organization
Voluntary association	Informal and local	Informal and local	Formal, regionally federated	Formal, interregionally federated
Scope of cultural standardization	Local	District	Regional	Inter-regional
Social importance of vicinage	Exclusive	Substantial	Attenuated	Minimal

latter developed first and most rapidly; the former followed by almost a century. Accordingly, the entire area over which regular exchanges could be sustained expanded in the urban phase, while the expansion of the zone of daily interactions comes primarily in the metropolitan phase. With the enlargement of territory the number of subordinate territorial units increased and the importance of any one place as a determinant of individual experience declined.

The village system can accommodate not many more than 250 persons. At the other extreme, the metropolitan system involves upwards of 1,000 times as many. The difference in sizes of population is understandable in part in the light of differences in the proportions of the economically active population engaged in primary industry, i.e., agriculture. A range from 95 to less than 20 percent reflects increases in the amount of surplus product available for the support of non-agricultural activities. The tools and sources of energy produce as little as $\frac{1}{12}$ of a horsepower unit per worker in the village system, larger amounts of energy outputs in the more extensive systems, and as much as 17 horsepower units per worker in the metropolitan system. A simple conversion to relative values, based on the assumption of one horsepower unit being equivalent to 10 to 15 workers, gives estimates of the difference in productivity ranging from 1 to 204. To attain the higher levels of productivity calls for increasingly refined specialization and work units free of traditional restraints, capable of mobilizing great amounts of capital and able to coordinate the labors of scores of workers. Specialization lengthens the functional sequences such that relationships are made increasingly indirect. That is facilitated by the widening scope of standardized ways of acting and communicating. It thus becomes possible to constitute associations of all kinds on a progressively broader territorial basis. Accordingly, territorial integration moves from mere exchanges of materials and goods to a thickening web of social and administrative linkages.

SUPPLEMENTARY READINGS

Bock, Kenneth. "Evolution, Function and Change," *American Sociological Review*, XXVIII (1963): 229–237.

Friedman, John. "Cities in Social Transformation," *Comparative Studies in Society and History*, IV (1961): 86–103.

Ogburn, W. F. "Technology and Cities: The Dilemma of the Modern Metropolis," *The Sociological Quarterly*, III (1960): 139–153.

Ryan, Bryce F. *Social and Cultural Change* (New York: The Ronald Press, 1969).

Wallerstein, Immanuel. *Social Change: The Colonial Situation* (New York: John Wiley, 1966).

Wilson, Godfrey and Monica. *The Analysis of Social Change* (Cambridge: The University Press, 1954).

Index

DATE DUE